Errata

In Part I, Learning Objective 2, the reference was quoted incorrectly. The following is a corrected version, which should be used in place of the original on page 44.

LO^2 Sources of Nonverbal Communication

There are a variety of sources or channels for the nonverbal messages that we interpret from others and display ourselves. These include the use of the body (kinesics), the use of the voice (vocalics/paralanguage), the use of space (proxemics), and self-presentation.

Use of Body: Kinesics

Of all the research on nonverbal behavior, you are probably most familiar with kinesics, the technical name for the interpretation of body motions as communications (Malmkjaer, 2004). Body motions are the movement of your body or body parts that others interpret and assign meaning. These include your gestures, eye contact, facial expression, posture, and your use of touch.

In the References section, one reference was omitted. The following reference should be added on page 259.

Malmkjaer, K. (2004). *The Linguistic Encyclopedia* (2nd ed.). New York: Routledge.

WHAT KIND OF COMMUNICATOR ARE YOU?

Take this quick and easy quiz to find out how you rank as a communicator.

On the line provided for each statement, indicate the response that best captures your behavior:
1, almost always; 2, often; 3, sometimes; 4, rarely; 5, never.

Add up your score and see where you stand.

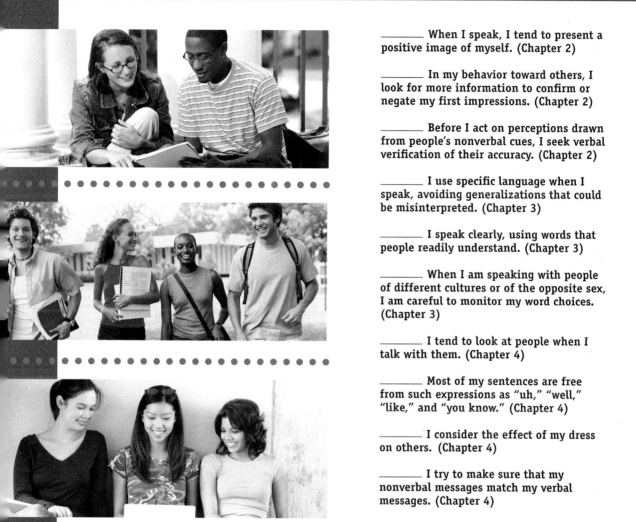

_____ When I speak, I tend to present a positive image of myself. (Chapter 2)

_____ In my behavior toward others, I look for more information to confirm or negate my first impressions. (Chapter 2)

_____ Before I act on perceptions drawn from people's nonverbal cues, I seek verbal verification of their accuracy. (Chapter 2)

_____ I use specific language when I speak, avoiding generalizations that could be misinterpreted. (Chapter 3)

_____ I speak clearly, using words that people readily understand. (Chapter 3)

_____ When I am speaking with people of different cultures or of the opposite sex, I am careful to monitor my word choices. (Chapter 3)

_____ I tend to look at people when I talk with them. (Chapter 4)

_____ Most of my sentences are free from such expressions as "uh," "well," "like," and "you know." (Chapter 4)

_____ I consider the effect of my dress on others. (Chapter 4)

_____ I try to make sure that my nonverbal messages match my verbal messages. (Chapter 4)

If your score is between 0-12 points: You're a communicating guru! Though we all have room to improve, it looks like you're confident in your abilities to listen, speak, and read people from all walks of life. Ask a friend or family member to rate you, and find out if they think you're all that!

13-40 points: You come to this course with a lot of life experience in communication, but you probably wouldn't be the first person to volunteer to present in front of class. Now, it's time to refine what you already know, learn the theories behind communication, and refine the communication skills you apply in your own life. You're on your way!

41-50 points: You have some communication strengths, but you just can't make the first move asking out that special someone because you're not sure they're into you. You're definitely ready to find areas to build confidence and improve your skills.

COMM 2008-2009 Edition
Rudolph F. Verderber
Kathleen S. Verderber
Deanna D. Sellnow

Sr. Publisher: Lyn Uhl

Editor-in-Chief: PJ Boardman

Director: Neil Marquardt

Executive Editor: Monica Eckman

Developmental Editors: David Ferrell &
    Jamie Bryant, B-books, Ltd.

Research Coordinator: Clara Goosman

Editorial Assistant: Colin Solan

Executive Marketing Manager:
    Mandee Eckersley

Marketing Manager: Erin Mitchell

Marketing Coordinator: Mary Anne Payumo

Executive Marketing Communications
    Manager: Talia Wise

Marketing Communications Manager:
    Christine Dobberpuhl

Production Director: Amy McGuire,
    B-books, Ltd.

Content Project Manager: Corinna Dibble

Media Editor: Jessica Badiner

Sr. Print Buyer: Susan Carroll

Production Service: B-books, Ltd.

Art Director: Linda Helcher

Internal Designer: Beckmeyer Design

Cover Designer: Didona Design

Cover Image: ©Getty Images

Photography Manager: Deanna Ettinger

Photo Researcher: Susan Van Etten

For product information and technology assistance, contact us at
Cengage Learning Academic Resource Center, 1-800-423-0563

For permission to use material from this text or product,
submit all requests online at **www.cengage.com/permissions.**
Further permissions questions can be e-mailed to
permissionrequest@cengage.com

Library of Congress Control Number: 2008934982

Student Edition:
ISBN-13: 978-0-495-57013-4
ISBN-10: 0-495-57013-3

Wadsworth
25 Thomson Place
Boston, MA 02210-1202
USA

Cengage Learning products are represented in Canada by
Nelson Education, Ltd.

For your course and learning solutions, visit **academic.cengage.com**
Purchase any of our products at your local college store or at our
preferred online store **www.ichapters.com**

Printed in the United States of America
3 4 5 6 7 11 10 09

COMM
Brief Contents

Learning Your Way

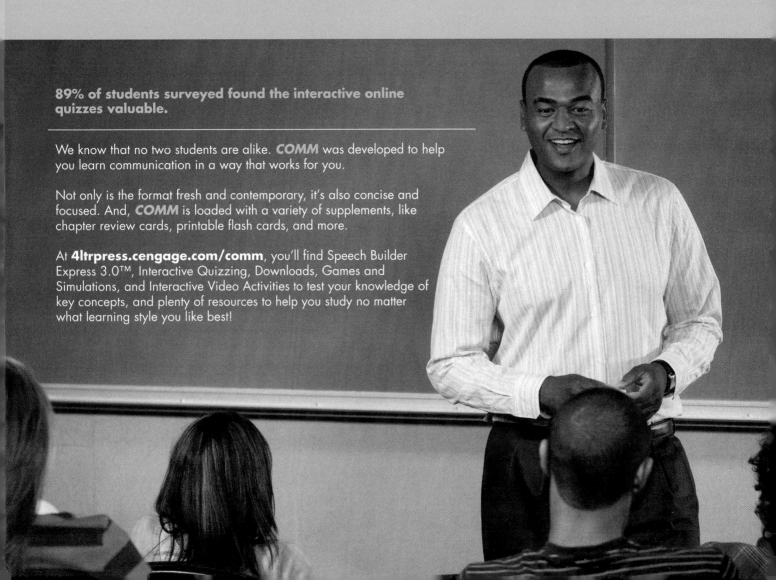

89% of students surveyed found the interactive online quizzes valuable.

We know that no two students are alike. *COMM* was developed to help you learn communication in a way that works for you.

Not only is the format fresh and contemporary, it's also concise and focused. And, *COMM* is loaded with a variety of supplements, like chapter review cards, printable flash cards, and more.

At **4ltrpress.cengage.com/comm**, you'll find Speech Builder Express 3.0™, Interactive Quizzing, Downloads, Games and Simulations, and Interactive Video Activities to test your knowledge of key concepts, and plenty of resources to help you study no matter what learning style you like best!

COMM Contents

PART **3** Group Communication 116

PART 4 Public Speaking 146

CHAPTER 1

Communication Perspectives

Learning Outcomes

LO   Define the communication process

LO   Discuss communication functions and settings

LO   Identify communication principles

LO   Discover how to increase communication competence

> **"** *The first skill that employers seek from college graduates is communication, including both speaking and writing.* **"**

Studies done over the years have concluded that, for almost any job, two of the most important skills sought by employers are oral communication skills and interpersonal abilities (Goleman, 1998, pp. 12–13). Even in fields not usually thought of as requiring strong communication skills, employers look for competence. For instance, an article on the role of communication in the workplace found that in engineering, a highly technical field, 72 percent of the employers surveyed indicated that speaking skills were very important (Darling & Dannels, 2003, p. 12). A survey by the National Association of Colleges and Employers (Koncz, 2006) reported the top 10 personal qualities and skills that employers seek from college graduates. The number-one skill was communication, including both speaking and writing, and the seventh item was interpersonal skills. So this course can significantly increase your ability to get a job and to be successful in your chosen career.

What do you think?

When sharing my ideas, I prefer to do so on a one-on-one basis.

Strongly Disagree   *Strongly Agree*

1	2	3	4	5	6	7

How effective you are in your communication with others is important to your career, but it is also the foundation for all of your personal relationships. Your ability to make and keep friends, to be a good family member, to have satisfying intimate relationships, to participate in or lead groups, and to prepare and present speeches depends on your communication skills. During this course, you will learn about the communication process and have an opportunity to practice basic communication skills that will help you improve your relationships.

In this first chapter, we explain the basic communication process, provide an overview of the functions communication serves, and explore the settings in which our communications occur. Then we describe the major principles of communication. Finally, we discuss communication competence and a process you can use for improving your communication skills.

LO^1 The Communication Process

Communication is the process of creating or sharing meaning in informal conversation, group interaction, or public speaking. To understand how this process works, we begin by describing its essential elements: participants (who), messages (what), context (where), channels (how), presence or absence of noise (distractions), and feedback (reaction).

communication
the process of creating or sharing meaning in informal conversation, group interaction, or public speaking

Participants

The participants are the individuals who assume the roles of senders and receivers during an interaction. As senders, participants form and transmit messages using verbal symbols and nonverbal behavior. As receivers, they interpret the messages and behaviors that have been transmitted to them.

Messages

Messages are the verbal utterances and nonverbal behaviors to which meaning is attributed during communication. To understand how messages are created and received, we need to understand meanings, symbols, encoding and decoding, and form or organization.

Meanings

Meanings include the thoughts in one person's mind as well as interpretations one makes of another's message. Meanings refer to the ways that communicators make sense of messages. It is important to realize that meanings are not transferred from one person to another, but are created together in an exchange. Some communication settings enable participants to verify that they have shared meanings; in other settings this is more difficult. For instance, if Sarah describes to Tiffany that her cat is old and fat, through the exchange of messages, they can together come to some degree of understanding of what "old" and "fat" mean. But if Tiffany is in an audience of 200 people listening to a speech Sarah is giving about cats, her ability to question Sarah and negotiate a mutual meaning is limited.

Symbols

To express yourself, you form messages comprising verbal symbols and nonverbal behaviors. **Symbols** are words, sounds, and actions that seek to represent specific ideas and feelings. As you speak, you choose word symbols to express your meaning. At the same time, facial expressions, eye contact, gestures, and tone of voice—all symbolic, nonverbal cues—accompany your words in an attempt to express your meaning. As a listener, you make interpretations or attribute meaning to the message you heard.

Encoding and Decoding

Encoding is the process of putting our thoughts and feelings into words and nonverbal cues. **Decoding** is the process of interpreting another's message. Ordinarily you do not consciously think about either the encoding or the decoding process. Only when there is a difficulty, such as speaking in a second language or having to use an easier vocabulary with children, do you become aware of encoding. You may not think about decoding until someone seems to speak in circles or uses unfamiliar technical words and you have difficulty interpreting or understanding what is being said.

Form or Organization

When the meaning we wish to share is complex, we may need to organize it in sections or in a certain order. Message form is especially important when one person talks without interruption for a relatively long time, such as in a public speech or when reporting an event to a colleague at work.

Contexts

Context is the setting in which a communication encounter occurs, including what precedes and follows what is said. The context affects the expectations of the participants, the meaning these participants derive, and their subsequent behavior. Context includes the (1) physical, (2) social, (3) historical, (4) psychological, and (5) cultural circumstances that surround a communication episode.

participants
individuals who assume the roles of senders and receivers during an interaction

messages
verbal utterances and nonverbal behaviors to which meaning is attributed during communication

meaning
thoughts in our minds and interpretations of others' messages

symbols
words, sounds, and actions that are generally understood to represent ideas and feelings

encoding
the process of putting our thoughts and feelings into words and nonverbal cues

decoding
the process of interpreting another's message

contexts
the settings in which communication occurs, including what precedes and follows what is said

{ Fast Facts—The Enigma Machine }

The Enigma machines were used during World War II by the German Army to transmit coded messages. Once a message was ready to be delivered, German intelligence officers would use the Enigma machines to encode the message so that people who did not know the code would not be able to understand it. Once the message was delivered, the receiver could use an Enigma machine to decode the message into its original form.

©GETTY IMAGES NEWS

Physical Context

The physical context includes its location, the environmental conditions (temperature, lighting, and noise level), the distance between communicators, seating arrangements, and time of day. Each of these factors can affect the communication. For instance, the meaning shared in a conversation may be affected by whether it is held in a crowded company cafeteria, an elegant candlelit restaurant, over the telephone, or on the Internet.

Social Context

The social context is the nature of relationship that may already exist between the participants. Whether communication takes place among family members, friends, acquaintances, work associates, or strangers influences what and how messages are formed, shared, and interpreted. For instance, most people change how they interact when talking with their parents or siblings as compared to how they interact when talking with their friends.

Historical Context

The historical context is the background provided by previous communication episodes between the participants. It influences understandings in the current encounter. For instance, suppose one morning Chad tells Shelby that he will get the draft of the report that they had left for their boss to read. As Shelby enters the office that afternoon, she sees Chad and says, "Did you get it?" Another person listening to the conversation would have no idea what the "it" is to which Shelby is referring. Yet Chad may well reply, "It's on my desk." Shelby and Chad would understand each other because of the contents of their earlier exchange.

Psychological Context

The psychological context includes the mood and feelings each person brings to the interpersonal encounter. For instance, suppose Corinne is under a lot of stress. While she is studying for an exam, a friend stops by and pleads with her to take a break and go to the gym with her. Corinne, who is normally good-natured, may explode with an angry tirade. Why? Because her stress level provides the psychological context within which she hears this message and it affects how she responds.

Cultural Context

The cultural context includes the values, attitudes, beliefs, orientations, and underlying assumptions prevalent among people in a society (Samovar, Porter, & McDaniel, 2007, p. 20). Culture penetrates

>> A student in an Asian culture might be quiet and respectful, while a student in a U.S. classroom might be more talkative and assertive.

into every aspect of our lives, affecting how we think, talk, and behave. Everyone is a part of one or more ethnic cultures, though we may differ in how much we identify with our ethnic cultures. When two people from different cultures interact, misunderstandings may occur because of the cultural variation between them. For example, the role of student in Asian cultures may mean being very quiet, respectful, and never challenging others' views, while the student role in U.S. classrooms may mean being talkative, assertive, and debating the views of others.

Channels

Channels are both the route traveled by the message and the means of transportation. Messages are transmitted through sensory channels. Face-to-face communication has two basic channels: verbal symbols and nonverbal cues. Online communication uses these same two channels, though some of the nonverbal cues like movements, touch, and gestures may be missing. Many aspects of the nonverbal channel such as facial expressions, aspects of voice, and use of time do occur online, however. We will explain more of these

physical context
its location, the environmental conditions (temperature, lighting, noise level), the distance between communicators, seating arrangements, and time of day

social context
the nature of the relationship that exists between the participants

historical context
the background provided by previous communication episodes between the participants that influence understandings in the current encounter

psychological context
the mood and feelings each person brings to the conversation

cultural context
the values, attitudes, beliefs, orientations, and underlying assumptions prevalent among people in a society

channel
both the route traveled by the message and the means of transportation

ONASIA/JUPITER IMAGES

concepts in Chapter 4, "Communicating through Nonverbal Behaviors."

Noise

Noise is any stimulus that interferes with the process of sharing meaning. Noise can be physical (based on external sounds) or it can be psychological (based on internal distractions).

Physical noise includes the sights, sounds, and other stimuli in the environment that draw people's attention away from intended meaning. For instance, while a friend is giving you directions on how to work the new MP3 player, your attention may be drawn away by the external noise of your favorite TV show, which is on in the next room. External noise does not have to be a sound, however. Perhaps, while the person gives the directions, your attention is drawn momentarily to an attractive man or woman. Such visual distractions are also physical noise.

Psychological noise includes internal distractions based on thoughts, feelings, or emotional reactions to symbols and can fall into two categories: internal noise and semantic noise. Internal noise refers to the thoughts and feelings that compete for attention and interfere with the communication process. If you have tuned out the lecture your professor is giving in class and tuned into a daydream or a past conversation, then you have experienced internal noise.

Semantic noise refers to the distractions aroused by certain symbols that take our attention away from the main message. If a friend describes a 40-year-old secretary as "the girl in the office," and you think "girl" is an odd and condescending term for a 40-year-old woman, you might not even hear the rest of what your friend has to say. Whenever we react emotionally to a word or a behavior, we are experiencing semantic noise.

Feedback

Feedback refers to the reactions and responses to messages that indicate to the sender whether and how that message was heard, seen, and interpreted. We can express feedback verbally through words or nonverbally through body language. We continuously give feedback when we are listening to another, if only by paying attention, giving a confused look, or showing signs of boredom. Or we may be very direct with feedback by saying, "I don't understand the point you are making" or "That's a great comment you just made."

A Model of the Basic Communication Process

Figure 1.1 illustrates the communication process between two people. In the minds of these people are meanings, thoughts, or feelings that they intend to share. The nature of those thoughts or feelings is created, shaped, and affected by their total field of experience, including such factors as values, culture, environment, experiences, occupation, sex, interests, knowledge, and attitudes. To communicate a message, the sender encodes thoughts or feelings into a message that is sent using one or more channels.

The receiver decodes or interprets the symbols in an attempt to understand the speaker's meaning. This decoding process is affected by the receiver's total field of experience—that is, by all the same factors that shape the encoding process. Feedback messages complete the process so that the sender and receiver can arrive at a similar understanding of the message.

The model depicts the context as the area around the participants. The physical, social, psychological, and cultural contexts permeate all parts of the process. Similarly, the model shows that during conversation physical and psychological noise, including internal and semantic distractions, may occur at various points and therefore affect the people's ability to arrive at similar meanings. As you might imagine, the process becomes much more complex when more than two people are conversing or when someone is speaking to a large and diverse audience.

noise
any stimulus that interferes with the process of sharing meaning

physical noise
sights, sounds, and other stimuli in the environment that draw people's attention away from intended meaning

psychological noise
internal distractions based on thoughts, feelings, or emotional reactions to symbols

internal noise
thoughts and feelings that compete for attention and interfere with the communication process

semantic noise
distractions aroused by certain symbols that take our attention away from the main message

feedback
reactions and responses to messages

©PHOTOSINDIA.COM/GETTY IMAGES

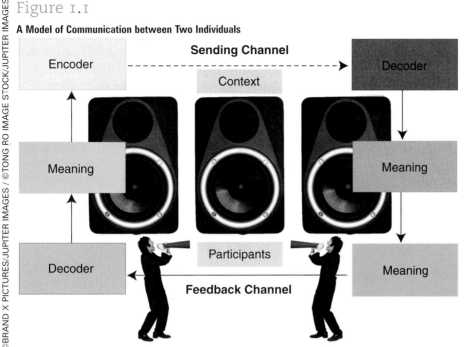

Figure 1.1

A Model of Communication between Two Individuals

Encoder — Sending Channel — Decoder

Context

Meaning — Meaning

Decoder — Participants — Meaning

Feedback Channel

LO² Communication Functions and Settings

Communication serves many functions and takes place in a variety of settings. When we know its various purposes, we are equipped to better understand the goals of the communication situation. When we recognize how settings affect the process, we can adapt our behavior so that we are more effective.

Communication Functions

Communication serves several functions for us, including social, developmental, and influential.

Meeting Social Needs

We communicate to meet our social needs. Just as we need food, water, and shelter, so too do we, as social animals, need contact with other people. Two people may converse happily for hours, gossiping and chatting about inconsequential matters that neither remembers afterward. When they part, they may have exchanged little real information and they may never meet again, but their communication has functioned to meet the important need simply to talk with another human being. Similarly, we greet others as we pass by to meet social obligations.

Developing and Maintaining Self

We communicate to develop and maintain our sense of self. Through our interactions, we learn who we are, what we are good at, and how people react to how we behave. We explore this important function of communication in detail in Chapter 2, "Perception of Self and Others."

Developing Relationships

We communicate to develop relationships. Not only do we get to know others through our communication with them but, more importantly, we develop relationships with them—relationships that grow and deepen or stagnate and wither away. We discuss how communication creates and maintains relationships in Chapter 6, "Communicating in Relationships."

Exchanging Information

We communicate to exchange information. Some information we get through observation, some through reading, some through media, and a great deal through direct communication with others either face-to-face or online. Whether we are trying to decide how warmly to dress or whom to vote for in the next presidential election, all of us have countless exchanges that involve sending and receiving information. We discuss communication as information exchange in Chapter 10, "Participating in Group Communication," and Chapter 16, "Informative Speaking."

Influencing Others

We communicate to influence others. It is doubtful that a day goes by in which you don't engage in behavior such as trying to convince your friends to go to a particular restaurant or to see a certain movie, to persuade your supervisor to alter your schedule, or to convince an instructor to change your course grade. We discuss the role of influencing

---

Communication Functions

1. Meet our social needs.
2. Develop and maintain our sense of self.
3. Develop relationships.
4. Exchange information.
5. Influence others.

others in Chapter 11, "Member Roles and Leadership in Groups," and in Chapter 17, "Persuasive Speaking."

Communication Settings

While the basic communication process describes how meanings are shared, various communication skills can be learned so that you are effective across a variety of settings. In this book, you will be introduced to skills that will help you achieve communication competence in interpersonal, problem-solving group, public speaking, and electronically mediated settings.

Interpersonal Communication Settings

Most of our communication takes place in **interpersonal communication settings**, which are characterized by informal interaction among a small number of people who have relationships with each other. Talking to a group of classmates on campus, chatting on the phone with your mother, arguing the merits of a movie with your brother, instant messaging with several friends, and comforting someone who has suffered a loss are all examples of interpersonal communication.

Our study of interpersonal communication begins by exploring how we develop, maintain, improve, or end our relationships with others. Then we will study the theory and skills of listening and responding empathically, sharing personal information, and self-disclosure and feedback. We will also discuss talking with people online and describe the skills you will need to be effective in interviews.

Problem-Solving Group Settings

Problem-solving group settings are characterized by participants who come together for the specific purpose of solving a problem or arriving at a decision. Much of this kind of communication takes place in formal or informal meetings.

Our study of problem-solving group settings includes a discussion of the characteristics of effective groups, the stages of group development, problem solving and decision making, and the roles participants play, including leadership.

Public Speaking Settings

Public speaking settings are characterized by one or more participants, the speakers, who deliver a prepared message to a group or audience who has assembled to hear the speakers.

Our discussion of public speaking settings focuses on the skills associated with effective speech preparation and delivery, including determining speaking goals, gathering and evaluating material, organizing and developing material, adapting material to a specific audience, and presenting the speech, as well as variations in procedure for information exchange and persuasion.

Electronically Mediated Communication (EMC) Settings

Today interpersonal communication, group discussion, and public speaking can all take place in **electronically mediated communication settings**, which are characterized by participants who do not share a physical context but communicate through the use of technology. Electronically mediated communication (EMC) can occur in real time or in delayed time, can involve as few as two people or as

interpersonal communication settings
interactions among a small number of people who have relationships with each other

problem-solving group settings
participants come together for the specific purpose of solving a problem or arriving at a decision

public speaking settings
one participant, the speaker, delivers a prepared message to a group or audience who has assembled to hear the speaker

electronically mediated communication settings
involves participants who do not share a physical context but communicate through the use of technology

e-mail
electronic correspondence conducted between two or more users on a network where the communication does not occur in real time

©STONE/GETTY IMAGES

many as millions of people, and can use one or multiple channels (written, voice, images).

Interpersonally, we may keep in touch with family and friends through e-mail, instant messaging, or text messaging. **E-mail** involves electronic correspondence conducted between two or more users on a network where the communication does not appear in real time. There is a delay between the sending and receiving of messages. **Instant messaging (IM)** involves electronic communication through maintaining a list of people that you can interact with in real time when they are online, with people that you have agreed to interact with by adding them to your IM list. **Text messaging** involves the sending of short, written messages between mobile phones and other handheld electronic devices. Messages may be exchanged in real time between phone users, or messages may be stored for later retrieval.

Group communication may occur through some of these types of EMC and through other types of online communication including listservs, chat rooms, weblogs, or interactive games. **Listservs** are electronic mailing lists sent through e-mail; they allow for widespread distribution of information to many Internet users. Any message sent to the listserv goes to all users, so online discussions can occur in a delayed time format. **Chat rooms** are web-based forums designed for interactive message exchange between two or more people who are logged into the room, where they exchange multiple messages in real time. **Weblogs** or **blogs** are online journals housed on a website. They include short, frequently updated postings arranged chronologically. They may be private and restricted to certain users who can read each other's blogs; or, they may be public, allowing any Internet user to read the messages. **Online games** are web-based sites where a group of people interact in real time to play common board games, games of chance, or fantasy role-playing games. Electronically mediated communication is particularly useful for conveying messages to a large public audience. The Internet has become the medium for posting job ads and résumés, for advertising and buying products, for political speechmaking and activism, for sharing social information

>> With over 10 million monthly subscribers worldwide, World of Warcraft, in which players create and assume the persona of an ingame fantasy character, go on quests, and interact with other players, is the world's largest massively multiplayer online role-playing game.

widely and establishing relationships, and for sending and retrieving information of all types.

LO³ Communication Principles

Principles are general truths. Understanding the principles of communication is important as you begin your study. In this section, we discuss seven principles: communication has purpose, communication is continuous, communication messages vary in conscious thought, communication is relational, communication is guided by culture, communication has ethical implications, and communication is learned.

Communication Has Purpose

When people communicate with each other, they have a purpose for doing so. The purpose of a given transaction may be either serious or trivial. One way to evaluate the success of the communication is to ask whether it achieved its purpose. When Beth calls Leah to ask whether she'd like to join her for lunch to discuss a project they are working on, her purpose may be to resolve a misunderstanding they've had. Speakers may not always be aware of their purpose. For instance, when Jamal passes Tony on the street and says lightly, "Tony,

instant messaging (IM) communication through maintaining a list of people that you can interact with in real time when they are online

text messaging short, written messages between mobile phones and other handheld electronic devices, exchanged in real time or stored for later retrieval

listservs electronic mailing lists through the use of e-mail that allow for widespread distribution of information to many Internet users, so online discussions can occur in a delayed time format

chat rooms interactive message exchange between two or more people where multiple messages are exchanged in real time

weblogs (blogs) online journals housed on a website

online games interaction among a group of people in real time to play common board games, games of chance, or fantasy role-playing games

what's happening?" Jamal probably doesn't consciously think, "Tony's an acquaintance and I want him to understand that I see him and consider him worth recognizing." In this case, the social obligation to recognize Tony is met spontaneously with the first acceptable expression that comes to Jamal's mind. Regardless of whether Jamal consciously thinks about the purpose, it still motivates his behavior. In this case, Jamal will have achieved his goal if Tony responds with an equally casual greeting.

Communication Is Continuous

Because communication is nonverbal as well as verbal, we are always sending behavioral messages from which others draw inferences or meaning. Even silence or absence is communication behavior if another person infers meaning from it. Why? It is because your nonverbal behavior represents reactions to your environment and to the people around you. If you are cold, you shiver; if you are hot or nervous, you perspire; if you are bored, happy, or confused, your face or body language probably will show it. As skilled communicators, we need to be aware of the explicit and implicit messages we are constantly sending to others.

Communication Messages Vary in Conscious Thought

As we discussed earlier in this chapter, sharing meaning with another person involves presenting verbal and nonverbal messages. Our messages may (1) occur spontaneously, (2) be based on a "script" we have learned or rehearsed, or (3) be carefully constructed based on our understanding of the unique situation in which we find ourselves.

Many of our messages are **spontaneous expressions**, spoken without much conscious thought. For example, when you burn your finger, you may blurt out "Ouch." When something goes right, you may break into a broad smile.

At other times, our messages are scripted, phrasings that we have learned from our past encounters and judge to be appropriate to the present situation. Many of these scripts are learned in childhood. For example, when you want the sugar bowl but cannot reach it, you may say, "Please pass the sugar," followed by "Thank you" when someone complies. This conversational sequence comes from your "table manners script," which may have been drilled into you at home. Scripts enable us to use messages that are appropriate to the situation and are likely to increase the effectiveness of our communication. One goal of this text is to acquaint you with general scripts (or skills) that can be adapted for use in your communication encounters across a variety of relationships, situations, and cultures.

Finally, our messages may be carefully constructed to meet the unique requirements of a particular situation. **Constructed messages** are those that we put together with careful thought when we recognize that our known scripts are inadequate for the situation.

Communication Is Relational

Saying that communication is relational means that in any communication setting, in addition to sharing content meaning, our messages also reflect two important aspects of our relationships: immediacy and control (dominance/submissiveness).

Immediacy is the degree of liking or attractiveness in a relationship. For instance, when José passes by Hal on campus he may say, "Hal, good to see you" (a verbal expression of friendliness); the nonverbal behavior that accompanies the words may show Hal whether José is genuinely happy to see him or is only expressing recognition. For instance, if José smiles, has a sincere sound to his voice, looks Hal in the eye, and perhaps pats him on the back or shakes hands firmly, then Hal will recognize these signs of friendliness. If, however, José speaks quickly with no vocal inflection and with a deadpan facial expression, Hal will perceive the comment as solely meeting some social expectation.

Control is the degree to which one participant is perceived to be more dominant or powerful. Thus, when Tom says to Sue, "I know you're concerned about the budget, but I'll see to it that we have

spontaneous expressions
spoken without much conscious thought

scripted messages
phrasings learned from past encounters that we judge to be appropriate to the present situation

constructed messages
messages put together with careful thought when we recognize that our known scripts are inadequate for the situation

immediacy
the degree of liking or attractiveness in a relationship

control
the degree to which one participant is perceived to be more dominant or powerful

money to cover everything," his words and the sound of his voice may be saying that he is "in charge" of finances—that he is in control. How Sue responds to Tom determines whether, on this issue, she submits to his perception of control. If Sue says, "Thanks, I know you have a better handle on finances than I do," then she accepts that on this issue, she is willing to submit to Tom at this time. A few days later, if Tom says to Sue, "I think we need to cut back on credit card expenses for a couple of months," and Sue responds, "No way! I need a new suit for work, the car needs new tires, and you promised we could replace the couch," then the nature of the relationship will require further discussion.

Communication Is Guided by Culture

Culture may be defined as systems of knowledge shared by a relatively large group of people. It includes a system of shared beliefs, values, symbols, and behaviors. How messages are formed and interpreted depends on the cultural background of the participants. We need to look carefully at ourselves and our communication behavior; as we interact with others whose cultural backgrounds differ from our own, we may unintentionally communicate in ways that are culturally inappropriate or insensitive and thereby undermine our relationships.

We must also be sensitive to how differences among people based on sex, age, class, physical characteristics, and sexual orientation affect communication. Failure to take those differences into account when we interact can also lead us to behave insensitively.

Throughout the history of the United States, we've experienced huge migrations of people from different parts of the world. According to the *New York Times Almanac* (Wright, 2002), the 2000 census shows that today, the largest number of new immigrants is from Latin America and Asia. At the end of the twentieth century, people of Latin and Asian descent constituted 12.5 percent and 3.8 percent, respectively, of the total U.S. population. About 2.4 percent of the population regards itself as multiracial. Combined with the approximately 13 percent of our population that is of African descent, these four groups account for nearly 32 percent of the total population. According to the U.S. Census Bureau, within the next 45 years, this figure is predicted to rise to nearly 50 percent.

> How messages are formed and interpreted depends on the cultural background of the participants.

According to Samovar, Porter, and McDaniel (2007) "three cultural elements have the potential to affect situations in which people from different backgrounds come together: (1) perception, (2) verbal processes, and (3) nonverbal processes" (p. 11). Because cultural concerns permeate all of communication, in each chapter of this book we will point out when the concepts and skills you are learning are viewed differently by other cultural groups.

Communication Has Ethical Implications

In any encounter, we choose whether or not we will communicate ethically. Ethics is a set of moral principles that may be held by a society, a group, or an individual. Although what is considered ethical is a matter of personal judgment, various groups still expect members to uphold certain standards. These standards influence the personal decisions we make. When we choose to violate the standards that are expected, we are viewed to be unethical. Here are five ethical standards that influence our communication and guide our behavior.

1. Truthfulness and honesty mean refraining from lying, cheating, stealing, or deception. "An honest person is widely regarded as a moral person, and honesty is a central concept to ethics as the foundation for a moral life" (Terkel & Duval, 1999, p. 122). Although most people accept truthfulness and honesty as a standard, they still confess to lying on occasion. We are most likely to lie when we are caught in a moral dilemma, a choice involving an unsatisfactory alternative. An example of a moral dilemma would be a boss asking us if our coworker arrived to work late today and knowing that telling the truth would get the coworker fired.
2. Integrity means maintaining a consistency of belief

culture
systems of knowledge shared by a relatively large group of people

ethics
a set of moral principles that may be held by a society, a group, or an individual

truthfulness and honesty
refraining from lying, cheating, stealing, or deception

moral dilemma
a choice involving an unsatisfactory alternative

integrity
maintaining a consistency of belief and action (keeping promises)

and action (keeping promises). Terkel and Duval (1999) say, "A person who has integrity is someone who has strong moral principles and will successfully resist the temptation to compromise those principles" (p. 135). Integrity, then, is the opposite of hypocrisy. A person who had promised to help a friend study for the upcoming exam would live up to this promise even when another friend offered a free ticket to a sold-out concert for the same night.

3. **Fairness** means achieving the right balance of interests without regard to one's own feelings and without showing favor to any side in a conflict. Fairness implies impartiality or lack of bias. To be fair to someone is to listen with an open mind, to gather all the relevant facts, consider only circumstances relevant to the decision at hand, and not let prejudice or irrelevancies affect how you treat others. For example, if two of her children are fighting, a mom is exercising fairness if she listens openly as the children explain "their side" before she decides what to do.

4. **Respect** means showing regard or consideration for others and their ideas, even if we don't agree with them. Respect is not based on someone's affluence, job status, or ethnic background. In a classroom, students show respect for others by attentively listening to another student's speech with a main point that violates their political or religious position.

5. **Responsibility** means being accountable for one's actions and what one says. Responsible communicators recognize the power of words. Messages can hurt and messages can soothe. Information is accurate or it may be faulty. A responsible communicator would not spread a false rumor about another friend.

In our daily lives, we often face ethical dilemmas and must sort out what is more or less right or wrong. In making these decisions, we usually reveal our ethical standards. The prep card for each chapter of this book includes a What Would You Do? A Question of Ethics that asks you to think about and resolve an ethical dilemma that relates to that chapter's content. Your instructor may use these as a vehicle for class discussions, or you may be asked to prepare a written report.

fairness
achieving the right balance of interests without regard to one's own feelings and without showing favor to any side in a conflict

respect
showing regard or consideration for others and their ideas, even if we don't agree with them

responsibility
being accountable for one's actions and what one says

> 1. TRUTHFULNESS & HONESTY
> 2. INTEGRITY
> 3. FAIRNESS
> 4. RESPECT
> 5. COMMUNICATION AND COMPETENCE

Communication Is Learned

Just as you learned to walk, so too you learned to communicate. But talking is a complex undertaking. You may not yet have learned all of the skills you will need to develop healthy relationships. Because communication is learned, you can improve your ability. Throughout this text, we identify interpersonal, group, and public speaking skills that can help you become a more competent communicator.

>> Just as children learn how to behave from their parents, so too do they learn to communicate. What specific communication behaviors can you identify that you learned at home?

©RADIUSIMAGES/JUPITER IMAGES

> > As a leading expert in the field of physics, most people would consider Stephen Hawking a person with credibility.

LO⁴ Increasing Our Communication Competence

Communication competence is the impression that communicative behavior is both appropriate and effective in a given situation (Spitzberg, 2000, p. 375). Communication is *effective* when it achieves its goals; it is *appropriate* when it conforms to what is expected in a situation. We create the perception that we are competent communicators through the verbal messages we send and the nonverbal behaviors that accompany them. Competence is an impression or judgment that people make about others. Because communication is at the heart of how we relate to each other, one of your goals in this course will be to learn strategies to increase the likelihood that others will view you as competent.

Motivation is important because we will only be able to improve our communication if we are *motivated*—that is, if we want to. People are likely to be more motivated if they are confident and if they see potential rewards.

> COMMUNICATION IS *effective* WHEN IT ACHIEVES ITS GOALS; IT IS *appropriate* WHEN IT CONFORMS TO WHAT IS EXPECTED IN A SITUATION.

Knowledge is important because we must know what is involved in increasing competence. The more knowledge people have about how to behave in a given situation, the more likely they are to be able to develop competence.

Skill is important because we must know how to act in ways that are consistent with our communication knowledge. **Skills** are goal-oriented actions or action sequences that we can master and repeat in appropriate situations. The more skills you have, the more likely you are to be able to structure your messages effectively and appropriately.

In addition to motivation, knowledge, and skills, credibility and social ease are important components of communication competence. **Credibility** is a perception of a speaker's knowledge, trustworthiness, and warmth. Listeners are more likely to be attentive to and influenced by speakers they see as credible. **Social ease** means communicating without

communication competence
the impression that communicative behavior is both appropriate and effective in a given situation

skills
goal-oriented actions or action sequences that we can master and repeat in appropriate situations

credibility
a perception of a speaker's knowledge, trustworthiness, and warmth

social ease
communicating without anxiety or nervousness

Goal Statement for Improving Skills

1. State the problem.
2. State the specific goal.
3. Outline a specific procedure for reaching the goal.
4. Devise a method of determining when the goal has been reached.

anxiety or nervousness. To be seen as a competent communicator, it is important that you can speak in a style that conveys confidence and poise. Communicators that are apprehensive or anxious are not likely to be regarded as competent, despite their motivation or knowledge.

The combination of our motivation, knowledge, skills, credibility, and social ease leads us to perform effectively in our encounters with others. The rest of this book is aimed at helping you increase the likelihood that you will be perceived as competent. In the pages that follow, you will learn about theories of interpersonal, group, and public speaking that can increase your knowledge and your motivation. You will also learn how to perform specific skills, and you will be provided with opportunities to practice them. Through this practice, you can increase the likelihood that you will be able to perform these skills when needed.

Develop Communication Skill Improvement Goals

To get the most from this course, we suggest that you write personal goals to improve specific skills in your own interpersonal, group, and public communication repertoire.

Before you can write a goal statement, you must first analyze your current communication skills repertoire. After you read each chapter and practice the skills described, select one or two skills to work on. Then write down your goal statement in four parts.

1. **State the problem.** Start by stating a communication problem that you have. For example: "Problem: Even though some of my group members in a team-based class project have not produced the work they promised, I haven't spoken up because I'm not very good at describing my feelings."
2. **State the specific goal.** A goal is specific if it is measurable and you know when you have achieved it. For example, to deal with the problem stated above, you might write, "Goal: To describe my disappointment to other group members about their failure to meet deadlines."
3. **Outline a specific procedure for reaching the goal.** To develop a plan for reaching your goal, first consult the chapter that covers the skill

you wish to hone (for instance, Describing Feelings in Chapter 8). Then translate the general steps recommended in the chapter to your specific situation. For example: "Procedure: I will practice the steps of describing feelings. (1) I will identify the specific feeling I am experiencing. (2) I will encode the emotion I am feeling accurately. (3) I will include what has triggered the feeling. (4) I will own the feeling as mine. (5) I will then put that procedure into operation when I am talking with my group members."
4. **Devise a method of determining when the goal has been reached.** A good goal is measurable, and the fourth part of your goal-setting effort is to determine your minimum requirements for knowing when you have achieved a given goal. For example: "Test of Achieving Goal: This goal will be considered achieved when I have described my disappointment to my group members about missed deadlines."

Figure 1.2 provides another example of a communication improvement plan, this one relating to a public speaking problem.

Figure 1.2

Communication Improvement Plan

Problem: When I speak in class or in the student senate, I often find myself burying my head in my notes or looking at the ceiling or walls.

Goal: To look at people more directly when I'm giving a speech.

More Bang for Your Buck

has it all, and you can too. Between the text and our online offerings, you have everything at your fingertips. Make sure you check out all that   has to offer:

- Speech Builder Express
- Printable Flash Cards
- Interactive Games
- Interactive Video Activities

- Chapter Review Cards
- Online Quizzing with Feedback
- Audio Downloads
- And More!

Visit **4ltrpress.cengage.com/comm**
to find the resources you need today!

Learning Outcomes

LO¹ Discuss the perception process

LO² Examine self-perceptions and how they affect communication

LO³ Examine what determines our perception of others

LO⁴ Describe how we perceive messages

Perception
of Self
and Others

"For each person, perception becomes reality. What one person sees, hears, and interprets is real and considered true to that person."

How can two people come to have different takes on the same event? Though the details might be the same, different people may be lead to focus on different parts of the situation, or their individual circumstances might affect the way that they see things. In this way different people may carry away different perceptions of the same event. Because much of the meaning we share with others is based on our perceptions, our study of communication begins with understanding the general perceptual process and the social perceptions that affect how we view others.

In this chapter, we discuss the perception process, perceptions of self including self-concept and self-esteem, and perceptions of others. We offer suggestions for improving the accuracy of your perceptions.

LO¹ The Perception Process

Perception is the process of selectively attending to information and assigning meaning to it. At times, our perceptions of the world, other people, and ourselves agree with the perceptions of others. At other times, our perceptions are significantly different from the perceptions of other people. For each person, perception becomes reality. What one person sees, hears, and interprets is real and considered true to that person. Another person who may see, hear, and interpret something entirely different from the same situation will regard that different perception as real and true. So when our perceptions are different from those with whom we interact, sharing meaning becomes more challenging.

Your brain selects the information it receives from your senses, organizes the information, and then interprets it.

Attention and Selection

Although we are subject to a constant barrage of sensory stimuli, we focus attention on relatively little of it. How we choose depends in part on our needs, interests, and expectations.

Needs

We are likely to pay attention to information that meets our biological and psychological needs. When you go to class, how well in tune you are to what is being discussed is likely to

perception
the process of selectively attending to information and assigning meaning to it

>> **So much stimuli can be overwhelming.**

©KUMAR SARSKANDAN/ALAMY

depend on whether you believe the information is important to you—that is, does it meet a personal need?

Interests

We are likely to pay attention to information that pertains to our interests. For instance, you may not even recognize that music is playing in the background until you find yourself suddenly listening to some old favorite. Similarly, when you are really attracted to a person, you are more likely to pay attention to what that person is saying.

Expectations

Finally, we are likely to see what we expect to see and to miss information that violates our expectations. Take a quick look at the phrases in the triangles in Figure 2.1. If you have never seen these triangles, you probably read "Paris in the springtime," "Once in a lifetime," and "Bird in the hand." But if you re-examine the words, you will see that what you perceived was not exactly what is written. Do you now see the repeated words? It is easy to miss the repeated word because we don't expect to see the word repeated.

Organization of Stimuli

Even though our attention and selection process limits the stimuli our brain must process, the absolute number of discrete stimuli we attend to at any one moment is still substantial. Our brains fol-

low certain organizing principles to arrange these stimuli so that they make sense. Two common principles we use are simplicity and pattern.

Simplicity

If the stimuli we attend to are very complex, the brain simplifies the stimuli into some commonly recognized form. Based on a quick look at what someone is

Figure 2.1

A Sensory Test of Expectation

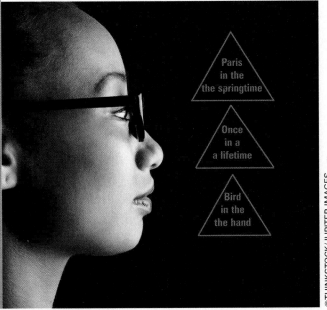

Paris
in the
the springtime

Once
in a
a lifetime

Bird
in the
the hand

©THINKSTOCK/JUPITER IMAGES

wearing, how she is standing, and the expression on her face, we may perceive her as a successful businesswoman, a doctor, or a soccer mom. Similarly, we simplify the verbal messages we receive. So, for example, Tony might walk out of an hour-long performance review meeting with his boss in which the boss described four of Tony's strengths and three areas for improvement and say to Jerry, his coworker, "Well, I better shape up or I'm going to get fired!"

Pattern

A second principle the brain uses when organizing information is to find patterns. A **pattern** is a set of characteristics used to differentiate some things from others. A pattern makes it easy to interpret stimuli. For example, when you see a crowd of people, instead of perceiving each individual, you may focus on a characteristic of sex and "see" men and women, or you may focus on age and "see" children, teens, adults, and seniors. In our interactions with others, we try to find patterns that will enable us to interpret and respond to their behavior. For example, each time Jason and Bill encounter Sara, she hurries over to them and begins an animated conversation. Yet when Jason is alone and runs into Sara, she barely says "Hi." After a while Jason may detect a pattern to Sara's behavior. She is warm and friendly when Bill is around and not so friendly when Bill is absent. Based on this pattern, Jason may interpret Sara's friendly behavior as flirting with Bill.

Interpretation of Stimuli

As the brain selects and organizes the information it receives from the senses, it also interprets the information by assigning meaning to it. Look at these three sets of numbers. What do you make of them?

A. 631 7348
B. 285 37 5632
C. 4632 7364 2596 2174

In each of these sets, your mind looked for clues to give meaning to the numbers. Because you use similar patterns of numbers every day, you probably interpret A as a telephone number. How about B? A likely interpretation is a Social Security number. And C? People who use credit cards may interpret this set as a credit card number.

Our interpretation of others' behavior in conversation affects how we interact with them. If Jason believes that Sara is only interested in Bill, he may not participate in conversations that she initiates.

In the remainder of this chapter, we will apply this basic information about perception to the study of perceptions of self and others in our communication.

LO^2 Perceptions of Self: Self-Concept and Self-Esteem

Self-concept and self-esteem are the two self-perceptions that have the greatest impact on how we communicate. Self-concept is your self-identity (Baron, Byrne, & Brascombe, 2006). It is the idea or mental image that you have about your skills, your abilities, your knowledge, your competencies, and your personality. Self-esteem is your overall evaluation of your competence and personal worthiness (based on Mruk, 1999, p. 26). In this section, we describe how you come to understand who you are and how you evaluate yourself. Then we examine what determines how well these self-perceptions match others' perceptions of you. Finally, we discuss the role self-perceptions play when you communicate with others.

Forming and Maintaining a Self-Concept

How do we learn what our skills, abilities, knowledge, competencies, and personality are? Our self-concept comes from the unique interpretations about ourselves that we have made based on our experience and from others' reactions and responses to us.

Self-Perception

We form impressions about ourselves based on our own perceptions. Through our experiences, we develop our own sense of our skills, our abilities, our knowledge, our competencies, and our personality. For example, if you perceive that it is easy for you to talk in front of a group of people, you may conclude that you are a "natural" as a public speaker.

We place a great deal of emphasis on the first experience we have with a particular phenomenon. For instance, someone who is rejected in his first try at dating may perceive himself to be unattractive to the opposite sex. If additional experiences produce results similar to the first experience, this first perception will be strengthened. Even if the first experience is not immediately repeated, it is

pattern
a set of characteristics used to differentiate some things from others

interpret
assigning meaning to information

self-concept
your self-identity

self-esteem
your overall evaluation of your competence and personal worthiness

©LJS PHOTOGRAPHY/ALAMY

Jackie

Sonya

likely to take more than one contradictory experience to change the original negative perception.

When we have positive experiences, we are likely to believe we possess the personal characteristics that we associate with that experience, and these characteristics become part of our picture of who we are. So if Sonya quickly debugs a computer program that Jackie has struggled with, she is more likely to incorporate "competent problem solver" into her self-concept. Her positive experience confirms that she has that skill, so it is reinforced as part of her self-concept.

Reactions and Responses of Others

In addition to our self-perceptions, our self-concept is formed and maintained by how others react and respond to us (Rayner, 2001, p. 43). We use other people's comments as a check on our own self-descriptions. They serve to validate, reinforce, or alter our perception of who and what we are. For example, if during a brainstorming session at work, one of your coworkers tells you, "You're really a creative thinker," you may decide that this comment fits your image of who you are. Such comments are especially powerful in affecting your self-perception if you respect the person making the comment. And the power of such comments is increased when the praise is immediate rather than delayed (Hattie, 1992, p. 251).

Some people have very strong self-concepts; they can describe numerous skills, abilities, knowledge, competencies, and personality characteristics that they possess. They think positively about themselves. Others have weak self-concepts; they cannot describe the skills, abilities, knowledge, competencies, or the personality characteristics that they have. They think negatively about themselves.

Our self-concept begins to form early in life, and information we receive from our families shapes our self-concept (Demo, 1987). One of the major responsibilities that family members have is to talk and act in ways that will help develop accurate and strong self-concepts in other family members. For example, the mom who says, "Roberto, your room looks very neat. You are very organized," or the brother who comments, "Kisha, lending Tomika 20 dollars really helped her out. You are very generous," is helping Roberto or Kisha to recognize important parts of their personalities.

Unfortunately, in some families, members do not fulfill these responsibilities. Sometimes family members actually do real damage to each other's self-image, especially to the developing self-images of children. Communicating blame, name-calling, and repeatedly pointing out another's shortcomings are particularly damaging.

Developing and Maintaining Self-Esteem

You'll recall that our self-esteem is our overall evaluation of our competence and personal worthiness—it is our positive or negative evaluation of our self-concept. Our evaluation of our personal worthiness is rooted in our values and develops over time as a result of our experiences. As Mruk (1999) points out, self-esteem is not just how well or poorly we do things (self-concept) but the importance or value we place on what we do well or poorly (p. 27). For instance, as part of Chad's self-concept, he believes he is physically strong. But if he doesn't believe that physical strength or other characteristics he possesses are worthwhile or valuable to have, then he will not have high self-esteem. Mruk explains that it takes both the perception of having a characteristic and a personal belief that the characteristic is of positive value to produce high self-esteem.

When we successfully use our skills, abilities, or knowledge in worthwhile endeavors, we raise our self-esteem. When we are unsuccessful in using our skills and abilities, or when we use them in unworthy endeavors, we lower our self-esteem.

Social Construction of Self

We create multiple selves in an ongoing manner through our relationships with many different people. All people progressively modify and reinvent their public personas. We create different characters to respond to different situations and change ourselves in the process. We socially construct ourselves through the roles we enact.

A **role** is a pattern of learned behaviors that people use to meet the perceived demands of a particular context. For instance, during the day you may enact the roles of student, brother/sister, and salesclerk. Let's look at all the different personas or selves that one person may create and present across a few days. Stephen presents certain aspects of himself at work as a restaurant server. There he is very polite, helpful, agreeable, and attentive to others. He does not talk about himself much or use cusswords. He is confident, moves quickly, and cares about being efficient and productive. When Stephen goes out with his friends after work, he is more casual and less concerned about time. Perhaps he is louder and more boisterous. He may talk about himself more, cuss occasionally, and get into heated debates of issues and ideas. When Stephen visits his grandmother, he may act more childlike, he may be cautious not to mention topics that may offend his grandmother, and he may listen more than he talks. Stephen will enact other selves at school, playing soccer, on a date, or with his siblings. Which is Stephen's real self? They all are. We are not unitary beings. Our sense of self is the total of all the selves we play and how others react to those selves. Stephen and society will create and recreate his sense of self continuously throughout his life.

Self-Monitoring

In any situation that we face, we can choose how we present ourselves to others. **Self-monitoring** is the internal process of observing and regulating your own behavior based on your analysis of the situation and others' responses to you. Because self-monitoring goes on inside your head, others don't know if or when you are doing it. Some people are very aware of other people's responses to their behavior. They notice people's expressions and reactions and use this feedback to adjust their own behavior so that they leave the impression they wish to leave. Other people are less aware of the impression they are making. As a result, they tend to do and say things that may be viewed as inappropriate or lead others to have an inaccurate impression of them.

We are more likely to self-monitor when we are in new situations. When we don't know what is expected, we look to others for cues to see if we are behaving appropriately, and we are likely to adjust our behavior accordingly. So when Mia, who is visiting her friend at another college, finds herself at a party with a bunch of strangers, she may want to show her sophisticated side so she can fit in. As a result, she may find her self-talk filled with self-monitoring statements like, "Why did I just make that comment—it sounded so lame?" or "Well, I sure scored points there; now I've got their attention." Being aware of and attentive to other's feedback is an important part of self-monitoring.

Accuracy of Self-Concept and Self-Esteem

The accuracy of our self-concept and self-esteem depends on the accuracy of our own perceptions and how we process others' perceptions of us. All of us experience success and failure, and all of us hear praise and criticism. If we are overly attentive to successful experiences and positive responses, our self-concept may become overdeveloped and our self-esteem

>> **Which one is the "real" Stephen?**

role
a pattern of learned behaviors that people use to meet the perceived demands of a particular context

self-monitoring
the internal process of observing and regulating your own behavior based on your analysis of the situation and others' responses to you

inflated. If, however, we perceive and dwell on failures and give little value to our successes, or if we only remember the criticism we receive, our self-image may be underdeveloped and our self-esteem low. In neither case does our self-concept or self-esteem accurately reflect who we are.

Incongruence, the gap between our inaccurate self-perceptions and reality, is a problem because our perceptions of self are more likely than our true abilities to affect our behavior (Weiten, 1998, p. 491). For example, Raul may actually possess all the skills, abilities, knowledge, competencies, and personality characteristics for effective leadership, but if he doesn't perceive that he has these characteristics, he won't step forward when leadership is needed. Unfortunately, individuals tend to reinforce their self-perceptions by adjusting their behavior to conform with their perceived self-conceptions. That is, people with high self-esteem tend to behave in ways that lead to more affirmation, whereas people with low self-esteem tend to act in ways that confirm the low esteem in which they hold themselves. The inaccuracy of a distorted picture of oneself is magnified through self-fulfilling prophecies and by filtering messages.

Self-Fulfilling Prophecies

Self-fulfilling prophecies are events that happen as the result of being foretold, expected, or talked about. They may be self-created or other-imposed.

Self-created prophecies are those predictions you make about yourself. We often talk ourselves into success or failure. For example, researchers have found that when people expect rejection, they are more likely to behave in ways that lead others to reject them (Downey, Freitas, Michaelis, & Khouri, 2004, p. 437). So Aaron, who sees himself as unskilled in establishing new relationships; says to himself, "I doubt I'll know hardly anyone at the party—I'm going to have a miserable time." Because he fears encountering strangers, he feels awkward about introducing himself and, just as he predicted, spends much of his time standing around alone thinking about when he can leave. In contrast, Stefan sees himself as quite social and able to get to know people easily. As a result of his positive self-esteem and prophecy, he looks forward to the party and, just as he predicted, makes several new acquaintances and enjoys himself.

incongruence
the gap between our inaccurate self-perceptions and reality

self-fulfilling prophecies
events that happen as the result of being foretold, expected, or talked about

Self-esteem has an important effect on the prophecies people make. For instance, people with positive self-esteem view success positively and confidently prophesy that they can repeat successes; people with low self-esteem attribute their successes to luck, and so prophesy that they will not repeat them (Hattie, 1992, p. 253).

The prophecies others make about you also affect your performance and self-image. For example, when teachers act as if their students are bright, students "buy into" this expectation and learn. Likewise, when teachers act as if students are not bright, students may live "down" to these imposed prophecies and fail to achieve. So how we talk to ourselves and how we treat others affects self-concepts and self-esteem.

Filtering Messages

A second way that our self-perceptions can become distorted is through the way we filter what others say to us. We are prone to pay attention to messages that reinforce our current self-image, whereas messages that contradict this image may not "register" or may be downplayed. For example, suppose you prepare an agenda for your study group. Someone comments that you're a good organizer. If you spent your childhood hearing how disorganized you were, you may not really hear this comment, or you may downplay it. If, however, you think you are good at organizing, you will pay attention to the compliment and may even reinforce it by responding, "Thanks, I'm a pretty organized person. I've learned it from my boss at work."

Changing Self-Concepts and Self-Esteem

Self-concept and self-esteem are enduring characteristics, but they can be changed. At times, comments that contradict your current self-concept and self-esteem are absorbed and lead you to slowly change your self-image. Certain situations seem to expedite this process. When you experience a profound change in your social environment, you are likely to be amenable to incorporating new information into your self-image. When children begin school or go to sleep-away camp; when teens start part-time jobs; when young adults go to college; or when people begin or end jobs or relationships, become parents, or grieve the loss of someone they love, they are more likely to absorb messages that are at odds with their current self-images.

Therapy and self-help techniques can assist us when we want to alter our self-concept and improve our self-esteem. In his analysis of numerous research studies, Christopher Mruk (1999, p. 112) found that self-esteem is increased through "hard work and practice, practice, practice—there is simply no escaping this basic existential fact."

So why is this important to communication? Because our self-esteem affects with whom we choose to form relationships, how we interact with them, how we participate when we are in small groups, and how comfortable we feel when we are called on to present a speech. Researchers have found that "people with high self-esteem are more committed to partners who perceive them very favorably, while people with low self-esteem are more committed to partners who perceive them less favorably" (Leary, 2002, p. 130).

In this book, we consider many specific communication behaviors that are designed to increase your communication competence. As you begin to practice and to perfect these skills, you may begin to receive positive responses to your behavior. If you continue to work on these skills, the posi-

Therapy can wring out absorbed messages.

©WORKBOOK STOCK/JUPITER IMAGES

tive responses you receive will help improve your self-concept and increase your self-esteem.

Self-Concept, Self-Esteem, and Communication

Just as our self-concept and self-esteem affect how accurately we perceive ourselves, so too do they influence our communication by moderating competing internal messages in our self-talk and influencing our personal communication style.

Self-perceptions moderate how we talk to ourselves. Self-talk is the internal conversations we have with ourselves. A lot of this conversation is also about ourselves. People who have high self-esteem are likely to engage in positive self-talk, such as "I know I can do it" or "I did really well on that test." They are also more likely to have self-talk that is more accurate. People with negative self-esteem are likely to overemphasize negative self-talk or, ironically, they may overinflate their sense of self-worth to compensate. So they may tell themselves that they are good at everything they do.

Self-perception influences how we talk about ourselves with others. If we feel good about ourselves, we are likely to communicate positively. For instance, people with a strong self-concept and higher self-esteem usually take credit for their successes. Likewise, people with healthy self-perceptions are inclined to defend their views even in the face of opposing arguments. If we feel bad about ourselves, we are likely to communicate negatively by downplaying our accomplishments.

Why do some people put themselves down regardless of what they have done? People who have low self-esteem are likely to be unsure of the value of their contributions and expect others to view them negatively. As a result, people with a poor self-concept or low self-esteem may find it less painful to put themselves down than to hear the criticism of others. Thus, to preempt the likelihood that others will comment on their unworthiness, they do it first.

Cultural and Gender Influences

A person's culture has a strong influence on the self-perception process (Samovar, Porter, & McDaniel, 2007, p. 130). In some cultures, described as individualistic, people stress the self and personal achievement. In these cultures, the individual is treated as the

self-talk
the internal conversations we have with ourselves

most important element in a social setting. In individualistic cultures, people care about self-concept, self-esteem, and self-image. The United States is considered an individualistic culture. In fact, all the information thus far in this chapter reflects an individualistic cultural perspective on perception and the self-concept. Other cultures are considered collectivist and they tend to downplay the individual. Groups and social norms are more important in collectivist cultures. People are expected to be interdependent and to see themselves in terms of the group. Notions of self-concept and self-esteem have little meaning in collectivist cultures. In an individualistic culture, you would think only of what is best for yourself when making a decision, such as taking a new job. You might move far away from family for the job. At work, you would want to be paid, judged, and promoted on your own work rather than how the group is performing. In a collectivist culture, your decision about taking a new job would be made collectively by your family, and you would be expected to live near the family. Your salary, performance evaluations, and promotions would naturally be based on how well the entire group, team, or department was functioning.

Similarly, men and women are socialized to view themselves differently and to value who they are based on whether their behavior corresponds to or challenges the behavior expected of their sex in their culture. There are norms of what it means to be feminine and what it means to be masculine in our society. Gender expectations in a society inevitably influence our perceptions, sense of self, and social construction of self. Generally in the United States, males are taught to base their self-esteem on their achievements, status, and income, while females are taught that their self-esteem derives from their appearance and their relationships (Wood, 2007). Thus, it is difficult to understand the process of social perception without taking into consideration the influences of culture and gender. The Internet offers a variety of sources on the topics of self-concept and self-esteem. Many of them offer suggestions that people have found useful. You can use a search engine like Google to find and view such sites.

Individualist

©RADIUS IMAGES/JUPITER IMAGES

Will others accept and value us? Will we be able to get along? Because this uncertainty makes us uneasy, we try to alleviate it. Charles Berger describes the process we use to overcome our discomfort as **uncertainty reduction**, the process of monitoring the social environment to learn more about self and others (Littlejohn & Foss, 2005). As people interact, they gain information and form impressions of others. For example, when Nicole and Justin meet for the first time at a party, they probably pay much attention to how each other looks, because that's the only source of information they have about each other at first. Then, they ask each other questions about their majors, jobs, hobbies, interests, and people they may know in common. This small talk helps them gain information so that they can find things they have in common. The more they learn about each other and find commonalities, the less uncertain they are about each other. These perceptions will be reinforced, intensified, or changed as their relationship develops. The factors likely to influence perceptions of others include their physical characteristics and social behaviors, their messages, your use of stereotyping, and your emotional state.

Observing Physical Characteristics and Social Behaviors

Social perceptions, especially first impressions, are often made on the basis of physical characteristics and social behaviors. On the basis of people's physical attractiveness (facial characteristics, height, weight, grooming, dress, sound of voice), we are likely to categorize people as friendly, trendy, intelligent, cool, or their opposites (Aronson, 1999, p. 380).

LO^3 Perception of Others

uncertainty reduction
the process of monitoring the social environment to learn more about self and others

As we encounter others, we are faced with a number of questions: Do we have anything in common?

> **" First impressions are formed not only in face-to-face communication, but in online interaction as well. "**

In one study, professional women dressed in jackets were assessed as more powerful than professional women dressed in other clothing (Temple & Loewen, 1993, p. 345). Show a friend a picture of your child, uncle, or grandmother, and your friend may well form impressions of your relative's personality on the basis of that photo alone!

Early impressions are also made on the basis of a person's social behaviors. If, on the first day of class, a fellow student strikes up conversations with strangers sitting near him, makes humorous remarks in class, and gives the best self-introduction in a class activity, you are likely to form the impression that he is confident, extroverted, and friendly.

First impressions are formed not only in face-to-face communication, but in online interaction as well. People care about creating the right impression online through the timeliness of their responses, the use of chat room nicknames, and their use of vocabulary, grammar, and manners (sometimes called *netiquette*). Initial interaction online often begins with the question A/S/L?, which asks for someone's age, sex, and location. This is a get-to-know-you question, which allows someone to reduce uncertainty about the other person. Creating personal home pages also relates to self-identity and first impressions. Creating a personal home page is an opportunity for people to reflect upon themselves and to think about how they want to represent themselves to the world. It is an

attempt to influence others' first impressions of you (Thurlow, Lengel, & Tomic, 2004).

Some judgments of other people are based on **implicit personality theories**, which are assumptions people have developed about which physical characteristics and personality traits or behaviors are associated with another (Michener & DeLamater, 1999, p. 106). Because your own implicit personality theory says that certain traits go together, you are likely to generalize and perceive that a person has a whole set of characteristics when you have actually observed only one characteristic, trait, or behavior. When you do this, your perception is exhibiting what is known as the **halo effect**. For instance, Heather sees Martina personally greeting and welcoming every person who arrives at the meeting. Heather's implicit personality theory views this behavior as a sign of the characteristic of warmth. She further associates warmth with goodness, and goodness with honesty. As a result, she perceives that Martina is good and honest as well as warm.

In reality, Martina may be a con artist who uses her warmth to lure people into a false sense of trust. This example demonstrates a "positive halo" (Heather assigned Martina positive characteristics), but we also use implicit personality theory to inaccurately impute bad characteristics. Given limited amounts of information, then, we fill in details. This tendency to fill in details leads to a second factor that explains social perception, stereotyping.

Using Stereotypes

Perhaps the most commonly known factor that influences our perception of others is stereotyping.

>> In what ways do you think the salesmen of these fraudulent medicines were able to play off the perceptions of their audiences in selling their products? What characteristics do you think they truly exhibited, and what characteristics do you think their clients filled in?

implicit personality theories
assumptions people have developed about which physical characteristics and personality traits or behaviors are associated with another

halo effect
to generalize and perceive that a person has a whole set of characteristics when you have actually observed only one characteristic, trait, or behavior

Stereotypes are "attributions that cover up individual differences and ascribe certain characteristics to an entire group of people" (Hall, 2002, p. 198). So, when we find out that someone is Hispanic or Muslim, a skateboarder, a chess player, an elementary school teacher, or a nurse—in short, any "identifiable group"—we use this information to attribute to the person a host of characteristics. These perceived group characteristics, taken as a whole, may be positive or negative, and they may be accurate or inaccurate (Jussim, McCauley, & Lee, 1995, p. 6).

We are likely to develop generalized perceptions about any group we come in contact with. Subsequently, any number of perceptual cues—skin color, style of dress, a religious medal, gray hair, a loud voice, an expensive car, and so on—can lead us to stereotype our generalizations onto a specific individual. A professor may see a student's purple spiked hair and numerous tattoos and assume the student defies authority, does not take school seriously, and seeks attention. In reality, this person may be a quiet, serious honor student who obeys rules and aspires to graduate school. A customer may generalize that her bank teller is professional and competent because the teller is wearing a business suit and speaks with proper grammar, while, in reality, the bank teller makes frequent mistakes and is about to be fired. According to B. J. Hall (2002, p. 201), we don't form most of the stereotypes we use from our personal experience. Instead we learn them from family, friends, coworkers, and the mass media. So we adopt stereotypes before we have any personal "proof." And because stereotypes guide what we perceive, they can lead us to attend to information that confirms them and to overlook information that contradicts them.

Stereotyping can lead to prejudice and discrimination. According to B. J. Hall (2002), **prejudice** is "a rigid attitude that is based on group membership and predisposes an individual to feel, think, or act in a negative way toward another person or group" (p. 208). Notice the distinction between a stereotype and a prejudice. Whereas a stereotype is a set of beliefs or expectations, a prejudice is a positive or negative attitude; both relate to group membership. Stereotypes and prejudice are cognitive—that is, things we think.

Discrimination, on the other hand, is a negative action toward a social group or its members on account of group membership (Jones, 2002, p. 8). Whereas prejudice and stereotypes deal with attitudes, discrimination involves negative action. For instance, when Laura discovers that Wasif, a man she has just met, is a Muslim, she may stereotype him as a chauvinist. If she is a feminist, she may use this stereotype to prejudge him and assume that he will expect women to be subservient. Thus she holds a prejudice about him. If she acts on her prejudice, she may discriminate against him by refusing to partner with him on a class project. So, without really having gotten to know Wasif, Laura uses her stereotype to prejudge him and discriminate. In this case, Wasif may never get the chance to be known for who he really is, and Laura may have lost an opportunity to get to work with the best student in class.

Emotional States

A final factor that affects how accurately we perceive others is our emotional state at the time of the interaction. Based on his research, Joseph Forgas (1991) has concluded that "there is a broad and pervasive tendency for people to perceive and interpret others in terms of their (own) feelings at the time" (p. 288). If, for example, you received the internship you had applied for, your good mood is likely to spill over so that you perceive other things and other people more positively than you might under different circumstances. If, however, you just learned that your car needs $1,500 in repairs, your perceptions of people around you are likely to be colored by your negative mood and anxiety about paying this bill.

Our emotions also cause us to engage in selective perceptions, ignoring inconsistent information. For instance, if Nick is physically attracted to Jessica, he is likely to focus on the positive aspects of Jessica's personality and may overlook or ignore the negative ones that are apparent to others.

Our emotional state also affects our attributions (Forgas, 2000, p. 397). **Attributions** are reasons we give for others' behavior. In making judgments about people, we attempt to construct reasons to explain

stereotypes
attributions that cover up individual differences and ascribe certain characteristics to an entire group of people

prejudice
a rigid attitude that is based on group membership and predisposes an individual to feel, think, or act in a negative way toward another person or group

discrimination
a negative action toward a social group or its members on account of group membership

attributions
reasons we give for others' behavior

why people behave as they do. According to attribution theory, what we determine—rightly or wrongly—to be the causes of others' behavior has a direct impact on our perceptions of them. For instance, suppose a coworker with whom you had made a noon lunch date has not arrived by 12:20 P.M. If you like and respect your coworker, you may attribute his lateness to something out of his control: an important phone call at the last minute, the need to finish a job before lunch, or some accident that may have occurred. If you are not particularly fond of your coworker, you are more likely to attribute his lateness to something in his control: forgetfulness, inconsiderateness, or malicious intent. In either case, your attribution will affect your perception of him and probably how you treat him.

Like prejudices, the attributions we make can be so strong that we ignore contrary evidence. If you are not particularly close to your coworker, when he does arrive and explains that he had an emergency long-distance phone call, you may believe he is lying or discount the urgency of the call.

Understanding that our physical characteristics and social behaviors, stereotyping, and emotional states affect our perceptions of others is a first step in improving our perceptual accuracy. Now we want to describe three guidelines and a communication skill you can use to improve the accuracy of your social perceptions of others.

Improving Social Perception

Because distortions in perception are common and because they influence how we communicate, improving perceptual accuracy is an important first step in becoming a competent communicator. The following guidelines can aid you in constructing accurate impressions of others and assessing your own perceptions of others' messages.

1. **Question the accuracy of your perceptions.** Questioning accuracy begins by saying, "I know what I think I saw, heard, tasted, smelled, or felt, but I could be wrong. What other information should I be aware of?" By accepting the possibility that you have overlooked something, you will become interested in increasing your accuracy.

2. **Seek more information to verify perceptions.** If your perception is based on only one or two pieces of information, try to collect further information so that your perceptions are better grounded. Note that your perception is tentative—that is, subject to change.

Improving Social Perception

1. Question the accuracy of your perceptions.
2. Seek more information to verify perceptions.
3. Realize that your perceptions of a person will change over time.

The best way to get additional information about people is to talk with them. It's OK to be unsure about how to treat someone from another group. But rather than letting your uncertainty cause you to make mistakes, talk with the person and ask for the information you need to become more comfortable.

3. **Realize that your perceptions of a person will change over time.** People often base their behavior on perceptions that are old or based on incomplete information. So when you encounter someone you haven't seen for a while, you will want to become reacquainted and let the person's current behavior rather than their past actions or reputation inform your perceptions. A former classmate who was "wild" in high school may well have changed and become a mature, responsible adult.

LO⁴ Perception of Messages

In the first chapter, we discussed how the communication process worked and explained that conversational partners or speakers and audiences use messages as the vehicle through which they attempt to create shared meanings. Their success at sharing meaning depends on the encoding and decoding processes, which, in turn, depend on how the messages are perceived. Although many things can affect the message perception process, three important factors are the context, the extent to which the participants share a common language and nonverbal code, and the skillfulness the message sender uses in preparing the message.

Context Rules!

The most important factor in determining how a message will be understood by the receiver is the context in which it is sent and received. We use contextual cues to help us understand the content and the intent of the speaker in sending the message. For example, several years ago at a family dinner Jeorge's dad, who dislikes conflict, sought to distract family members from a quarrel that had begun between two aunts by looking up at the elaborate crystal chandelier hanging above the table and asking, "How do you suppose they clean that chandelier?" Now, because the aunts were aware that Jeorge's dad hated conflict, they immediately understood "the message" and discontinued their argument. Thereafter, regardless of the situation, when anyone in the family wanted to avoid a brewing conflict, they would simply say, "How about that chandelier?" and the potential conflict would usually be diffused. Obviously, people who had not been present at the initial dinner would not have understood the historical context of this message and would likely be confused by what was said.

Obviously the better we know someone, the more likely we are to share an understanding of the context in which our messages are sent and received. When we don't know someone well or when we are speaking with several people or a large audience, there are expanded opportunities for messages to be perceived differently.

Shared Language

It is obvious that for people to be able to decode messages, they need to be able to understand the language in which they were encoded. But because of the nature of language and nonverbal symbols, it is possible for receivers to understand the language in which a message is encoded and yet misperceive the meaning of the sender. This can occur because the sender is using a word with which the receiver is unfamiliar, using a word that has multiple meanings in an ambiguous way, misusing a symbol, or using a personal and idiosyncratic definition of a word. So when Justin tells his wife that he's "going out with the guys for an hour or so," she may expect him home in 60–90 minutes. When he shows up 5 hours later, she will probably be distraught. Justin may have figured that his "or so"

perception check
a message that reflects your understanding of the meaning of another person's nonverbal behavior

would cover any additional time he was away, while his wife viewed it as something less than 2 hours. In this case, while the message was sent in a language that both "understood," they did not share meaning because they perceived the message to mean different lengths of time.

Skillfulness in Encoding and Decoding Messages

Although a multitude of factors can conspire to make accurately perceiving and decoding the messages of others difficult, we can help each other as we strive to share meaning when we thoughtfully construct the messages we send. This means that we need to choose specific, concrete, and precise words as we form our messages. We need to provide details and use examples. We must be careful to adapt our language to the specific listener or group of listeners so that the words we use are likely to be perceived as we intended. When we are giving a speech to an audience where the likelihood of misperception is greatest, we need to make our messages vivid, using similes and metaphors to help our audience "picture" what we are hoping to convey. In addition, we need to help our audience perceive what is important by giving parts of our speech messages more emphasis through the proportion of time spent discussing an idea, repetition, and the use of guiding transitional phrases. We will discuss each of these techniques in depth in Chapter 3.

Perception Checking

Whether we are trying to accurately perceive ourselves, others, or messages that we receive, one way to assess the accuracy of a perception is to verbalize it and see whether others agree with what you see, hear, and interpret. A **perception check** is a message that reflects your understanding of the meaning of another person's nonverbal behavior. It is a process of describing what you have seen and heard and asking for feedback from the other person.

The following examples illustrate the use of perception checking. In each of the examples, the final sentence is a perception check. Notice that the perception-checking statements do not express approval or disapproval of what is being

Perception checking calls for you to

1. watch the behavior of the other person.

2. ask yourself "What does that behavior mean to me?"

3. describe the behavior and put your interpretation into words to verify your perception.

received—they are purely descriptive statements of the perceptions.

Valerie walks into the room with a completely blank expression. She does not speak to Ann or even acknowledge that Ann is in the room. Valerie sits down on the edge of the bed and stares into space. Ann says, "Valerie, did something happen? You look like you're in a state of shock. Am I right? Is there something I can do?"

While Marsha is telling Jenny about the difficulty of her midterm exam in chemistry class, she notices Jenny smiling. She says to Jenny, "You're smiling. I'm not sure how to interpret it. What's up?" Jenny may respond that she's smiling because the story reminded her of something funny or because she

had the same chemistry teacher last year and he purposely gave an extremely difficult midterm to motivate students, but then he graded them on a really favorable curve.

Cesar, speaking in short, precise sentences with a sharp tone of voice, gives Bill his day's assignment. Bill says, "From the sound of your voice, Cesar, I get the impression that you're upset with me. Are you?"

So when we use the skill of perception checking, we encode the meaning that we have perceived from someone's behavior and feed it back so that it can be verified or corrected. For instance, when Bill says, "I can't help but get the impression that you're upset with me. Are you?" Cesar may say: (1) "No, whatever gave you that impression?" in which case Bill can further describe the cues that he received; (2) "Yes, I am," in which case Bill can get Cesar to specify what has caused the feelings; or (3) "No, it's not you, it's just that three of my team members didn't show up for this shift." If Cesar is not upset with him, Bill can examine what caused him to misinterpret Cesar's feelings; if Cesar is upset with him, Bill has the opportunity to change the behavior that caused Cesar to be upset.

"Are you upset with me?"

"No, it's not you, it's just my team didn't show up."

©BRAND X RUBBER BALL/JUPITER IMAGES

Learning Outcomes

LO^1 Discuss the nature and use of language

LO^2 Identify methods for improving language skills

LO^3 Understand what is and is not appropriate in speech

Communicating Verbally

"Language is one of those things that we often take for granted."

—Thomas Holtgraves

Sometimes, for a variety of reasons, the way we form our messages makes it difficult for others to understand. Sometimes the problem is what we say; other times it's how we say it. As Thomas Holtgraves (2002), a leading scholar in language use, reminds us, "Language is one of those things that we often take for granted" (p. 8). Yet we could all improve our use of language. In this chapter, we discuss the nature and use of language and improving our verbal language skills.

What do you think?

It is more important to communicate precise details rather than general ideas.

Strongly Disagree					Strongly Agree	
1	2	3	4	5	6	7

LO¹ The Nature and Use of Language

Language is both a body of symbols (most commonly words) and the systems for their use in messages that are common to the people of the same speech community.

A **speech community**, also called a language community, is a group of people who speak the same language. There are between 3,000 and 4,000 speech communities in the world, with the number of native speakers in a community ranging from a hundred million or more to communities with only a few remaining native speakers. Around 60 percent of the world's speech communities have fewer than 10,000 speakers. The five largest speech communities in order are Mandarin Chinese, English, Spanish, Arabic, and Hindi (Encyclopedia.com, 2002).

Words are symbols used by a speech community to represent objects, ideas, and feelings. While the exact word used to represent the object or idea is arbitrary, for a word to be a symbol it must be recognized by members of the speech community as standing for a particular object, idea, or feeling. So different speech communities use different word symbols for the same phenomenon. For example, the season for planting is called *spring* in English-speaking communities but *printemps* in French-speaking communities.

Speech communities vary in the words that they use, and they also vary in how words are put together to form messages. The structure a message takes depends on the rules of grammar and syntax that have evolved in a particular speech community. For example, in English a sentence must have at least a subject (a

language
a body of symbols (most commonly words) and the systems for their use in messages that are common to the people of the same speech community

speech community
a group of people who speak the same language (also called a language community)

words
symbols used by a speech community to represent objects, ideas, and feelings

{ Fast Facts—
Language Games }

The mid-20th century German philosopher Ludwig Wittgenstein created what he called "language games" to imagine how the symbols of language (words) acquire their objects or meanings as individuals attempt to convey messages to one another. Wittgenstein's games pictured a builder on a construction project providing commands to his assistant, who supplied materials. When the builder called for a "block," a "pillar," a "slab," or a "beam," the assistant would retrieve the material corresponding with the name in the order that it was requested. Can you imagine a scenario that might illustrate how people might establish a common understanding of the language they are using?

clear: We select the correct words, structure them using the rules of syntax and grammar agreed upon by our speech community, and people will interpret our meanings correctly. In fact, the relationship between language and meaning is not nearly so simple for several reasons.

One reason is that the meaning of words is in people, not in the words themselves. If Juan describes to Julia that the restaurant is expensive, each of them probably has a different meaning of the word expensive in this context. Maybe Julia thinks one meal will cost $40, while, for Juan, expensive might mean a $20 meal. All words, especially abstract ones, have multiple meanings depending on who is using them and who is hearing them. Think of all the variations of meaning that people bring to words such as responsibility, freedom, and love.

A second factor complicating language and meaning is the fact that words have two levels of meaning: denotation and connotation. **Denotation** is the direct, explicit meaning a speech community formally gives a word—it is the meaning found in a dictionary. Different dictionaries may define words in slightly different ways. For instance, whereas the *Encarta World English Dictionary* defines "bawdy" as "ribald in a frank, humorous often crude way," the *Cambridge American English Dictionary* defines "bawdy" as "containing humorous remarks about sex." Similar? Yes, but not the same. Second, for many words there are multiple definitions. For instance, the *Random House Dictionary of the English Language* lists 23 definitions for the word "great." Connotation, the feelings or evaluations we associate with a word, may be even more important to our understanding of meaning than denotation. C. K. Ogden and I. A. Richards (1923) were among the first scholars to consider the misunderstandings resulting from the failure of communicators to realize that their subjective reactions to words are based on their life experiences. For instance, when Tina says, "We bought an SUV; I think it's the biggest one Chevy makes," Kim might think "Why in the world would anyone want one of those gas guzzlers that take up so much space to park?" and Lexia might say, "Oh, I envy you. I'd love

noun or pronoun) and a predicate (a verb). To make a statement in English, the subject is placed before the predicate.

Language affects how people think and what they pay attention to. This concept is called the Sapir–Whorf hypothesis, named after two theorists, Edward Sapir and Benjamin Lee Whorf (Littlejohn & Foss, 2005). Language allows us to perceive certain aspects of the world by naming them and allows us to ignore other parts of the world by not naming them. For instance, if you work in a job such as fashion or interior design that deals with many different words for color distinctions, you will be able to perceive finer differences in color. Knowing various words for shades of white, such as ecru, eggshell, cream, ivory, pearl, bone china white, or antique white actually helps you see differences in shades of white. Similarly, there are concepts that people and society did not fully perceive until a word was coined to describe that concept. Think of the relatively new words added to American English vocabulary in the last few decades such as *date rape* or *male bashing*. Whatever behaviors to which those words refer certainly existed before the terms were coined. But as a society, we did not collectively perceive these behaviors until language allowed us to name them.

Sapir–Whorf hypothesis
a theory claiming that language influences perception

denotation
the direct, explicit meaning a speech community formally gives a word

connotation
the feelings or evaluations we associate with a word

Language and Meaning

On the surface, the relationship between language and meaning seems perfectly

Uses of Language

Although language communities vary in the words that they use and in their grammar and syntax systems, all languages serve the same purposes.

1. **We use language to designate, label, define, and limit.** So, when we identify music as "techno," we are differentiating it from other music labeled rap, punk, pop, goth, or grunge.

2. **We use language to evaluate.** Through language we convey positive or negative attitudes toward our subject. For instance, if you see Hal taking more time than others to make a decision, you could describe Hal positively as "thoughtful" or negatively as "dawdling." Kenneth Burke, a prominent language theorist, describes this as the power of language to emphasize hierarchy and control (1968). Because language allows us to compare things, we tend to judge those things as better or worse, which leads to social hierarchy or a pecking order.

3. **We use language to discuss things outside our immediate experience.** Language enables us to talk about ourselves, discuss things outside our immediate experience, speak hypothetically, talk about past and future events, and communicate about people and things that are not present. Through language, we can discuss where we hope to be in five years, analyze a conversation two acquaintances had last week, or learn about the history that shapes the world we live in. Language enables us to learn from others' experiences, to share a common heritage, and to develop a shared vision for the future.

4. **We can use language to talk about language.** We can use language to discuss how someone phrased a statement and whether different wording would have had a better outcome or a more positive response. Think of the power of language when we can communicate about how we are communicating. For instance, if your friend said she would see you "this afternoon," but she didn't arrive until 5 o'clock, and you ask her where she's been, the two of you are likely to discuss your communication and the different interpretations you each bring to the words "this afternoon."

> > The SUV: a powerful, off-road utility or a gas-guzzling, waste of space? It all depends on connotations.

©AP PHOTO/BEN MARGOT

to afford a vehicle that has so much power and sits so high on the road." Word denotation and connotation are important because the only message that counts is the message that is understood, regardless of whether it is the one you intended.

A third complication of language and meaning is that meaning may vary depending on the **syntactic context** (the position of a word in a sentence and the other words around it) in which the word is used. For instance, in the same sentence a person might say, "I love to vacation in the mountains where the mornings are really cool and when you hike you're likely to see some really cool animals." Most listeners would understand that "mornings are really cool" refers to temperature and "see some really cool animals" refers to animals that are uncommon or special.

A fourth factor affecting language meaning is that the language used by any speech community will change over time. Language changes in many ways, including the creation of new words, the abandonment of old words, changed word meanings developed by segments of society, and the influx of words from the mixing of cultures. For instance, the latest edition of *Merriam-Webster's Collegiate Dictionary* contains ten thousand new words and usages.

New words are created to express new ideas. For example, younger generations, businesspeople, and scientists, among others, will invent new words or assign different meanings to the words they learn to better express the changing realities of their world. For example, *bling bling* is used to describe flashy jewelry and decorations, *e-tailing* is Internet retail selling, and *bioinformatics* is a field of study concerned with the creation and maintenance of databases of biological information. In the past 20 years, entire vocabularies have been invented to allow us to communicate about the explosion of new technologies. So we *google* to get information, use the *wi-fi* on our *laptop*, and *listen* to a *podcast* while we write our *blog*. Words frequently used by older generations may fade as they no longer describe current realities or are replaced by newer words. *Cellophane* was the word used years ago for

syntactic context
the position of a word in a sentence and the other words around it

what we call plastic wrap today. We once used a *mimeograph* but now we use a *copy machine*. In addition, some members of the speech community will invent new meanings for old words to differentiate themselves from other subgroups of the language community. For instance, in some parts of the country, teenagers use *stupid* to mean *cool*, as in "That's a really stupid shirt" and *played* to mean *tiresome* or *boring*, as in "This party is played; let's go."

As a society absorbs immigrants who speak different languages and becomes more multicultural, the language gradually adopts some words from the native language of the immigrants. So in English we now use and understand what were once foreign words, such as *petite, siesta, mench, kindergarten,* and *ciao,* among thousands of others. Similarly, the slang or jargon used by a subgroup may also eventually be appropriated by the larger speech community. So the African American slang term for athletic shoes, *kicks,* is now used and understood by a more diverse group of American speakers.

Cultural and Gender Influences on Language Usage

Culture and gender both influence how words are used and interpreted. Cultures vary in how much meaning is embedded in the language itself and how much meaning is interpreted from the context in which the communication occurs. In low-context cultures, like the United States and most northern European countries, messages are direct and language is very specific. Speakers say exactly what they mean and the verbal messages are very explicit, with lots of details provided. In low-context cultures, what the speaker intends the message to mean is not heavily influenced by the setting or context; rather, it is embedded in the verbal message. In **high-context cultures**, like Latin American, Asian, and Native American, what a speaker really means you to understand from the verbal message depends heavily on the setting or context in which it is sent. So verbal messages in high-context cultures may be indirect, using more general and ambiguous language. Receivers in high-context cultures, then, rely on contextual cues to help them understand the speaker's meaning (Chen & Starosta, 1998).

When people from low-context cultures interact with others from high-context cultures, problems of understanding often occur. Imagine that Isaac from a German company and Zhao from a Chinese company are trying to conduct business.

ISAAC: "Let's get right down to it. We're hoping that you can provide 100,000 parts per month according to our six manufacturing specifications spelled out in the engineering contract I sent you. If quality control finds more than a 2-percent error, we will have to terminate the contract. Can you agree to these terms?"

ZHAO: "We are very pleased to be doing business with you. We produce the highest quality products and will be honored to meet your needs."

ISAAC: "But can you supply that exact quantity? Can you meet all of our engineering specifications? Will you consistently have less than a 2-percent error?"

ZHAO: "We are an excellent, trustworthy company that will send you the highest quality parts."

Isaac is probably frustrated with what he perceives as general, evasive language used by Zhao, while Zhao may be offended by the direct questions, specific language, and perceived threat in the message. Global migration, business, and travel are increasing the interactions that occur between people accustomed to high- or low-context expectations. As this happens, the likelihood of misunderstanding increases. So to be a competent communicator, you will need to be aware of, compensate for, or adapt to the cultural expectations of your conversational partner.

Societal expectations for masculinity and femininity influence language use. According to Wood (2007), **feminine styles of language** typically use words of empathy and support, emphasize concrete

low-context cultures
cultures in which messages are direct, specific, and detailed

high-context cultures
cultures in which messages are indirect, general, and ambiguous

feminine styles of language
use words of empathy and support, emphasize concrete and personal language, and show politeness and tentativeness in speaking

>> For these soldiers, the success of their missions often depends on whether they are able to accurately communicate information or not.

and personal language, and show politeness and tentativeness in speaking. **Masculine styles of language** often use words of status and problem solving, emphasize abstract and general language, and show assertiveness and control in speaking.

Feminine language often includes empathic phrases like, "I can understand how you feel," or "I've had a similar experience, so I can sense what you are going through." Likewise, feminine language often includes language of support such as, "I'm so sorry that you are having difficulty," or "please let me know if I can help you in any way." Feminine language often goes into detail by giving specific examples and personal disclosures. To appear feminine is to speak politely by focusing on others and by not being too forceful with language. Words and phrases like "I may be wrong but . . . it's just my opinion . . . maybe . . . perhaps . . . I don't want to step on anyone's toes here . . . " are associated with feminine styles of speaking.

By contract, masculine styles of speaking often emphasize status through phrases like "I know that . . . my experience tells me . . . " and communicates problem solving or advice giving through such language as "I would . . . you should . . . the way you should handle this is . . ." Masculine styles of communication may favor theoretical or general discussions and avoid giving personal information about oneself. To appear masculine, one's language must be forceful, direct, and in control through such phrases as "definitely, I have no doubt, it is clear to me, I am sure that . . . "

Women and men can use both masculine and feminine language, though, generally, society expects women to use feminine language and men to use masculine language. One style is not inherently better than another, but each may be better suited to certain communication situations.

LO² Improving Language Skills

Regardless of whether we are conversing with a friend, working on a task force, or giving a speech, we should strive to use language in our messages that accurately conveys our meanings.

masculine styles of language
use words of status and problem solving, emphasize abstract and general language, and show assertiveness and control in speaking

We can improve our messages by choosing specific language, developing verbal vividness and emphasis, providing details and examples, dating information, and indexing generalizations.

Choose Specific Language

When we speak in specific language, we help listeners assign meaning to our words similar to what we intended. Compare these two descriptions of a near miss in a car: "Some nut almost got me a while ago" versus "An hour ago, an older man in a banged-up Honda Civic ran the light at Calhoun and Clifton and almost hit me broadside while I was in the intersection waiting to turn left at the cross street." In the second example, the message used language that was much more specific, so both parties are likely to have a more similar perception of the situation than would be possible with the first description.

Often as we try to express our thoughts, the first words that come to mind are general in nature. **Specific words** clear up confusion caused by general words by narrowing what is understood from a general category to a particular group within that category. Specific words are more concrete and precise than general words. What can we do to speak more specifically?

We speak more clearly when we select a word that most accurately or correctly captures the sense of what we are saying. At first I might say, "Waylon was angry at the meeting today." Then I might think, "Was he really showing anger?" So I say, "To be more accurate, he wasn't really angry. Perhaps he was more frustrated or impatient with what he sees as lack of progress by our group." What is the difference between the

two statements in terms of words? By carefully choosing words, you can show shades of meaning. Others may respond quite differently to your description of a group member showing anger, frustration, or impatience. The interpretation others get of Waylon's behavior is very much dependent on the word or words you select. Specific language is achieved when words are concrete or precise or when details or examples are used.

Concrete words are words that appeal to our senses. Consider the word *speak*. This is an abstract word—that is, we can speak in many different ways. So instead of saying that Jill *speaks in a peculiar way*, we might be more specific by saying that Jill *mumbles, whispers, blusters,* or *drones.* Each of these words creates a clearer sense of the sound of her voice.

We speak more specifically when we use **precise words**, narrowing a larger category to a smaller group within that category. For instance, if Nevah says that Ruben is a "blue-collar worker," she has named a general category; you might picture an unlimited number of occupations that fall within this broad category. If, instead, she is more precise and says he's a "construction worker," the number of possible images you can picture is reduced; now you can only select your image from the specific subcategory of construction worker. So your meaning is likely to be closer to the one she intended. To be even more precise, she may identify Ruben as "a bulldozer operator"; this further limits your choice of images and is likely to align with the one she intended you to have.

Choosing specific language is easier when we have a large working vocabulary. One way to increase your vocabulary is to study vocabulary-

Ruben

©PHOTOS.COM/JUPITER IMAGES

specific words
words that clarify meaning by narrowing what is understood from a general category to a particular item or group within that category

concrete words
words that appeal to the senses and help us see, hear, smell, taste, or touch

precise words
words that narrow a larger category

building books, which are available in most libraries and bookstores. A second way is to use a dictionary to look up the meanings of words that you read or hear that you do not understand and add them to a vocabulary list that you keep and study. A third way to increase your vocabulary is to use a thesaurus (a list of words and their synonyms) to identify related words that are more concrete and precise than the ones you use most frequently.

Develop Verbal Vividness and Emphasis

Because your listeners cannot simply re-read what you have said, effective verbal messages use vivid wording and appropriate emphasis to help listeners understand and remember the message.

Vivid wording is full of life, vigorous, bright, and intense. For example, a novice baseball announcer might say, "Jackson made a great catch," but a more experienced commentator's vivid account would be, "Jackson leaped and made a spectacular one-handed catch just as he crashed into the center field wall." The words *spectacular, leaped, one-handed catch,* and *crashed* paint an intense verbal picture of the action. Vivid messages begin with vivid thoughts. You are much more likely to *express* yourself vividly when you have physically or psychologically *sensed* the meanings you are trying to convey.

Vividness can be achieved quickly through using similes and metaphors. A simile is a direct comparison of dissimilar things and is usually expressed with the words *like* or *as.* Clichés such as "She walks like a duck." And "She sings like a nightingale" are both similes. A metaphor is a comparison that establishes a figurative identity between objects being compared. Instead of saying that one thing is like another, a metaphor says that one thing *is* another. Thus, problem cars are "lemons" and a team's porous infield is a "sieve." As you think about and try to develop similes and metaphors, stay away from trite clichés. Although we use similes and metaphors frequently in conversations, they are an especially powerful way to develop vividness when we are giving a speech. Try developing and practicing one or two different original metaphors or similes when you rehearse a speech to see which works best.

Finally, while your goal is to be vivid, make sure that you use words that are understood by all your listeners. Novice speakers can mistakenly believe they will be more impressive if they use a large vocabulary, but using "big" words can be off-putting to the audience and make the speaker seem pompous, affected, or stilted. When you have a choice between a common vivid word or image and one that is more obscure, choose the more common.

Emphasis is the weight or importance given to certain words or ideas. Emphasis tells the audience what it should seriously pay attention to. Ideas are emphasized through proportion, repetition, and use of transitions. You emphasize an idea by the proportion of time you spend discussing it. Ideas to which you devote more time are perceived by listeners to be more important, whereas ideas that are quickly mentioned are perceived to be less important. Emphasizing by repeating means saying important words or ideas more than once. You can either repeat the exact words, "A ring-shaped coral island almost or completely surrounding a lagoon is called an atoll—an atoll," or you can restate the idea in different language, "The test will comprise about four essay questions; that is, all the questions on the test will be the kind that require you to discuss material in some detail." Emphasizing through transitions means using words that show the relationship between your ideas. Some transitions summarize, some clarify, and others forecast. Simple word transitions add material (*also, and, likewise, again, in addition, moreover, similarly, further*); add up, show consequences, summarize, or show results (*therefore, and so, so, finally, all in all, on the whole, in short, thus, as a result*); indicate changes in direction or provide contrasts (*but, however, on the other hand, still, although, while, no doubt*); indicate reasons (*because, for*); show causal or time relationship (*then, since, as*); or explain, exemplify, or limit—in other words (*in fact, for example, that is to say, more specifically*).

> **Emphasis tells the audience what it should seriously pay attention to.**

Provide Details and Examples

Sometimes clarity can be achieved by adding detail or examples. For instance,

vivid wording
wording that is full of life, vigorous, bright, and intense

simile
a direct comparison of dissimilar things

metaphor
a comparison that establishes a figurative identity between objects being compared

emphasis
the weight or importance given to certain words or ideas

Linda says, "Rashad is very loyal." The meaning of "loyal" (faithful to an idea, person, company, and so on) is abstract, so to avoid ambiguity and confusion, Linda might add, "He defended Gerry when Sara was gossiping about her." By following up her use of the abstract concept of loyalty with a concrete example, Linda makes it easier for her listeners to "ground" their idea of this personal quality in a concrete or "real" experience. Likewise by providing details, we clarify our messages. Saying, "He lives in a really big house," can be clarified by adding details: "He lives in a 14-room Tudor mansion on a 6-acre estate."

Date Information

Dating information means to specify the time or time period that a fact was true or known to be true. Because nearly everything changes with time, not dating our statements can lead someone to conclude that what we are saying is current, when it is not. For instance, Parker says, "I'm going to be transferred to Henderson City." Laura replies, "Good luck—they've had some real trouble with their schools." On the basis of Laura's statement, Parker may worry about the effect his move will have on his children. What he doesn't know is that Laura's information about this problem in Henderson City is over five years old! Henderson City still may have problems, but again, the situation may have changed. Had Laura replied, "Five years ago, I know they had some real trouble with their schools. I'm not sure what the situation is now, but you may want to check," Parker would look at the information differently.

Here are two additional examples:

1 **Undated:** Professor Powell is really enthusiastic when she lectures.

Dated: Professor Powell is really enthusiastic when she lectures—at least she was *last quarter* in communication theory.

2 **Undated:** You think Mary's depressed? I'm surprised. She seemed her regular, high-spirited self when I talked with her.

Dated: You think Mary's depressed? I'm surprised. She seemed her regular, high-spirited self when I talked with her *last month.*

To date information, before you make a statement, (1) consider or find out when the information was true and (2) verbally

©WORKBOOK STOCK/JUPITER IMAGES

>> Have you ever been inconvenienced by information that was out of date? As you form messages, the skill of dating can help you be more accurate with the information you share.

acknowledge the date or time period when the information was true. When we date our statements, we increase the effectiveness of our messages and enhance our own credibility.

Index Generalizations

Indexing generalizations is the mental and verbal practice of acknowledging the presence of individual differences when voicing generalizations. While we might generally think that people who buy a Mercedes are rich, that may not be true for all Mercedes buyers. Thus, just because we learn that Brent has bought a top-of-the-line, very expensive Mercedes, it does not mean that Brent is rich. So, if we were to say, "Brent bought a Mercedes; he must be rich," we should add, "of course not all people who buy Mercedes are rich."

Let's consider another example:

Generalization: Your Toyota should go 50,000 miles before you need a brake job; Jerry's did.

Indexed Statement: Your Toyota may well go 50,000 miles before you need a brake job; Jerry's did, *but of course, all Toyotas aren't the same.*

dating information
specifying the time or time period that a fact was true or known to be true

indexing generalizations
the mental and verbal practice of acknowledging the presence of individual differences when voicing generalizations

To index, consider whether what you are about to say applies a generalization to a specific person, place, or thing. If so, qualify it appropriately so that your assertion does not go beyond the evidence that supports it.

LO³ Speaking Appropriately

Speaking appropriately means choosing language and symbols that are adapted to the needs, interests, knowledge, and attitudes of the listeners and avoiding language that alienates them. Through appropriate language, we communicate our respect and acceptance of those who are different from us. There are times when we use words that our listeners do not understand or that offend others. Some words are so familiar to us that we forget that others are unaware of their meaning. It is also important that we consider the effect that our words may have on others.

Use Vocabulary the Listener Understands

People vary in the extent to which they know and use a large variety of words. If you have made a conscious effort to expand your vocabulary, are an avid reader, or have spent time conversing with others who use a large and varied selection of words, then you probably have a large vocabulary. As a speaker, the larger your vocabulary, the more choices you have from which to select the words you want. Having a larger vocabulary, however, can present challenges when communicating with people whose vocabulary is more limited. As a speaker, you must try to adapt your vocabulary to the level of your listener so that your words will be understood. One strategy for assessing another's vocabulary level is to listen to the types and complexity of words the other person uses and to take your signal from your communication partner. When you have determined that your vocabulary exceeds that of your partner, you can use simpler synonyms for your words or use

word phrases composed of more familiar terms. Adjusting your vocabulary to others does not mean talking down to them. It is merely polite behavior and effective communication to try to select words that others understand.

Use Jargon Sparingly

Jargon refers to technical terms whose meanings are understood only by a select group of people based on their shared activity or interests. We may form a special speech community, which develops a common language (jargon) based on a hobby or occupation. Medical practitioners speak a language of their own, which people in the medical field understand and those outside of the medical field do not. The same is true of lawyers, engineers, educators, and virtually all occupations. If you are an avid computer user, you may know many terms that noncomputer users do not. Likewise, there is a lingo associated with sports, theatre, wine tasting, and science fiction, to name just a few interest groups. The key to effective use of jargon is to employ it only with other people who speak the same jargon. When people understand the same jargon, then its use facilitates communication. If you must use jargon with people who are not members of the occupation or special interest group, remember to explain the terms you are using. Without explanation to outsiders, jargon becomes a type of foreign language.

Use Slang Appropriate to the Situation

Slang refers to informal vocabulary developed and used by particular groups in society. It is casual and sometimes playful language that is deliberately used in place of standard terms. Slang is a type of alternative vocabulary that performs an important social function. Slang bonds those in an inner circle who use the same words to emphasize a shared experience. But slang simultaneously excludes others who don't share the terminology. The simultaneous inclusion of some and exclusion of others is what makes slang popular with youth and marginalized people in all cultures. Slang may emerge from teenagers, urban life,

speaking appropriately choosing language and symbols that are adapted to the needs, interests, knowledge, and attitudes of the listeners and avoiding language that alienates them

jargon technical terms understood only by select groups

slang informal vocabulary used by particular groups in society

---

To speak appropriately,

1. use vocabulary the listener understands.

2. use jargon sparingly.

3. use slang appropriate to the situation.

4. use inclusive language.

5. use nonoffensive language.

>> Can you identify these different types of glasses and what they are used for? Many activities or occupations, such as wine-tasting, have a particular lingo associated with them, that not everyone will be familiar with.

college life, gangs, or other contexts. A teenager might say, "My bad" for "I made a mistake." That's "tight" could be translated, as "That's great, fine, or excellent." You can even find slang dictionaries online. Using slang appropriately means using it in situations where people understand the slang but avoiding it with people who do not share the slang terminology.

There is a new type of slang developing with digital and Internet technology. Experts in computer-mediated communication (Thurlow, Lengel, & Tomic, 2004) explain the unique features of this language, which goes by various names including Weblish, netlingo, e-talk, techspeak, wired style, or netspeak. Because of the need for speed in instant messaging, for example, many of the rules of grammar, style, and spelling are broken. Many people adopt a phonetic type of spelling, which increasingly is understandable to this speech community, but may not be understandable to others. Consider the language used in cyberspace versus traditional wording for the following question: wen wud u b hm (When would you be home?). New abbreviations have emerged such as jk (just kidding), bbl (be back later),

generic language
using words that may apply only to one sex, race, or other group as though they represent everyone

and lol (laugh out loud). Some communication experts who emphasize traditional styles of communication regard this new language of cyberspace as incorrect, deficient, or inferior. While it is natural that people in cyberspace would develop their own alternative, using these terms in other settings is problematic.

Demonstrate Linguistic Sensitivity

You demonstrate linguistic sensitivity when you choose language that respects others and avoid usages that others perceive as offensive because they are sexist, racist, or otherwise biased. Generic and nonparallel languages are common types of insensitive language that can be easily corrected.

Generic Language

Generic language uses words that may apply only to one sex, race, or other group as though they represent everyone. This usage is a problem because it linguistically excludes a portion of the population it ostensibly includes. The following paragraphs contain some examples of generic language.

Traditionally, English grammar called for the use of the masculine pronoun, *he*, to stand for the entire class of humans regardless of gender. Using this rule, we would say, "When a person shops, he should have a clear idea of what he wants to buy." Despite traditional usage, it is hard to picture people of both sexes when we hear the masculine pronoun "he."

You can avoid generic language in one of two ways. First, use plurals. For instance, instead of saying, "Because a doctor has high status, his views may be believed regardless of the topic," you could say, "Because doctors have high status, their views may be believed regardless of the topic." Secondly, you can use both male and female pronouns: "Because a doctor has high status, his or her views may be believed regardless of the topic." Stewart, Cooper, Stewart, and Friedley (1998, p. 63) cite research to show that when speakers refer to people using "he and she," and to a lesser extent "they," listeners often visualize *both* women and men. Thus, when speakers avoid generic language, it's more likely that listeners will perceive a message that is more gender balanced.

Another problem results from the traditional use of the generic word *man* when referring to all humans. Many of the words that have become a common part of our language are inherently sexist in that they refer to only one gender. Consider the term *man-made*. What this really means is that a product was produced by human beings, but its underlying connotation is that a male human being made the item. Research has demonstrated that people usually visualize men (not women) when they read or hear these words. Moreover, when job titles end in "man," their occupants are

©SUSAN VAN ETTEN

assumed to have stereotypically masculine personality traits (Gmelch, 1998, p. 51).

For most sex-biased expressions, you can use or create suitable alternatives. For instance, use police officer instead of policeman and substitute synthetic for man-made. Instead of saying mankind, change the construction—for example, from "All of mankind benefits" to "All the people in the world benefit."

Nonparallel Language

Nonparallel language is language in which terms are changed because of the sex, race, or other characteristic of the individual. Because it treats groups of people differently, nonparallel language is also belittling. Two types of nonparallel language are *marking* and *unnecessary association*.

Marking is the addition of sex, race, age, or other designations to a description. For instance, a doctor is a person with a medical degree who is licensed to practice medicine. Notice the difference between the following two sentences:

Jones is a good doctor.

Jones is a good black doctor.

In the second sentence, use of the marker "black" is offensive; it has nothing to do with doctoring. Marking is inappropriate because you trivialize the person's role by introducing an irrelevant characteristic. The speaker may be intending to praise Jones, but listeners may interpret the sentence as saying that Jones is a good doctor "for a black person" (or woman, or old person, and so on) but not that Jones is as good as a white doctor (or a male, or young person, and so forth).

A second form of nonparallel language is emphasizing one person's relationship to another when that relationship is irrelevant. Introducing a speaker as "Gladys Thompson, whose husband is CEO of Acme Inc., is the chairperson for this year's United Way campaign," for example, is inappropriate. Using her husband's status implies that Gladys Thompson is chairperson because of her husband's accomplishments, not her own.

By monitoring yourself, you can become more inclusive in your language choices. How can you speak more appropriately? (1) Use vocabulary the listener understands, (2) use jargon sparingly, (3) use slang situationally, and (4) demonstrate linguistic sensitivity by avoiding generic and nonparallel language.

nonparallel language
terms are changed because of the sex, race, or other characteristic of the individual

marking
the addition of sex, race, age, or other designations to a description

CHAPTER 4

Communicating through Nonverbal Behaviors

Learning Outcomes

LO **1**   Identify characteristics of nonverbal communication

LO **2**   Identify channels through which we communicate nonverbally

LO **3**   Discuss how our self-presentation affects communication

LO **4**   Examine how nonverbal communication varies based on culture and gender

LO **5**   Understand guidelines for improving nonverbal communication

"In face-to-face communication as much as 60 percent of the social meaning is a result of nonverbal behavior."

We've all heard—and said—"actions speak louder than words." Actions are so important to our communication that researchers have estimated that in face-to-face communication as much as 60 percent of the social meaning is a result of nonverbal behavior (Burgoon & Bacue, 2003, p. 179). In other words, the meaning we assign to any communication is based on both the content of the verbal message and our interpretation of the nonverbal behavior that accompanies and surrounds the verbal message. And interpreting these nonverbal actions is not always the easiest thing to do.

We begin this chapter by briefly identifying the characteristics of nonverbal communication. Next, we describe the sources of nonverbal information that we use when we interpret and assign meaning to the behavior of others: body language (kinesics), nonsymbolic vocal sounds (paralanguage), our use of space (proxemics), and self-presentation cues. Then we explore how the meaning of nonverbal communication may vary based on culture, sex, and gender. Finally, we offer suggestions to help you improve your accuracy at interpreting nonverbal messages and for increasing the likelihood that others are able to accurately interpret your behavior.

In the broadest sense, the term *nonverbal communication* is commonly used to describe all human communication events that transcend spoken or written words (Knapp & Hall, 2006). Specifically, **nonverbal communication behaviors** are those bodily actions and vocal qualities that typically accompany a verbal message. The behaviors are usually interpreted as intentional and have agreed-upon interpretations in a particular culture or speech community (Burgoon & Hoobler, 2002, p. 244).

LO¹ Characteristics of Nonverbal Communication

Nonverbal communication is distinct from verbal communication in that it is continuous and multichanneled. It may be unintentional and ambiguous. The nonverbal part of the message is the primary conveyer of emotion.

First, nonverbal communication is *continuous*. Although you can choose to form and send a verbal message, you do not control whether your nonverbal behavior is interpreted as a communication message. As long as you are in the presence of someone else, that person may perceive your behavior as communication. When Austin yawns and stares off into the distance during a meeting at work, his coworkers will notice this behavior and assign meaning to it. One coworker may interpret it as a sign of

> **What do you think?**
>
> **I don't like it when people stand too close to me when they're talking to me.**
>
> *Strongly Disagree*   *Strongly Agree*
> 1   2   3   4   5   6   7

nonverbal communication behaviors
bodily actions and vocal qualities that typically accompany a verbal message

boredom, another might see it as a sign of fatigue, and yet another may view it as a message of disrespect. Meanwhile, Austin is oblivious to all of the messages that his behavior is sending.

Second, nonverbal communication is *multichanneled*. We perceive meaning from a variety of nonverbal behaviors including posture, gestures, body movements, body appearance, non-language vocal mannerisms, and so on. When we interpret nonverbal behavior, we usually base our perception on a combination of these behaviors. So, Anna observes Mimi's failure to sustain eye contact, her bowed head, and her repetitive toe stubbing in the dirt, as cues that mean her daughter is lying about not hitting her brother.

Third, nonverbal communication can be *intentional* or *unintentional*. Although we can carefully control the verbal messages we send, because nonverbal behavior is continuous, we often display behaviors that we are not controlling. For example, President George W. Bush's noted "smirk," a nonverbal facial mannerism, may be an intentional message conveying contempt for another's opinion, or it may be an unintentional nervous reaction to speaking in public. Whether the smirk is intentional or unintentional, however, when we see it, we interpret and assign it meaning. Because nonverbal behavior is not easily controlled, it is perceived to be more accurate than verbal communication. So when your nonverbal behavior contradicts your verbal message, people are more likely to believe the nonverbal communication they perceive.

Fourth, the meaning of a particular nonverbal communication can be *ambiguous*. Any particular behavior can have many meanings. So regardless of what President Bush intends, the smirk is an ambiguous message and may be interpreted differently by different audience members.

Finally, nonverbal communication is the *primary conveyor of our emotions*. When we listen to others, we base our interpretation of their feelings and emotions almost totally on their nonverbal behavior. In fact, about 93 percent of the emotional meaning of messages is conveyed nonverbally. (Mehrabian,

kinesics
the interpretation of body motions used in communication

gestures
movements of our hands, arms, and fingers that we use to describe or to emphasize

illustrators
gestures that augment a verbal message

1972). So, when Janelle says, "I'm really fine, but thanks for asking," her sister Renee will understand the real message based on the nonverbal behaviors that accompany it. For example, if Janelle uses a sarcastic tone, Renee will understand that Janelle is angry about something. If Janelle sighs, averts her eyes, tears up, and almost whispers her message, Renee will understand that Janelle is really sad and emotionally upset.

LO² Sources of Nonverbal Communication

There are a variety of sources or channels for the nonverbal messages that we interpret from others and display ourselves. These include the use of the body (kinesics), the use of the voice (vocalics/paralanguage), the use of space (proxemics), and self-presentation.

Use of Body: Kinesics

Of all the research on nonverbal behavior, you are probably most familiar with **kinesics**, the technical name for the interpretation of body motions as communications (Wikipedia, 2006). Body motions are the movement of your body or body parts that others interpret and assign meaning. These include your gestures, eye contact, facial expression, posture, and your use of touch.

Gestures

Gestures are the movements of your hands, arms, and fingers that you use to describe or to emphasize. People vary, however, in the amount of gesturing that accompanies their spoken messages; for example, some people "talk with their hands" far more than others. Some gestures, called **illustrators**, augment the verbal message. So when you say "about this high" or "nearly this round," we expect to see a gesture accompany your verbal description. One type of gesture, called **emblems**, can stand alone and substitute completely for words. When you raise your finger and place it vertically across your lips, it signifies "Quiet." Emblems have automatic agreed-upon meanings in a particular culture, but the specific meaning assigned to a specific gesture can vary greatly across cultures. For example, the American hand sign for "OK" has an obscene sexual meaning in some European countries. Gestures called **adaptors** occur unconsciously as a response to a physical need. For example, you may scratch an itch, adjust your glasses, or rub your hands together when they are cold. You do not mean to communicate a message with these gestures, but others do notice them and attach meaning to them.

Our facial expressions are especially important in conveying emotions. What is the message on these faces?

Eye Contact

Eye contact, also referred to as **gaze**, is how and how much we look at others when we are communicating. Although the amount of eye contact differs from person to person and from situation to situation, studies show that talkers hold eye contact about 40 percent of the time and listeners nearly 70 percent of the time (Knapp & Hall, 2006).

Through our eye contact, we both express our emotions and we monitor what is occurring in the interaction. How we look at a person can convey a range of emotions such as anger, fear, or affection. Shakespeare acknowledged how powerfully we express emotions through eye contact when he said, "The eyes are the windows of the soul." With eye contact, you can tell when or whether a person or audience is paying attention to you, whether a person or audience is involved in what you are saying, and the reaction a person or audience is having to your comments.

Although the use and meaning of eye contact varies from one cultural group to another, in the United States,

effective public speakers not only use direct eye contact with audience members to monitor how their speech is being received, but also to establish rapport and demonstrate their sincerity. Speakers who fail to maintain eye contact with audience members are perceived as ill at ease and often as insincere or dishonest (Burgoon, Coker, & Coker, 1986).

Facial Expression

Facial expression is the arrangement of facial muscles to communicate emotional states or reactions to messages. Our facial expressions are especially important in conveying the six basic human emotions of happiness, sadness, surprise, fear, anger, and disgust. It appears that the particular facial expression for each of these emotions is universal and does not vary by culture. But we can consciously choose to mask the feeling expressed by our face or to feign feelings that we do not have (Ekman, 1999).

Facial expressions are so important to communicating the emotional part of a message that people have invented **emoticons**, a system of typed symbols to convey facial expressions online. For example, :-) conveys a smile, while : -(conveys a frown (Walther & Parks, 2002).

Posture

Posture is the position and movement of your body. From your posture, others interpret how attentive, respectful, and dominant

emblems
gestures that can substitute for words

adaptors
gestures that respond to a physical need

eye contact (gaze)
how and how much we look at people with whom we are communicating

facial expression
the arrangement of facial muscles to communicate emotional states or reactions to messages

emoticons
typed symbols that convey emotional aspects of an online message

posture
the position and movement of the body

you are. **Body orientation** refers to your posture in relation to another person. If you face another person squarely, this is called direct body orientation. When two people's postures are at angles to each other, this is called indirect body orientation. In many situations, direct body orientation signals attentiveness and respect, while indirect body orientation shows nonattentiveness and disrespect. Think of how you would sit in a job interview. You are likely to sit up straight and face the interviewer directly because you want to communicate your interest and respect. Interviewers tend to interpret a slouched posture and indirect body orientation as inattentiveness and disrespect. Yet, in other situations, such as talking with friends, a slouched posture and indirect body orientation may be appropriate and may not carry messages about attention or respect. When you are making a speech, an upright stance and squared shoulders will help your audience perceive you as poised and self-confident. So when you are giving a speech, be sure to distribute your weight equally on both feet so that you maintain a confident bearing.

Haptics

Haptics is the interpretation of touch. Touching behavior is a fundamental aspect of nonverbal communication. We use our hands, our arms, and other body parts to pat, hug, slap, kiss, pinch, stroke, hold, embrace, and tickle others. Through touch we communicate a variety of emotions and messages. In Western culture, we shake hands to be sociable and polite, we pat a person on the back for encouragement, we hug a person to show love, and we clasp raised hands to demonstrate solidarity.

Because of individual preference, family background, or culture, people differ in their use of touching behavior and their reactions to unsolicited touch from others. Some people like to touch others and be touched; other people do not. Although American culture is relatively noncontact oriented, the kinds and amounts of touching behavior within our society vary widely. Touching behavior that seems appropriate to one person may be perceived as overly intimate or threatening by another. Moreover, the perceived appropriateness of touch differs with the context. Touch that is considered appropriate in private may embarrass a person when done in public or with a large group of people.

Use of Voice: Vocalics

The interpretation of a verbal message based on the paralinguistic features is called **vocalics**. **Paralanguage** is the voiced but not verbal part of a spoken message. Six vocal characteristics that comprise paralanguage are pitch, volume, rate, quality, intonation, and vocalized pauses.

Pitch

Pitch is the highness or lowness of vocal tone. People raise and lower vocal pitch and change volume to emphasize ideas, indicate questions, and show nervousness. They may also raise the pitch when they are nervous or lower the pitch when they are trying to be forceful. Lower pitch voices tend to convey more believability and credibility.

Volume

Volume is the loudness or softness of tone. Whereas some people have booming voices that carry long distances, others are normally soft-spoken. Regardless of their normal volume level, however, people do vary their volume depending on the situation and topic of discussion. For example, people talk loudly when they wish to be heard in noisy settings. They may vary their volume when they are angry, or they may speak more softly when they are being romantic or loving.

Rate

Rate is the speed at which a person speaks. People tend to talk more rapidly when they are happy,

body orientation
posture in relation to another person

haptics
the interpretation of touch

vocalics
the interpretation of a message based on the paralinguistic features

paralanguage
the voiced but not verbal part of a spoken message

pitch
the highness or lowness of vocal tone

volume
the loudness or softness of tone

rate
the speed at which a person speaks

frightened, nervous, or excited and more slowly when they are problem solving out loud or are trying to emphasize a point.

Quality

Quality is the sound of a person's voice. Each human voice has a distinct tone. Some voices are raspy, some smoky, some have bell-like qualities, while others are throaty or nasal.

Intonation

Intonation is the variety, melody, or inflection in one's voice. Some voices have little intonation and sound monotone. Other voices have a great deal of melody and may have a childlike quality to them. People prefer to listen to voices with a moderate amount of intonation.

Vocalized Pauses

Vocalized pauses are extraneous sounds or words that interrupt fluent speech. The most common vocalized pauses that creep into our speech include "uh," "um," "er," "well," "OK," and those nearly universal interrupters of American conversations, "you know" and "like." At times we may use vocal pauses to hold our turn when we momentarily search for the right word or idea. Because they are not part of the intended message, occasional vocalized pauses are generally ignored by those who are interpreting the message. However, when you begin to use them to excess, others will perceive you as nervous or unsure of what you are saying. As your use increases, people will be less able to understand what you are saying, and they may perceive you as confused and your ideas as not well thought out. For some people, the use of vocalized pauses presents interferences that are so pervasive that listeners are unable to concentrate on the meaning of the message.

We can interpret the paralinguistic part of a message as complementing, supplementing, or contradicting the meaning conveyed by the verbal message. So when Joan says, "Well, isn't that an interesting story." How we interpret her meaning will depend on the paralanguage that accompanies it. If she alters her normal voice so that the "Well" is varied both in pitch and tone while the rest of her words are spoken in a staccato monotone, we might interpret the vocalics as contradicting the words and

perceive her message as sarcasm. But if her voice pitch rises with each word, we might perceive the vocalics as supplementing the message and understand that she is asking a question.

Use of Space: Proxemics

Have you ever been in the midst of a conversation with someone that you felt was "standoffish" or "pushy"? If you had analyzed your feeling, you might have discovered that your impression of the person or what was being said stemmed from how far the person chose to stand from you. If the person seemed to be farther away than you are accustomed to, you might have interpreted the distance as aloofness. If the distance was less than you would have expected, you might have felt uncomfortable and perceived the person as being overly familiar or pushy. Proxemics is the formal term for the interpretation someone makes of your use of space. People will interpret how you use the personal space around you, the physical spaces that you control and occupy, and the artifacts that you choose to decorate your space.

How much space you need or view as appropriate depends on your individual preference.

Personal Space

Personal space is the distance you try to maintain when you interact with other people. Our need for and use of personal space stems from our biological territorial natures, which view space as a protective mechanism. How much space you need or view as appropriate depends on your individual preference, the nature of your relationship to the other person or people, and your culture. While the absolute amount of space varies from person to person, message to message, and from culture to culture, in general the amount of personal space we view as appropriate decreases as the intimacy of our relationship increases. For example, in the dominant U.S. culture, four distinct distances are generally perceived as appropriate

quality
the sound of a person's voice

intonation
the variety, melody, or inflection in one's voice

vocalized pauses
extraneous sounds or words that interrupt fluent speech

proxemics
the interpretation of a person's use of space

personal space
the distance you try to maintain when you interact with other people

Figure 4.1

Distance Levels of Personal Space in the Dominant U.S. Culture

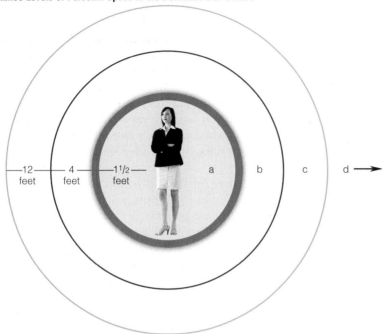

Zone a, **intimate space**: spouses, significant others, family members, and others with whom we have an intimate relationship

Zone b, **personal distance**: friends

Zone c, **social distance**: business associates and acquaintances

Zone d, **public distance**: strangers

the unwritten rules. For instance, people will tolerate being packed into a crowded elevator or subway and even touching others they do not know, provided that the others follow the "rules." The rules may include standing rigidly, looking at the floor or the indicator above the door, but not making eye contact with others. The rules also include ignoring or pretending that they are not touching.

Physical Space

Physical space is the part of the physical environment over which you exert control. Our territorial natures not only lead us to maintain personal distance, but also lead us to assert ownership claims to parts of the physical space that we occupy. Sometimes we do not realize the ways that we claim space as our own; in other instances, we go to great lengths to visibly "mark" our territory. For example, Ramon arrives early for the first day of class, finds an empty desk, and puts his backpack next to it on the floor and his coat on the seat. He then makes a quick trip to the restroom. If someone comes along while Ramon is gone, moves his backpack and coat, and sits down at the desk, that person is violating what Ramon has "marked" as his territory. If you regularly take the same seat in a class, that habit becomes a type of marker, signaling

and comfortable, depending on the nature of the conversation. These distances are illustrated in Figure 4.1. *Intimate distance* is defined as up to 18 inches and is appropriate for private conversations between close, intimate friends. *Personal distance,* from 18 inches to 4 feet, is the space in which casual conversation occurs. *Social distance,* from 4 to 12 feet, is where impersonal business such as a job interview is conducted. *Public distance* is anything more than 12 feet (Hall, 1969).

Of greatest concern to us is the intimate distance—that which we regard as appropriate for intimate conversation with close friends, parents, and younger children. People usually become uncomfortable when "outsiders" violate this intimate distance. For instance, in a movie theater that is less than one-quarter full, people will tend to leave one or more seats empty between themselves and others whom they do not know. If a stranger sits right next to you in such a setting, you are likely to feel uncomfortable or threatened and may even move away. Intrusions into our intimate space are acceptable only in certain settings and then only when all involved follow

physical space
the physical environment over which you exert control

> >What do the artifacts in this room and their arrangement tell you about the person who works there? How do you think they influence this person's interactions with other people?

©AP PHOTO/J. SCOTT APPLEWHITE

to others that a particular seat location is yours. Other students will often leave that seat empty because they have perceived it as yours. Not only can we interpret someone's ownership of space by their markers, but we also can understand a person's status in a group by noting where the person sits and the amount of space over which ownership is claimed. In a well-established group, people with differing opinions will often choose to sit on opposite sides of the table, while allies will sit in adjacent spots. So if you are observant, you can tell where people stand on an issue by noticing where they have chosen to sit. There are many other meanings that can be discerned from how people use physical space.

Artifacts

Artifacts are the objects and possessions we use to decorate the physical space we control. When others enter our homes, our offices, or our dorm rooms, they look around and notice what objects we have chosen to place in the space and how we have arranged them. Then they assign meaning to what they see. For example, when Katie visited her boyfriend Peter at school, the first thing she noticed was a picture hanging on his bulletin board of him hugging a really cute woman that she did not recognize. The second thing she noticed was that the framed picture she had given him of her before he left for school was nowhere to be found. From this, she concluded that Peter wasn't honoring his promise not to see anyone at school.

The way that we arrange the artifacts in our space also can nonverbally communicate to others. Professors and businesspeople have learned that by choosing and arranging the artifacts in their space, they can influence interactions. We once knew a professor who was a real soft touch. So when he had to handle the students who were petitioning to enter closed classes, he turned his desk, which normally faced out the window, so that it was directly in front of the door. That way, the students couldn't get into his office, sit down, and break his resolve with their sad stories. Instead, they had to plead their case standing in the very public hall. In this case, his desk served as a barrier and protected him from his soft-hearted self.

People choose artifacts not just for the function of the object, but also for the message that the object conveys about them. So when Lee, the baby of his family, got his first job, the first items he purchased for his new apartment were a large, flat-screen TV and a stuffed leather couch and chair. He chose these primarily to impress his older and already successful brother. Whether the artifacts you choose are conscious attempts to impress or whether they simply reflect your taste or income, when others enter your space, they will notice the artifacts and draw conclusions.

LO³ Self-Presentation Cues

People learn a lot about us based on how we look. This includes our physical appearance, our clothing and grooming, and our use of time.

Physical Appearance

People make judgments about others based on how they look. We can control our physique to some extent through exercise, diet, cosmetic surgery, and so on. But we also inherit much of our physical appearance, including our body type, and physical features such as hair and eyes. Our body is one of the first things that others notice about us and there are culture-based stereotypes associated with each of the three general body shapes. Endomorphs, who are shaped round and heavy, are stereotyped as kind, gentle, and jovial. Mesomorphs, who are muscular and strong, are believed to be energetic, outgoing, and confident. Ectomorphs, whose bodies are lean and have little muscle development, are stereotyped as brainy, anxious, and cautious. While not everyone fits perfectly into one of these categories, each person tends toward one body type. Even though these stereotypes are far from accurate, there is ample anecdotal evidence to suggest that many of us form our first impression of someone using body type stereotypes. Yet, the messages we infer from body type also vary by culture.

Clothing and Grooming

Your clothing and personal grooming communicate a message about you. Today, more than ever, people use

artifacts
objects and possessions we use to decorate the physical space we control

endomorph
round and heavy body type

mesomorph
muscular and athletic body type

ectomorph
body type that is lean and has little muscle development

clothing choices, body art, and other personal grooming to communicate who they are and what they stand for. Likewise, when we meet someone, we are likely to form our impression of them from how they are dressed and groomed. Because we can alter our clothing and grooming to suit the occasion, others rely heavily on these nonverbal cues to help them understand who we are and how to treat us. As a result, you can change how people perceive you by altering your clothing and grooming. For example, a successful sales representative may wear an oversize white T-shirt, baggy shorts, and a backward ball cap when hanging with his friends; put on khakis and a golf shirt to go to the office; and dress in a formal blue suit to make a major presentation to a potential client group. In each case, he uses what he is wearing to communicate who he is and how others should treat him.

Use of Time

Chronemics is the way others interpret your use of time. Cultures differ in how they view time (Hall, E. T., 1959). Some of us have a **monochronic time orientation**, or a "one thing at a time" approach to time. We concentrate our efforts on one task, and only when it is finished or when the time we have allotted to it is complete, do we move on to another task. If we are monochronic, we see time as "real" and think about "spending time," "losing time," and so on. As a result, we subordinate our interpersonal relationships to our schedule (Dahl, 2004, p. 11). So when Margarite's sister, who is excited to share some good news, comes into the room and interrupts her "study time," Margarite, who is monochronic, screams, "Get out! Can't you see I'm studying!" Others of us have a **polychronic time orientation** and tackle multiple tasks at once. We see time as flexible and fluid. So we view appointment times and schedules as variable and subordinate to our interpersonal relationships, and we easily alter or adapt our schedule to meet the needs of our relationships (Dahl, 2004, p. 11).

chronemics
the interpretation of a person's use of time

monochronic time orientation
a time orientation that emphasizes doing one thing at a time

polychronic time orientation
a time orientation that emphasizes doing multiple things at once

For example, George, who is polychronic, shows up for a noon lunch with Raoul at 12:47 p.m. because as he was leaving his office, his coworker stopped him to ask for help on a problem.

How Margarite's sister or Raoul interpreted the time behavior they experienced depends on their own time orientation. If Margarite's sister is also monochronic, she probably apologized, perceiving her own behavior to have been at fault. If Raoul is polychronic, he will not be offended by George's arrival time because he will have viewed George's delay as understandable. We tend to view other's use of time through the lens of the culture from which we come. So if we are monochronic in our orientation to time, we will view the polychronic time behavior of someone else as being "rude" and vice versa.

LO⁴ Cultural and Gender Variations in Nonverbal Communication

Culture and gender often play a role in how we communicate nonverbally. Cultural and gender variations are seen in the use of kinesics, paralanguage, proxemics and territory, artifacts and physical appearance, and chronemics.

Kinesics

As we have said, the use of kinesics, or body motions and the meanings they convey, differs among cultures. Several cultural differences in body motions are well documented.

Eye Contact

A majority of people in the United States and other Western cultures expect those with whom they are communicating to "look them in the eye." Samovar, Porter, and McDaniel (2007) explain, however, that direct eye contact is not a custom throughout the world (p. 210). For instance, in Japan, prolonged eye contact is considered rude, disrespectful, and threatening. People from Latin America, Caribbean cultures, and Africa tend to avoid eye contact as a sign of respect.

In the United States, women tend to have more frequent eye contact during conversations than men do (Cegala & Sillars, 1989). Moreover, women tend to hold eye contact longer than men, regardless of the sex of the person they are interacting with (Wood, 2007). It is important to note that these differences, which we have described according to biological sex, are also related to

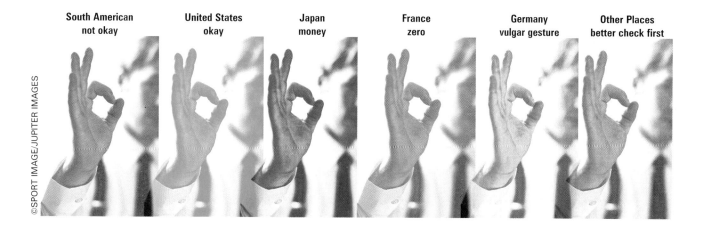

| South American
not okay | United States
okay | Japan
money | France
zero | Germany
vulgar gesture | Other Places
better check first |

notions of gender and standpoint in society. In other words, people (male or female) will give more eye contact when they are displaying feminine-type behaviors than when they are displaying masculine-type behaviors.

Facial Expression and Gestures

Studies show that there are many similarities in nonverbal communication across cultures, especially in facial expressions. For instance, several facial expressions seem to be universal, including a slight raising of the eyebrow to communicate recognition, wriggling one's nose, and a disgusted facial look to show social repulsion (Martin & Nakayama, 2000, pp. 183–184).

Across cultures, people also show considerable differences in the meaning of gestures. For instance, the forming of a circle with the thumb and forefinger signifies the OK sign in the United States, but means zero or worthless in France, is a symbol for money in Japan, and is a vulgar gesture in Germany and Brazil (Axtell, 1999, pp. 44, 143, 212).

Displays of emotion may also vary. For instance, in some Eastern cultures, people have been socialized to downplay emotional behavior cues, whereas members of other cultures have been socialized to amplify their displays of emotion. Research has shown some sex and gender effects in facial expressions and gestures. Women and men using a feminine style of communication tend to smile frequently. Gender differences in the use of gestures are so profound that people have attributed masculinity or femininity on the basis of gesture style alone (Pearson, West, & Turner, 1995, p. 126). For instance, women are more likely to keep their arms close to the body, are less likely to lean forward with the body, play more often with their hair or clothing, and tap their fingers more often than men.

Haptics

According to Samovar, Porter, and McDaniel (2007), touching behavior is closely linked to culture. In some cultures, lots of contact and touching is normal behavior, while in other cultures, individual space is respected and frequent touching is not encouraged. According to Neuliep (2006), some cultures such as South and Central American countries, as well as many southern European countries, encourage contact and engage in frequent touching. By contrast, many northern European cultures are medium to low in contact, and Asian cultures are mainly low-contact cultures. The United States, which is a country of immigrants, is generally perceived to be medium in contact, though there are wide differences among individual Americans due to variations in family heritage.

Women tend to touch others less than men do, but women value touching more than men do. Women view touch as an expressive behavior that demonstrates warmth and affiliation, whereas men view touch as instrumental behavior, so that touching females is considered as leading to sexual activity (Pearson, West, & Turner, 1995, p. 142).

Paralanguage

There are a few cultural and gender variations in the use of paralanguage. It is in the use of volume where cultural differences are most apparent (Samovar, Porter, & McDaniel, 2007). Arabs speak with a great deal of volume to convey strength and sincerity, while soft voices are preferred in Britain, Japan, and Thailand.

In the United States, there are stereotypes about what are considered to be masculine and feminine voices. Masculine voices are expected to be low-pitched and loud, with moderate to low intonation; feminine voices are expected to be higher-pitched, softer in volume, and more expressive. The voice characteristic of breathiness is associated with femininity. Although both sexes have the option to portray a range of masculine and feminine paralanguage, most people probably conform to the expectations for their sex (Wood, 2007).

Proxemics and Territory

As is the case with most forms of nonverbal communication, one's use of space and territory is associated with culture (Samovar, Porter, & McDaniel, 2007). Recall our discussion of individualistic and collectivist cultures in Chapter 2. Cultures that stress individualism generally demand more space than do collectivist cultures and will defend space more closely (p. 217). Seating and furniture placement may also vary by cultural expectations. For example, Americans in groups tend to talk to those seated opposite them, but Chinese prefer to talk to those seated next to them. Furniture arrangement in the United States and Germany often emphasizes privacy. In France or Japan, furniture is arranged for group conversation or participation (pp. 218–219).

Artifacts and Physical Appearance

There are cultural and gender influences regarding artifacts and physical appearance. Different clothing styles signify masculinity and femininity within a culture. In the United States, women's and feminine clothing is more decorative, while men's and masculine clothing is more functional (Wood, 2007).

Chronemics

As you probably recognize, the dominant U.S. culture has a monochronic time orientation; Swiss and German cultures are even more oriented in this way. On the other hand, many Latin American and Arab cultures have polychronic orientation. The large-scale immigration that is occurring across the globe is leading to an influx of Arab workers into northern Europe and Latin American workers into the U.S. As a result, it is likely that you will encounter people whose use of time is different from your own.

LO⁵ Guidelines for Improving Nonverbal Communication

Because nonverbal messages are inherently continuous, ambiguous, multichanneled, and sometimes unintentional, it can be tricky to accurately decode them. Add to this the fact that the meaning for any nonverbal behavior can vary by situation, culture, and gender, and you begin to understand why we so often "misread" the behavior of others. The following guidelines can help you improve the likelihood that you will make accurate interpretations of others' behavior, and that your own behavior will lead others to perceive your nonverbal messages correctly.

Interpreting Nonverbal Messages

When interpreting nonverbal messages, here are some things you might want to remember.

- **Do Not Assume**
  When interpreting others' nonverbal cues, do not automatically assume that a particular behavior means a certain thing. Except for the category of emblems, there is no automatic meaning of nonverbal behavior. And even the meaning of emblems varies culturally. There is much room for error when people make quick interpretations or draw rapid conclusions about an aspect of nonverbal behavior. Instead of making automatic interpretations of nonverbal cues, we should consider cultural, gender, and individual influences on nonverbal behavior.

- **Consider Influences**
  Consider cultural, gender, and individual influences when interpreting nonverbal cues. We have shown how nonverbal behavior varies widely based on culture or expectations of masculinity and femininity. Note also that some people are totally unique in their display of nonverbal behavior. You may have learned over time that your friend grinds her teeth when she is excited. You may never encounter another person who uses this behavior in this way.

- **Pay Attention to Nonverbal Communication**
  Pay attention to multiple aspects of nonverbal communication and their relationship to verbal communication. You should not take nonverbal cues out of context. In any one interaction, you are likely to get simultaneous messages from a person's eyes, face, gestures, posture, voice, and use of space and touch. Even in electronic communication, where much of the nonverbal communication is absent, there can be facial expression and touch communicated through emoticons, paralanguage through capitalization of words, and chronemics through the timing and length of an electronic message. By taking into consideration all aspects of communication, you will be more effective in interpreting others' messages.

- **Use Perception Checking**
  As we discussed in Chapter 2, the skill of perception checking lets you see if your interpretation of another person's message is accurate or not. By describing the nonverbal behavior you have noticed and tentatively sharing your interpretation of it,

you can get confirmation or correction of your interpretation. It may be helpful to use perception checking when faced with gender or cultural variations in nonverbal behavior.

Sending Nonverbal Messages

When considering what kinds of nonverbal messages you are sending, here are some things you should be aware of.

- **Be Conscious**
Be conscious of the nonverbal behavior you are displaying. Remember that you are always communicating nonverbally. Some nonverbal cues will always be out of your level of consciousness, but you should work to bring more of your nonverbal behavior into your conscious awareness. It is a matter of just paying attention to what you are doing with your body, voice, space, and self-presentation cues. If you initially have difficulty paying attention to your nonverbal behavior, ask a friend to point out the nonverbal cues you are displaying.

- **Be Purposeful**
Be purposeful or strategic in your use of nonverbal communication. Sometimes, it is important to control what you are communicating nonverbally. For instance, if you want to be persuasive, you should use nonverbal cues that demonstrate confidence and credibility. These may include direct eye contact, a serious facial expression, a relaxed posture, a loud and low-pitched voice with no vocal interferences, and a professional style of clothing and grooming. While there are no absolute prescriptions for communicating nonverbally, there are strategic choices we can make to convey the message we desire.

- **Do Not Distract**
Make sure that your nonverbal cues do not distract from your message. Sometimes, when we are not aware of what nonverbal cues we are displaying or when we are anxious, certain nonverbal behaviors will hinder our communication. Fidgeting, tapping your fingers on a table, pacing, mumbling, using vocal interferences, and using adaptors can hinder the other person's interpretation of your message. It is especially important to use nonverbal behaviors that enhance rather than distract from your message during a formal speech.

- **Make Communication Match**
Make your nonverbal communication match your verbal communication. When nonverbal messages contradict verbal messages, people are more likely to believe the nonverbal, so it is important to have your verbal and nonverbal communication match. In addition, the various sources of nonverbal communication behavior should match each other. If you are feeling sad, your voice should be softer and less expressive, and you should avoid letting your face contradict your voice by smiling. People get confused and frustrated when receiving inconsistent messages.

- **Adapt**
Adapt your nonverbal behavior to the situation. Situations vary in their formality, familiarity among the people, and purpose. Just like you would select different language for different situations, you should adapt your nonverbal messages to the situation. Assess what the situation calls for in terms of body motions, paralanguage, proxemics and territory, artifacts, physical appearance, and use of time. Of course, you already do some situational adapting with nonverbal communication. You do not dress the same way for a wedding as you would to walk the dog. You would not treat your brother's space and territory the same way you would treat your doctor's space and territory. But the more you can consciously adapt your nonverbal behavior to what seems appropriate to the situation, the more effective you will be as a communicator.

Learning Outcomes

LO[1]   Examine how culture affects communication

LO[2]   Discuss how to identify cultural norms and values

LO[3]   Explain barriers to effective intercultural communication

LO[4]   Analyze the development of intercultural communication competence

Communicating *across* Cultures

> **"As a nation of immigrants, the United States is defined as a multicultural society."**

Many of our judgments are based on our perceptions of people who are culturally different from us. Because culture has a profound impact on not only our perceptions but also our communication behavior, in this chapter we are going to study how culture affects our communication behavior and how it influences our perception of the communication we receive from others. We begin by taking a look at some basic concepts of culture, identifying important values and norms that set cultures apart. Then we discuss the barriers that arise from cultural difference and offer strategies for improving intercultural communication competence.

LO¹ Culture and Communication

How often have we heard people observe that the world is getting smaller and smaller and the people in it increasingly similar? Today, through the globalization of trade, the Internet and the World Wide Web, our lives are affected by the decisions and actions of people in other parts of the world and we can make instant personal contact with people around the globe through the click of a mouse. Some people celebrate this trend as a step toward world unity, while others mourn the loss of local cultures, traditions, and control and feel overwhelmed by the pervasiveness of communication.

You will recall from Chapter 1, that we defined *culture* as the values, attitudes, beliefs, orientations, and underlying assumptions prevalent among people in a society (Samovar, Porter, & McDaniel, 2007, p. 20). Yet, we do not have to journey to other countries to discover people of different cultures. As a nation of immigrants, the United States is defined as a multicultural society. Our population not only includes recent immigrants from Asia, Latin America, Eastern Europe, and other countries, but also the descendents of earlier immigrants, the descendents of Africans brought here against their will, and native peoples. So understanding how cultural groups vary in their approach to communication can help us as we interact with the people we meet each day.

Intercultural Communication

People are so familiar with their own language, gestures, facial expressions, conversational customs, and norms that they may experience anxiety when these familiar aspects of communication are disrupted. Yet, this occurs frequently when we interact with people from different cultures. **Culture shock** is the psychological discomfort you may feel when you attempt to adjust to a

culture shock
the psychological discomfort of adjusting to a new cultural situation

> > > A case of culture shock?

new cultural situation (Klyukanov, 2005, p. 33). Because culture shock is caused by an absence of shared meaning, you are likely to feel it most profoundly when you are thrust into another culture through travel, business, or when studying abroad. But it can also occur when you have contact with people from other cultures within your home country. For example, Brittney, who is from a small town in Minnesota, may experience culture shock when she visits Miami for the first time. She may be overwhelmed by the distinct Hispanic flavor of the city, by hearing Spanish spoken among people on the street, the prevalence of Latin beat music, the prominence of outdoor advertisements written in Spanish, and the ways people look and are dressed. Not only is Brittney likely to be disoriented because of the prominence of Spanish, but also because the values, attitudes, beliefs, and behaviors of the people she encounters might seem quite foreign to her.

Intercultural communication refers to interactions that occur between people whose cultural assumptions are so different that the communication between them is altered (Samovar, Porter, & McDaniel, 2007, p. 10). In other words, when communicating with people whose attitudes, values, beliefs, customs, and behaviors are culturally different from ours, we are communicating across cultural boundaries, which can lead to misunderstandings that would not commonly occur between people who are culturally similar. It is important to recognize that not every exchange between persons of different cultures exemplifies intercultural communication. For example, when

intercultural communication interaction between people whose cultural assumptions are distinct enough to alter the communication event

dominant culture the attitudes, values, beliefs, and customs that the majority of people in a society hold in common

co-cultures groups of people living within a dominant culture but exhibiting communication that is sufficiently different to distinguish them from the dominant culture

Brittney is on the beach in Miami and joins a group of Hispanics in a friendly game of beach volleyball, the cultural differences between her and the others are unlikely to affect their game-related exchanges. However, should Brittney decide to join the group for a night of club hopping, she is likely to experience conversations in which cultural differences lead to difficulty in understanding or interpreting what is said.

Dominant Cultures and Co-Cultures

Although the United States is a multicultural society, there are many attitudes, values, beliefs, and customs that a majority of people hold in common. This shared system of meaning comprises our **dominant culture**, and like the dominant culture of any country, ours has evolved over time. The dominant culture of the United States once reflected the values of white, western European, English-speaking, Protestant, heterosexual men. But as we have recognized our diversity, the dominant culture has evolved and incorporated aspects of other cultural groups. The result is a dominant culture that better reflects the diversity of the people in the United States.

In the United States, however, there are people who strongly identify with cultural groups whose values, attitudes, beliefs, and customs differ from the dominant culture. These groups, called **co-cultures**, exhibit communication that is sufficiently different to distinguish them from the dominant culture.

The following are some of the major contributors to co-cultures in United States society today:

Gender

Men and women have different cultural identities because they are biologically different and because they are differently socialized throughout their lives (through clothes, games, toys, education, roles, and so on). Women and men communicate differently in a number of ways because of these cultural differences. For instance, research shows that women are primarily concerned with personal relationships when they communicate. They talk more about relationships and feelings, tend to include others in conversations, and actively respond to others. Men more often focus on tasks or outcomes when they communicate. They talk more about content and problem solving, tend to emphasize control and status, and are less responsive to others (Wood, 2007).

Race

Traditionally, the term race has been used to classify people in terms of biological characteristics, such a skin and eye color, hair texture, and body shape.

©SUSAN VAN ETTEN

However, scientific justifications for such divisions have proven elusive, and the classification system itself has changed drastically over time (Hotz, 1995). Despite the difficulty of scientifically defining race, people have experienced the social effects of perceived race, and have formed communities and cultures based on racialized experiences. So race is an important cultural signifier for many people and racial identity can influence communication in a number of ways. The book, *African American Identities and Communication,* edited by Ronald Jackson (2004), describes linguistic and nonverbal patterns of African Americans who may switch from the communication styles of the dominant culture to communication forms unique to their race, depending on attitude, topics, or co-participants (Bonvillain, 2003). Other co-cultures based on gender, ethnicity, or social class may also change their communication from time to time, to be more similar to that of the dominant culture.

Ethnicity

Like race, ethnicity is an inexact distinction. Ethnicity refers to a classification of people based on combinations of shared characteristics such as nationality, geographic origin, language, religion, ancestral customs, and tradition. People vary greatly in terms of the importance they attach to their ethnic heritage and the degree to which it affects their attitudes, values, and behavior. You may descend from an Italian heritage and this may affect your closeness to family, your religion, the foods you eat, and many other aspects of your identity. Your roommate may also have Italian ancestors but may not identify herself as Italian and may not follow any family traditions based on this ethnicity.

Language or mother tongue is an obvious influence of ethnicity on communication. Immigrants bring with them the language of their original country and they may or may not speak English when they arrive. Even after they learn English, many immigrants choose to speak their mother language at home, intentionally live in close proximity to other people from their home country, and interact with those people in their mother language. Although the United States is an English-speaking country, it now has the third largest Spanish-speaking population of

>> Immigrants approaching New York City's Ellis Island.

any country in the world; furthermore, 70 percent of Hispanics in the United States mainly speak Spanish at home (Carlo-Casellas, 2002).

Sexual Orientation

In the United States, the dominant culture values heterosexuality. So, for example, most Americans are not offended when they see a man and a woman holding hands or kissing in public. Displays of affection between gay or lesbian couples may not be met with such tolerance. While the dominant culture has modified some of its most homophobic beliefs, people of other sexual orientations still face discrimination. So many gay, lesbian, bisexual, and transgender people participate in and identify with nonheterosexual communities whose distinct attitudes, values, customs, rites, rituals, and language markers provide social support that is absent in the dominant culture.

Religion

A religion is a system of beliefs that is shared by a group and that supplies the group with an object (or objects) for devotion, rituals for worshipping the object of devotion, and a code of ethics. Although the dominant culture of the United States values religious freedom and diversity, historically it has reflected

Major Contributors to Co-Cultures

- Gender
- Race
- Ethnicity
- Sexual Orientation
- Religion
- Class
- Age
- Cultural Identity

ethnicity
a classification of people based on combinations of shared characteristics such as nationality, geographic origin, language, religion, ancestral customs, and tradition

religion
a system of beliefs shared by a group with objects for devotion, rituals for worship, and a code of ethics

Judeo-Christian values and practices. All observant practitioners of a religion participate in co-culture. Those who strongly identify with a religious group that is outside the Judeo-Christian tradition will have different orientations that shape their relationships and their communication behavior. For example, Buddhism advises individuals to embrace rather than to resist personal conflict. Adversity, emotional upheaval, and conflict are seen as natural parts of life (Chuang, 2004). So a Buddhist is apt to communicate openly and calmly during an interpersonal conflict and embrace the positive aspects of conflict in strengthening interpersonal ties.

Social Class

Social class is a level in the power hierarchy of a society. Membership in each social class is determined by income, education, occupation, and social habits. The dominant culture of the United States reflects the culture of the middle class. Because social class often determines where people live, people of the same social class often establish communities where they develop and reinforce co-cultures with distinct values, rituals, and communication practices. For example, lower-class parents tend to emphasize obedience, acceptance of what others think, and hesitancy in expressing desires to authority figures, while middle-class parents more often emphasize self-control, self-direction, and intellectual curiosity. Such differences in values based on social class may lead those from middle-class backgrounds to speak more directly and assertively than do people from working-class backgrounds (Gilbert & Kahl, 1982).

Age

The time period in which we are born and raised can have a strong formative influence on us. People of the same generation form a cultural cohort group whose personal values, beliefs, and behaviors have been influenced by the common life experiences and events they encountered as they aged. People who grew up influenced by the Great Depression tend to be frugal; those alive during World War II value sacrifice of self for cause and country; those who came of age during the counterculture sixties are likely to question authority; and those we call Generation X, who experienced latchkey childhoods and the consequences of widespread divorce, value self-sufficiency.

Whether in family relationships or in the workplace, when people from different generations interact, their co-

social class
an indicator of a person's position in a social hierarchy, as determined by income, education, occupation, and social habits

{ **Fast Facts— The Dalits** }

Under the Indian caste system, the Dalits, or untouchables, were the lowest caste, and were allowed to occupy only the most menial jobs in Indian society. The untouchable castes were constitutionally outlawed in 1950.

©AP PHOTO/MANISH SWARUP

cultural orientations can create communication difficulties. For example, when members of different generational cohorts work together, miscommunication, misunderstandings, and conflict are likely to occur more than when people work with others of their same generation. Generally, people from earlier generations are less likely to question authority figures like parents, teachers, religious leaders, or bosses. They demonstrate their respect by using formal terms of address, such as referring to people by Mr., Ms., Dr., sir, and so on. People who came of age in the 1960s or later, on the other hand, tend to be more skeptical of authority and less formal in dealing with authorities. They are more likely to question their managers and to openly disagree with decisions that are made by those in authority (Zempke, Raines, & Filipczak, 2000).

Cultural Identity

As we saw in Chapter 2, our self-concept is the mental image that we have of ourselves, and that image is negotiated and reinforced through our communication with others. Membership in the cultural groups described above can contribute to our cultural identity, but it need not do so. Someone may greatly identify with their religion, ethnicity, or generation, while another person may scarcely think about those cultural groupings of which they are a part. Research has shown that cultural identity is determined by the importance that we assign to our membership in those cultural groups (Ting-Toomey et al., 2000). Shauna is a devoutly religious 20-year-old who attends prayer group every morning and is a leader in

her church youth group. She is a counselor at her church summer camp, dates men of her same religion only, and listens exclusively to Christian music. Religion would be a large part of Shauna's cultural identity, guiding how she sees herself and her actions. For her coworker, Nicole, who practices religion only during major religious holidays, her cultural identity would not be shaped by her religion.

LO² Identifying Cultural Norms and Values

Some aspects that identify the member of a culture may be easy to spot. We may be able to figure out someone's cultural background by the language spoken, their dress, or artifacts such as religious markers worn as jewelry or placed in the home. For example, when people meet Shimon, from his side curls, his yarmulke, and his black clothes, they can quickly discern that he is a Hassidic Jew. But beyond how one dresses, what does it really mean to be a Hassidic Jew? How do Hassidic Jews differ from the dominant culture and from other cultural groups? What are the other cultural groups to which they are similar? The work of Geert Hofstede gives us a way to understand how cultures are similar and different from one another and to understand how that variation affects communication.

Geert Hofstede (1980) identifies four major dimensions of culture that affect communication: individualism–collectivism, uncertainty avoidance, power distance, and masculinity–femininity. Table 5.1 (page 60) shows where the United States falls on each of these dimensions.

Individualism–Collectivism

In Chapter 2 we briefly discussed individualism and collectivism's effects on our self-perceptions. So you will recall that individualistic cultures are those in which people place primary value on the self and personal achievement. In an individualistic society, people consider the interests of others only in rela-

>> Hassidic reggae singer Matisyahu displays an interesting blend of cultural identities. He wears clothing that signifies how important his Jewish faith is to him. At the same time, he performs reggae music, inspired by the reggae culture's sense of optimism and emphasis on social reform.

tionship to how they affect the interest of the self. If you come from an individualistic culture, you may consider your family and close friends when you act, but only because your interests and theirs align. People in individualistic cultures view competition between people as desirable and useful. Because of this, individualistic cultures emphasize personal rights and responsibilities, privacy, voicing one's opinion, freedom, innovation, and self-expression (Andersen, Hecht, Hoobler, & Smallwood, 2003).

In contrast, collectivist cultures place primary value on the interests of the group and group harmony. In a collectivist society, an individual's decision is shaped by what is best for the group whether it serves the individual's interests or not. Collectivist societies are highly integrated and maintaining harmony and cooperation are valued over competitiveness and personal achievement. As a result, members of collectivist societies will probably have stronger bonds within the groups to which they belong (family, workplace, and community). Collectivist cultures emphasize community, collaboration, shared interest, harmony, the public good, and maintaining the avoidance of embarrassment (Andersen, Hecht, Hoobler, & Smallwood, 2003). According to Hofstede (1997), individualistic cultures include the United States, Australia, Great Britain, Canada, and northern and eastern European countries. Collectivist cultures are found in South and Central America, east and southeast Asia, and Africa.

Notions of individualism and collectivism influence many aspects of communication, including most notably our self-concept formation, assertiveness behavior, and group communication (Samovar, Porter, & McDaniel, 2007). In individualistic cultures, people stress the self and personal achievement, and the individual is treated as the most important element in a social setting. In

individualistic culture
emphasizes personal rights and responsibilities, privacy, voicing one's opinion, freedom, innovation, and self-expression

collectivist culture
emphasizes community, collaboration, shared interest, harmony, the public good, and avoiding embarrassment

©AP PHOTO/CHRIS PIZZELLO

individualist cultures like the United States, our self-concept and self-esteem are rooted in how successfully we have advanced our own interests without respect to how our actions have affected others. In a collectivist culture, what affects self-concept and self-esteem is not individual achievement; rather, it is whether the group thrives and how people's actions have contributed to their group's success. So if Marie is raised in an individualist culture and she is the highest scoring player on her basketball team, she will feel good about herself and identify herself as a "winner" even if her team has a losing season. But if Marie is from a collectivist culture, the fact that she is the highest scoring player will have little effect on her self esteem, but the fact that her team had a losing season will likely cause her to feel less personal esteem.

People coming from each of these cultural perspectives also view conflict differently. The emphasis that is placed on the individual leads members of individualistic cultures to value and practice assertiveness and confrontational argument, while members of collectivist cultures value accord and harmony and so practice tentativeness and collaboration or avoidance in arguments. In the United States, we teach assertiveness and argumentation as useful skills and expect them to be used in interpersonal and work relationships, politics, consumerism, and other aspects of civic life. By contrast, to maintain harmony and avoid interpersonal clashes, Japanese business has evolved an elaborate process called "nemawashii," a term that also means binding the roots of a plant before pulling it out. In Japan, any subject that might cause conflict at a meeting should be discussed in advance, so that the interaction at the meeting will not

low uncertainty-avoidance cultures cultures characterized by greater acceptance of, and less need to control, unpredictable people, relationships, or events

Table 5.1

Relative Comparison of Dimension Levels Between Ten Countries

Individualsim	High Uncertainty Avoidance	High Power Distance	Masculinity
USA	Japan	Russia	Japan
Netherlands	Russia	China	Germany
France	West Africa	Indonesia	USA
Germany	France	West Africa	Hong Kong
Russia	Germany	France	China
Japan	China	Hong Kong	Indonesia
Hong Kong	Netherlands	Japan	West Africa
China	Indonesia	USA	France
West Africa	USA	Netherlands	Russia
Indonesia	Hong Kong	Germany	Netherlands
Collectivism	**Low Uncertainty Avoidance**	**Low Power Distance**	**Femininity**

Source: G.H. Hofstede, "Cultural Constraints in Management Theories," *Academy of Management Executive* 7, no. 1 (1993): 81–94.

seem rude or impolite (Samovar & Porter, 2001). In collectivist societies, a style of communication that respects the relationship is more important than the information exchanged (Jandt, 2001). In collectivist societies, group harmony, sparing others embarrassment, and a modest presentation of oneself are important ways to show respect. A person does not speak directly if it might hurt others in the group.

> In collectivist societies, a style of communication that respects the relationship is more important than the information exchanged.

How people work in groups also depends on the type of culture they come from. Because members of collectivist cultures see group harmony and the welfare of the group to be of primary importance, they strive for consensus on group goals and may, at times, sacrifice optimal outcomes for the sake of group accord. Your cultural assumptions affect how you work to establish group goals, how you interact with other group members, and how willing you are to sacrifice for the sake of the group. Groups whose members come from both individualistic and collectivist cultures may experience difficulties due to their varying cultural assumptions.

Uncertainty Avoidance

Cultures differ in how their members feel about and deal with unpredictable people, relationships, or events. Low uncertainty-avoidance cultures (such as the United States, Sweden, and Denmark) are more tolerant of uncertainty in how people behave, in relationships, and in events, and so put little cultural emphasis on reducing unpredictability. People from cultures with low uncertainty avoidance more easily accept the unpredictability and ambiguity in life. They tend to be tolerant of the unusual, prize initiative, take risks, and think that there should be as few rules as possible. People who come from high uncertainty-avoidance cultures have a lower tolerance for unpredictable people, relationships, and events. These cultures create systems of formal rules and believe in absolute truth as the way to provide more security and reduce the risk. They also tend to be less tolerant of people or groups with deviant ideas or behavior. Because their culture emphasizes the importance of avoiding uncertainty, they often view life as hazardous and experience anxiety and stress when confronted with unpredictable people, relationships, or situations. Nations whose cultures are marked by high uncertainty avoidance include Japan, Portugal, Greece, Peru, and Belgium (Samovar, Porter, & McDaniel, 2007).

How our culture has taught us to view uncertainty affects our communication with others. It shapes how we use language, develop relationships, and negotiate with others. People from high uncertainty-avoidance cultures use and value specific and precise language because they believe that through careful word choice, we can be more certain of what a person's message means. Imagine a teacher declaring to a class that "the paper must be well researched, with evidence cited, and professional in format and appearance." Students from high uncertainty-avoidance cultures would find the teacher's remarks to be too general and vague. They would most likely experience anxiety and ask a lot of questions about what kind of research is appropriate, how to cite evidence, how much evidence is needed, what writing style to use, and the length of the paper in order to reduce their uncertainty. These students would welcome a specific checklist or rubric that enumerated the exact criteria by which the paper would be graded. By contrast, students from a low uncertainty-avoidance cultural background would be annoyed by an overly specific list of rules and guidelines, viewing it as a barrier to creativity and initiative. As you can imagine, a teacher with students from both of these backgrounds faces a difficult challenge when trying to explain an assignment.

How people approach new relationships and how they communicate in developing relationships is also affected by their culture's view of uncertainty. As you would expect, people from high uncertainty-

> > **Does uncertainty make you uncomfortable?**

avoidance cultures are wary of strangers and may not seek out new relationships or relationships with others they perceive as different (unpredictable). They generally prefer meeting people through friends and family and refrain from being alone with strangers. When developing relationships, people from high uncertainty-avoidance cultures tend to guard their privacy, refrain from self-disclosure early in a relationship, and proceed more slowly through relationship development. Members of low uncertainty-avoidance cultures, on the other hand, are likely to initiate new relationships with people who differ from them, and enjoy the excitement of disclosing personal information in earlier stages of relationship development.

Power Distance

Cultures differ in how accepting they are of wide differences in power held by different groups of people in the culture and how people of unequal power expect to be treated. In cultures characterized as having high power distance, inequalities in power, status, and rank are viewed as "natural" and these differences are acknowledged and accentuated by all members of the culture. These cultures believe that everyone in the culture has a rightful "place" and that members who have higher power, status, and rank should be deferred to by those having less power, status, and rank. High power-distance

high uncertainty-avoidance cultures cultures characterized by a low tolerance for, and a high need to control, unpredictable people, relationships, or events

high power distance the cultural belief that inequalities in power, status, and rank are "natural" and that these differences should be acknowledged and accentuated

cultures include most Arab countries of the Middle East, Malaysia, Guatemala, Venezuela, and Singapore, among other countries.

In cultures characterized as having **low power distance**, inequalities in power, status, and rank are underplayed and muted. People know that some individuals have more clout, authority, and influence, but lower ranking people are not in awe of, are not more respectful toward, and do not fear higher power people. Even though power differences exist, these cultures value democracy and egalitarian behavior. Austria, Finland, Denmark, Norway, the United States, New Zealand, and Israel are examples of countries whose dominant cultures are characterized by low power distance.

Our cultural beliefs about power distance affect how we interact with others, including how we communicate with authority figures, our language use, and our nonverbal behavior. If you are a student, unskilled worker, or average citizen in a high power-distance culture you would not challenge a person in authority, because you would expect to be punished for doing so. You would expect the more powerful person to control the interaction and would listen to what that person said and do what was ordered without question. When talking with a more powerful person, you would address them formally by using their title as a sign of respect. Formal terms of address like Mr. or Mrs., proper and polite forms of language, as well as nonverbal signals of your status differences would be evident in the exchange. If you come from a low power-distance culture, because differences in status are muted, you are more comfortable challenging those in authority. When interacting with a higher-power person, you will feel comfortable directing the course of the conversation and will question or confront the powerbroker if you need to. You would not feel compelled to use formal titles when addressing the more powerful member.

Masculinity–Femininity

Cultures differ in how strongly they value traditional sex role distinctions. Cultures that Hofstede called masculine cultures expect people to maintain traditional sex roles and maintain different standards of behavior for men and women. Hofstede called these cultures "masculine" because, for the most part, groups that maintain distinct sex-based roles also value masculine roles more highly than feminine ones. If you come from a masculine culture like the ones that are dominant in Mexico, Italy, and Japan, you are likely to value men when they are assertive and dominant and to value women when they are nurturing, caring, and service oriented. When you encounter people who don't meet these expectations, you are likely to be uncomfortable. Overall, however, if you come from a masculine culture regardless of your sex, you will see masculine behaviors to be more worthwhile, so you are likely to value the masculine characteristics of performance, ambition, assertiveness, competitiveness, and material success more than you value traditionally feminine traits such as service, nurturing, investment in relationships, and helping behaviors (Hofstede, 2000). **Feminine cultures** expect that people, regardless of sex, will assume a variety of roles depending on the circumstances and their own choices, rather than any sex-role expectations. If you are from a feminine culture, like the national cultures of Sweden, Norway, and Denmark, not only will you feel free to act in ways that are not traditionally assigned to people of your sex, but you will also value those traits that have traditionally been associated with feminine roles (Hofstede, 1998).

Whether you come from a masculine or a feminine culture has a significant effect on how much behavioral flexibility you demonstrate. People from masculine cultures have strict definitions of appropriate behavior for people of a particular sex. As a result, they learn and are reinforced only for those behaviors that are seen to be appropriate for their sex. So men in these cultures are unprepared to engage in nurturing and caring behaviors, such as empathizing and comforting, and women are unprepared to be assertive and argue persuasively. Both men and women in feminine cultures learn and are reinforced for demonstrating both traditionally masculine and feminine behaviors. As a result, people from feminine cultures are more flexible in their communication behavior. Both men and women learn to nurture, empathize, assert, and argue, although any single individual may still lack skill in one or more behaviors.

LO³ Barriers to Effective Intercultural Communication

Now that we have developed an understanding of culture and the variations that can exist among cultures and co-cultures, we are in a

low power distance
the cultural belief that inequalities in power, status, and rank should be underplayed and muted

masculine culture
a culture in which people are expected to adhere to traditional sex roles

feminine culture
a culture in which people, regardless of sex, are expected to assume a variety of roles based on the circumstances and their own choices

better position to appreciate the specific barriers that cultural differences give rise to including anxiety, assumptions of similarity or difference, ethnocentrism, stereotypes and prejudice, incompatible communication codes, and incompatible norms and values.

Anxiety

It is normal to feel some level of discomfort or apprehension when we recognize that we are different from most everyone else or when we enter a cultural milieu that has unfamiliar customs. Most people experience fear, dislike, and distrust when first interacting with someone from a different culture (Luckmann, 1999). So when Marissa, who is from a barrio in Los Angeles, decided to attend a small, liberal arts college in New England, she was nervous and questioned if her decision to attend school in the northeast had been a good one. Sure, the other students had been friendly enough during orientation week, but it had become clear that she didn't really have much in common with them. While the others easily shared stories of spring-break trips they had taken with their families and joked about the cars they had wrecked, Marissa found she had little to add—her family always went to see her grandmother back in Mexico when her parents took time off from their jobs. She didn't even have a driver's license. When she hesitantly mentioned her quinceañera party, everyone turned and stared at her and one guy said, "What's a 'quicky

hairy' party?" And all of the guys laughed. At first, the other women listened politely, but by that time Marissa was so nervous that she stumbled over her words and really didn't do a good job of explaining this coming-of-age tradition that was so important to her community. Most of us are like Marissa when we are anxious—we don't do a good job of sharing our ideas and feelings. So, our anxiety becomes a barrier to our communication.

Assuming Similarity or Difference

When people cross into an unfamiliar cultural environment, they often assume that the norms, values, and traditions that applied in their familiar situation match those that apply in the new one. When traveling internationally from the United States, for example, many people expect to eat their familiar hamburgers and fries, provided with rapid and efficient service. Likewise, they may be annoyed with shops and restaurants closing during midday in countries that observe the custom of siesta.

It can be just as great a mistake to assume that everything about an unfamiliar culture will be different. With time, Marissa is likely to find that the other students really aren't as different from her friends at home, and that school is still school even when there is snow on the ground. As she makes friends, she learns that although Rachel, who is Jewish, didn't have a quinceañera party, she did have a bat mitzvah celebration and Kate, who is Irish Catholic, had a big party when she made her confirmation. Because our assumptions guide our communication behavior, incorrectly assuming similarities that are not accurate or differences that do not exist can lead to miscommunication. The wisest way to overcome this barrier is not to assume anything, but to be aware of the feedback you receive, which provides cues to the real similarities and differences that exist between your cultural expectations and those of your interaction partners.

Common Barriers

- Anxiety
- Assuming similarity or difference
- Ethnocentrism
- Stereotypes and prejudice
- Incompatible communication codes
- Incompatible norms and values

Ethnocentrism

Ethnocentrism is the belief that one's own culture is superior to others. The stereotype of the immigrant in the host country, loudly complaining of how much better everything is back home, is the classic example of ethnocentrism. In varying degrees, ethnocentrism is found in every culture (Haviland, 1993) and can occur in co-cultures as well. An ethnocentric view of the world leads to attitudes of superiority and messages that are directly and subtly condescending in content and tone. As you would expect, these messages are offensive to receivers from other cultures or co-cultures.

Stereotypes and Prejudice

In Chapter 2, we defined stereotypes as attributions that cover up individual differences and ascribe certain characteristics to a group of people. Basing our interactions on stereotypes can lead to misunderstandings and can strain relationships. For example, when Laura anticipates meeting Joey, who she has heard is gay, she may expect him to be effeminate in his mannerisms and interested in fashion. So she embarrasses him and herself when, early in their conversation, she attempts to find common ground and asks him for advice on what type of cologne to buy her boyfriend—to which he replies, "What is your problem? I may be gay, but I'm not that Carson Kressley dude from *Queer Eye!*"

ethnocentrism
the belief that one's own culture is superior to others

> >Prejudice and stereotypes can negatively affect not only our relationships with people we know personally, but also with our larger communities. How do you suppose this protester's sign will affect the young girls in the photo?

Also you will recall that in Chapter 2, we defined prejudice as a rigid attitude based on group membership that predisposes us to think, feel, or act in a negative way toward another person or group. Thinking that a Chinese student in your class will get the best grade in the course because all Chinese students excel intellectually, or assuming that Alberto, who is Mexican, is working in the United States as an illegal, undocumented worker, would be examples of prejudice. Colin is prejudiced and believes that all white people try to take advantage of people of color. So when his coworker John, who is white, offers to refer a client to Colin, Colin replies, "Forget it—you're not going to pawn off a deadbeat on me." When we interact based on stereotypes and prejudice, we risk creating messages that are inaccurate and damage our relationships; when we listen with our stereotypes and prejudices in mind, we may misperceive the intent of the person with whom we are talking.

Incompatible Communication Codes

Zeke could not understand why those Chinese guys always sat together in the dining hall. They were always fighting—screaming at each other and waving their arms. He had no idea what they were saying because he did not understand Mandarin, but he could tell that they were pretty angry. He was always expecting a fight to break out.

Zeke was judging the conversation of the Chinese students based on their use of paralanguage and body movement. He could not understand the words they used, but he interpreted their nonverbal communication as hostile and angry. Zeke did not understand that Mandarin is a tonal language. How the words are voiced affects their meaning. The great changes in pitch and volume that he heard did not represent the expression of strong emotion, but only the expression of different meanings.

When our conversational partners, people in our group, or audience members speak a different language, it is easy to see that we have incompatible communication codes, but even when people speak the same language, there will be cultural variations that result from the co-cultures to which they belong. For example, people from Great Britain take a "lift" to reach a higher floor, while Americans ride an elevator. Even within a national group, co-cultural use of the language can lead to incompatible communication codes. In fact, less powerful co-cultural groups will often purposefully develop "in group" codes that are easily understood by co-culture members but unintelligible to those from the outside. Just

©COURTESY OF B-BOOKS, LTD.

try to have a conversation about your computer problem with your friend Sam who is a "techno geek." As an insider, Sam is likely to talk in a vocabulary that is as foreign to you as if Sam were speaking Icelandic. People who speak different languages quickly comprehend their inability to communicate verbally, and invariably turn to some type of nonverbal signing in an effort to overcome the language barrier. As we have seen, however, there are also significant differences in the use and meaning of nonverbal behaviors. Not only do incompatible verbal communication codes create barriers to intercultural communication, so do our differences in how we use and interpret nonverbal behavior. For example, in some cultures, belching after eating signifies that the meal did not agree with the diner, while in other cultures it is a compliment to the cook. In some cultures, the gesture used in the United States to mean "OK" is obscene. Such differences in nonverbal behavior across cultures often account for misunderstandings or embarrassment when people from different cultures attempt to communicate with each other.

Incompatible Norms and Values

All cultures base their communication behaviors on cultural norms and rules and on personal values based on those cultural norms and rules. Sometimes the norms and values of two people of different cultures create barriers that make it difficult for them to understand each other. For example, Imad, who is from Lebanon, works in the United States. When he first begins working at his new job, his coworkers, George and Simon, who are very interested in getting to know him, ask him if he would like to join them for lunch. In Imad's culture, when such an invitation is given, it would be customary for him to decline; accepting the first time would be considered impolite. After he declined, then George and Simon would invite him again.

When Imad declines their invitation, however, George and Simon, who have a cultural orientation that values being direct and objective in conveying information, assume that Imad is truly not interested in joining them for lunch, so they leave. After, several more encounters like this, in which Imad declines to join them, George and Simon stop inviting Imad to lunch all together. Imad does not understand this, because his cultural orientation values relationships and politeness. He thinks that George and Simon don't actually want him to join them for lunch, and that they were asking just to be polite. George and Simon are disappointed, because they think their new coworker is entirely uninterested in them. Both parties fail to realize that their cultural expectations in these situations are different, and this prevents them from developing their relationships.

LO⁴ Intercultural Communication Competence

Competent intercultural communicators overcome cultural barriers by adopting the correct attitudes toward other cultures, acquiring accurate information about other cultures' values and practices, and developing specific skills needed to be effective across cultures.

> We must be willing to try and must have a desire to succeed when communicating interculturally. We must be willing to try new behaviors, rather than expecting the other person to adjust to our style of communicating.

Adopt Correct Attitudes

The right attitudes for intercultural communication, according to Neuliep (2006) involve one's motivations and flexibility in interacting with others from different cultures. In other words, we must be willing to try and must have a desire to succeed when communicating interculturally. We must be willing to try new behaviors, rather than expecting the other person to adjust to our style of communicating. When we tolerate ambiguity, are open-minded, and act altruistically, these attitudes enable us to effectively communicate across cultural differences.

1. **Tolerate ambiguity.** Communicating with strangers creates uncertainty, and when we recognize that the stranger also comes from a different culture, we can become anxious about what they will expect of us. People beginning

intercultural relationships must be prepared to tolerate a high degree of uncertainty about the other person and to tolerate it for a long period of time. If we enter an intercultural interaction with the belief that it is OK for us to be unsure about how to proceed, we are likely to pay closer attention to the feedback we receive from the other person and we can then work to adjust our behavior and messages so that together we can achieve understanding. Accepting the ambiguity in the interaction can help us work hard to make the conversation successful; we are much less apt to become frustrated or discouraged by the inevitable false starts and minor misunderstandings.

When Jerome read the Partner Assignment List posted on the bulletin board outside of the lab, he discovered that his lab partner had an Indian-sounding name, but he resolved to work hard to make the relationship a success. So when he met Meena in class and found that she was an exchange student from Mumbai, he worked hard to attune his ear to her accent and was pleased to discover that although her accent was at first difficult to understand, her command of English was as good as his. Over the semester, Jerome worked hard to understand Meena's English. He was rewarded, because she really had a much better grasp of chemistry than he did and was willing to tutor him as they worked on assignments.

2. **Be open-minded.** An open-minded person is someone who is willing to dispassionately receive the ideas and opinions of others. Open-minded people are aware of their own

cultural values and recognize that other people's values are different. They resist the impulse to judge the values of other cultures in terms of those of their own culture. In other words, they resist ethnocentrism.

3. **Be altruistic. Altruism** is a display of genuine and unselfish concern for the welfare of others. The opposite of altruism is **egocentricity**, a selfish interest in one's own needs to the exclusion of everything else. Egocentric people are self-centered, while altruistic people are other-centered. Altruistic communicators do not neglect their own needs, but they recognize that for a conversation to be successful, both parties must be able to contribute what they want and take what they need from the exchange.

Acquire Knowledge about Other Cultures

The more we know about other cultures, the more likely we are to be competent intercultural communicators (Neuliep, 2006). There are various ways to learn about other cultures.

Observe

You can simply watch as members of another culture interact with each other. As you watch, you can notice how their values, rituals, and communication styles are similar and different from your own and other cultures with which you are familiar. Passive observers study the communication behaviors that are used by members of a particular culture.

altruism
a display of genuine and unselfish concern for the welfare of others

egocentricity
a selfish interest in one's own needs, to the exclusion of everything else

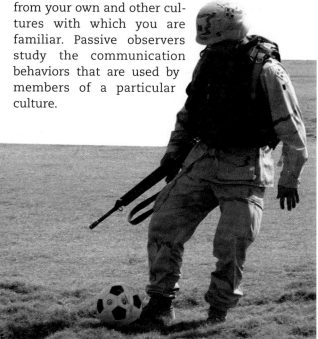

©AP PHOTO/ROB GRIFFITH

Formally Study

You can learn about other cultures by reading accounts of cultural members such as ethnographic research studies, by taking courses, or by interviewing members of the culture about their values, rituals, and so on.

Immerse Yourself in the Culture

You can learn a great deal about another culture by actively participating in it. When you live or work with people whose cultural assumptions are different from yours, you not only acquire obvious cultural information, but you also learn the nuances that escape passive observers and are generally not accessible through formal study alone. One reason that study abroad programs often include home stays is to insure that students become immersed in the culture of the host country. We hope that you will consider participating in a study abroad experience. The international or global studies office at your college or university can point you to a variety of study abroad opportunities and may even guide you to scholarships or grants to help pay your expenses.

Develop Culture-Specific Skills

To be effective in intercultural situations, you may need to adapt the communication skills that you will learn in this course to the demands of a particular culture. To this end, three of the specific skills that you will study that will be most useful are listening, empathy, and flexibility.

Practice Listening

By carefully listening and demonstrating your listening, you can improve your communication with people from other cultures. Because language and nonverbal communication vary across cultures, it is vitally important that you focus closely on the other and listen attentively. In Chapter 7, you will learn the skills associated with active listening. It is important to note that there are cultural differences in how people engage in listening and the value that cultures place on listening. In the United States, we listen closely for concrete facts and information and often ask questions while listening. In other cultures, such as Japan, Finland, and Sweden, listeners are more reserved and do not ask as many questions (Samovar, Porter, & McDaniel, 2007). For many cultures in the Far East, listening is much more valued than speaking. Regardless of your cultural background, however, becoming a more skillful listener will help you in your intercultural encounters.

Practice Intercultural Empathy

Intercultural empathy means imaginatively placing yourself in the other person's cultural world to attempt to experience what he or she is experiencing (Ting-Toomey, 1999). The Native American saying, "Don't judge another person until you have walked two moons in his moccasins," captures this idea. By paying close attention to the other person and focusing on the emotions displayed, we can improve our empathic skills. We will elaborate on how to communicate empathy in Chapter 7.

Develop Flexibility

We discussed the concept of flexibility as part of an appropriate attitude toward intercultural encounters, but we can also provide concrete strategies for becoming more flexible in your communication. Flexibility is the ability to adjust your communication to fit the other person and the situation. With flexibility, you can use a wide variety of communication skills during an interaction and modify your behavior within and across situations. Being flexible means analyzing a situation, making good decisions about how to communicate in that situation, and then modifying your communication when things are not going well.

intercultural empathy imaginatively placing yourself in the dissimilar other person's cultural world to attempt to experience what he or she is experiencing

flexibility the ability to adjust your communication to fit the other person and the situation

Learning Outcomes

LO Describe the major types of relationships

LO Explain how disclosure and feedback
affect relationships

LO Examine levels of communication at
various stages in relationships

Communicating
in Relationships

"We behave differently depending on whether our relationships are personal or impersonal."

Interpersonal skills help you start, build, and maintain healthy **relationships**, sets of expectations two people have for their behavior based on the pattern of interaction between them (Littlejohn & Foss, 2005). Relationships run the gamut from acquaintances to intimate friends. Regardless of the level of a relationship with a person, we seek **good relationships**, ones in which the interactions are satisfying to and healthy for those involved.

In this chapter, we describe three types of relationships and provide guidelines for developing acquaintance, friendship, and intimate relationships. Also, we examine disclosure and feedback in relationships and explain the stages that typical relationships go through.

What do you think?

Maintaining a relationship is harder than ending one.

Strongly Disagree						Strongly Agree
1	2	3	4	5	6	7

LO¹ Types of Relationships

We behave differently depending on whether our relationships are personal or impersonal. Moving on a continuum from impersonal to personal (Dindia & Timmerman, 2003, p. 687), we can classify our relationships as acquaintances, friendships, and close friends or intimates. There are specific communication competencies that help establish and maintain each type of relationship.

Acquaintances

Acquaintances are people we know by name and talk with when the opportunity arises, but with whom our interactions are limited. Many acquaintance relationships grow out of a particular context. We become acquainted with those who live in our apartment building or dorm or in the house next door, who sit next to us in class, who go to our church,

relationships
sets of expectations two people have for their behavior based on the pattern of interaction between them

good relationships
ones in which the interactions are satisfying to and healthy for those involved

acquaintances
people we know by name and talk with when the opportunity arises, but with whom our interactions are largely impersonal

>> Some guidelines for becoming more competent in conversation are to initiate conversations by introducing yourself, develop an "other-centered" focus, and engage in appropriate turn-taking. What techniques do you use in conversations when you're getting to know others?

or who belong to our club. Thus Melinda and Paige, who meet in biology class, may talk with each other about class-related issues, but they make no effort to share personal ideas or to see each other outside of class.

Acquaintanceship Guidelines

To meet other people and develop acquaintance relationships, it helps to be good at starting and developing conversations. The following guidelines can help you become more competent in conversing with others:

- Initiate conversations by introducing yourself, referring to the physical context, referring to your thoughts or feelings, referring to another person, or making a joke. For example, "Hi, I'm Kathie. Have you ever had this professor for a class before?"
- Develop an "other-centered" focus by asking questions, listening carefully, and following up on what has been said.
- Engage in appropriate turn-taking. Effective conversationalists balance talking with listening and do not interrupt the other. Not only do we need to avoid dominating the conversation, but we also need to uphold our part by talking enough.
- Make your comments relevant to what has previously been said before you change subjects.
- Be polite. Consider how your conversational partner will feel about what you say and work to phrase your comments in a way that allows your partner to "save face."

Friends

Over time, some acquaintances become our friends. Friends are people with whom we have voluntarily negotiated more personal relationships (Patterson, Bettini, & Nussbaum, 1993, p. 145). As friendships develop, people move toward interactions that are less role bound

friends
people with whom we have negotiated more personal relationships that are voluntary

and more interpersonally satisfying. For example, Melinda and Paige, who are acquaintances in biology class and have only talked about class-related subjects, may decide to get together after school to go to the gym. If they find that they enjoy each other's company, they may continue to meet outside of class and eventually become friends.

Some of our friendships are context bound. Thus, people often refer to their tennis friends, office friends, or neighborhood friends. These context friendships may fade if the context changes. For instance, your friendship with a person at the office may fade if you or your friend takes a job with a different company.

Friendship Guidelines

For friendships to develop and continue, some key behaviors must occur. The following guidelines can help you develop and maintain your friendships. Samter (2003) explains five important competencies necessary to friendship relationships.

- **Initiation.** Be proactive in setting up times to spend together. One person must get in touch with the other and the interaction must be smooth, relaxed, and enjoyable. A friendship is not likely to form between people who rarely interact or who have unsatisfying interactions.
- **Responsiveness.** Each person must listen. Listen to others and respond to what they say. It is difficult to form friendships with people who focus only on themselves or their issues, and it is equally difficult to maintain relationships with someone who is uncommunicative. In Chapter 7 you will be introduced to skills that can help you be more effective in listening to others.
- **Self-disclosure.** Friends share feelings with each other. Although acquaintances can be maintained by conversations that discuss surface issues or abstract ideas, a friendship is based on the exchange of more personal and specific information including personal history, opinions, and feelings. In Chapter 8 you will learn the skills associated with effective disclosure and feedback.
- **Emotional support.** Provide comfort and support when needed. When we are emotionally or psychologically vulnerable, we expect to be helped by those we call friends. When your friends are

> **"**Intimacy is not synonymous with "love" or exclusivity, and both platonic and romantic relationships may become intimate. **"**

hurting, they need you to support them by confirming their feelings and helping them work through making sense of what has happened. You will learn more about comforting and supporting in Chapter 7.

- **Conflict management.** Manage conflicts so that both parties' needs are met. It is inevitable that friends will disagree about ideas or behaviors. Friendship depends on successfully handling these disagreements. In fact, by competently managing conflict, people can strengthen their friendships. You will learn more about conflict management in Chapter 8.

Close Friends or Intimates

Close friends or intimates are those few people with whom we share close, caring, and trusting relationships characterized by a high degree of commitment, trust, interdependence, disclosure, and enjoyment. We may have countless acquaintances and many friends, but we are likely to have only a few truly intimate relationships. Intimacy is not synonymous with "love" or exclusivity, and both platonic and romantic relationships may become intimate. A platonic relationship is one in which the partners are not sexually attracted to each other or do not act on an attraction they feel. Conversely, a romantic relationship is one in which the partners act on their sexual attraction.

Regardless of whether the relationship is platonic or romantic, for the relationship to remain intimate, both partners must continue to trust the other. Trust is placing confidence in another in a way that almost always involves some risk. As we disclose personal information, we monitor how well our partner keeps our confidence. Once we perceive our partner to be untrustworthy, we are likely to withdraw and not continue to disclose. As a result, over time the intimacy in the

©BOTANICA/JUPITER IMAGES

relationship will decrease. When there is a severe breach of our trust, we may even abruptly end the relationship. With close friends, we show commitment by pledging ourselves and our time to each other. We show trust by having positive expectations of the other person and believing that he or she will behave fairly and honestly. With our close friends, our lives are interdependent or intertwined. We rely upon each other. We are more likely to share personal, private information about ourselves to close friends. In close relationships, there is some fusion of the self and the other. The partner is perceived as part of yourself. In other words, you come to define who you are, in part, through your close relationships (Aron, Aron, Tudor, & Nelson, 2004).

Research shows that women and men tend to differ on the factors that lead to intimacy in relationships. This may be because society teaches women and men to behave differently, to follow norms of femininity and masculinity. Women tend to develop close relationships with others based on talking, opening up with the other, and sharing personal feelings. By gaining knowledge of the innermost being of their partner, women develop a sense of "we-ness" with others. Men tend to develop close friendships through joint activities, doing favors for each other, and being able to depend on one another.

©COMSTOCK IMAGES/JUPITER IMAGES

close friends (intimates)
people with whom we share a high degree of commitment, trust, interdependence, disclosure, and enjoyment

platonic relationship
an intimate relationship in which the partners are not sexually attracted to each other or do not act on an attraction they feel

romantic relationship
an intimate relationship in which the partners act on their sexual attraction

trust
placing confidence in another in a way that

Men are less likely to define a close friend as someone with whom you can share feelings. For men, close friends are the people you can depend on to help you out of a jam and the people you regularly choose for pursuing enjoyable activities together (Wood & Inman, 1993). It is important to note that these differences are more pronounced in same-sex friendships. When men and women develop close friendships or intimate relationships with each other, these distinctions may not apply.

Intimacy Guidelines

Maintaining intimacy depends on developing and maintaining trust in your partner and commitment to your relationship. The following guidelines can help you establish and maintain trust (Boon, 1994, pp. 97–101).

- Be dependable so your partner knows they can rely on you at all times and under all circumstances.
- Be responsive in meeting your partner's needs. At times, this will require you to put their needs before your own.
- Be an effective partner in conflict by managing the conflict in a collaborative manner.
- Be faithful by maintaining your partner's confidential information and by abiding to sexual or other exclusivity agreements between you and your partner.
- Be transparent by honestly sharing your real ideas and feelings with your partner.
- Be willing to give up other activities or relationships to spend time with your partner.

LO² Disclosure and Feedback Ratios in Relationships

As people interact in a relationship, they will engage in some degree of disclosure with each other and they will also give some amount of feedback to each other.

self-disclosure
sharing biographical data, personal ideas, and feelings that are unknown to the other person

feedback
verbal and physical responses to people (and/or their messages) within the relationship

Johari window
a tool for examining the relationship between disclosure and feedback in the relationship

A healthy interpersonal relationship is marked by an appropriate balance of **self-disclosure** (sharing biographical data, personal ideas, and feelings that are unknown to the other person) and **feedback** (the verbal and physical responses to people and/or their messages) within the relationship. The **Johari window**,

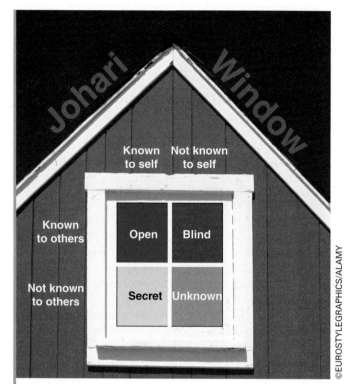

Figure 6.1

The Johari Window

named after its two originators, Jo Luft and Harry Ingham, is a tool for examining the relationship between disclosure and feedback in the relationship (Luft, 1970). The window represents all of the information about you that can be known. You and your partner each may know some (but not all) of this information.

The window has four "panes" or quadrants, as shown in Figure 6.1. The first quadrant is called the "open" pane of the window because it represents the information about you that both you and your partner know. It includes information that you have disclosed and the observations about you that your partner has shared with you. It might include mundane information that you share with most people, such as your college major, but it also may include information that you disclose to relatively few people. Similarly, it could include simple observations that your partner has made, such as how cute you look when you wrinkle your nose, or more serious feedback you have received from your partner about your interpersonal style.

The second quadrant is called the "secret" pane. It contains all those things that you know about yourself but that your partner does not yet know about you. Secret information is made known through the process of self-disclosure. The information moves into the open pane of the window when you choose to share the information with your partner. For example, suppose that you had been engaged to be married, but on the day of the wedding your fiancé(e) had backed out. You may not want to share this part of your history with casual acquaintances, so it will be in the secret pane of your window in many of your relationships. But when you disclose this fact to a friend, it moves into the open part of your Johari window with this person. As you disclose information, the secret pane of the window becomes smaller and the open pane is enlarged.

The third quadrant is called the "blind" pane. This is the place for information that the other person knows about you, but about which you are unaware. Most people have blind spots—parts of their behavior or the effects of their behavior of which they are unaware. Information moves from the blind area of the window to the open area through feedback from others. When someone gives you an insight about yourself and you accept the feedback, then the information will move into the open pane of the Johari window you have with this person. Thus, like disclosure, feedback enlarges the open pane of the Johari window, but in this case, it is the blind pane that becomes smaller.

The fourth quadrant is called the "unknown" pane. It contains information about you that you don't know and neither does your partner. Obviously, you cannot develop a list of this information. So how do we know that it exists? Well, because periodically we "discover" it. If, for instance, you have never tried hang gliding, then neither you nor anyone else can really know how you will react at the point of takeoff. You might chicken out or follow through, do it well or crash, love every minute of it or be paralyzed with fear. But until you try it, all of this information is unknown. Once you try it, you gain information

> ## Obviously, to get a complete "picture" of a relationship, each partner's Johari window would need to be examined.

about yourself that becomes part of the secret pane, which you can move to the open pane through disclosure. Also, once you have tried it, others who observe your flight will have information about your performance that you may not know unless they give you feedback.

As you disclose and receive feedback, the sizes of the various windowpanes change. These changes reflect the relationships. So the panes of the Johari window you have with different people will vary in size.

In Figure 6.2A we see an example of a relationship where there is little disclosure or feedback occurring. This person has not shared much information with the other, and has received little feedback from this partner as well. We would expect to see this pattern in a new relationship or one between casual acquaintances.

Figure 6.2

Sample Johrai Windows

O = Open   S = Secret (Hidden)
B = Blind   U = Unknown

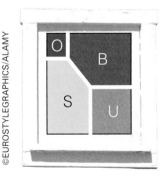

A
low disclosure, low feedback

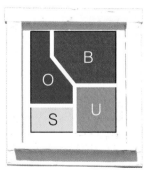

B
high disclosure, low feedback

C
low disclosure, high feedback

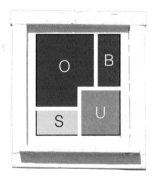

D
high disclosure, high feedback

Figure 6.2B shows a relationship in which a person is disclosing to a partner, but the partner is providing little feedback. As you can see, the secret pane is smaller, but the hidden pane is unchanged. A window like this indicates that the individual is able to disclose information but the partner is unable or unwilling to give feedback (or, perhaps, that the individual refuses to accept the feedback that is being given). Because part of the way that we learn about who we are comes from the feedback we receive from others, relationships in which one partner does not provide feedback can become very unsatisfying to the other individual.

Figure 6.2C shows a relationship where a partner is good at providing feedback, but where the individual is not disclosing. Since most of us disclose only when we trust our partners, this pattern may be an indication that the individual does not have confidence in the relational partner.

Figure 6.2D shows a relationship in which the individual has disclosed information and received feedback. So the open pane of the window has enlarged as a result of both processes. Windows that look like this indicate that there is sufficient trust and interest in the relationship that both partners are willing to risk by disclosing and giving feedback.

Obviously, to get a complete "picture" of a relationship, each partner's Johari window would need to be examined. A healthy interpersonal relationship is marked by a balance of disclosure and feedback, so that both people are participating.

LO³ Communication in the Stages of Relationships

Regardless of whether a relationship is an acquaintanceship, a friendship, or an intimate relationship, every relationship develops and changes with time. Even though no two relationships develop in exactly the same manner, they tend to follow a "life cycle" that has three identifiable stages: beginning and developing, maintaining, and a deteriorating stage (Baxter, 1982; Duck, 1987; Knapp & Vangelisti, 2000; Taylor & Altman, 1987). How quickly any relationship moves through these stages depends on the interpersonal communication between the relationship partners. Relationships can alternate between maintenance, development (greater closeness), and deterioration (distancing) in almost imperceptible ways, so it may be difficult at any point in time to accurately label a stage of the relationship. At times, relationship stages may merge and at other times, they may be quite distinct. But if you are observant over time, you can detect which way the relationship is moving.

Beginning and Developing a Relationship

The early stage of a relationship depends on increasing your knowledge of the other person and beginning to feel relaxed and confirmed. As the relationship grows, there will be feelings of relaxation and confirmation, and more physical contact and psychological closeness will develop. As relationships develop, you will increase disclosure and support. The earliest communication in relationships focuses on learning about the other person so that uncertainty is reduced and you start to feel comfortable with each other (Littlejohn & Foss, 2005). As the relationship develops, there will be additional time spent together, with disclosures of a more personal nature. Both of you will experience a sense of support (Duck, 1999). As the relationship develops, partners will identify and capitalize on their similarities and tolerate or negotiate their differences.

As you know from your own experience, communication during the earliest stage of a relationship, beginning and building relationships, is initially focused on getting information about the other person. We do this information exchanging as a way to reduce uncertainty (Berger & Bradac, 1982; Littlejohn & Foss, 2005). If we don't know anything about another person, we don't know how to act with them. Let's look at an example of two college roommates, Whitney and Madeline. During their first few conversations, they each are nervous, wondering if they will be compatible. To reduce this uncertainty, they will want to get to know each other. So they may talk about what they did in high school, what majors each is pursuing, what hobbies they like, and their favorite foods, movies, and music. As they learn more about each other, they find that although Whitney is majoring in fine arts and Madeline is in pre-med, they both are passionate environmentalists and vegetarians. As they learn more, they begin to relax and find that although they have many differences, they like and respect each other. Over the semester, they each find other friends that they socialize with alone, but they continue to have evening meals in the dining hall together. Life in the room they share begins to take on a

©IMAGE SOURCE

>> Many people enjoy the beginning stages of a relationship, when they're having fun getting to know another person.

predictable pattern. When Whitney is working on an art project for class, materials are strewn all over the room, so Madeline accommodates her by studying in the library. When Madeline is freaking out over her mid-term exam in chemistry, Whitney gets her a double latte from the coffee shop.

In the beginning stages of relationship formation, we also look for feelings of relaxation and confirmation. It should be more comfortable conversing with someone over time. We want conversation to flow smoothly and we want to feel enjoyment during the interaction. Each person wants the other to listen and to confirm one's sense of self and one's ideas. When relaxation and confirmation happen, we consider that we are connecting with the other person. Only when both parties experience relaxation and confirmation is the relationship likely to proceed to a deeper level.

If a relationship is growing deeper, then people perceive it to have closeness. They perceive that the relationship is developing to more interpersonally intimate levels. This also can happen via online relationships. Some people report that they achieve more closeness in online relationships than in equivalent, offline relationships (Walther, 1996). Indeed, rapid and exaggerated intimacy can be part of the fun of online relationships (Rabby & Walther, 2003).

As the relationship escalates, it deepens and grows closer and partners tend to share greater physical contact. Physical contact may involve sitting closer together, leaning toward each other, more eye contact, and more touch. Such physical behaviors may or may not involve romantic feelings. Even friends increase physical contact with each other as the relationship develops, though females and males may differ in how they show physical contact in same- and opposite-sex friendships. Females may hold hands or hug other female friends, whereas males may slap hands in a high-five gesture or

punch each other's arms as examples of physical contact in a developing relationship. Of course, cultural norms and age also affect how people engage in physical contact in relationships. Let's say the relationship between Whitney and Madeline is working out well. They spend time together, get to know each other well, and consider themselves to be close friends. By second semester, they hug each other when they return from spring break, share clothes, and do each other's hair, makeup, or nail polish.

Learning about another and developing a sense of relaxation and confirmation during interaction can occur in face-to-face or in online exchanges. Increasingly, the initial stage of relationship development may occur electronically (Ward & Tracy, 2004). Online communication may present a potentially less difficult way to meet and interact with others than traditional, face-to-face interactions. The initial interaction can occur in the comfort of your own home and at your own pace. You need not be concerned about physical aspects of the self or the other, and you can more precisely select what you are going to say (Ward & Tracy, 2004).

The need for physical contact seems to be an important aspect of relationship development, even for relationships that begin online. Two researchers of online relationships, James Katz and Philip Aspden (2004), have found that Internet relationships frequently lead to face-to-face meetings.

Many people who are escalating their relationship begin to share feelings and disclose more personal information, as well as depend upon each other for favors and support. At this stage, they are likely to seek each other out for help with a problem or talk for hours, sharing both the joys and the sorrows of their lives. Over time, Whitney and Madeline may share their innermost feelings with each other, cry on each others' shoulders during hard times, or lend each other money.

Maintaining a Relationship

Maintaining a relationship means that both people behave and communicate in ways that keep the relationship at a particular level of closeness or intimacy. Generally, the maintenance stage involves keeping the relationship from escalating to greater closeness or from moving to less closeness. Researchers have catalogued many strategies that people use to maintain relationships, including continuing to spend time with our partner, merging our social networks, and reciprocating unselfish acts

maintaining a relationship
behaving and communicating in ways that preserve a particular level of closeness or intimacy in a relationship

(Rusbult, Olsen, Davis, & Hannon, 2004). Other ways that people maintain their relationships include continuing mutually acceptable levels of affection, self-disclosure, favors, and support.

You probably unconsciously use many of these techniques to maintain your relationships. In stable relationships, we choose to spend time with the other person. Most of the time, we do this in face-to-face conversations or on the phone, but increasingly, people are enjoying spending time in online interactions as well. We also maintain relationships by merging our social networks. As you become acquainted with other people who are important to your partner and your partner becomes acquainted with those you have relationships with, not only do you begin to appreciate your partner in a different context, but these mutual friends and relationships will act like a web that surrounds and supports your relationship with your partner. Finally, whatever type of relationship we are in (acquaintanceship, friendship, or intimacy), we will have established expectations for the kinds and frequency of unselfish acts that each of us will perform. Though individuals differ in the extent to which they will act selflessly, generally we are most likely to act selflessly with intimates, somewhat less willing with friends, and least willing with acquaintances.

Let's see how our roommates, Whitney and Madeline, use these strategies to maintain their friendship. Because they are both committed to the environment, they decide to join the campus chapter of the Student Environmental Action Coalition (SEAC), where they make a group of common friends. On parents' weekend they meet each other's parents, and when Whitney's best friend from high school visits, Madeline joins them at the gym and goes dancing with them in the evening. When Whitney falls and hurts her arm, perhaps Madeline breaks a date so that she can go with her to the emergency room.

De-Escalating and Ending a Relationship

Just as partners can develop their relationships to greater levels of intimacy and support, we can also behave in ways that weaken intimacy and support. Sometimes a relationship may become less satisfying to one or both relational partners. When this happens, one or both partners make a conscious decision to spend less time together, to develop more independence in social networks, and to engage in less selfless behavior. Other times, relationships deteriorate without either partner consciously feeling dissatisfied and deciding to change the relationship. Rather, deterioration occurs because the partners are not vigilant in doing those things necessary to maintain the relationship at its current level.

As your relationship becomes less intimate, it may devolve to a different level and stabilize there, or it may end. The communication in deteriorating relationships is marked by three phases: the recognition signs and hints of dissatisfaction, the process of disengaging behavior, and ending. Subtle signs of dissatisfaction include losing interest in the opinions and feelings of the other person, recognizing and emphasizing the other's faults while downplaying their virtues, and increasing the number of subjects that are off-limits or sources of conflict. As partners disengage, they become less willing to share ideas and feelings that were once commonly exchanged. They become more independent, less supportive, and indifferent to their partner.

Recognition of Dissatisfaction

The first sign that a relationship is de-escalating is a subtle indication of dissatisfaction. When one person begins to lose interest in the opinions and feelings of the other, the orientation of that person changes from *we* to *I*. The partners may begin to emphasize each other's faults and downplay virtues. Subjects that once yielded free and open discussion become off-limits or sources of conflict. As the relationship begins to be characterized by an increase in "touchy" subjects and more unresolved conflicts, partners become more defensive and less willing to foster a positive communication climate.

Disengaging

If the relationship continues to be dissatisfying, people begin to drift apart. They become less willing to sacrifice for each other and they show less forgiveness. Their communication changes from deep sharing of ideas and feelings to small talk and other "safe" communication, to no significant communication at all. It may seem strange that people who had so much to share can find themselves with nothing to talk about. Not only are they no longer interested in exchanging significant ideas, they may begin to avoid each other altogether, seeking out other people with whom to share interests and activities. They depend less on each other and more upon other people for favors and support. Hostility need not be present; rather, this stage is likely to be marked by indifference.

So even though Whitney and Madeline have been very close during their first year at college, perhaps they develop new friendships and they each arrive at the separate decision that they want to room with someone different next year. As effective communicators, they would discuss their decisions with each other without blame or manipulation and acknowledge that their relationship is not as close as it once was. Over the summer, they may not interact and may drift apart. They move in with new roommates for the second year of college and see each other infrequently on campus. They talk at SEAC meetings and at a few parties, but they no longer have personal conversations, do not depend on each other for support, and do not have the same circle of friends. By the time they graduate, they have become so disengaged that there is little chance that they will continue to see each other.

Whitney

Ending

If the relationship can't be maintained at a less intimate level, it will end. A relationship has ended when the people no longer interact with each other. As Cupach and Metts (1986) show, people give many reasons for terminating relationships, including poor communication, lack of fulfillment, differing lifestyles and

©GOODSHOOT/JUPITER IMAGES

>> How relationships end depends on the interpersonal competence of both people. Do you know people who have amicable divorces? How do they differ from people who have hostile divorces? How do you think this person's separation just went?

interests, rejection, outside interference, absence of rewards, and boredom.

At some point, one or both partners may decide that the relationship should end. Because many of us aren't skilled communicators, we may use manipulation ("This is really the best thing for you"), withdrawal (spend less and less time together until you don't see each other at all), or avoidance (purposefully dodging the other) (Baxter, 1982). To end a deteriorating relationship, competent communicators should engage in a direct, open, and honest conversation. It is important to clearly state your wish to end the relationship, while being respectful of the other person and sensitive to the resulting emotions.

Madeline

©PHOTODISC/GETTY IMAGES

Listening
and **Responding**

Learning Outcomes

LO¹   List techniques for improving focus in the listening process

LO²   Examine ways for improving understanding of messages

LO³   Discuss how to better retain information

LO⁴   Explain how to evaluate and critically analyze the truthfulness of messages

LO⁵   Identify steps for responding supportively and giving comfort

> ## "Listening is a key communication skill, yet less than 2 percent of us have had any formal listening training."

Are you a good listener when you are under pressure? Or do you occasionally find that your mind wanders when others are talking to you? Listening is a key communication skill, yet less than 2 percent of us have had any formal listening training (Listening Factoid, 2003). Most of us can improve our listening skills. We must not underestimate the importance of listening, which can provide clarification, connect us to others, build trust and empathy, help us learn and remember material, and improve our evaluation of information (Donoghue & Siegel, 2005).

Judi Brownell (2002) points out that members of the International Listening Association offer this definition of listening: "Listening is the process of receiving, constructing meaning from, and responding to spoken and/or nonverbal messages" (p. 48). Incorporated within this definition are the processes of attending, understanding, remembering, evaluating, and responding.

LO¹ Attending

Attending is the perceptual process of selecting and focusing on specific stimuli from the countless stimuli reaching the senses. Recall from Chapter 2 that we attend to information that interests us and meets physical and psychological needs. But to be a good listener, we must train ourselves to attend to what people are saying regardless of our interest or needs. Let's consider four techniques for consciously focusing attention.

1 **Get physically and mentally ready to listen.** Physically, good listeners create a physical environment helpful for listening and adopt a listening posture. Creating a physical environment means eliminating distractions. If the music is playing so loudly that it competes with your roommate who is trying to talk with you, turn it down. The physical posture that is helpful when listening is one that moves the listener toward the speaker, allows direct eye contact, and stimulates the senses. For instance, when the professor tells the class that the next bit of information will be on the test,

What do you think?

I'd rather be the listener than the speaker.

Strongly Disagree						Strongly Agree
1	2	3	4	5	6	7

listening
the process of receiving, constructing meaning from, and responding to spoken and/or nonverbal messages

attending
the perceptual process of selecting and focusing on specific stimuli from the countless stimuli reaching the senses

©CORBISRF/JUPITER IMAGES

©BLEND IMAGES/JUPITER IMAGES

effective listeners are likely to sit upright in their chairs, lean slightly forward, cease any extraneous physical movement, and look directly at the professor. Likewise, mentally they will focus their attention by blocking out miscellaneous thoughts.

2. **Make the shift from speaker to listener a complete one.** In conversation, we are called on to switch back and forth from speaker to listener so frequently that we may find it difficult at times to make these shifts completely. Instead of listening, it is easy to rehearse what you are going to say as soon as you have a chance. It is especially important when trying to be a good listener that you let the other person finish before you take your turn to speak. Good listeners resist interrupting others. Especially when you are in a heated conversation or excited about what you just heard, you will consciously need to stop yourself from preparing a response or interrupting the speaker instead of listening completely.

3. **Hear a person out before you react.** Far too often, we stop listening before the person has finished speaking because we think we know what the person is going to say. Yet often we are wrong. In addition, we often stop listening to people because their mannerisms and words "turn us off." Think of the times you may have stopped listening to a professor's lecture and missed important information because of the teacher's accent or gestures. Most of us need to learn the value of patience and silence in freeing others to express themselves and helping us to listen closely and carefully.

4. **Observe nonverbal cues.** Listeners interpret messages more accurately when they observe the nonverbal behaviors accompanying the words. For instance, when Deborah says, "Don't worry about me. I'm fine, really," we must interpret cues such as tone of voice, body actions, and facial expression to tell whether she is really fine or whether she is upset but reluctant to tell you about it.

Attending

1. Get physically and mentally ready to listen.
2. Make the shift from speaker to listener a complete one.
3. Hear a person out before you react.
4. Observe nonverbal cues.

LO² Understanding

Understanding is decoding a message accurately to reflect the meaning intended by the speaker. Sometimes we do not understand because the message is encoded in words that are not in our vocabulary, but most of our misunderstanding stems from passive listening. *Active listening* requires us to use empathy, questioning, and paraphrasing so that we understand both the message content and the speaker's intent.

Empathy

Empathy is intellectually identifying with or vicariously experiencing the feelings or attitudes of another. Or, as Jon Hayes (2002) says, letting people "know that they have been understood from within their own frame of reference and that they can see the world as they see it while remaining separate from it" (p. 183). To empathize, we generally try to put aside our own feelings or attitudes about another. Three approaches people use when empathizing are empathic responsiveness, perspective taking, and sympathetic responsiveness (Weaver & Kirtley, 1995, p. 131).

Empathic responsiveness occurs when you experience an emotional response parallel to, and as a result of observing, another person's actual or anticipated display of emotion (Omdahl, 1995, p. 4; Stiff et al., 1988, p. 199). For instance, when Jackson tells James that he is in real trouble financially, and James senses the stress and anxiety that Jackson is feeling, we would say that James has experienced empathic responsiveness.

understanding
decoding a message accurately to reflect the meaning intended by the speaker

empathy
intellectually identifying with or vicariously experiencing the feelings or attitudes of another

empathic responsiveness
experiencing an emotional response parallel to, and as a result observing, another person's actual or anticipated display of emotion

> SOMETIMES WE DO NOT UNDERSTAND BECAUSE THE MESSAGE IS ENCODED IN WORDS THAT ARE NOT IN OUR VOCABULARY, BUT MOST OF OUR MISUNDERSTANDING STEMS FROM PASSIVE LISTENING.

{ Fast Facts—
Professional Mourning }

In ancient cultures, particularly in Egypt and the Near East, it was a common practice to hire professional mourners when someone died, both to lament at the funeral process and sometimes to offer a eulogy. A group of female mourners can be seen in this relief from a tomb in Luxor, Egypt. What empathy roles do you think these kinds of people perform, and what effect do you think they have on others who are mourning, both individually and collectively?

conclusion? Consciously asking these questions helps you focus your attention on the nonverbal aspects of messages, which convey most of the information on the person's emotional state.

To further increase the accuracy of reading emotions, we can use the skill of perception checking (introduced in Chapter 2). This is especially helpful when the other person's culture is different from our own. Let's consider an example. Suppose Jerry says that he feels embarrassed when people comment on how old he is to be wearing braces. His friend Mary might empathize by concentrating on the feelings he shows with both his verbal and nonverbal messages, and then she may show that she understands by saying, "I can understand your embarrassment—I might even be depressed if that kept happening to me."

Perspective taking, imagining yourself in the place of another, is the most common form of empathizing. Although perspective taking is difficult for many of us (Holtgraves, 2002, p. 122), with conscious effort we can learn to imagine ourselves in the place of another. For example, if James personalizes the message by picturing himself in serious financial debt, anticipates the emotions he might experience, and then assumes that Jackson might be feeling the same way, then James is empathizing by perspective taking.

Sympathetic responsiveness is feeling concern, compassion, or sorrow for another because of the other's situation or plight. Having *sympathy* differs from the other two approaches. Rather than attempting to experience the feelings of the other, when you sympathize, you translate your intellectual understanding of what the speaker has experienced into your own feelings of concern, compassion, and sorrow for that person. In our previous example, James has sympathy for Jackson when he understands that Jackson is embarrassed and worried, but instead of trying to feel those same emotions, he feels concern and compassion for his friend. Because of this difference in perspective, many scholars differentiate sympathy from empathy.

How well you empathize also depends on how observant you are of others' behavior and how clearly you "read" the nonverbal messages they are sending. To improve your observational skills, try this. When another person begins a conversation with you, develop the habit of silently posing two questions to yourself: (1) What emotions do I believe the person is experiencing right now? and (2) What cues is the person giving that I am using to draw this

Questioning

Active listeners ask questions to get the information they need to understand. A **question** is a statement designed to get further information or to clarify information already received. Although you may have asked questions for as long as you can remember, you may notice that, at times, your questions don't get the information you want or irritate, fluster, or cause defensiveness. We can increase the chances that our questions will get us the information we want and reduce negative reactions if we observe these guidelines.

Recognize the Kind of Information You Need to Increase Your Understanding

Suppose Maria says to you, "I am totally frustrated. Would you stop at the store on the way home and buy me some more paper?" At this point, you may be a bit confused and need more information to understand. Yet if you simply respond "What do you mean?" Maria, who is already uptight, may become defensive. To solicit the information you need, you might recognize one of the three types of information needs you have, and form a question to meet that need. You probably will not know precisely what you do not understand. To increase your understanding, you might ask Maria one of these three types of questions:

perspective taking
imagining yourself in the place of another; the most common form of empathizing

sympathetic responsiveness
feeling concern, compassion, or sorrow for another because of the other's situation or plight

question
a statement designed to get further information or to clarify information already received

> >When asking questions, pay attention not just to what you say but how you say it. Think about the message you are trying to convey and how your nonverbal cues might be perceived.

- *Get details:* "What kind of paper would you like me to get, and how much will you need?"

- *Clarify word meanings:* "Could you tell me what you mean by 'frustrated'?"

- *Clarify feelings:* "What's frustrating you?"

Monitor Your Nonverbal Cues so That They Convey Genuine Interest and Concern

Ask questions with a tone of voice that is sincere—not a tone that could be interpreted as bored, sarcastic, cutting, superior, dogmatic, or evaluative. We need to constantly remind ourselves that the way we speak may be even more important than the words we use. Sometimes, asking several questions in a row can seem like an interrogation. If you need to ask several questions, you might explain why you are asking them by saying something like, "I really want to understand what you are saying, so I need to ask a few questions. Is that OK?"

Put the "Burden of Ignorance" on Your Own Shoulders

paraphrasing
putting into words the ideas or feelings you have perceived from the message

content paraphrase
one that focuses on the denotative meaning of the message

feelings paraphrase
a response that captures the emotions attached to the content of the message

To minimize defensive reactions, especially when people are under stress, phrase your questions to put the burden of ignorance on your own shoulders. Preface your question with a short statement that suggests that any problem of misunderstanding may be the result of *your* listening skills. For instance, when Drew says "I've really had it with Malone screwing up all the time," you might say, "Drew, I'm sorry, I'm missing some details that would help me understand your feelings better—what kinds of things has Malone been doing?"

Here are two more examples that contrast inappropriate with more appropriate questioning responses.

TAMARA: They turned down my proposal again!
ART [Inappropriate]: Well, did you explain it the way you should have? [This question is a veiled attack on Tamara in question form.]
[Appropriate] Did they tell you why? [This question is a sincere request for additional information.]

RENEE: With all those executives at the party last night, I really felt strange.
JAVIER [Inappropriate]: Why? [With this abrupt question, Javier is making no effort to be sensitive to Renee's feelings or to understand them.]
[Appropriate] What is it about your bosses' presence that makes you feel strange? [Here the question is phrased to elicit information that will help Javier understand, and it also may help Renee understand.]

Paraphrasing

In addition to being skilled questioners, active listeners are also adept at **paraphrasing**, that is, putting into words the ideas or feelings you have perceived from the message. For example, during an argument with your sister, after she has stated her concern about your behavior, you might paraphrase what she has said as follows: "You say that you are tired of my talking about work and that you feel that I try to act better than you when I talk about my successes at work." Paraphrases may focus on content, on feelings underlying the content, or on both. A **content paraphrase** focuses on the denotative meaning of the message. The first part of the example above (You say that you are tired of my talking about work) is a content paraphrase. A **feelings paraphrase** is a response that captures the emotions attached to the content of

To paraphrase effectively:

1. listen carefully to the message.
2. notice what images and feelings you have experienced from the message.
3. determine what the message means to you.
4. create a message that conveys these images or feelings.

the message. The second part of the example (you feel that I try to act better than you) is a feelings paraphrase.

By paraphrasing, you give the speaker a chance to verify your understanding. The longer and more complex the message, the more important it is to paraphrase. When the speaker appears to be emotional or when English is not the speaker's native language, paraphrasing is also important.

LO³ Remembering: Retaining Information

Remembering is being able to retain information and recall it when needed. Too often, people forget almost immediately what they have heard. For instance, you can probably think of many times when you were unable to recall the name of a person to whom you were introduced just moments earlier. Think of how much the education system depends on listening and recalling information. Given the common use of lectures, class discussions, and other listening-based learning experiences, it is not surprising that research shows a link between effective listening and school success (Bommelje, Houston, & Smither, 2003). Three techniques that can help you improve your ability to remember information are repeating, constructing mnemonics, and taking notes.

Jack McNeil, Jack McNeil, Jack McNeil

Repeat Information

Repetition—saying something two, three, or even four times—helps listeners store information in long-term memory by providing necessary reinforcement (Estes, 1989, p. 7). If information is not reinforced, it will be held in short-term memory for as little as 20 seconds and then forgotten. So, when you are introduced to a stranger named Jack McNeil, if you mentally say "Jack McNeil, Jack McNeil, Jack McNeil, Jack McNeil," you increase the chances that you will remember his name. Likewise, when you receive the directions "Go two blocks east, turn left, turn right at the next light, and it's in the next block," you can immediately repeat to yourself "two blocks east, turn left, turn right at light, next block—that's two blocks east, turn left, turn right at light, next block."

Construct Mnemonics

Constructing mnemonics helps listeners put information in forms that are more easily recalled. A **mnemonic device** is any artificial technique used as a memory aid. One of the most common ways of forming a mnemonic is to use the first letters of a list of items you are trying to remember to form a word. For example, an easy mnemonic for remembering the five Great Lakes is HOMES (Huron, Ontario, Michigan, Erie, Superior).

When you want to remember items in a sequence, you can form a sentence with the words themselves or assign words using the first letters of the words in sequence to form an easy-to-remember statement. For example, when you studied music the first time, you may have learned the notes on the lines of the treble clef (E, G, B, D, F) with the saying "*Every good boy does fine.*" And for the notes on the treble clef spaces, F, A, C, E, you may have remembered the word *face*.

Take Notes

Although note taking would be inappropriate in the most casual interpersonal encounters, it represents a powerful tool for increasing your recall of information when you are involved in conversations where important information you need to remember is being shared. Note taking has been shown to be an important strategy for learners when they attempt to listen to and

remembering
being able to retain information and recall it when needed

mnemonic device
any artificial technique used as a memory aid

Taking notes is a great tool to increase recall.

absorb information from lecture-type speech (Dunkel & Pialorsi, 2005). Note taking does more than provide a written record that you can go back to; it also allows you to take an active role in the listening process (Wolvin & Coakley, 1996, p. 239).

Useful notes may consist of a brief list of main points or key ideas, plus a few of the most significant details. Or they may be a short summary of the entire concept (a type of paraphrase) after the message is completed. For lengthy and rather detailed information, however, good notes likely will consist of a brief outline of what the speaker has said, including the overall idea, the main points of the message, and key developmental material. Good notes are not necessarily very long. In fact, many classroom lectures can be reduced to a short outline of notes. Figure 7.1 is an example of this and is based on the material in this chapter.

LO⁴ Evaluate, or Critically Analyze

The fourth listening process is to critically analyze what has been said. **Critical analysis** is the process of evaluating what you have heard to determine its truthfulness. Critical listening is especially important when you are asked to believe, act on, or support what is being said. For instance, if a person is trying to convince you to vote for a particular candidate, or support efforts to legalize gay marriage, or buy an expensive gadget, you will want to listen critically so that you can evaluate the information and arguments presented. If you don't critically analyze what you hear, you risk going along with ideas or plans that may violate your values, are counterproductive to your interests, or mislead others (including the speaker) who value your judgment.

One important skill of critical analysis is to separate statements of fact from statements based on inference. **Factual statements** are those whose accuracy can be verified or proven. **Inferences** are statements made by the speaker that are based on facts or observations. If we comment "You are reading this sentence," we have stated a fact. If we say "You are understanding and enjoying what you are reading," we have made an inference.

Separating factual statements from inferences begins by recognizing whether what has been said

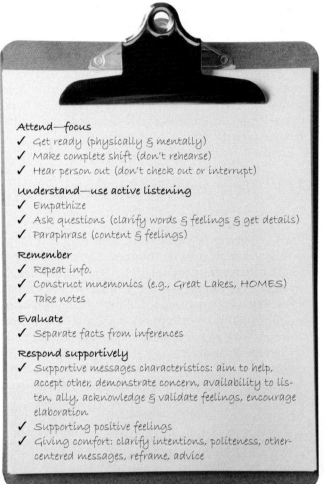

Attend—focus
✓ Get ready (physically & mentally)
✓ Make complete shift (don't rehearse)
✓ Hear person out (don't check out or interrupt)

Understand—use active listening
✓ Empathize
✓ Ask questions (clarify words & feelings & get details)
✓ Paraphrase (content & feelings)

Remember
✓ Repeat info.
✓ Construct mnemonics (e.g., Great Lakes, HOMES)
✓ Take notes

Evaluate
✓ Separate facts from inferences

Respond supportively
✓ Supportive messages characteristics: aim to help, accept other, demonstrate concern, availability to listen, ally, acknowledge & validate feelings, encourage elaboration
✓ Supporting positive feelings
✓ Giving comfort: clarify intentions, politeness, other-centered messages, reframe, advice

Figure 7.1

Notes Based on a Lecture on Listening

is an established fact, or whether it is an opinion that may be related to a fact. If the statement is a fact, we need to determine if the fact that was stated is true, because people sometimes make things up and pass them off as facts. If the statement is an inference, then we need to further evaluate it to see if the inference is valid. An inference may be false, even when it is based on observable facts. For instance, you are reading this sentence, you may even be nodding your head and smiling, but these facts do not alone provide proof of either your understanding or your enjoyment.

When we have determined that a statement is an inference, we need to test to see whether it is a valid inference. To do this we can ask ourselves (or the speaker) three questions: (1) What are the facts that support this inference? (2) Is this information really central to the inference? (3) Are there other facts or information that would contradict this inference? For example, when we hear "Better watch it—Katie's in one bad mood today. Did you catch the look on her

---

critical analysis
the process of evaluating what you have heard to determine its truthfulness

factual statements
statements whose accuracy can be verified or proven

inferences
statements made by the speaker that are based on facts or observations

face? That's one unhappy girl," we should stop and think, is Katie really in a bad mood? The fact that supports this is her facial expression. Is this fact accurate? Is Katie really looking unhappy or angry? Is the look on her face enough to conclude that she's in a bad mood? Or does Katie normally look unhappy? Is the look on her face really key to determining her mood? Or are there other cues that those of us who know her would expect to see? Is there anything else about Katie's behavior today that could lead us to believe that she's not in a bad mood?

LO⁵ Responding Supportively to Give Comfort

Many times as we are listening, we recognize that the speaker is emotionally distressed and in need of comfort. We can respond supportively by confirming the speaker's feelings and providing emotional comfort. To comfort means to help people feel better about themselves and their behavior. Comforting occurs when one feels respected, understood, and confirmed.

Characteristics of Effective and Ineffective Emotional Support Messages

Supportive messages are comforting statements that have a goal to reassure, bolster, encourage, soothe, console, or cheer up. Supportive messages are helpful and provide comfort because they create a conversational environment that encourages the person needing support to talk about and make sense of the situation that is causing distress. Over the years, much of the groundbreaking scholarship on comforting has been done by Brant Burleson and his colleagues. In recent studies, Burleson found that effective supportive messages had these characteristics (Burleson, 2003, pp. 565–568):

1. They clearly state that the speaker's aim is to help the other.
   Example: "I'd like to help you, what can I do?"

> **Supporting does not mean making false statements or only telling someone what he or she wants to hear.**

2. They express acceptance or affection for the other; they do not condemn or criticize.
   Example: "I understand that you just can't seem to accept this."
3. They demonstrate care, concern, and interest in the other's situation; they do not focus on a lengthy recount of a similar situation.
   Example: "What are you planning to do now?" Or "Gosh, tell me more; what happened then?"
4. They indicate that the speaker is available to listen and support the other without intruding.
   Example: "I know we've not been that close, but sometimes it helps to have someone to listen, and I'd like to do that for you."
5. They state that the speaker is an ally.
   Example: "I'm with you on this." Or "Well, I'm on your side; this isn't right."
6. They acknowledge the other's feelings and situation as well as express sincere sympathy; they do not condemn or criticize the other's behavior or feelings.
   Example: "I'm so sorry to see you feeling so bad; I can see that you're devastated by what has happened."
7. They assure the other that what he or she is feeling is legitimate; they do not tell the other how to feel or that the other should ignore his or her feelings.
   Example: "With what has happened to you, you have a right to be angry."
8. They encourage the other to elaborate on his or her story.
   Example: "Uh-huh," "yeah," or "I see. How did you feel about that?" or "Well, what happened before that, can you elaborate?"

Supporting does not mean making false statements or only telling someone what he or she wants to hear. Effective supporting responses are in touch with the facts but focus on how those facts can provide emotional support for the speaker.

comfort
to help people feel better about themselves and their behavior

supportive messages
comforting statements that have a goal to reassure, bolster, encourage, soothe, console, or cheer up

>> Recall an occasion when you were feeling especially happy and chose to share your feelings with someone. How did the person react? Was it what you hoped for? How did that person's reaction affect your feelings?

Giving Comfort

Comforting is helping people feel better about themselves, their behavior, or the situation they are in by creating a safe conversational space where they can express their feelings and work out a plan for the future. Comforting rarely happens in single statements. Instead, it usually occurs over several turns in a conversation or over several conversations that span weeks, months, and occasionally years. Supportive messages that comfort have the eight characteristics previously discussed, but they also draw from the five specific comforting message skills listed in the box below.

clarify supportive intentions
openly stating that your goal in the conversation is to help your partner

buffering
cushioning the effect of messages by utilizing both positive and negative politeness skills

positive face needs
the desire to be appreciated and approved, liked, and honored

Giving Comfort

1. Clarifying supportive intentions
2. Buffering face threats with politeness
3. Encouraging understanding through other-centered messages
4. Reframing the situation
5. Giving advice

Clarifying Supportive Intentions

When people are experiencing turmoil, they may have trouble understanding the motives of those who want to help. You can **clarify your supportive intentions** by openly stating that your goal in the conversation is to help your partner. Notice how David does this in the following conversation:

DAVID *[noticing Paul sitting in his cubicle with his head in his lap and his hands over his head]:* Paul, is everything OK?

PAUL *[sitting up with a miserable but defiant look on his face]:* Like you should care. Yeah, everything is fine.

DAVID: Paul, I do care. You've been working for me for five years; you're one of our best technicians. So if something is going on, I'd like to help, even if all I can do is listen. Now, what's up?

Buffering Face Threats with Politeness

Buffering cushions the effect of messages by utilizing both positive and negative politeness skills. The very act of providing comfort can threaten the positive and negative face needs of your partner. (**Positive face needs** refer to the desire to be appreciated and approved, liked, and honored. **Negative face needs** refer to the desire to be free from imposition or intrusion.) On one hand, your partner can feel that you will respect, like, or value him less because of his situation. On the other hand, the very act of comforting suggests that the other person cannot independently handle the situation. So comforting messages are phrased very politely in ways that address the other person's face needs. Notice how David says to Paul, "You're one of our best technicians," which reaffirms his admiration for Paul's work. David also attends to Paul's need for independence by stating that maybe all he "can do is listen," which implies that Paul will be able to do the rest.

Encouraging Understanding through Other-Centered Messages

To reduce emotional distress, people need to make sense out of what has happened (Burleson & Goldsmith, 1998). People feel better if they can re-evaluate specific parts of the situation or change their opinion about what happened. An important way for people to do this is by repeatedly telling and elaborating on the story (what happened to them). We can help people do this by using **other-centered messages**, those that encourage our partners to talk about and elaborate on what happened and how they feel about it. Many of us find this difficult to do because we have been taught it is rude to pry or we are uncomfortable hearing someone's problems, so our gut reaction is to change the subject.

Other-centered messages may ask questions that allow the other to elaborate, they may simply be vocalized encouragement (um, uh-huh, wow, I see), they encourage the person to explore their feelings, and they demonstrate understanding and empathy.

Reframing the Situation

When people are vulnerable and are in the midst of strong emotions, they are likely to perceive events in a limited way. At times, their limited vision prevents them from viewing the situation in ways that would enable them to re-evaluate the situation or their feelings. In these cases, it may be helpful for you to **reframe** the situation by offering ideas, observations, information, and alternative explanations that might help your partner understand the situation in a different light. For example, imagine that Travis returns from class and tells his roommate Abe, "Well, I'm flunking calculus. It doesn't matter how much I study or how many of the online problems I do, I just can't get it. This level of math is above me. I might as well just drop out of school before I flunk out completely. I can ask for a full-time schedule at work and not torture myself with school anymore."

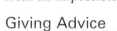
>> Sometimes strong emotions can act like situational "blinders."

©DESIGNPICS.COM/ALAMY

To reframe this situation, Abe might remind Travis that he has been putting in many hours at work and maybe his work schedule is interfering with his calculus grades. Or he might tell Travis that he heard calculus instructors curve grades at the end of the term because the material is so difficult. In each case, Abe is offering new observations and providing alternative explanations that can help Travis reframe the situation from an impossible one to a manageable one.

Giving Advice

At times, we can comfort people by **giving advice**—presenting relevant suggestions and proposals that a person can use to satisfactorily resolve a situation. Unfortunately, we often rush to give advice before we really understand the problem. Advice should not be given until our supportive intentions have been understood, we have attended to our partner's face needs, and we have sustained an other-centered interaction for some time. Only when your partner has had time to understand and make his or her own sense out of what has happened should you offer advice to help with unresolved issues. Before giving advice, always ask permission and acknowledge that your advice is only one suggestion of many that might work. Present the potential risks or costs associated with your advice, and let your partner know that it's OK if he or she chooses to ignore what you have said.

negative face needs the desire to be free from imposition or intrusion

other-centered messages statements that encourage our partners to talk about and elaborate on what happened and how they feel about it

reframing offering ideas, observations, information, and alternative explanations that might help your partner understand the situation in a different light

giving advice presenting relevant suggestions and proposals that a person can use to satisfactorily resolve a situation

Gender and Cultural Considerations in Comforting

It is popularly thought that men and women differ in the value they place on emotional support, with women expecting, needing, and providing more. However, Burleson (2003, p. 572) reports that a growing body of research finds that both men and women of various ages place a high value on emotional support from their partners in a variety of relationships (siblings, same-sex friendships, opposite-sex friendships, and romantic relationships). Studies also find that men and women have similar ideas about what messages do a better or worse job of reducing emotional distress. Both men and women find that messages encouraging them to explore and elaborate on their feelings provide the most comfort. Research has also found that men are less likely to use other-centered messages when comforting.

Researchers have also examined cultural differences in comforting. Burleson (p. 574) reports that members of all social groups find solace strategies, especially other-centered messages, the most sensitive and comforting way to provide emotional support. Burleson has identified these cultural differences:

1. European Americans, more than other American ethnic groups, believe that openly discussing feelings will help a person feel better.
2. Americans are more sensitive to other-centered messages than are Chinese.
3. Both Chinese and Americans view avoidance strategies as less appropriate than approach strategies, but Chinese see avoidance as more appropriate than Americans do.
4. Married Chinese and married Americans both view the emotional support provided by their spouse to be the most important type of social support they receive.
5. African Americans place lower value on partner emotional support skills than do European or Asian Americans. This was especially true for African American women.

Overall, it appears that we are more alike than different concerning our desire to be supported by our partners and the types of messages we find to be emotionally comforting.

Table 7.1 summarizes how good listeners and poor listeners deal with the five aspects of listening: attending, understanding, remembering, evaluating, and responding supportively.

Table 7.1

A Summary of the Five Aspects of Listening

	Good Listeners	Bad Listeners
ATTENDING	Attend to important information	May not hear what a person is saying
	Ready themselves physically and mentally	Fidget in their chairs, look out the window, and let their minds wander
	Listen objectively regardless of emotional involvement	Visibly react to emotional language
	Listen differently depending on situations	Listen the same way regardless of the type of material
UNDERSTANDING	Assign appropriate meaning to what is said	Hear what is said but are either unable to understand or assign different meaning to the words
	Seek out apparent purpose, main points, and supporting information	Ignore the way information is organized
	Ask mental questions to anticipate information	Fail to anticipate coming information
	Silently paraphrase to solidify understanding	Seldom or never mentally review information
	Seek out subtle meanings based on nonverbal cues	Ignore nonverbal cues
REMEMBERING	Retain information	Interpret message accurately but forget it
	Repeat key information	Assume they will remember
	Mentally create mnemonics for lists of words and ideas	Seldom single out any information as especially important
	Take notes	Rely on memory alone
EVALUATING	Listen critically	Hear and understand but are unable to weigh and consider it
	Separate facts from inferences	Don't differentiate between facts and inferences
	Evaluate inferences	Accept information at face value
RESPONDING SUPPORTIVELY	Provide supportive comforting statements	Pass off joy or hurt; change the subject
	Give alternative interpretations	Pass off hurt; change the subject

Speak Up!

COMM was built on a simple principle: to create a new teaching and learning solution that reflects the way today's faculty teach and the way you learn.

Through conversations, focus groups, surveys, and interviews, we collected data that drove the creation of the current version of COMM that you are using today. But it doesn't stop there—in order to make COMM an even better learning experience, we'd like you to SPEAK UP and tell us how COMM worked for you. What did you like about it? What would you change? Are there additional ideas you have that would help us build a better product for next semester's communication students?

At **4ltrpress.cengage.com/comm** you'll find all of the resources you need to succeed in principles of communication— **Printable Flash Cards, Speech Builder Express 3.0™, Interactive Quizzing, Downloads, Games and Simulations, Interactive Video Activities,** and more!

Speak Up! Go to **4ltrpress.cengage.com/comm**.

Learning Outcomes

LO¹ Discuss the balance between self-disclosure and privacy

LO² Examine guidelines for disclosing feelings

LO³ Develop effective ways to give personal feedback

LO⁴ Describe assertive behavior

LO⁵ Discuss conflict management styles

Developing Intimacy in Relationships:
Self-Disclosure, Feedback, and Conflict Resolution

66 *It is normal to sometimes feel a need to connect with someone, and at other times to feel the need to be independent.* 99

Every day in your new and ongoing relationships you make decisions about the information you will share with your partners and how you will handle issues on which you disagree. The decisions that you make will affect the degree of intimacy and satisfaction you experience in your relationships. It

is normal to sometimes feel that you want to be open and share with someone, yet feel at other times that you want to maintain your privacy. It is normal to sometimes feel a need to connect with someone, and at other times to feel the need to be independent. It is normal to sometimes want to have your partner act in predictable ways and at other times wish that your partner would do something to surprise you. These seemingly opposing forces (openness–closedness, autonomy–connection, and novelty–predictability) that you feel are called **relational dialectics** and they naturally occur in all interpersonal relationships. How we choose to deal with them causes changes in our relationship. Think of these tensions as a pendulum making a wide swing. When a relationship moves toward too much openness, too much connection, or too much predictability, it will naturally swing back toward its opposite of closedness, independence, or novelty.

In this chapter, we will explore the interpersonal processes that affect the ebb and flow of our relational dialectics. We begin by describing how self-disclosure and personal feedback affect the level of openness–closedness in a relationship. Then we explain how assertiveness helps us to maintain our autonomy. Finally, we discuss various styles of conflict management that we can use as we manage the tension that arises from these natural relationship dialectics.

LO¹ Self-Disclosure and Privacy

As we saw in Chapter 6, we develop and grow our relationships through self-disclosure. Self-disclosure leads to openness and intimacy in our relationships. **Self-disclosure** is the process of revealing your biographical data, personal experiences, ideas, and feelings to someone else. Statements such as "I was 5′ 6″ in seventh grade" provide biographical information—facts about you as an individual. "I don't think prisons ever really rehabilitate criminals" discloses a personal idea. "I get scared whenever I have to make a speech" discloses feelings. Biographical disclosures may be the easiest to make, and some biographical information is public. Most of us find it more difficult to talk about our personal ideas and feelings (Rosenfeld, 2000, p. 6).

relational dialectics seemingly opposing forces (openness–closedness, autonomy–connection, and novelty–predictability) that occur in all interpersonal relationships

self-disclosure sharing biographical data, personal experiences, ideas, and feelings

Guidelines for Appropriate Self-Disclosure

We know that self-disclosure increases the intimacy of a relationship. But at the same time, it's risky. So we sometimes choose to avoid disclosure rather than risk personal or relationship consequences (Affifi and Guerrero, 2000, p. 179). The following guidelines can help you manage the dialectical tensions surrounding openness and closedness in your decisions about making a self-disclosure.

Self-Disclose the Kind of Information You Want Others to Disclose to You

When people are getting to know others, they begin by sharing information that they perceive to be low risk. This is information usually shared freely among people with that type of relationship in that culture and might include information about hobbies, sports, school, and views of current events. One way to determine what information is appropriate to disclose is to ask yourself whether you would feel comfortable having the person disclose that kind of information to you.

Self-Disclose More Intimate Information Only When the Disclosure Represents an Acceptable Risk

There is always some risk that disclosure will distress or alarm your partner and damage your relationship, but the better you know your partner, the more likely it is that a difficult disclosure will be well received. Incidentally, this guideline explains why people sometimes engage in inappropriate intimate self-disclosure with bartenders or with people they meet in travel. They perceive the disclosures as safe (representing reasonable risk) because the person either does not know them or is in no position to use the information against them. Some people who are extremely shy find it very difficult to self-disclose.

Continue Self-Disclosure Only If It Is Reciprocated

Research suggests that people expect a kind of equity in self-disclosure (Derlega et al., 1993, p. 33). When it is apparent that self-disclosure is not being returned, you should consider limiting the amount of disclosure you make. Someone's choice not to reciprocate indicates that the person does not yet feel comfortable with this level of self-disclosure. If the response you receive to your self-disclosure implies that it was inappropriate, try to find out why so that you may avoid this problem in the future.

©BLEND IMAGES/JUPITER IMAGES

Self-Disclose at Deeper Levels Gradually

Because receiving self-disclosure can be as threatening as giving it, most people who receive it become uncomfortable when the level of disclosure exceeds their expectations. As a relationship develops, the depth of disclosure should gradually increase. So we disclose biographical and demographic information early in a relationship and more closely held, personal information later, in a more developed relationship (Dindia, Fitzpatrick, & Kenny, 1997, p. 408).

Reserve Intimate or Very Personal Self-Disclosure for Ongoing Relationships

Disclosures about intimate matters are appropriate in close, well-established relationships. When people disclose very personal information to acquaintances or business associates, they are not only taking a risk of being exposed; the disclosure may also threaten their partner. Making intimate disclosures before a bond of trust is established risks alienating the other person. Moreover, people are often embarrassed by and hostile toward others who try to saddle them with intimate information in an effort to establish a personal relationship where none exists.

Guidelines for Appropriate Self-Disclosure

1. Self-disclose the kind of information you want others to disclose to you.
2. Self-disclose more intimate information only when the disclosure represents an acceptable risk.
3. Continue self-disclosure only if it is reciprocated.
4. Self-disclose at deeper levels gradually.
5. Reserve intimate or very personal self-disclosure for ongoing relationships.

Managing Privacy

At times, a relationship can feel too intimate and you may become uncomfortable with the openness; at these times, you may want to reduce the intimacy by distancing yourself and refraining from disclosure. So, it is equally important to understand how to manage your privacy in both developing and ongoing relationships. Privacy is the right of an individual to keep biographical data, personal ideas, and feelings secret. Managing privacy is a conscious decision to avoid disclosure and to withhold information or feelings from a relational partner. You may choose privacy over self-disclosure for many legitimate reasons, including protecting your partner's or another person's feelings, avoiding unnecessary conflict, helping another save face, and protecting the relationship. So when Will, who knows that his partner, Celeste, has worried to the point of weight loss and insomnia over a minor unpaid bill, becomes aware that there is a slight chance that he may lose his job due to a merger, he may decide to keep this information to himself unless the rumor is confirmed. If he later finds out that he will be laid off, he will, of course, need to tell Celeste, but he may not tell her that he has suspected this would happen for some time.

What can you do when you don't want to disclose? First, you can change the subject. For example, if your partner makes a disclosure that seems to invite a parallel disclosure that you are uncomfortable making, just introduce a new topic. So if Pat says, "I got an 83 on the test, how about you?" and you don't want to share your score, you can simply reply, "Hey, that's a 'B'. Good going! Did you finish the homework for calculus?" Second, you can tell a white lie, which is a false or misleading statement that is acceptable to use when telling the truth would embarrass you or your partner and when the untruth you tell does not cause serious harm to either of you or to your relationship. So you might tell Pat, "Gosh, I'm not sure I remember; I got several tests back this week." Third, you can establish a boundary by telling the other person that you don't want to share the information and perhaps why you choose to keep it private. So you might say to Pat, "I know that everyone is different, but because I am so competitive, I've adopted the policy of not asking anyone about their grades and not telling them mine."

> ## What can you do when you don't want to disclose?

Cultural and Gender Differences

Some people, by virtue of their culture, gender, or family upbringing, may readily self-disclose; others may have distinct privacy rules and customs. People from formal cultures, like Germany or Japan, value privacy and are less likely to disclose personal information. The United States is considered an informal culture (Samovar, Porter, & McDaniel, 2007), so most Americans tend to disclose information about themselves.

Particularly in the beginning stages of a cross-cultural friendship, cultural differences can easily lead to misperceptions and discomfort. For instance, an American student may perceive an exchange student from China to be reserved and not interested in establishing a genuine friendship because the exchange student doesn't volunteer personal information. At the same time, the Chinese exchange student may be feeling embarrassed by the American's personal disclosures. When we are aware of cultural differences, we can vary our level of disclosure so that it is appropriate for our partner.

Regardless of these cultural differences, however, Gudykunst and Kim (2003) have discovered that, across cultures, as relationships become more intimate, self-disclosure increases. In addition, they found that the more partners disclosed to each other, the more they were attracted to each other and the less uncertain they felt about each other (p. 329).

Differences in learned patterns of self-disclosure can create misunderstandings between men and women, especially in intimate relationships. In *You Just Don't Understand*, Deborah Tannen (1990, p. 48) argues that in their disclosure patterns, men are more likely to engage in **report-talk** (sharing information, displaying knowledge, negotiating, and preserving independence), whereas women engage in **rapport-talk** (sharing experiences and stories to establish bonds with others). When men and women fail to recognize these differences in disclosure patterns, the stage is set for misunderstandings about whether or not they are being truly open and intimate with each other.

privacy
the right of an individual to keep biographical data, personal ideas, and feelings secret

managing privacy
a conscious decision to avoid disclosure and to withhold information or feelings from a relational partner

report-talk
a way to share information, display knowledge, negotiate, and preserve independence

rapport-talk
a way to share experiences and establish bonds with others

LO² Disclosing Feelings

At the heart of intimate self-disclosure is sharing our personal emotions, which is a risky business. Why? When we share our feelings, we usually give the other person potent knowledge about us that he or she might use to harm us. So all of us have to decide whether and how we disclose our feelings. Obviously, one option in managing our privacy is to withhold our emotions. If we decide to disclose our feelings, we can either display them or describe them.

Masking Feelings

We mask our feelings by concealing the verbal and nonverbal cues that would enable our partners to understand what we are really feeling. The straight-faced poker player who develops the neutral look that is impossible to decipher has become a master of masking feelings. Habitually masking your feelings leads to a variety

describing feelings
the skill of naming the emotions you are feeling without judging them

of physical and psychological problems, such as heart disease and anxiety, and can prevent you from experiencing openness in your relationships. At times, masking your feelings is appropriate such as when a situation or relationship is inconsequential or when disclosing your feelings would pose an unreasonable risk to your physical or emotional safety. For example, it may be appropriate to mask your anger when a stranger cuts in line ahead of you at the theater concession stand, especially if the stranger appears to be menacing.

Displaying Feelings

We display our feelings when we express them through facial expressions, body responses, and verbal outbursts. Cheering over a great play at a sporting event, howling when you bang your head against the car doorjamb, and patting a coworker on the back for doing something well are all displays of feelings. Displaying feelings often serves as an escape valve for very strong emotions, so in some sense it is healthier to display feelings than to withhold them because we "get them out of our system." Unfortunately, although we may feel better, these displays usually stress our relational partners. Because most people are not able to interpret the emotional displays of others with consistent accuracy, misinterpretation of feelings often results. Displays of feelings harm relationships when negative feelings such as anger, disgust, or hatred are displayed in ways that frighten or threaten others. In addition, displays of feelings can damage our relationships and cause stress for our relationship partners. At times, displaying our feelings can rise to the level of abuse, both verbal and physical. Rather than masking or displaying our emotions, we can use the self-disclosure skill of describing feelings to help us share our feelings with others in an appropriate manner.

Describing Feelings

Describing feelings is the skill of naming the emotions you are feeling without judging them. When we describe our feelings, we teach others how to treat us by explaining how we are affected by what has happened. This knowledge gives our relational partners information they can use to help us deal with our emotions. For example, if you tell Paul that you enjoy his visits, your description of how you feel should encourage him to visit you again. Likewise, when you tell Gloria that you are annoyed when she borrows your MP3 player without asking, she is more likely to ask the next time. Describing your feelings allows you to exercise a measure of control over others' behavior simply by making them aware of the effects their actions have on you.

Many times, people think they are describing their feelings when they are actually displaying their feelings or evaluating the other person's behavior. For instance, an outburst like "Who the hell asked you for your opinion?" is a display of feelings, not a description. Simply beginning a sentence with "I feel . . ." may not guarantee that you are describing your feelings. In many cases, these statements can end up evaluating, blaming, or scapegoating someone or something. For example, "I feel like you don't respect me" actually blames the speaker. It doesn't let the speaker know how you feel about what happened. You might have felt hurt, betrayed, or angry. But you haven't disclosed this.

Sometimes we can't describe our emotions because we don't have an active vocabulary that allows us to name or accurately describe what we are feeling. What we are feeling may be similar to anger, but are we annoyed, betrayed, cheated, crushed, disturbed, furious, outraged, or shocked? Each of these words more richly describes a feeling that might less precisely be labeled anger. Figure 8.1 provides a short vocabulary of common emotions.

>> Describing feelings is difficult for many people because it makes them vulnerable. Can you recall a situation in which you masked your feelings because you didn't trust others? Was your fear justified?

To describe your feelings: (1) Identify the behavior that has triggered the feeling. The feeling results from some specific behavior—what someone has done to or said about you. (2) Identify the specific emotion you are experiencing as a result of the behavior. The vocabulary of emotions provided in Figure 8.1 can help you develop your ability to select specific words to describe your feelings. (3) Frame

Figure 8.1

The Vocabulary of Emotions

Words Related to Angry
annoyed	enraged	incensed	infuriated
irate	livid	mad	outraged

Words Related to Loving
affectionate	amorous	aroused	caring
fervent	heavenly	passionate	tender

Words Related to Embarrassed
flustered	humiliated	mortified	overwhelmed
rattled	shamefaced	sheepish	uncomfortable

Words Related to Surprised
astonished	astounded	baffled	jolted
mystified	shocked	startled	stunned

Words Related to Fearful
afraid	anxious	apprehensive	frightened
nervous	scared	terrified	worried

Words Related to Disgusted
aghast	appalled	dismayed	horror-struck
nauseated	repulsed	revolted	sickened

Words Related to Hurt
abused	damaged	forsaken	hassled
mistreated	offended	pained	wounded

Words Related to Happy
cheerful	contented	delighted	ecstatic
elated	glad	joyous	pleased

Words Related to Lonely
abandoned	alone	deserted	desolate
forlorn	isolated	lonesome	lost

Words Related to Sad
blue	depressed	downcast	gloomy
low	miserable	morose	sorrowful

Words Related to Energetic
animated	bouncy	brisk	lively
peppy	spirited	sprightly	vigorous

your response as an "I" statement: "I feel *happy, sad, irritated, vibrant.*" "I" statements help neutralize the impact of an emotional description because they do not blame the other or evaluate the other's behavior. Instead, a first-person message accurately conveys what you are expressing and why. (4) Verbalize the specific feeling.

Here are two examples of describing feelings. Notice that the first one begins with the trigger, and the second one begins with the feeling—either order is acceptable: (1) "Thank you for your compliment [trigger]; I [the person having the feeling] feel gratified [the specific feeling] that you noticed the effort I made." (2) "I [the person having the feeling] feel very resentful [the specific feeling] when you criticize my cooking on days I've worked as many hours as you have [trigger]."

To begin with, you may find it easier to describe positive feelings: "As a result of your taking me to the movie, I really feel cheered up" or "When you offered to help me with the housework, I really felt relieved." As you become comfortable describing positive feelings, you can move to describing negative feelings caused by environmental factors: "It's cold and cloudy; I feel gloomy" or "When there's a thunderstorm, I get jumpy." Finally, you can risk describing the difficult emotions you feel resulting from what people have said or done: "When you use a sarcastic tone while you are saying that what I did pleased you, I really feel confused."

LO³ Giving Personal Feedback

Sometimes in our interactions and relationships, it is appropriate to comment on another's message or behavior. When personal feedback is conveyed with sensitivity, it can help the other person to develop a more accurate self-concept, and it can increase the openness in the relationship. There are three skills that we use to give personal feedback: describing behavior, praising the positive behaviors of others, and constructively criticizing negative behaviors of others.

describing behavior
accurately recounting the specific behaviors of another without commenting on their appropriateness

praise
describing the specific positive behaviors or accomplishments of another and the effect that behavior has on others

Describing Behavior

Effective praising and critiquing are both based on being descriptive rather than evaluative. Just as we must learn to describe our feelings as part of effective self-disclosure, so we must learn to describe the specific behavior of others if we are to give effective feedback. Unfortunately, people are quick to share generalized conclusions and evaluations. "You're so mean," "She's a tease," "You're a real friend," and countless statements like these are attempts to provide feedback but are stated as evaluative and vague.

Describing behavior is accurately recounting the specific behaviors of another without commenting on their appropriateness. When we describe behavior, we hold ourselves accountable for our observations and conclusions. To describe behavior, we move backward through the perceptual process by identifying the specific behaviors that have led to our generalized perception. What led you to conclude someone was "mean"? Was it something the person said? Did? If so, what? What did the person do or say that led you to conclude that he or she is a "real friend"? Once you have identified the specific behaviors, actions, or messages that led to your conclusion, you can share that information as feedback. For example, "Georgio, you called me a liar in front of the team, and you know I have no way to prove that I told the truth." "Shana, you came to my graduation even though it was on your twenty-first birthday." "You stayed and comforted me when Tyrone left, and you even volunteered to stay with my son so I could job hunt. You're a real friend."

Praising

Praise is describing the specific positive behaviors or accomplishments of another and the effect that behavior has on others. Too often, we fail to acknowledge the positive and helpful things people say and do. Yet our view of who we are—our identity as well as our behavior—is shaped by how others respond to us. Praise can be used to reinforce posi-

tive behavior and to help another develop a positive self-concept.

Praise is not the same as flattery. When we flatter someone, we use insincere compliments to ingratiate ourselves to that person. When we praise, our compliments are sincere. We express only admiration that we genuinely feel.

For praise to be effective, we need to focus the praise on the specific behavior and accomplishments and word the message according to the significance or value of the accomplishment or behavior. If your sister, who tends to be forgetful, remembers your birthday, that is a behavior that you will want to praise so that it is reinforced. But saying, "You're so wonderful, you're on top of everything" reinforces nothing because it is an overly general statement that does not identify a particular behavior or accomplishment. Simply saying something like, "Thanks for the birthday card; I really appreciate it" would be appropriate. The response acknowledges the accomplishment by describing the specific behavior and the positive feeling of gratitude that the behavior has caused. Although effective praise can enhance self-esteem, unnecessary praise can actually lower self-esteem.

Praise, when appropriate, doesn't cost much, and it is usually valued and appreciated. Praise provides feedback and builds esteem; it can also deepen our relationship with that person because it increases the openness of the relationship. To increase your effectiveness in using praise, follow these steps: (1) identify the specific behavior or accomplishment that you want to reinforce; (2) describe the specific behavior or accomplishment; (3) describe any positive feelings or outcomes that you or others experienced as a result of the behavior or accomplishment; and (4) phrase the response so that the level of praise appropriately reflects the significance of the behavior or accomplishment. Let's look at two more examples.

Behavior: Sonya takes responsibility for selecting and buying a group wedding present for a friend. The gift is a big hit.

Praise: "Sonya, the present you chose for Stevie was really thoughtful. Not only did it fit our price range, but Stevie really liked it."

Accomplishment: Cole has just received a letter inviting him to a reception at which he is to receive a scholarship award given for academic accomplishments and community service work.
Praise: "Congratulations, Cole. I'm proud of you. It's really great to see that the effort you put into studying, as well as the time and energy you have devoted to the Second Harvest Food Program and Big Brothers, is being recognized and valued."

Giving Constructive Criticism

Research on reinforcement theory has found that people learn faster and better through positive rewards such as praise. Nevertheless, there are times when you need to give personal feedback to address negative behaviors or actions. Constructive criticism is describing specific behaviors of another that hurt the person or that person's relationships with others. Although the word *criticize* can mean judgment, constructive criticism does not condemn or judge but is based on empathy and a sincere desire to help someone understand the impact of his or her behavior. Use the following guidelines when giving constructive criticism.

Ask the Person's Permission before Giving Criticism

Before you give constructive criticism, you should make sure the person wants to hear what you have to say. A person who has agreed to hear constructive criticism is likely to be more receptive to it than is someone who is not accorded respect by being asked.

>>When offering constructive criticism, be careful not to be condemning or judgemental but to try to help the other person understand the effects of their behavior.

constructive criticism describing specific behaviors of another that hurt the person or that person's relationships with others

Describe the Behavior by Accurately Recounting Precisely What Was Said or Done without Labeling the Behavior Good or Bad, Right or Wrong

By describing behavior, you lay an informative base for the feedback and increase the chances that the person will listen receptively. Feedback that is preceded with detailed description is less likely to be met defensively. Your description shows that you are criticizing the behavior rather than attacking the person, and it points the way to a solution. For example, if DeShawn asks, "What did you think of the visuals I used when I delivered my report?" replying, "They weren't very effective" would be general and evaluative. Replying "Well, the type on the first two was small, and I had trouble reading them" is descriptive. Notice this constructive criticism does not attack DeShawn's competence. Instead, it points out a problem and in so doing enables DeShawn to see how to improve.

Preface Constructive Criticism with an Affirming Statement

Remember, by its nature even constructive criticism threatens the needs all of us have to be liked and admired. So, prefacing constructive criticism with statements that validate your respect or admiration of the other is important. One way to do this is to offer praise before criticism. In our example, you could begin your feedback to DeShawn by saying, "First, the charts and graphs were useful, and the color really helped us to see the problems. Second, the type size on the first two slides was small, and I had trouble reading them." Here the praise is relevant and significant. If you cannot preface feedback with significant praise, don't try. Prefacing feedback with empty praise will not help the person accept your feedback.

When Appropriate, Suggest How the Person Can Change the Behavior

Because the focus of constructive criticism is helping, it is appropriate to provide the person with your suggestions that might lead to positive change. In responding to DeShawn's request for feedback, you might also add, "When I make slides, I generally try to use 18-point font or larger. You might want to give that a try." By including a positive

passive behavior not expressing personal preferences or defending our rights because we fear the cost and are insecure in the relationships, have very low self-esteem, or value the other person above ourself

suggestion, you not only help the person by providing honest information, you also show that your intentions are positive.

Consider How the Feedback Will Affect Your Relationship

Although appropriate personal feedback generally deepens a relationship, there are times when, by avoiding feedback, we may actually strengthen the relationship. For example, studies show that one of the most common problems in relationships is expressing complaints about one's partner too freely (Petronio, 2002). So before you offer constructive criticism, consider the context of your relationship. If you are overly free in your criticism, you risk having your partner become defensive or distant.

Giving Constructive Criticism

1. Ask the person's permission before giving criticism.
2. Describe the behavior by accurately recounting precisely what was said or done without labeling the behavior good or bad, right or wrong.
3. Preface constructive criticism with an affirming statement.
4. When appropriate, suggest how the person can change the behavior.
5. Consider how the feedback will affect your relationship.

LO⁴ Assertiveness

A second dialectical tension in relationships is the tension we experience between wanting to be autonomous or independent and our need to be connected. At times, our desire for connectedness pushes us to subordinate our needs and opinions to the needs and opinions of our partner. At other times, our desire for autonomy pushes us to stand up for what we want and think. As we deal with this dialectical tension, we may find ourselves behaving passively, aggressively, or assertively.

Passive, Aggressive, and Assertive Behavior

We behave **passively** when we do not express our personal preferences or defend our rights because we value our connection with the other person more than we value our independence and we fear that we will lose our connection if we stand up for ourselves. We behave passively when we submit to other people's demands, even when doing so is inconvenient, against our best interests, or when it violates our rights. For example, Aaron and Katie routinely go to the gym at 10 a.m. Saturday mornings, but Aaron's Friday work schedule has changed and he doesn't get home until 3 a.m. on Saturday morning. Aaron behaves passively if he doesn't say anything to Katie but drags himself out of bed even though he'd much rather sleep.

We behave **aggressively** when we forcefully make claims for our preferences, feelings, needs, or rights with little or no regard for the situation or for the feelings or rights of our partner. People can behave aggressively when they perceive themselves to be powerful, do not value the other person, lack emotional control, or feel defensive. Although aggressive behavior may stem from the need to establish more independence in a relationship, it also weakens feelings of connection and damages relationships. Research shows that people who receive aggressive messages from their partner are likely to feel hurt by them regardless of their relationship (Martin, Anderson, & Horvath, 1996, p. 24). Suppose that, without letting her know of his schedule change, Aaron has continued to meet Katie at the gym. If Katie suggests they meet next week at 8 a.m. instead of 10 a.m., Aaron may explode and aggressively reply, "No way! In fact, I don't care if I ever work out on Saturday again!" Katie, who has no context for understanding this aggressive outburst, may be startled, hurt, and confused.

Assertive behavior is expressing your personal preferences and defending your personal rights while respecting the preferences and rights of others. Assertiveness is an effective way of establishing our independence while continuing to nurture the relationship because our assertive messages teach our partners how to treat us. When we assert our

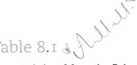

Table 8.1

Characteristics of Assertive Behavior

Own your feelings	Assertive individuals acknowledge that the thoughts and feelings expressed are theirs.
Avoid confrontational language	Assertive individuals do not use threats, evaluations, or dogmatic language.
Use specific statements directed to the behaviors at hand	Instead of focusing on extraneous issues, assertive individuals use descriptive statements that focus on the issue that is most relevant.
Maintain eye contact and firm body position	Assertive individuals look people in the eye rather than shifting gaze, looking at the floor, swaying back and forth, hunching over, or using other signs that may be perceived as indecisive or lacking conviction.
Maintain a firm but pleasant tone of voice	Assertive individuals speak firmly but at a normal pitch, volume, and rate.
Avoid hemming and hawing	Assertive individuals avoid vocalized pauses and other signs of indecisiveness.

needs and preferences effectively, we provide our partners with the honest and truthful information they need to understand and meet our needs. When Aaron's schedule changed, he could have behaved assertively and called Katie, explained his situation, and negotiated a more convenient time for working out together.

Assertive messages balance our rights and needs with the rights and needs of others. For a review of the characteristics of assertive behavior, see Table 8.1.

Cultural Variations in Passive, Aggressive, and Assertive Behavior

Assertiveness is valued and practiced in Western cultures. Whereas North American culture is known for its assertive communication style, Asian and South American cultures value accord and harmony (Samovar, Porter, & McDaniel, 2007). In fact, in collectivist societies typical of Asia and South America, there is "a style of communication in which respecting the relationship through communication is more important than the information exchanged" (Jandt, 2001, p. 37). Jandt goes on to explain that these societies use group harmony, avoidance of loss of face to others and oneself, and a modest presentation of oneself as

aggressive behavior belligerently or violently confronting another with your preferences, feelings, needs, or rights with little regard for the situation or for the feelings or rights of others

assertive behavior expressing your personal preferences and defending your personal rights while respecting the preferences and rights of others

Guidelines for Practicing Assertive Behavior

1. Identify what you are thinking or feeling.
2. Analyze the cause of these feelings.
3. Identify what your real preferences and rights are.
4. Use describing feelings and describing behavior skills to make "I" statements that explain your position politely.

means of respecting the relationship. "One does not say what one actually thinks when it might hurt others in the group" (p. 37).

On the other hand, in Latin and Hispanic societies, men, especially, are frequently taught to exercise a form of self-expression that goes far beyond the guidelines presented here for assertive behavior. In these societies, the concept of "machismo" guides male behavior. Thus, the standard of assertiveness considered appropriate in the dominant American culture can seem inappropriate to people whose cultural frame of reference leads them to perceive it as either aggressive or weak.

Thus, when we use assertiveness—as with any other skill—we need to be aware that no single standard of behavior ensures that we will achieve our goals. Although what is labeled appropriate behavior varies across cultures, the results of passive and aggressive behaviors seem universal. Passive behavior can cause resentment and aggressive behavior leads to fear and misunderstanding. When talking with people whose culture, background, or lifestyle differs from your own, you may need to observe their behavior and their responses to your statements before you can be sure about the kinds of behavior that are likely to communicate your intentions effectively.

LO⁵ Managing Conflict in Relationships

When two people have an honest relationship, it is inevitable that there will be times when one person's attempt to satisfy his or her own needs will conflict with the other person's desires. When this happens, the partners experience conflict. **Interpersonal conflict** exists when the needs or ideas of one person are at odds or in opposition to the needs or ideas of another. In these conflict situations, participants have choices about how they act and how they communicate with each other.

Many people view conflict as a sign of a bad relationship, but the reality is that conflicts occur in all relationships. Although cultures differ in how they view conflict (for example, Asian cultures see it as dysfunctional), whether conflict hurts or strengthens a relationship depends on

how we deal with it. In this section, we discuss five styles people use to manage conflict and how you can skillfully initiate and respond to conflict in your relationships.

Think about the last time you experienced a conflict. How did you react? Did you avoid it? Give in? Force the other person to accept your will? Did you compromise? Or did the two of you use a problem-solving approach. When faced with a conflict, you can withdraw, accommodate, force, compromise, or collaborate (Lulofs & Cahn, 2000, pp. 101–102).

One of the most common and easiest ways to deal with conflict is withdrawing or avoiding the conflict. **Withdrawing** involves physically or psychologically removing yourself from the conflict. You withdraw physically by leaving the site. For instance, imagine Eduardo and Justina get into an argument about their financial situation. Eduardo may withdraw physically by saying, "I don't want to talk about this" and walk out the door. Psychological withdrawal occurs when you simply ignore what the other person is saying. So, when Justina begins to talk about their financial situation, Eduardo may ignore her and act as though she has not spoken. When you repeatedly use withdrawing, you risk damaging your relationship. First, in terms of the dialectical tension in the relationship, withdrawing signals closedness rather than openness and autonomy rather than connection. Further, withdrawing doesn't eliminate the source of the conflict and it often increases the tension. In many cases, not confronting the problem when it occurs only makes it more difficult to deal with in the long run. Nevertheless, as a temporary strategy, withdrawing allows tempers to cool and may be appropriate when neither an issue nor a relationship is important.

A second style of managing conflict is **accommodating**, which means satisfying others' needs or accepting others' ideas while neglecting your own. So people who adopt the accommodating style of conflict will use passive behavior. For instance, during a discussion of their upcoming vacation, Mariana and Juan disagree in their thinking about whether to invite friends to join them. Juan uses accommodation when Mariana says, "I think it would be fun to go with another couple, don't you?" and he replies, "OK, whatever you want."

Accommodating can result in poor communication because important facts, arguments, and positions are not voiced. There are situations, of course, in which it is appropriate and effective to accommodate. When the issue is not important to you, but the relationship is, accommodating is the preferred style. Hal and Yvonne are trying to decide where to go for dinner. Hal says, "I really have a craving for some Thai food tonight." Yvonne, who prefers pizza, says,

interpersonal conflict
when the needs or ideas of one person are at odds or in opposition to the needs or ideas of another

withdrawing
managing conflict by physically or psychologically removing yourself

accommodating
managing conflict by satisfying others' needs or accepting others' ideas while neglecting our own

Do you have to have pizza . . . **can you accommodate?**

©PHOTODISC/GETTY IMAGES V20

©FOOD PIX/JUPITER IMAGES

"OK, that will be fine." Yvonne's interest in pizza was not very strong, and because Hal really seemed excited by Thai food, Yvonne accommodated.

A third style of dealing with conflict is forcing or competing. **Forcing** means satisfying your own needs or advancing your own ideas with no concern for the needs or ideas of the other and no concern for the harm done to the relationship. Forcing may use aggressive behavior such as physical threats, verbal attacks, coercion, or manipulation. If you use forcing in a conflict and your partner avoids or accommodates, the conflict seems to subside. If, however, your partner answers your forcing style with a forcing style, the conflict escalates.

Although forcing may result in a person getting her or his own way, it usually hurts a relationship, at least in the short term. There are times, however, when forcing is an effective means to resolve conflict. In emergencies, when quick and decisive action must be taken to ensure safety or minimize harm, forcing is useful. When an issue is critical to your own or the other's welfare and you know you are right, you may find forcing necessary. Finally, if you are interacting with someone who will take advantage of you if you do not force the issue, this style is appropriate. For example, David knows that, statistically speaking, the likelihood of death or serious injury increases dramatically if one does not wear a helmet when riding a motorcycle. So he insists that his sister wear one when she rides with him, even though she complains bitterly about wearing one.

A fourth way to manage conflict is through **compromising**, which involves giving up part of what each wants, to provide at least some satisfaction for both parties. Under this approach, both people have to give up part of what they really want or believe, or they have to trade one thing they want to get something else. For example, if Heather and Paul are working together on a class project and need to meet outside of class but both have busy schedules, they may compromise on a time to meet.

Although compromising is a popular and effective style, there are drawbacks associated with it. One drawback is that the quality of a decision is affected if one of the parties "trades away" a better solution to find a compromise. Compromising is appropriate when the issue is moderately important, when there are time constraints, and when attempts at forcing or collaborating have not been successful.

A fifth style of dealing with conflict is through problem-solving discussion, or collaboration. When you **collaborate**, you both try to fully address the needs and issues of each of you and arrive at a solution that is mutually satisfying. In this approach, both of you view the disagreement as a problem to be solved, so you discuss the issues, describe your feelings, and identify the characteristics of an effective solution. With collaboration, both people's needs are met and both sides feel that they have been heard. For example, if Juan and Mariana decide to collaborate on their conflict about asking friends to join them on vacation, Mariana may explain to Juan how she thinks that, by vacationing with friends, they can share expenses and lower their costs. Juan may describe his desire to have "alone time" with Mariana. As they explore what each wants from the vacation, they may arrive at a plan that meets both of their needs. So, they may end up vacationing alone, but spending several nights camping to lower their expenses.

©SUSAN VAN ETTEN

forcing
managing conflict by satisfying your own needs or advancing your own ideas, with no concern for the needs or ideas of the other and no concern for the harm done to the relationship

compromising
managing conflict by giving up part of what you want, to provide at least some satisfaction for both parties

collaborating
managing conflict by fully addressing the needs and issues of each party and arriving at a solution that is mutually satisfying

Learning Outcomes

LO ^{1} Identify different kinds of questions to use in an interview

LO ^{2} Explain how to prepare for and conduct an information interview

LO ^{3} Explain how to conduct a job interview

LO ^{4} Explain how to present yourself when being interviewed for a job

LO ^{5} Discuss how to participate in a media interview

Interviewing

> **"The success of any interview depends on preparing a list of good questions."**

Interviewing is a powerful method you can use to collect or present firsthand information that may be unavailable elsewhere. So, it is an important communication skill to master. An interview is a planned, structured conversation in which one person asks questions and another person answers them. Unlike most interpersonal communication, interview participants usually prepare for the interview conversation.

What do you think?

I'd rather do an interview over the phone than in person.

Strongly Disagree						Strongly Agree
1	2	3	4	5	6	7

We begin this chapter by describing interview planning, especially how you can construct good interview questions. Then we explain how you can prepare for and conduct an interview where the goal is to gather information. Next we discuss employment interviews from the perspective of both the interviewer and the interviewee. Finally, we provide information on how you can prepare for and participate in media interviews.

LO¹ Questions Used in Interviewing

The success of any interview depends on preparing a list of good questions. You may want to ask questions about (1) behaviors (what a person has done or is doing), (2) demographics (such as age, education), (3) opinions or values, (4) knowledge (facts), (5) experiences, and (6) feelings. But regardless of content, your interview question list is likely to have a mix of open-ended and closed questions, which may be phrased neutrally or may be leading. Some of your questions will be primary and others secondary or follow-up questions.

Open versus Closed Questions

Open questions are broad-based probes that call on the interviewee to provide perspective, ideas, information, feelings, or opinions as he or she answers the question. For example, in a job interview you might be asked, "What one

interview
a planned, structured conversation in which one person asks questions and another person answers them

open questions
broad-based probes that call on the interviewee to provide perspective, ideas, information, feelings, or opinions as he or she answers the question

accomplishment has best prepared you for this job?" In a customer service interview, a representative might ask, "What seems to be the problem?" or "Can you tell me the steps you took when you first set this product up?" Interviewers ask open questions to encourage the person to talk, allowing the interviewer an opportunity to listen and observe. Open questions take time to answer and give respondents more control, which means that interviewers can lose sight of their original purpose if they are not careful (Tengler & Jablin, 1983).

By contrast, **closed questions** are narrowly focused and require the respondent to give very brief (one- or two-word) answers. Closed questions range from those that can be answered "yes" or "no," such as "Have you had a course in marketing?" to those that require only a short answer, such as "Where did you buy the product?" By asking closed questions, interviewers can control the interview and obtain specific information quickly. The answers to closed questions cannot reveal the nuances behind responses, nor are they likely to capture the complexity of the story. Effective interview conversations contain a combination of open and closed questions.

Neutral versus Leading Questions

Open and closed questions may be either neutral or leading. **Neutral questions** do not direct a person's answer. "What can you tell me about your work with Habitat for Humanity?" or "What symptoms did you experience?" are both neutral questions. The neutral question gives the respondent free rein to answer the question without any knowledge of what the interviewer thinks or believes.

By contrast, **leading questions** guide respondents toward providing certain types of information and imply that the interviewer prefers one answer over another. "What do you like about working for Habitat for Humanity?" steers the respondent to describe only the positive aspects of the work. "Was this as painful as a migraine?" directs the answer by providing the standard for comparison. In most types of interviews, neutral questions are preferred.

Primary versus Secondary Questions

Primary questions are the lead-in questions that you use to introduce one of the major topics of the interview conversation. When planning interview questions, you should carefully choose the major topics you want to cover and then prepare at least one primary question for each topic. **Secondary or follow-up questions** are designed to probe the answers given to primary questions. When you expect a specific answer, you can preplan your secondary questions. Usually, however, your secondary questions will be spontaneous and you will construct them in response to an answer to a primary question. Some follow-up questions encourage the person to continue ("And then?" or "Is there more?"); some probe into what the person has said ("What does 'frequently' mean?" or "What were you thinking at the time?"); and some probe the feelings of the person ("How did it feel to get the prize?" or "Did it last longer than 15 minutes?"). The major purpose of follow-up questions is to encourage the person to expand on an answer that seems incomplete or vague. Sometimes the person may not understand how much detail you are looking for, and occasionally he or she may be purposely evasive.

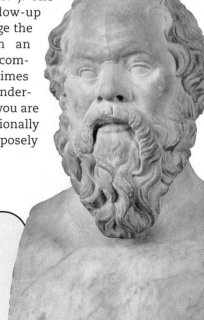

©YSIPPOS/THE BRIDGEMAN ART LIBRARY/GETTY IMAGES

Socrates

closed questions
narrowly focused questions that require the respondent to give very brief (one- or two-word) answers

neutral questions
questions that do not direct a person's answer

leading questions
questions that guide respondents toward providing certain types of information and imply that the interviewer prefers one answer over another

primary questions
lead-in questions that introduce one of the major topics of the interview conversation

secondary (follow-up) questions
questions designed to probe the answers given to primary questions

> { Fast Facts—
> Plato's Dialogues }
>
> In Plato's *Meno*, Socrates tells Meno that he, Socrates, does not know what virtue is, nor has he ever met anyone who he thought knew. Meno responds, "What? Didn't you meet Gorgias when he was here?" Socrates answers, "I did." to which Meno responds, "And you didn't think that he knew?" Do you think that Meno's questions are leading questions? What answers do you think he expects, and what indicates this?

LO² Interviewing for Information

Interviewing can be a valuable method for obtaining information on nearly any topic. Lawyers and police interview witnesses to establish facts; health care providers interview patients to obtain medical histories before making diagnoses; reporters interview sources for their stories; social workers and sales representatives interview clients; managers interview current and perspective employees; and students interview experts to obtain information for papers. Your interviews are more likely to achieve the desired result if they are carefully planned. Planning includes clearly defining the purpose of the interview, selecting the person (people) to interview, planning the interview protocol, and conducting the interview.

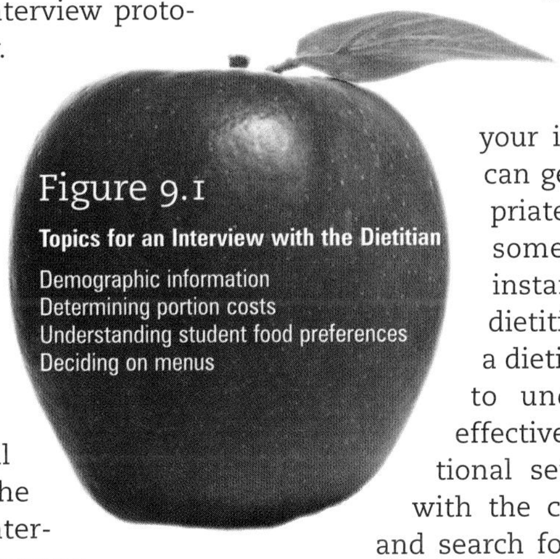

Defining the Purpose of the Interview

Informative interviews require a clear, identified purpose that can be summarized in one sentence. Without such a statement of purpose, your questions will probably have no direction, and the information derived from the interview may not fit together well. Your purpose may be to obtain expert information, investigate a complaint, get the story of someone's experience, or evaluate someone. Suppose you wanted to learn about the commercial food service business. Possible specific purposes would be:

1. To find out what criteria were used for selecting a commercial food service provider for this college.
2. To learn the most efficient means of food distribution in a dining hall.
3. To understand how dietitians create cost-effective menus that provide good nutrition.

Each of these topics covers an entirely different aspect of food service and will direct you toward who to interview and the types of questions to ask.

Selecting the Best Person to Interview

In some situations, it is obvious who you should interview. At other times, locating the right person to interview can be a challenge, especially when you need expert answers. You may have to do research before you can identify the right people. Suppose your purpose is to learn how dietitians create cost-effective menus that provide good nutrition. You might begin by asking one of the food service workers at the campus dining hall for the name of the food service manager. Or you could find the manager by calling the student center. In any case, the manager could give you the name and phone number (or e-mail address) of the dietitian. Once you have identified the person or people to be interviewed, you should contact them to make an appointment. Be sure to clearly state the purpose of the interview, how the interview information will be used, and how long you expect the interview to take. When setting a time and date, be flexible by suggesting several dates and time ranges.

You don't want to bother your interviewee with information you can get elsewhere. So to prepare appropriate questions, you will need to do some research on the topic. If, for instance, you are going to interview a dietitian, you will want to find out what a dietitian is and does. If your purpose is to understand how nutritious, cost-effective menus are planned in an institutional setting, you can acquaint yourself with the current FDA nutritional standards and search for articles on cost factors in commercial food service operations. Interviewees will be more likely to enjoy talking with you if you're well informed, and familiarity with your subject will also enable you to ask better questions.

Figure 9.1

Topics for an Interview with the Dietitian

Demographic information
Determining portion costs
Understanding student food preferences
Deciding on menus

Developing the Interview Protocol

The heart of the interview plan is the **interview protocol**, an ordered list of questions that you have selected to meet the specific purpose of the interview. Preparation of the interview protocol begins by listing the topic areas to be covered in the interview. Once topics are listed, they need to be prioritized for importance. Figure 9.1 presents a list of topics for the interview with the dietitian.

For each topic, a list of questions should be generated. Questions should be revised until they are a mixture of open and closed questions that are phrased

interview protocol
an ordered list of questions that have been selected to meet the specific purpose of the interview

Do you know the cost of each portion of all items?
How are portion costs determined?
Do you have a budget for each meal plan serving?
Suppose you'd planned a menu and it turned out to be more expensive than you anticipated; what would happen?
How important is portion control?
What are some of the less expensive foods you use that are both nutritious and tasty?

Figure 9.2

Questions to Determine Portion Costs

neutrally. Figure 9.2 shows some questions that could be asked about the topic "Determining Portion Costs."

Once a complete question list has been generated, you will need to estimate how long it will take to ask and answer all of the questions. A rule of thumb is to allow four minutes for each open-ended question and one minute for each close-ended question. If your realistic guess exceeds the time you have allotted for the interview, cull your questions by eliminating some from each topic list and by severely trimming those from less important topics.

The final step in creating the interview protocol is to develop a sequence for the questions. Your initial questions should be short and designed to get the interviewee involved in the conversation. In general, these opening questions should ask for facts. It is better to leave more complex or controversial questions until later, after you have established rapport. Answering fact questions can be boring for the interviewee, so you might consider spreading these throughout the interview. It is usually easier for people to talk about things in the present than it is for them to remember things in the past or to hypothesize about the future, so begin by asking about current practices or events, then work backward or forward. Be sure to place topics of great importance early in the interview, so you will have plenty of time for follow-up questions.

When you have finalized your interview protocol, reproduce it, leaving enough space between your questions for you to take complete notes of the answers.

Conducting the Interview

By applying the interpersonal skills we have discussed in this book, you'll find that you can turn your careful planning into an excellent interview.

First, of course, you will want to be courteous during the interview. Start by thanking the person for taking the time to talk to you. Remember, although the interviewee may enjoy talking about the subject, may be flattered, and may wish to share knowledge, that person has nothing to gain from the interview. Encourage the person to speak freely. Most of all, respect what the person says regardless of what you may think of the answers.

Second, listen carefully. At key places in the interview, you should paraphrase what the person has said to assure yourself that you really understand him or her.

Third, keep the interview moving. You do not want to rush the person, but you do want to get your questions answered during the allotted time.

>> Focus groups are marketing interviews with a group of consumers. What adjustments do you think an interviewer must make in a group, versus a one-on-one, interview?

Fourth, make sure that your nonverbal reactions—your facial expressions and your gestures—are in keeping with the tone you want to communicate. Maintain good eye contact with the person. Nod to show understanding, and smile occasionally to maintain the friendliness of the interview. How you look and act is likely to determine whether the person will warm up to you and give you an informative interview.

Finally, if you are going to publish the substance of the interview, be sure to get written permission for exact quotes; as a courtesy, offer to let the person see a copy of the article (or at least tell the person exactly when it will be published). Under some circumstances, you may want to show the interviewee a draft of your report about the interview before it goes into print, if only to allow him or her to double-check the accuracy of direct quotations. If so, provide a draft well before the deadline, to give the person the opportunity to read it and to give you time to deal with any suggestions. At times, you may wish to conduct an electronic interview by using e-mail.

LO³ Conducting Employment Interviews

Almost all organizations use interviewing as part of their hiring process. Employment interviews help organizations assess which applicants have the knowledge, experience, and skills to do a job and which applicants will "fit" into the organization's culture. Interviews allow organizations to evaluate personal characteristics (such as ambition, energy, and enthusiasm) and interpersonal skills (such as conversing and listening) that cannot be judged from a résumé.

Historically, most employment interviewing was done by human resource professionals or managers, but today organizations are using coworkers as interviewers. You may have already helped to conduct employment interviews, or you may be asked to do so in the near future.

Preparing for the Interview

As with information interviews, your preparation begins by doing research. In the case of employment interviewing, this means becoming familiar with the knowledge, skills, and aptitudes that someone must have to be successful in the job. It also means studying the résumés, references, and, if available, the test scores for each person you will interview.

In most employment interviewing situations, you will be seeing several candidates. You will want to make sure that all applicants are asked the same (or very similar) questions and that the questions selected allow applicants to disclose information you will need to know to make an informed hiring decision. To accomplish this, you will want to use a highly structured to moderately structured interview. This means that you will prepare a general interview protocol to use with all interviewees. Your protocol should have questions designed to probe the interviewees' knowledge, skills, and experiences that are relevant to the job.

It is important that you avoid questions that violate fair employment practice legislation. The Equal Opportunity Commission has detailed guidelines that spell out what questions are unlawful.

Conducting the Interview

A well-planned employment interview is carefully orchestrated. It has an introduction designed to establish rapport and help the interviewee relax. As the interviewer, you should warmly greet the applicant by name, shake hands, and introduce yourself. If you will be taking notes or recording the interview, you should explain that to the candidate. During the early part of the interview, you will want to establish rapport with the applicant. If the applicant is extremely nervous, you may want to ask a couple of "warm-up" questions designed to put the applicant at ease. If the applicant seems comfortable, you may move directly into the body of the interview, using the interview protocol.

In the body, or main part of the interview, candidates are carefully questioned to determine whether their knowledge, skills, experiences, personal characteristics, and interpersonal style fit with the demands of the job and with the organizational culture. During this period it is important for you, the interviewer, to keep the interview moving. You will want to give applicants sufficient time to answer your questions, but you don't want to waste time by allowing applicants to over-answer questions. One way to help applicants understand the scope of the interview is to preview each of the topic areas to be covered and the time you expect to spend in this conversation.

As you ask the questions, strive to sound spontaneous and to speak in a voice that is easily heard. Be sensitive to the nonverbal messages you are sending. Be careful that you are not "leading" applicants through nonverbal cues. Use follow-up questions to probe answers that are vague. Remember, your goal is to understand the applicant.

As the interview comes to an end, tell the applicant what will happen next. Explain how and approximately when the hiring decision will be made, and how the applicant will be notified. Unless you are the person with hiring authority, remain neutral about the candidate. You don't want to mislead the candidate with false hope or discouragement.

LO⁴ Interviewing to Get a Job

Being able to present yourself successfully in a job interview is an essential skill that you may engage in repeatedly during the course of a career. In this section, we present strategies for writing a cover letter, preparing a résumé, and participating in a job interview.

Getting the Interview

Because interviewing is time consuming, most organizations do not interview all the people who apply for a job. Rather, they use a variety of screening devices to eliminate people who don't meet their qualifications. Chief among these are evaluating the qualifications presented in the résumé and in the cover letter. The goal of your résumé with cover letter "is to communicate your qualifications in writing and sell yourself to prospective employers" (Kaplan, 2002, p. 6).

cover letter
a short, well-written letter expressing your interest in a particular job

résumé
a written summary of your skills and accomplishments

It All Begins with Research

To write an effective cover letter and résumé that high-

>> Early in the interview, the interviewer should establish rapport. In addition to a welcoming greeting, what other methods have interviewers used to put you at ease?

light your qualifications for a particular job, you need to know something about the job requirements and about the company. The career center advisers at your college or university can assist you with your research.

Write an Effective Cover Letter

A **cover letter** is a short, well-written letter expressing your interest in a particular job. In a cover letter, it is important to focus on the employer's needs, and not your own needs. The letter should capture the reader's attention, demonstrate your qualifications, and request an interview.

Prepare a Professional Résumé

The **résumé** is a summary of your skills and accomplishments and is your "silent sales representative" (Stewart & Cash, 2000, p. 274). Although there is no universal format for résumé writing, there is some agreement on what should be included. The following information should be included:

- **Contact information:** Information including your name, addresses (current and permanent), telephone numbers, and e-mail address.
- **Career objective:** A one-sentence objective focusing on your job search goals.
- **Employment history:** List of your paid and unpaid experiences, beginning with the most recent. List the name and address of the organization, your employment dates, your title, key duties, and noteworthy accomplishments.
- **Education:** List the names and addresses of the schools you have attended (including specialized military schools), the degrees or certificates earned (or expected), and the dates of attendance and graduation. Also list academic honors received with degrees or certificates.
- **Relevant professional affiliations:** List the names of the organizations, dates of membership, and any offices held.
- **Military background:** List branch and dates of service, last rank held, significant commendations, and discharge status.

Figure 9.3

Sample Cover Letter

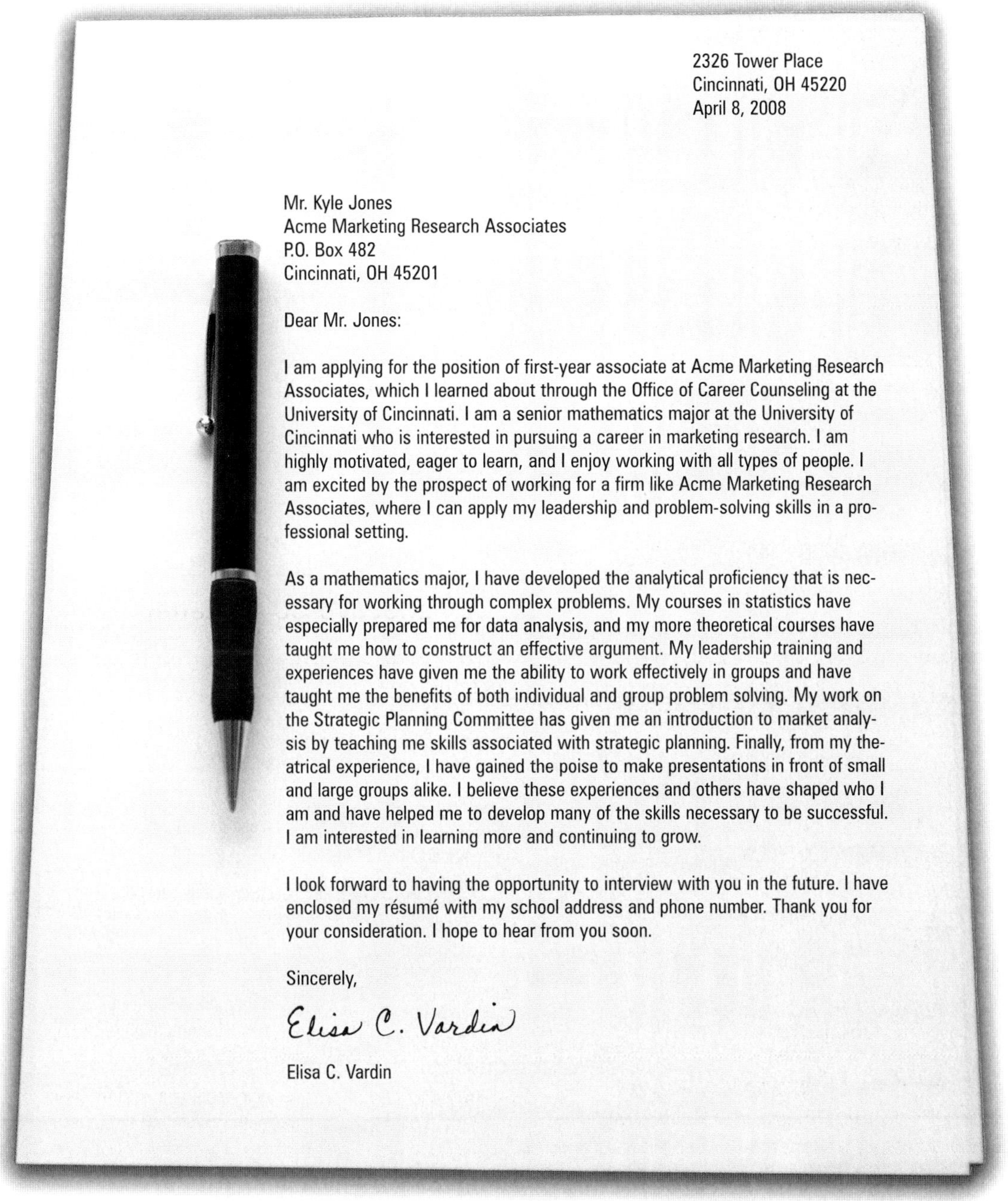

2326 Tower Place
Cincinnati, OH 45220
April 8, 2008

Mr. Kyle Jones
Acme Marketing Research Associates
P.O. Box 482
Cincinnati, OH 45201

Dear Mr. Jones:

I am applying for the position of first-year associate at Acme Marketing Research Associates, which I learned about through the Office of Career Counseling at the University of Cincinnati. I am a senior mathematics major at the University of Cincinnati who is interested in pursuing a career in marketing research. I am highly motivated, eager to learn, and I enjoy working with all types of people. I am excited by the prospect of working for a firm like Acme Marketing Research Associates, where I can apply my leadership and problem-solving skills in a professional setting.

As a mathematics major, I have developed the analytical proficiency that is necessary for working through complex problems. My courses in statistics have especially prepared me for data analysis, and my more theoretical courses have taught me how to construct an effective argument. My leadership training and experiences have given me the ability to work effectively in groups and have taught me the benefits of both individual and group problem solving. My work on the Strategic Planning Committee has given me an introduction to market analysis by teaching me skills associated with strategic planning. Finally, from my theatrical experience, I have gained the poise to make presentations in front of small and large groups alike. I believe these experiences and others have shaped who I am and have helped me to develop many of the skills necessary to be successful. I am interested in learning more and continuing to grow.

I look forward to having the opportunity to interview with you in the future. I have enclosed my résumé with my school address and phone number. Thank you for your consideration. I hope to hear from you soon.

Sincerely,

Elisa C. Vardin

Elisa C. Vardin

- **Special skills:** List language fluencies, technical expertise, computer expertise, multimedia competencies, and so forth.
- **Community service:** List significant involvement in community service organizations, clubs, and other volunteer efforts.
- **References:** List or have available the names, addresses, e-mail addresses, and phone numbers of at least three people who will speak well of your ability, your work product, and your character.

Prepare your résumé so that it is easy to read, highlights your accomplishments, and is short. Figure 9.3 and Figure 9.4 display a sample cover letter and a sample résumé for a recent college graduate.

Electronic Cover Letters and Résumés

Electronic cover letters and résumés are sent online. Electronic résumés have become quite popular with employers and job seekers. For example, from 1995 to 1999 the number of résumés that were received electronically by Microsoft increased from 5 percent to 50 percent (Criscito, 2000, p. 2). Employers like electronic résumés because they can

electronic cover letters and résumés
these contain the same information as traditional cover letters and résumés but are sent online

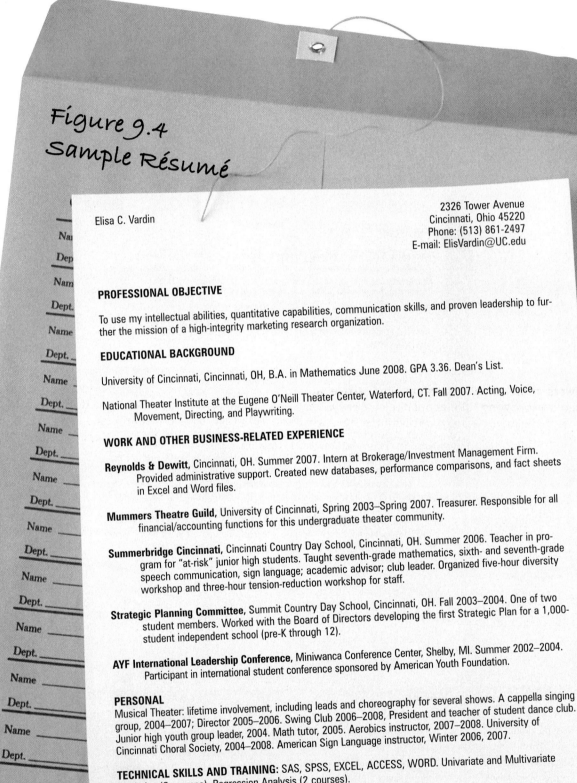

Figure 9.4
Sample Résumé

Elisa C. Vardin

2326 Tower Avenue
Cincinnati, Ohio 45220
Phone: (513) 861-2497
E-mail: ElisVardin@UC.edu

PROFESSIONAL OBJECTIVE

To use my intellectual abilities, quantitative capabilities, communication skills, and proven leadership to further the mission of a high-integrity marketing research organization.

EDUCATIONAL BACKGROUND

University of Cincinnati, Cincinnati, OH, B.A. in Mathematics June 2008. GPA 3.36. Dean's List.

National Theater Institute at the Eugene O'Neill Theater Center, Waterford, CT. Fall 2007. Acting, Voice, Movement, Directing, and Playwriting.

WORK AND OTHER BUSINESS-RELATED EXPERIENCE

Reynolds & Dewitt, Cincinnati, OH. Summer 2007. Intern at Brokerage/Investment Management Firm. Provided administrative support. Created new databases, performance comparisons, and fact sheets in Excel and Word files.

Mummers Theatre Guild, University of Cincinnati, Spring 2003–Spring 2007. Treasurer. Responsible for all financial/accounting functions for this undergraduate theater community.

Summerbridge Cincinnati, Cincinnati Country Day School, Cincinnati, OH. Summer 2006. Teacher in program for "at-risk" junior high students. Taught seventh-grade mathematics, sixth- and seventh-grade speech communication, sign language; academic advisor; club leader. Organized five-hour diversity workshop and three-hour tension-reduction workshop for staff.

Strategic Planning Committee, Summit Country Day School, Cincinnati, OH. Fall 2003–2004. One of two student members. Worked with the Board of Directors developing the first Strategic Plan for a 1,000-student independent school (pre-K through 12).

AYF International Leadership Conference, Miniwanca Conference Center, Shelby, MI. Summer 2002–2004. Participant in international student conference sponsored by American Youth Foundation.

PERSONAL
Musical Theater: lifetime involvement, including leads and choreography for several shows. A cappella singing group, 2004–2007; Director 2005–2006. Swing Club 2006–2008, President and teacher of student dance club. Junior high youth group leader, 2004. Math tutor, 2005. Aerobics instructor, 2007–2008. University of Cincinnati Choral Society, 2004–2008. American Sign Language instructor, Winter 2006, 2007.

TECHNICAL SKILLS AND TRAINING: SAS, SPSS, EXCEL, ACCESS, WORD. Univariate and Multivariate Statistics (2 courses), Regression Analysis (2 courses).

REFERENCES: Available on request.

sift through large numbers, looking only for particular qualifications or characteristics. Candidates like electronic résumés because they can send essentially the same materials online, saving time and money. Your electronic résumé is the same résumé that you will send to employers and take to your interview, only you will need to alter the format so it is easy to post to the web (Dikel, 2006).

Preparing to Be Interviewed

Although the résumé and cover letter make you an attractive candidate for an employer, it is your behavior at the interview that will solidify your chances of receiving an offer. The following guidelines will help you prepare for the interview.

Do Your Homework

If you haven't yet done extensive research on the position and the company, do so before you go to the interview. Be sure you know the company's products and services, areas of operation, ownership, and financial health. Nothing puts off interviewers more than applicants who arrive at an interview knowing little about the company. Today, most medium and large organizations have a web presence so you can easily begin your research by looking online.

Based on Your Research, Prepare a List of Questions about the Organization and the Job

The employment interview should be a two-way street, where you size up the company as they are sizing you up. So you will probably have a number of specific questions to ask the interviewer. For example, "Can you describe a typical workday for the person in this position?" or "What is the biggest challenge in this job?" Make a list of your questions and take it with you to the interview.

Rehearse the Interview

Several days before the interview, spend time outlining the job requirements and how your knowledge, skills, and experiences meet those requirements. Practice answering questions commonly asked in interviews, such as those listed in Figure 9.5.

Dress Appropriately

You want to make a good first impression, so it is important to be well groomed and neatly dressed. Although "casual" or "business casual" is common in many workplaces, some organizations still expect employees to be more formally dressed. If you don't

>> It's important to dress appropriately for an interview. Make sure you know the dress code of the place you will be working.

know the dress code for the organization, call the Human Resources department and ask.

Plan to Arrive on Time

The interview is the organization's first exposure to your work behavior, so you don't want to be late. Find out how long it will take you to travel by making a dry run several days before. Plan to arrive 10 or 15 minutes before your appointment.

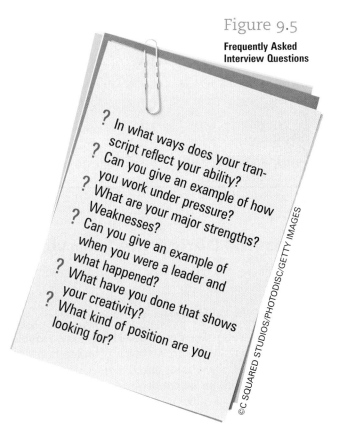

Figure 9.5

Frequently Asked Interview Questions

? In what ways does your transcript reflect your ability?

? Can you give an example of how you work under pressure?

? What are your major strengths?

? Weaknesses?

? Can you give an example of when you were a leader and what happened?

? What have you done that shows your creativity?

? What kind of position are you looking for?

Think Before Answering

If you have prepared for the interview, you want to make sure that as you answer the questions posed, you also tell your story. So take a moment to consider how your answer will portray your skills and experiences. "Tell me about yourself" is not an invitation to give the interviewer your life history. Rather, you can focus your answer on presenting your experiences and qualifications that are related to the job.

Be Enthusiastic

If you come across as bored or disinterested, the interviewer is likely to conclude that you would be an unmotivated employee.

Ask Questions

As the interview is winding down, be sure to ask the questions you prepared that have not already been answered. You may also want to ask how well the interviewer believes your qualifications match the position, and what your strengths are.

Avoid Discussing Salary and Benefits

The time to discuss salary is when you are offered the job. If the interviewer tries to pin you down, simply say something like, "I'm really more interested in talking about how my experiences map onto your needs and would like to defer talking about salary until we know we have a match." Similarly, discussions of benefits are best held until an offer is made.

Interview Follow-Up

When the interview is complete, there are several important steps to follow:

Write a Thank-You Note

It is appropriate to write a short note thanking the interviewer for the experience and re-expressing your interest in the job.

Self-Assess Your Performance

Take time to critique your performance. How well did you do? What can you do better next time?

Contact the Interviewer for Feedback

If you don't get the job, you might call the interviewer and ask for feedback. Be sure to be polite and to indicate that you are only calling to get some help on your interviewing skills. Actively listen to the feedback, using questions and paraphrases to clarify what is being said. Be sure to thank the interviewer for helping you.

Bring Supplies

Gather and bring extra copies of your résumé, cover letter, and references as well as the list of questions you plan to ask. You will also want to have paper and a pen so that you can make notes.

Behavior During the Interview

Interviewing is a crucial step in obtaining a job. Use these guidelines to help you put your best foot forward.

Use Active Listening

When we are anxious, we sometimes have trouble listening well. Work on attending, understanding, and remembering what is asked. Remember that the interviewer will be aware of your nonverbal behavior, so be sure to make and keep eye contact as you listen.

TO REVIEW

LO⁵ Media Interviews

Today we live in a media-saturated environment where any individual may be approached by a newsperson and asked to participate in an on-air interview. For example, we have a friend who became the object of media interest when the city council in his town refused to grant him a zoning variance so he could complete building a new home on his property. In the course of three days, his "story" became front-page news in his town and reports about his situation made the local radio and TV news shows. You might be asked for an interview when you attend public meetings, and at the mall, or within the context of your work or community service. For example, you may be asked to share your knowledge of your organization's pro-

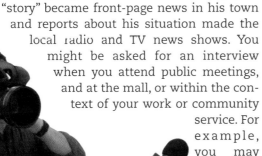

TODAY WE LIVE IN A MEDIA-SATURATED ENVIRONMENT WHERE ANY INDIVIDUAL MAY BE APPROACHED BY A NEWSPERSON AND ASKED TO PARTICIPATE IN AN ON-AIR INTERVIEW.

grams, events, or activities. Because media interviews are likely to be edited in some way before they are aired and because they are reaching a wider audience, there are specific strategies you should use as you prepare for and participate in a media interview.

Before the Interview

The members of the media work under very tight deadlines, so it is crucial that you respond immediately to media requests for an interview. When people are insensitive to media deadlines, they can end up looking like they have purposefully evaded the interview and have something to hide. When you speak with the media representative, clarify what the focus of the interview will be and how the information will be presented. At times, the entire interview will be presented; however, it is more likely that the information from the interview will be edited or paraphrased, and all of your comments will not necessarily be reported.

talking points
the three or four central ideas you will present as you answer the questions that are asked during a media interview

As you prepare for the interview, identify three or four **talking points**, that is, the central ideas you will present as you answer the questions asked during a media interview. For example, before our friend was interviewed by the local TV news anchor, he knew that he wanted to emphasize that he was a victim of others' mistakes: (1) he had hired a licensed architect to draw the plans, (2) the city inspectors had repeatedly approved earlier stages of

>> It's more common than many of us think to be in a position to be interviewed by the media. By following a few simple guidelines, even the most novice interviewee can give a successful media interview.

©PHOTOEDIT

©ON ASIA/JUPITER IMAGES

the building process, (3) the city planning commission had voted unanimously to grant him the variance, and (4) he would be out half the cost of the house if he were forced to tear it down and rebuild. Consider how you will tailor your information to the specific audience in terms they can understand. Consider how you will respond to tough or hostile questions.

During the Interview

Media interviews call for a combination of interviewing, nonverbal communication, and public speaking skills (Boyd, 1999). There are many strategies to be followed during a media interview:

1. Present appropriate nonverbal cues. Inexperienced interviewees can often look or sound tense or stiff. By standing up during a phone interview, your voice will sound more energetic and authoritative. With on-camera interviews, when checking your notes, move your eyes but not your head. Keep a small smile when listening. Look at the interviewer, not into the camera.

2. Make clear and concise statements. It is important to speak slowly, to articulate clearly, and to avoid technical terms or jargon. Remember that the audience is not familiar with your area of expertise.

3. Realize that you are always "on the record." So, nothing should be said as an aside or confidentially to a reporter. Do not say anything that you would not want quoted. If you do not know an answer, do not speculate, but indicate that the question is outside of your area of expertise. Do not ramble during the interviewer's periods of silence. Do not allow yourself to be rushed into an answer.

4. Learn how to bridge. Media consultant Joanna Krotz (2006) defines a **bridge** as a transition you create so that you can move from the interviewer's subject to the message you want to communicate. To do this, you first answer the direct question and then use phrases such as "what's important to remember, however . . . ," "let me put that in perspective . . . ," or "it's also important to know . . ."

With careful preparation, specific communication strategies during the interview, and practice, one can skillfully deliver a message in any media interview format.

bridge
a transition you create in a media interview so that you can move from the interviewer's subject to the message you want to communicate

Test coming up? Now what?

With COMM you have a multitude of study aids at your fingertips. After reading the chapters, check out these ideas for further help.

Chapter in Review Cards include all learning outcomes, definitions, and visual summaries for each chapter.

Printable Flash Cards give you three additional ways to check your comprehension of key communication concepts.

Other great ways to help you study include **Speech Builder Express 3.0™**, **Interactive Quizzing, Downloads, Games and Simulations,** and **Interactive Video Activities**.

You can find it all at **4ltrpress.cengage.com/comm**

Learning Outcomes

LO¹ Analyze the characteristics of an effective work group

LO² Explain various stages of group development

LO³ Explain the steps in group problem solving

Participating in
Group
Communication

> **“** *Because most of us spend some of our time interacting in groups, we need to learn how group process works and how to participate in ways that maximize group effectiveness.* **”**

Perhaps you have been part of a work group at school, at work, or in a volunteer organization. When group meetings are ineffective, it is easy to point the finger at the leader; often, however, the responsibility for the "waste of time" or other ineffectiveness lies not with one person but with the complex nature of communication in a group setting. Because most of us spend some of our time interacting in groups, we need to learn how group process works and how to participate in ways that maximize group effectiveness.

In this chapter, we examine the characteristics of effective work groups, the stages of group development, and the problem-solving process in groups.

LO¹ Characteristics of Effective Work Groups

A **work group** is a collection of three or more people who must interact and influence each other to solve problems and to accomplish a common purpose. Effective work groups have clearly defined goals, an optimum number of diverse members, cohesiveness, norms, a good working environment, and synergy. Let's consider each of these.

Clearly Defined Goals

An effective work group has clearly defined group goals. A group goal is a future state of affairs desired by enough members of the group to motivate the group to work toward its achievement (Johnson & Johnson, 2003, p. 73). Goals become clearer to members, and members become more committed to goals, when they are discussed. Through goal discussions, members are able to make sure goal statements are specific, consistent, challenging, and acceptable.

First, goal statements must be specific. A specific goal is precisely stated, measurable, and behavioral. For example, the crew at a local fast food restaurant that began with the goal of "increasing profitability of the store" made the goal more specific and meaningful by revising the goal statement to read: "During the next quarter, the second shift night crew will increase the profitability of the store by reducing food costs on their shift by

work group
a collection of three or more people who must interact and influence each other to solve problems and to accomplish a common purpose

group goal
a future state of affairs desired by enough members of the group to motivate the group to work toward its achievement

specific goal
a precisely stated, measurable, and behavioral goal

>> Reducing food costs by 1 percent by reducing the amount of food thrown away due to precooking is an example of a specific goal.

1 percent through reducing the amount of food thrown away due to precooking."

Second, goal statements must be consistent. **Consistent goals** are complementary; that is, achieving one goal does not prevent the achievement of another. To meet the consistency test, the team will have to believe that reducing the amount of precooking will not interfere with maintaining their current level of service. If they do not believe that these two goals can be accomplished simultaneously, they will need to reformulate the goals so that they are compatible.

Third, goal statements must be challenging. **Challenging goals** require hard work and team effort; they motivate group members to do things beyond what they might normally accomplish. The crew determined that a goal of 1 percent was a significant challenge.

Fourth, goal statements must be acceptable. **Acceptable goals** are seen as meaningful by team members and are goals to which members feel personally committed. People support things that they help to create. So group members who participate in setting their own goals are likely to exert high effort to see that the goals are achieved. Likewise, a group member who does not believe a goal is reasonable or just, is likely to be unmotivated or to resist working toward accom-

consistent goals
complementary goals; achieving one goal does not prevent the achievement of another

challenging goals
goals that require hard work and team effort; they motivate group members to do things beyond what they might normally accomplish

acceptable goals
goals to which members feel personally committed

homogeneous group
group in which members have a great deal of similarity

heterogeneous group
group in which various demographics, levels of knowledge, attitudes, and interests are represented

plishing the goal. Because the members of the crew helped to formulate the profitability goal, they are more likely to work to achieve it.

Optimum Number of Diverse Members

Effective groups are composed of enough diverse members to ensure good interaction but not so many members that discussion is stifled. In general, as the size of a group grows, so does the complexity it must manage. Bostrom (1970) noted that the addition of one member to a group has a geometric effect on the number of relationships. When only Jeff and Sue are in a group, there is only one relationship to manage. But when a third person, Bryan, joins them, the group now has four relationships to manage (Jeff–Sue; Bryan–Jeff; Bryan–Sue; Bryan–Sue–Jeff). As groups grow in size and complexity, the opportunities for each member to participate drop. People tend to be more satisfied in groups in which they can actively participate (Bonito, 2000). When many people cannot or will not contribute, the resulting decision is seldom a product of the group's collective thought (Beebe et al., 1994, p. 125).

So what is the right size for a group? It depends. In general, research shows that the best size for a group is the smallest number of people capable of effectively achieving the goal (Sundstrom et al., 1990). For many situations, this might mean as few as three to five people. As the size of the group increases, the time spent discussing and deciding also increases. This argues for very small groups because they will be able to make decisions more quickly. However, as the goals, problems, and issues become complex, it is unlikely that very small groups will have the diversity of information, knowledge, and skills needed to make high-quality decisions. For many situations, then, a group of five to seven or more might be desirable.

More important than having a certain number of people in a group is having the right combination of people in the group. Notice the heading of this section was "optimum number of *diverse* members." To meet this test, it is usually better to have a heterogeneous group rather than a homogeneous group. A **homogeneous group** is one in which members have a great deal of similarity. By contrast, a **heterogeneous group** is one in which various demographics, levels of knowledge, attitudes, and interests are represented. For example, a group composed of seven nurses who are all young, white females would be considered a homogeneous group; a group composed of nurses, doctors, nutritionists, and physical therapists who differ in age, race, and sex would be considered a heterogeneous group.

Effective groups are likely to be composed of people who bring different but relevant knowledge and skills into the group discussion (Valacich et al., 1994). In homogeneous groups, members are likely to know the same things, come at the problem from the same perspective, and, consequently, be likely to overlook some important information or take shortcuts in the problem-solving process. In contrast, groups composed of heterogeneous members are more likely to have diverse information, perspectives, and values, and, consequently, discuss issues more thoroughly before reaching a decision. The heterogeneous medical group described above would probably make a more comprehensive decision about a patient's care than the homogeneous group of nurses who were all similar demographically.

Cohesiveness

Effective work group are also cohesive. **Cohesiveness** is the degree of attraction members have to each other and to the group's goal. In a highly cohesive group, members genuinely like and respect each other, work cooperatively to reach the group's goals, and generally perform better than noncohesive groups (Evans & Dion, 1991). In contrast, a group that is not cohesive may have members who are indifferent toward or dislike each other, have little interest in what the group is trying to accomplish, and may even work in ways that prevent the group from being successful.

>> **When forming groups, we should give people some control over joining.**

Research (Balgopal, Ephross, & Vassil, 1986; Widmer & Williams, 1991; Wilson, 2005) has shown that several factors lead to developing cohesiveness in groups: attractiveness of the group's purpose, voluntary membership, feeling of freedom to share opinions, members reinforcing each other, and progress and celebration of accomplishments.

1. **Attractiveness of the group's purpose.** Social or community groups, for example, build cohesiveness out of friendship or devotion to service. In a decision-making group, attractiveness is likely to be related to how important the task is to members. If Daniel is part of a campus group raising money for needy children, the cohesiveness of the group will depend, in part, on how motivated the group is to complete the task.

2. **Voluntary membership.** When we are forming groups, we should give people some control over joining. Even at work, group effectiveness may be enhanced if employees have some choice regarding team projects. Likewise, Daniel's group is likely to develop cohesiveness more easily if members are volunteering rather than being required to work on a fundraising project.

   If group members are appointed, or if they have some discomfort in working together, a group may benefit from **team-building activities** designed to help the group work better together (Midura & Glover, 2005). Often, this means having the group meet someplace outside of its normal setting, where members can engage in activities designed to help them recognize each other's strengths, share in group successes, and develop rituals. As group members learn to be more comfortable with each other socially, they are also likely to become more comfortable in the group setting.

3. **Feeling of freedom to share opinions.** Feeling comfortable in disagreeing with the ideas and positions of others is an important aspect of group cohesion. If Daniel's fundraising group members

cohesiveness
the degree of attraction members have to each other and to the group's goal

team-building activities
activities designed to help the group work better together

are comfortable sharing contrasting ideas without fear of being chastised, they are likely to develop better group cohesiveness. Moreover, group members should feel free to converse about their goals very soon after the group is formed. During this discussion, individual members should be encouraged to express their ideas about group goals and to hear the ideas of others. Through this discussion process, the group can clarify goals and build group commitment.

4. **Members reinforcing each other.** A group will be more cohesive if members feel that others are listening to them and that their ideas count. Groups that provide support, encouragement, and positive feedback will become highly cohesive. No one wants to offer a suggestion in a group and have it be ignored. Even if the group decides not to pursue the idea, the careful consideration of each suggestion will send a reinforcing message that group members respect each other.

5. **Progress and celebration of accomplishments.** Groups should be encouraged to set subgoals that can be achieved early. Groups that feel good about the progress they are accomplishing develop a sense of unity. Once early subgoals are accomplished, the group can celebrate these achievements. Celebrations of early achievements cause members to more closely identify with the group and to see it as a "winner" (Renz & Greg, 2000, p. 54).

Keep in mind that the more heterogeneous the group, the more difficult it is to build cohesiveness. We know that heterogeneous groups generally arrive at better decisions, so we need to structure group conversations that can develop cohesiveness in all types of groups. This is why team-building activities, freedom to express controversial ideas, members reinforcing each other, and progress and celebration of achievements are so important with heterogeneous groups.

In addition, members should be taught to communicate in ways that foster supportive patterns of cooperative interaction. Groups become cohesive when individual members feel valued and respected. By using the skills of active listening, empathizing, describing, and collaborative conflict management, you can help heterogeneous groups become cohesive.

norms
expectations for the way group members will behave while in the group

ground rules
prescribed behaviors designed to help the group meet its goals and conduct its conversations

---

Factors in Group Cohesiveness

1. Attractiveness of the group's purpose
2. Voluntary membership
3. Feeling of freedom to share opinions
4. Members reinforcing each other
5. Progress and celebration of accomplishments

Productive Norms

Norms are expectations for the way group members will behave while in the group. Effective groups develop norms that support goal achievement (Shimanoff, 1992) and cohesiveness (Shaw, 1981). Norms begin to be developed early in the life of the group. Norms grow, change, and solidify as people get to know each other better. Group members usually comply with norms and are sanctioned by the group when they do not.

Norms can be developed through formal discussions or informal group processes (Johnson & Johnson, 2003, p. 27). Some groups choose to formulate explicit **ground rules**, prescribed behaviors

>> Most group norms, such as this group's on-time norm, will evolve informally.

©COMSTOCK PICTURES/JUPITER IMAGES

designed to help the group meet its goals and conduct its conversations. These may include sticking to the agenda, refraining from interrupting others, making brief comments rather than lengthy monologues, actively listening to others, expecting everyone to participate, focusing arguments on issues rather than personalities, and sharing decision making.

In most groups, however, norms evolve informally. When we become part of a new group, we try to act in ways that were considered appropriate in other groups in which we have participated. If the other members of our new group behave in ways that are consistent with our interpretation of the rules for behavior, an informal norm is established. For example, suppose Daniel and two other group members show up late for a meeting. If the group has already begun discussion and the latecomers are greeted with cold looks, showing that other members of this group do not abide by being late, then this group will develop an on-time norm. A group may never discuss informal norms that develop, but all veteran group members understand what they are and behave in line with the expectations of these informally established norms.

When group members violate a group norm, they are usually sanctioned. The severity of the sanction depends on the importance of the norm that was violated, the extent of the violation, and the status of the person who violated the norm. Violating a norm that is central to a group's performance or cohesiveness will generally receive a harsher sanction than will violating a norm that is less central. Minor violations of norms, or violation of a norm by a newcomer, or violations of norms that are frequently violated will generally receive more lenient sanctions. Group members who have achieved higher status in the group (for example, those with unique skills and abilities needed by the group) receive more lenient sanctions or escape sanctioning.

Some norms turn out to be counterproductive. For example, at the beginning of the first meeting of a work group, suppose a few folks cut up, tell jokes and stories, and generally ignore attempts by others to begin more serious discussion. If the group seems to encourage or does not effectively sanction this behavior, then this dallying behavior will become a group norm. As a result, the group may become so involved in these behaviors that work toward the group's goals is delayed, set aside, or perhaps even forgotten. If counterproductive behavior such as this continues for several meetings and becomes a norm, it will be very difficult to change.

What can a group member do to try to change a norm? Renz and Greg (2000) suggest that you can help your group change a counterproductive norm

{ Fast Facts—The Miracle on Ice }

At the 1980 Winter Olympics, a United States ice hockey team made up largely of collegiate and amateur players defeated the much more experienced team from the Soviet Union, and eventually went on to win the gold medal. The U.S. team's cohesiveness played a major role in their victory over a Soviet team, which had dominated international and Olympic competition.

by (1) observing the norm and its outcome, (2) describing the results of the norm to the group, and (3) soliciting opinions of other members of the group (p. 52). For instance, you might observe whether every meeting begins late, note how long dallying tends to continue, determine whether discussion is productive, and judge whether extra meetings are necessary. Then you could start the next meeting by reporting the results of your observations and asking for reaction from group members.

Although norms are important mechanisms for guiding group behavior, social norms also influence our behavior in other, less-structured group settings. Social norm theory has been used to guide recent successful alcohol, tobacco, and violence interventions on college campuses.

Synergy

The old saying "two heads are better than one" captures an important characteristic of effective groups. **Synergy** is the multiplying force created by having a common purpose and complementariness of each others' efforts; it results in a group outcome that is more than what we would expect the individuals in the group to be capable of producing (Henman, 2003). When a group has synergy, the whole is more than the sum of its parts. For instance, a synergistic symphony orchestra may be able to outplay an orchestra that has more talented members. And the sports record books are replete with "no-name teams" that have won major championships over more talented rivals. An effectively functioning group can develop a collective intelligence and a dynamic energy that translate into an outcome

synergy
a commonality of purpose and a complementariness of each other's efforts that produces a group outcome greater than an individual outcome

that exceeds what even a highly talented individual could produce. When group members bring diversity and differing perspectives to a clearly defined and accepted group goal, and they develop cohesiveness and positive norms, the group is well on its way toward achieving synergy.

Appropriate Environment

The environment for group meetings may be face-to-face, where all members come together in one physical location to make a decision or solve a problem, or it may be virtual, where people in various locations use technology to work together on a decision or problem. In either case, there are issues you need to consider in order to create an environment conducive to effective communication.

Face-to-Face Meetings

When your group meets face-to-face on an ongoing basis, it will want to choose a location that is convenient for its members, is an appropriate size for the group, has comfortable seating and temperature, and allows everyone to see and hear everyone else.

The physical setting can affect both group interaction and decision making (Figure 10.1). Seating can be too formal. When seating approximates a board of directors style, as illustrated in Figure 10.1A, where people sit indicates their status. In this style, a dominant–submissive pattern emerges that can inhibit group interaction. People who sit at the head of the table are likely to be looked to for leadership and are seen as having more influence than those members who sit on the side. People who sit across the table from each other interact with each other more frequently, but they also find themselves disagreeing with each other more often than they disagree with others at the table.

Excessively informal seating can also inhibit interaction. For instance, in Figure 10.1B, the three people sitting on the couch form their own little group; the two people seated next to each other form another group; and two members

face-to-face meeting
a meeting in which all members come together in one physical location to make a decision or solve a problem

virtual meeting
a meeting in which people in various locations use technology to work together on a decision or problem

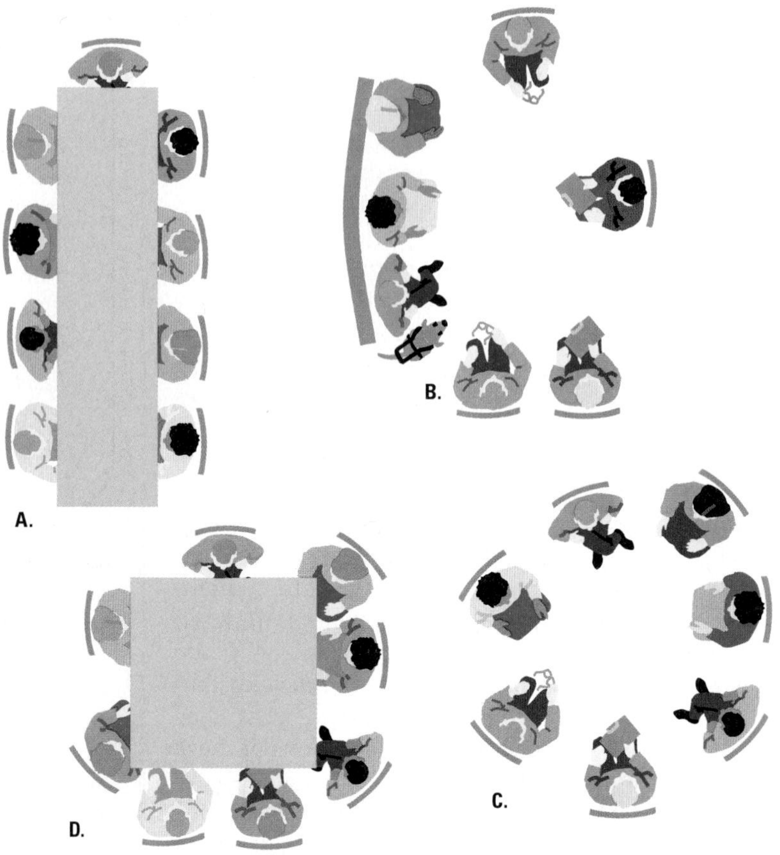

Figure 10.1

Group Seating Arrangements
Which group members do you think will be able to arrive at a decision easily? Why or why not?

have placed themselves out of the main flow. In arrangements such as these, people are more likely to communicate with the people adjacent to them than with others. In such settings, it is more difficult to make eye contact with every group member. Johnson and Johnson (2003) maintain that "easy eye contact among members enhances the frequency of interaction, friendliness, cooperation, and liking for the group and its work" (p. 171)

The circle, generally considered the ideal arrangement for group discussions and problem solving, is depicted in Figure 10.1C. Circle configurations increase participant motivation to speak because sight lines are better for everyone and everyone appears to have equal status. When the location of the group meeting does not have a round table, the group may be better off without a table or with an arrangement that approximates a circle using square tables, as shown in Figure 10.1D.

Virtual Meetings

In virtual meetings, technologies such as e-mail, teleconferencing, and videoconferencing allow members who are dispersed geographically to communicate as a group. Awareness of several issues related to virtual meetings can improve the effectiveness of your group communication in mediated formats.

In group discussions via e-mail listervs, members post comments for others to read at a later time and ideas are shared without interruption. Individual comments can be saved for everyone to read at a later point in time. Because it takes time to type comments, some discussion may be reduced in e-mail formats. However, e-mail discussions encourage equal participation and are less influenced by a member's status or dominance. They are also convenient because they allow members to participate on their own schedule and pace (Patton & Downs, 2003).

E-mail discussions are most productive when a discussion leader posts one question or decision at a time, with a deadline for response. Each person's comments should go to all members of the discussion group and a member should read all previous comments before posting a comment. The discussion leader should summarize responses or point out emerging differences of opinion periodically and then close the discussion by posting the decision reached by the deadline.

Teleconferencing is a form of meeting that allows geographically separated participants to enter a discussion in real time via speaker telephones. In a teleconference, you can hear but not see the other participants. Therefore, it is important to announce your name and location before making a comment so that listeners can recognize you. Because of the absence of nonverbal cues that signal turn-taking, you may have trouble avoiding interruptions. Announcing your name before making a remark also signals your intent to take a speaking turn. A skilled teleconference moderator can help overcome these obstacles by calling on members by name.

In videoconferencing, which is the most sophisticated of virtual meeting formats, all members of your group can see and hear all other members, even though they may be at different physical locations. Videoconferencing relies on expensive technology involving cameras, monitors, and microphones that must be available at the locations of all members, so it is usually reserved for meetings in which it is critical to approximate face-to-face interaction. Although you can see and hear other participants in videoconferences, there is no direct eye contact. Some of the nonverbal information available in face-to-face settings (such as to whom comments are directed) is not available. In addition, some people may feel self-conscious about maintaining an "on-screen image" and not react as they might in a face-to-face setting (Jones, Oyung, & Pace, 2005). But all three of these mediated forms of virtual meetings can save travel time and expense in conducting group communication when members are located around the globe. The issues of group goals, cohesiveness, and norms discussed so far apply to both virtual group discussions and face-to-face group discussions.

LO^2 Stages of Group Development

Although some groups are brought together on a one-time-only basis to make a quick decision, most work groups convene regularly to consider a variety of issues. Once assembled, these typical work groups tend to move through stages of development. Although numerous models have been proposed to describe the stages of group

{ **Fast Facts—**
The Mercury Space Project }

The Mercury Space Project ran from 1959–1963, with the purpose of putting a man in orbit around the earth. The face of the Mercury project came from the astronauts, who called themselves the Mercury 7 and put 7 at the end of the names of their spacecraft to emphasize that they were a team.

©NASA

Alan Shepard   John Glenn Jr.   Scott Carpenter   Gordo Cooper   Gus Grissom   Deke Slayton   Walter Schirra

development, Tuckman's (1965) model has been widely accepted because it identifies the central issues facing a group at each stage in its development. Tuckman named these stages forming, storming, norming, performing, and adjourning. Research by Wheelen and Hochberger (1996) has confirmed that groups can be observed moving through each of these stages. In this section, we describe each of the stages of group development and discuss the nature of communication during each phase.

Forming

Forming is the initial stage of group development during which people come to feel valued and accepted so that they identify with the group. At the beginning of any group, individual members will experience feelings of discomfort caused by the uncertainty they are facing in this new social situation.

Politeness and tentativeness on the part of members may characterize group interactions as members try to understand the task before them, become acquainted with others, understand how the group will work, and find their place in the group. During forming, there may be awkward silences because people may feel unsure about how to act. Any real disagreements between people often remain unacknowledged because members strive to be seen as flexible. During this stage, if the group has formally appointed group leaders, group members depend on them for clues as to how they should behave. Members work to fit in and to be seen as likable.

Anderson (1988) suggests that during forming, we should express positive attitudes and feelings while refraining from abrasive or disagreeable comments; we should make appropriately benign self-disclosures and wait to see if they are reciprocated; and we should try to be friendly, open, and interested in others. So active listening and empathizing skills should be used to become better acquainted with other members of the group. Members should smile, nod, and maintain good eye contact, to make conversations a bit more relaxed.

Storming

Storming is the stage of group development during which the group clarifies its goals and determines the roles each member will have in the group power structure. The stress and strain that arise when groups begin to make decisions are a natural result of the conflicting ideas, opinions, and personalities that begin to emerge during decision making. There may be underlying or expressed tension as members struggle to determine each other's status and role in the group. In the forming stage, members are concerned about fitting in, whereas in the storming stage, members are concerned about expressing their ideas and opinions and finding their place. One or more members may begin to question or challenge the formal leader's position on issues. In groups that do not have formally appointed leaders, two or more members may vie for informal leadership of the group. During this phase, the overpoliteness exhibited during forming may be replaced by snide comments, sarcastic remarks, or pointedly aggressive exchanges between some members. While storming, members may take sides, forming cliques and coalitions.

Storming, if controlled, is an important stage in a group's development. During periods of storming, the group is confronted with alternative ideas, opinions, and ways of viewing issues. Although storming will occur in all groups, some groups will manage it better than others. When storming in a group is severe, it can threaten the group's survival. When a group does not storm, it may experience **groupthink**, a deterioration of mental efficiency, reality testing, and moral judgment that results from in-group pressure (Janis, 1982, p. 9). To avoid groupthink, we should encourage constructive disagreement, self-monitor what we say to avoid name-calling and using inflammatory language, and use the active listening skills

forming
the initial stage of group development during which people come to feel valued and accepted so that they identify with the group

storming
the stage of group development during which the group clarifies its goals and determines the roles each member will have in the group power structure

groupthink
a deterioration of mental efficiency, reality testing, and moral judgment that results from in-group pressure

discussed earlier with emphasis on paraphrasing and honest questioning (Anderson, 1988).

Norming

Norming is the stage of group development during which the group solidifies its rules for behavior, especially those that relate to how conflict will be managed. As the group successfully completes a storming phase, it moves into a phase where members begin to apply more pressure on each other to conform. During this phase, the norms or standards of the group become clear. Members for the most part comply with norms, although those who have achieved higher status or power may continue to occasionally deviate from them. Members who do not comply with norms are sanctioned.

During norming, competent communicators pay attention to the norms that are developing. Then, they adapt their communication styles to the norms of the group. Members increasingly go along with stated and unstated expectations and all aspects of the group function fairly smoothly. When communicators who are monitoring norm development determine that a norm is too rigid, too elastic, or in other ways counterproductive, they initiate a group discussion about their observations. As you would expect, these conversations are best received when the person initiating them uses the skills of describing behavior, using specific and concrete language.

Performing

Performing is the stage of group development when the skills, knowledge, and abilities of all members are combined to overcome obstacles and meet goals successfully. Through each of the stages, groups are working to accomplish their goals. Once members

> Performing is the most important stage of group development. This is the stage in which members freely share information, solicit ideas from others, and work to solve problems.

have formed social bonds, settled power issues, and developed their norms, however, they "get in the groove," becoming more effective at creative problem solving and task performance. During this stage, conversations are focused on problem solving and sharing task-related information, with little energy directed to relationship building. Members who spend the group's time in chitchat not only detract from the effectiveness of the group but risk being perceived as unprepared or lazy. Performing is the most important stage of group development. This is the stage in which members freely share information, solicit ideas from others, and work to solve problems. This is the most productive stage of the group as members jointly arrive at an outcome.

Adjourning

Adjourning is the stage of group development in which members assign meaning to what they have done and determine how to end or maintain interpersonal relations they have developed. Some groups are brought together for a finite time period, whereas for other groups, work is continuous. Regardless of whether a group is short term or ongoing, all groups experience endings. A short-term project team will face adjourning when it has completed its work within the time period specified for its existence.

Ongoing groups also experience endings. When the team has reached a particular goal, finished a specific project, or lost members to reassignments or resignations, it will confront the same developmental challenges faced by short-term groups in this phase.

Keyton's (1993) study of the adjourning phase of group development points to two challenges that groups face during this phase. First, groups need to construct meaning from their shared experience by evaluating and reflecting on the experience. They may discuss what led to their successes or failures, recall events and share memories of stressful times, and celebrate accomplishments. Second, members will need to find ways to sever or maintain interpersonal relationships that have developed during the

norming
the stage of group development during which the group solidifies its rules for behavior, especially those that relate to how conflict will be managed

performing
the stage of group development when the skills, knowledge, and abilities of all members are combined to overcome obstacles and meet goals successfully

adjourning
the stage of group development in which members assign meaning to what they have done and determine how to end or maintain interpersonal relations they have developed

group's life together. During this phase, people in the group may explore ways to maintain contact with those they have particularly enjoyed working with. They may continue the relationship on a purely social level or plan to undertake additional work together.

Keyton thinks it is especially important for groups to have a termination ritual, which can range from an informal debriefing session to formalized celebrations with group members and their friends, family, and colleagues. Whatever form the ritual takes, Keyton believes such a ritual "affects how they [members] will interpret what they have experienced and what expectations they will take with them to similar situations" (p. 98).

The phases of group development explain the work that groups must do to aid the social and emotional development of the group. How the group develops through these phases is important to how effectively it works. But achieving group goals is also the result of how well the group uses the problem-solving process. We now turn our attention to understanding the problem-solving process and the communication skills that provide the focus for the performing stage of group development.

LO^3 Problem Solving in Groups

Research shows that groups follow many different approaches to problem solving. Some groups move linearly through a series of steps to reach consensus, and some move in a spiral pattern in which they refine, accept, reject, modify, and combine ideas as they go along. Whether groups move in something approximating an orderly pattern or go in fits and starts, those groups that arrive at high-quality decisions are likely to accomplish certain tasks during their deliberations. These tasks include identifying a specific problem, analyzing the problem, arriving at criteria that an effective solution must meet, identifying possible alternative solutions to the problem, comparing the alternatives to the criteria, and determining the best solution or combination of solutions.

Defining the Problem

Much wheel spinning takes place during the early stages of group discussion because the specific goal may not be understood by all group members. It is the duty of the person, agency, or parent group that forms a particular work group to give the group a charge, such as "work out a new way of selecting peo-

Much wheel spinning takes place during the early stages of group discussion.

ple for merit pay increases." However, rarely will the charge be stated in such a way that the group does not need to do some clarification of its own. Even when the charge seems clear, effective groups will want to make sure they are focusing on the real problem and not just symptoms of the problem. Let's look again at the charge "work out a new way of selecting people for merit pay increases." What is wrong with this as a problem definition? "Work out a new way of selecting" is too general to be meaningful. A clearer question would be "What are the most important criteria for selecting people for merit pay increases?"

Even when a group is given a well-defined charge, it will need to gather information before it can accurately define the specific problem. Accurately defining the problem requires the group to understand the background, history, and status of the problem. This means collecting and understanding a variety of information. Some groups, however, rush through defining the problem and end up working to solve symptoms, not root causes.

It helps if the group formally states the problem in writing. This written statement can help the group avoid being sidetracked by tangential or unrelated issues. Unless the group can agree on a formal definition of the problem, there is little likelihood of the group's being able to work together toward a solution.

Effective problem definitions have these four characteristics.

1. **They are stated as questions.** Problem-solving groups begin from the assumption that solutions are not yet known, so problems should be stated as questions to be answered. For example, the merit pay committee might define the problem it will solve as follows: What are the most important criteria for determining merit pay increases? Phrasing the group's problem as a question furthers the spirit of inquiry.
2. **They contain only one central idea.** If the charge includes two questions—"Should the college abolish its foreign language and physical education requirements?"—the group should

break it down into two separate questions: Should the college abolish its foreign language requirement? Should the college abolish its physical education requirement?

3. **They use specific and precise language to describe the problem.** For instance, the problem definition "What should the department do about courses that aren't getting the job done?" may be well intentioned, and participants may have at least some idea about their goal, but such vague wording as "getting the job done" can lead to problems later. Notice how this revision makes the intent much clearer: "What should the department do about courses that receive low scores on student evaluations?"

4. **They can be identified as a question of fact, value, or policy.** How we organize our problem-solving discussion will depend on the kind of question we are addressing: a question of fact, value, or policy.

Questions of fact are concerned with discovering what is true or to what extent something is true. Implied in such questions is the possibility of determining truth through the process of examining facts by way of directly observed, spoken, or recorded evidence. For instance, "Did Smith steal equipment from the warehouse?" "Did Mary's sales report follow the written guidelines for sales reports?" and "Do the data from our experiment support our hypothesis?" are all questions of fact. The group will discuss the validity of the evidence it has to determine what is true.

Questions of value concern subjective judgments of what is right, moral, good, or just. Questions of value can be recognized because they often contain evaluative words such as *good, reliable, effective,* or *worthy.* For instance, the program development team for a TV sitcom aimed at young teens may discuss: "Is the level of violence in the scripts we have developed appropriate for programs designed to appeal to children?" or "Is the proposed series of ads too sexually provocative?" Although we can establish criteria for "too sexually provocative" and "effectively" and measure material against those criteria, the criteria we choose and the evidence we accept depend on our judgment. A different group of people using different values might come to a different decision.

Questions of policy concern what courses of action should be taken or what rules should be adopted to solve a problem. "Should the university offer online degrees?" and "Where should the new landfill be built?" are both questions of policy. The inclusion of the word *should* in questions of

Effective problem definitions:

1. are stated as questions.
2. contain only one central idea.
3. use specific and precise language to describe the problem.
4. can be identified as a question of fact, value, or policy.

policy makes them the easiest to recognize and the easiest to phrase of all problem statements.

Analyzing the Problem

Analysis of a problem entails finding out as much as possible about the problem and determining the criteria that must be met to find an acceptable solution. Three types of information can be helpful in analyzing problems. Most groups begin by sharing the information individual members have acquired through their experience. This is a good starting place, but groups that limit their information gathering to the existing knowledge of members often make decisions based on incomplete or faulty information.

A second source of information that should be examined includes published materials available through libraries, electronic databases, and the Internet. From these sources, a group can access information about the problem that has been collected, analyzed, and interpreted by others. Just because information is published, however, does not mean that it is accurate or valid. Accuracy and validity are especially an issue when the information comes from an Internet source, and the group will also have to evaluate the relevance and usefulness of the information.

A third source of information about a problem can be gathered from other people. At times, the group may want to interview experts for their ideas about a problem or conduct a survey to gather information from a particular target group.

Once group members have gathered information, it must be shared with other members. It is important for group members to share

questions of fact questions concerned with discovering what is true or to what extent something is true

questions of value questions that concern subjective judgments of what is right, moral, good, or just

questions of policy questions that concern what courses of action should be taken or what rules should be adopted to solve a problem

Questions are a key element of defining problems.

>>One source of information includes published materials that can be found available through libraries, electronic databases, and the Internet.

new information to fulfill the ethical responsibility that comes with group discussion. A study by Dennis (1996) shows that groups tend to spend more time discussing information common to group members if those with information don't work to get the information heard. The tendency to discuss common information while ignoring unique information leads to less effective decisions. To overcome this, groups need to ask each member to discuss the information he or she has uncovered that seems to contradict his or her personal beliefs about the issue. When addressing a complex issue, separate information sharing from decision making by holding separate meetings spaced far enough apart to enable members to think through their information.

Determining Solution Criteria

Once a group understands the nature of the problem, it is in a position to determine what tests a solution must pass to solve the problem. The criteria become the decisive factors in determining whether a particular solution will solve the problem. The criteria that are selected should be ones that the information gathered has suggested are critical to successfully solving the problem.

The criteria that the group decides on will be used to screen alternative solutions. Solutions that do not meet the test of all criteria are eliminated from further consideration. For example, a local citizens' committee is charged with selecting a site for a new county jail. The group arrives at the following phrasing for the problem: "Where should the new jail be located?" After the group agrees on this wording, they can then ask the question, "What are the criteria for a good site for a new jail?"

In that discussion, suppose members contribute information related to the county's budget, the need for inmates to maintain family contact, concerns about proximity to schools

brainstorming
an uncritical, nonevaluative process of generating associated ideas

and parks, and space needs. After considering this kind of information, the group might then select the following criteria for selecting a site:

- Maximum cost of $1 million for purchasing the land.
- A location no more than three blocks from public transportation.
- A location that is one mile or more from any school, day care center, playground, or youth center.
- A lot size of at least 10 acres.

Kathryn Young and her colleagues (2000) suggest that when groups discuss and decide on criteria before they think about specific solutions, they increase their ability to avoid becoming polarized and are more likely to come to a decision that all members can accept.

Identifying Possible Solutions

For most policy questions, many solutions are possible. The trick is to tap the creative thinking of group members so that many ideas are generated. At this stage of discussion, the goal is not to worry about whether a particular solution fits all the criteria, but to come up with a large list of ideas.

One way to identify potential solutions is to brainstorm for ideas. **Brainstorming** is an uncritical, nonevaluative process of generating associated ideas. It involves verbalizing your ideas as they come to mind, without stopping to evaluate their merits. Members are encouraged, however, to build on the ideas presented by others. In a 10- or 15-minute brainstorming session, a group may come up with 20 or more possible solutions, depending on the nature of the problem. For instance, the group working on the jail site question might mention 10 or more in just a few minutes of brainstorming, such as sites that individual members have thought of or have heard others mention.

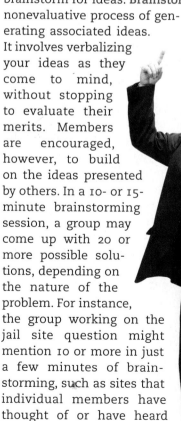

Evaluating Solutions

Once the group has a list of possible solutions, it needs to compare each solution alternative to the criteria that it developed. During this phase, the group must determine whether each criterion is equally important or whether certain criteria should be given more weight in evaluating alternative solutions. Whether a group weighs certain criteria more heavily or not, it should use a process that ensures that each alternative solution is thoroughly assessed against all criteria.

Research by Randy Hirokawa (1987) confirmed that high-quality decisions are made by groups that are "careful, thoughtful, and systematic" in evaluating their options (p. 10). In another study, Hirokawa (1988) noted that it is common for groups to begin by eliminating solutions that clearly do not meet important criteria and then to compare the positive features of solutions that remain.

Deciding

A group brought together for problem solving may or may not be responsible for making the actual decision, but it is responsible for presenting its recommendation. Decision making is the process of choosing among alternatives. The following five methods differ in the extent to which they require all members to agree with the decision and the amount of time it takes to reach a decision.

The Expert Opinion Method

Once the group has eliminated alternatives that do not meet the criteria, the group asks the member with the most expertise to select the final choice. This method is quick, and it is useful when one member is much more knowledgeable about the issues or has a greater stake in implementation of the decision.

The Average Group Opinion Method

When using this approach, each member of the group ranks the alternatives that meet all the crite-ria. These rankings are then averaged, and the alternative receiving the highest average ranking becomes the choice. This method is useful for routine decisions or when a decision needs to be made quickly. It can also be used as an intermediate straw poll to enable the group to eliminate low-scoring alternatives before moving to a different process for making the final decision.

The Majority Rule Method

When using this method, the group votes on each alternative, and the one that receives the majority of votes (50 percent +1) is selected. Although this method is considered democratic, it can create problems for implementation. If the majority voting for an alternative is slight, there may be nearly as many members who do not support the choice as there are those that do. If these minority members object strongly to the choice, they may sabotage implementation of the solution either through active or passive means.

The Unanimous Decision Method

In this method, the group must continue deliberation until every member of the group believes the same solution is the best. As you would expect, it is very difficult to arrive at truly unanimous decisions, and to do so takes a lot of time. When a group reaches unanimity, however, it can expect that each member of the group will be fully committed to selling the decision to others and to helping implement the decision.

The Consensus Method

This method is an alternative to the unanimous decision method. In consensus, the group continues deliberation until all members of the group find an acceptable variation—one they can support and are committed to helping implement. Members of a consensus group may believe that there is a better solution than the one that has been chosen, but they feel they can support and help implement the one they have agreed to. Although easier to achieve than reaching unanimity, arriving at consensus is still difficult. Although the majority rule method is widely used, selecting the consensus method is a wise investment if the group needs everyone's support to implement the decision successfully.

decision making
the process of choosing among alternatives

Methods for Decision Making

1. Expert opinion method
2. Average group opinion method
3. Majority rule method
4. Unanimous decision method
5. Consensus method

Member Roles and Leadership in Groups

Learning Outcomes

LO¹ Discuss the roles of members in groups

LO² Discuss member responsibilities in group meetings

LO³ Examine the importance of leadership in groups

LO⁴ Describe leadership responsibilities in group meetings

LO⁵ Examine the process for evaluating group effectiveness

> **"** *The roles that group members play depend on their personalities and the requirements or needs of the group.* **"**

If you listen closely to group interactions, you may typically hear the members of the group not only discussing the topic at hand, but also acting in the ways expected of them by others in the group. Our goal in this chapter is to explain how members of groups take on specific roles that help or detract from the effectiveness of the group. We describe the types of roles members assume, and the responsibilities that group members have during meetings. Then we discuss group leadership, including understanding its functions, identifying several leadership roles, describing how members gain and maintain leadership, and the responsibilities of meeting leaders. Finally, we discuss ways to evaluate group effectiveness.

What do you think?

I'd rather lead the group than be told what to do.

Strongly Disagree						Strongly Agree
1	2	3	4	5	6	7

LO¹ Members' Roles

A **role** is a specific pattern of behavior that one group member performs based on the expectations of other members. The roles that group members play depend on their personalities and the requirements or needs of the group. Three common types of roles are task-related, maintenance, and self-centered roles.

Task-Related Roles

Task-related roles require specific patterns of behavior that directly help the group accomplish its goals. Task roles include initiator, information or opinion giver, information or opinion seeker, analyzer, and orienter.

Initiator

You play the initiator role when your comment gets the discussion started or moves it in a new direction. You would be performing the initiating role by suggesting, "Let's begin by looking at the current problems in our inventory control system." Or by saying, "Perhaps we should move on to a discussion of quality concerns we have related to our vendors and suppliers."

role
a specific pattern of behavior that one group member performs based on the expectations of other members

task-related roles
specific patterns of behavior that directly help the group accomplish its goals

initiator
a group member who gets the discussion started or moves it in a new direction

Information or Opinion Giver

You play the information or (opinion) giver role when you provide content for the discussion. People who perform these roles well are those who have expertise or who are well informed on the content of the task and share what they know with the group. An example of this role performance is "In my experience, telling a customer that it's against company policy just makes them angrier, so I don't think that is what we want to say in this situation."

Information or Opinion Seeker

You play the information or (opinion) seeker role when you ask questions that probe others for their ideas and opinions. Typical comments by those performing these roles include remarks such as, "Before going further, what information do we have about how raising dues is likely to affect membership?" or, "How do members of the group feel about this idea?"

Analyzer

In the analyzer role, you probe the content, reasoning, and evidence of members during discussion. To make good decisions, group members must critically examine ideas or suggestions provided by members and also the facts and data gathered by the group. A member would be performing this role by saying, "We need to be sure the numbers we have here on annual enrollment in our program are consistent with monthly totals."

information (opinion) giver
a group member who provides content for the discussion

information (opinion) seeker
a group member who probes others for their factual ideas and opinions

analyzer
a group member who probes the content, reasoning, and evidence of members during discussion

orienter
a group member who indicates to the group that it is off track or summarizes points of agreement and disagreement among members

maintenance roles
patterns of behavior that help the group develop and maintain good member relationships, group cohesiveness, and effective levels of conflict

gatekeeper
a group member who ensures that everyone has an opportunity to speak and be heard

Orienter

The orienter indicates to the group that it is off track, and summarizes points of agreement and disagreement among members. It's easy for a group to get so involved in a discussion that it loses track of the "big picture" or goes off on many tangents and wastes time with irrelevant issues. Thus, it is important that someone in the group monitors the group process. A member would be performing an ori-

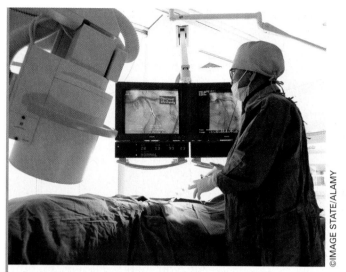

>> It's important to have someone in the group monitor the group process, determining how well the group is performing and whether it is staying on track or not.

enting role by making a comment such as, "We might want to finish our listing of fund-raising sources before we move to talking about hiring a fund-raising consultant," or "We seem to be coming back again and again to the basic disagreement between having customer support functions at each location or consolidating them centrally. Is that the point we're stuck on right now?"

Maintenance Roles

The Gatekeeper

Maintenance roles require specific patterns of behavior that help the group develop and maintain good member relationships, group cohesiveness, and effective levels of conflict. Members who play maintenance roles are likely to be gatekeepers, encouragers, and harmonizers.

Gatekeeper

As the gatekeeper, you ensure that everyone has an opportunity to speak and be heard. In some group discussions, certain people may talk more than their fair share while others remain silent, contributing little or nothing. By performing the gatekeeping role, you help to create more balanced participation among members so that the group can benefit from a variety of viewpoints and information sources. An example of gatekeeping is: "Let me interrupt you, Doug. We haven't heard from Juanita, and she seems to have something she wants to say."

Encourager

You are the encourager when your messages provide support for the contributions of other team members. Participants in a group discussion need to have their ideas acknowledged and supported from time to time. Otherwise, they are unsure if they are being heard and their ideas are being taken seriously. Examples of encouraging include: "That was a really good suggestion that Kent just made because it deals exactly with the problem we have in meeting client specifications." Or, "I think we should keep in mind Miranda's point about maintaining requirements until the next quarter. She made some good observations about the dangers of moving too quickly."

Harmonizer

You act as the harmonizer when you help the group relieve tension and manage conflict. It is inevitable that team decision making will become stressful at times, and conflicts may emerge. A member who acts as a harmonizer may temporarily relieve the tension by saying something witty or may help the group effectively deal with an emerging conflict. Examples of harmonizing behavior include: "The task of planning this product launch reminds me of dealing with Godzilla. Anyone see that movie?" Or, "We seem to be at odds around the issue of partnering with other schools. It seems that Elana and Nils strongly represent alternate perspectives. Before we get too polarized around these two options, maybe we should look at a range of possibilities."

Self-Centered Roles

Self-centered roles reflect specific patterns of behavior that focus attention on individuals' needs and goals at the expense of the group. Task-related and maintenance roles must be played for groups to be effective, but self-centered roles detract from group effectiveness. Members who play self-centered roles are likely to be aggressors, jokers, withdrawers, or blockers.

Aggressors

Aggressors seek to enhance their own status by criticizing almost everything or blaming others when things get rough and by deflating the ego or status of others. Aggressors should be confronted and encouraged to assume a more positive role. They should be asked if they are aware of their actions and the effect their behavior is having on the group.

Jokers

Jokers attempt to draw attention to themselves by clowning, mimicking, or generally making a joke of everything. Unlike tension relievers, the joker is not focused on helping the group relieve stress or tension. Rather, a joker disrupts work when the group is trying to focus on the task. Jokers should also be confronted; they should be encouraged to use their abilities when the group needs a break, but to refrain from disrupting the group when it is being productive.

Withdrawers

Withdrawers seek to meet their own goals at the expense of group goals by not participating in the discussion or the work of the group. Sometimes, withdrawers play their role by physically missing meetings or not participating in virtual meetings. At other

encourager
a group member who provides support for the contributions of other team members

harmonizer
a group member who helps the group relieve tension and manage conflict

self-centered roles
patterns of behavior that focus attention on individuals' needs and goals at the expense of the group

aggressor
a group member who seeks to enhance his or her own status by criticizing almost everything or blaming others when things get rough and by deflating the ego or status of others

joker
a group member who attempts to draw attention to himself or herself by clowning, mimicking, or generally making a joke of everything

withdrawer
a group member who meets his or her own goals at the expense of group goals by not participating in the discussion or the work of the group

times, withdrawers are present but remain silent in discussion or refuse to take responsibility for doing work. When a person has assumed this role, the group needs to find out why the person is choosing not to participate and find ways to get the member either involved in the group or removed from the group.

Blockers

Blockers routinely reject others' views and stubbornly disagree with emerging group decisions. They may hold out as a lone voice refusing to go along with the rest of the group. They may attempt to sabotage a group decision on which they do not agree. If a member has had ample opportunity to express his or her views and the rest of the group has genuinely listened to and considered those views, then the group must proceed without the blocker. The group should acknowledge and respect a member's right to disagree, but should assert the group's right to proceed with its work.

> WE CAN APPLY TWO NORMS AS GUIDELINES FOR EFFECTIVE GROUP FUNCTIONING: (1) APPROXIMATELY HALF OF ALL DISCUSSION TIME SHOULD BE DEVOTED TO INFORMATION SHARING, AND (2) GROUP AGREEMENT TIME SHOULD FAR OUTWEIGH GROUP DISAGREEMENT TIME.

Normal Distribution of Roles

What proportion of time in a "normal" group should be devoted to the various roles described in this section? According to Robert Bales (1971), a leading researcher in group interaction processes, 40 to 60 percent of discussion time is spent giving and asking for information and opinion; 8 to 15 percent of discussion time is spent on disagreement, tension, or unfriendliness; and 16 to 26 percent of discussion time is characterized by agreement or friendliness (positive maintenance functions). We can apply two norms as guidelines for effective group functioning: (1) approxi-

blocker
a group member who routinely rejects others' views and stubbornly disagrees with emerging group decisions

mately half of all discussion time should be devoted to information sharing, and (2) group agreement time should far outweigh group disagreement time.

LO² Member Responsibilities in Group Meetings

Although members specialize in particular roles during group meetings, members of effective groups also assume common responsibilities for making their meetings successful. Here are some guidelines to help group members prepare for, participate in, and follow up on a meeting in order to increase its effectiveness.

Preparing

Too often, people think of meetings as a "happening" that requires attendance but no particular preparation. People often arrive at a meeting unprepared, even though they are carrying packets of material that they received before the meeting. The reality is that meetings should not be treated as impromptu events, but as carefully planned interactions that pool information from well-prepared individuals. Here are some important steps to take before attending a meeting.

1. **Study the agenda.** Consider the purpose of the meeting and determine what you need to do to be prepared. The agenda is an outline for your preparation.
2. **Study the minutes.** If this is one in a series of meetings, study the minutes and your own notes from the previous meetings. Because each meeting is not a separate event, what happened at one meeting should provide the basis for preparation for the next meeting.
3. **Prepare for your contributions.** Read the material distributed before the meeting and do your own research to become better informed about items on the agenda. If no material is provided, you should identify the issues and learn what you

Preparing for Meetings

1. Study the agenda.
2. Study the minutes.
3. Prepare for your contributions.
4. Prepare to play a major role.
5. List questions.

need to know to be a productive member of the group. Bring any materials you have uncovered that will help the group accomplish the agenda. If appropriate, discuss the agenda with others who will not be attending the meeting and solicit their ideas concerning issues to be discussed in the meeting.

4. **Prepare to play a major role.** Consider which roles you are assigned or which you are interested in playing. What do you need to do to play those roles to the best of your ability?

5. **List questions.** Make a list of questions related to agenda items that you would like to have answered during the meeting.

Participating

Be involved in the meeting with the expectation that you will be a full participant. If there are five people in the group, all five should be participating.

1. **Listen attentively.** Concentrate on what others are saying so that you can use your material to complement, supplement, or counter what has been presented.

2. **Stay focused.** In a group setting, it is easy to get the discussion going in nonproductive directions. Keep your comments focused on the specific agenda item under discussion. If others have gotten off the subject, do what you can to get people back on track.

3. **Ask questions.** "Honest" questions that have answers you do not already know help to stimulate discussion and build ideas.

4. **Take notes.** Even if someone else is responsible for providing the official minutes, you will need notes that help you follow the line of development. Also, these notes will help you remember what has been said and any responsibilities you have agreed to take on.

5. **Play devil's advocate.** When you think an idea has not been fully discussed or tested, be willing to voice disagreement or encourage further discussion.

6. **Monitor your contributions.** Especially when people are well prepared, they have a tendency to dominate discussion. Make sure that you are neither dominating the discussion nor abdicating your responsibility to share insights and opinions.

Boring presentations aren't always the reason that meetings go poorly. Group members share a common responsibility for making sure meetings are successful.

©BIG CHEESE PHOTO/JUPITER IMAGES

Following Up

When meetings end, too often people leave and forget about what took place until the next meeting. But what happens in one meeting provides a basis for what happens in the next; be prepared to move forward at the next meeting.

1. **Review and summarize your notes.** Try to do this shortly after the meeting has concluded, while ideas are still fresh in your mind. Make notes of what needs to be discussed next time.
2. **Evaluate your effectiveness.** How effective were you in helping the group move toward achieving its goals? Where were you strong? Where were you weak? What should you do next time that you did not do in this meeting?
3. **Review decisions.** Make note of what your role was in making decisions. Did you do all that you could have done?
4. **Communicate progress.** Inform others who need to know about information conveyed and decisions that were made in the meeting.
5. **Follow up.** Make sure you complete all assignments you received in the meeting.
6. **Review minutes.** Compare the official minutes of the meeting to your own notes, and report any significant discrepancies that you find.

Meeting Follow-Up

1. Review and summarize your notes.
2. Evaluate your effectiveness.
3. Review decisions.
4. Communicate progress.
5. Follow up.
6. Review minutes.

LO^3 Leadership

Although performance of all task, maintenance, and procedural roles helps groups to accomplish their goals, good leadership is also necessary to accomplish group goals. Scholars have offered numerous definitions of leadership, but common to most definitions is the notion that leadership is a process of influencing members to accomplish group goals (Shaw, 1981, p. 317). In this section, we will discuss various perspectives of leadership, types of leaders, and ways of becoming informal leaders.

leadership
a process of influencing members to accomplish group goals

Perspectives of Leadership

There are various ways to think about leadership. Each perspective focuses on different aspects of leadership, but taken together, these perspectives provide insight into characteristics and behaviors that can help you become an effective leader. The various perspectives emphasize different aspects such as leadership traits, situations, functions, and transformations.

Leadership Traits

This approach examines personality characteristics or traits that are associated with effective leaders. It is believed that certain leadership traits or abilities can reside within a person and are universal and constant. Some studies have shown that leaders typically possess achievement orientation, adaptability, energy, responsibility, self-confidence, intelligence, verbal communication ability, sociability, persistence, and innovativeness (Bass, 1981; Baker, 1990; Stogdill, 1981). To be an effective leader, you might think about some of the leadership traits you possess and be sure to demonstrate them in group decision-making situations.

Situational Leadership

This approach says that leadership depends on the situation. Unlike the trait approach, this view says there is no one style of effective leadership. Rather, effective leadership is a match between what a situation calls for and how a person behaves. Some situations, like an emergency, may call for a strong, task-oriented leader to be very directive and take charge. Another situation, like a decision-making team of very technically skilled people, may call for a nondirective leader who emphasizes maintenance behaviors and a sharing of information. To employ situational leadership, it is important to analyze what behaviors are needed in a group discussion, to employ those behaviors, and to monitor outcomes to see if alternative behaviors might be demonstrated.

Functional Leadership

The functional perspective suggests that leadership involves acting in a way that helps the group achieve its goals. It might mean that the leader performs certain task or maintenance roles that are not being handled by other members. Or it may involve the leader performing separate functions such as preparing the agenda, scheduling meetings, making assignments, and distributing minutes. Later in this chapter, we will discuss leader roles before, during, and after group meetings. As a functional leader, you will pay close attention to what group roles are

How Members Gain and Maintain Informal Leadership

According to research by Ernest Bormann (1990), leaders emerge through a two-step elimination process. During the first step of the process, members form crude impressions about each other based on early interactions. During this phase, members who do not demonstrate the commitment or skillfulness necessary to fulfill leadership roles are eliminated. Group members less likely to emerge as leaders include those who do not participate (either due to shyness or indifference); those who are overly strong and bossy in their opinions and positions; those who are perceived to be uninformed, less intelligent, or unskilled; and those with irritating interpersonal styles.

{ Fast Facts—
Martin Luther King Jr. }

Martin Luther King Jr. was a famous leader during the civil rights movement in the late 1950s and into the 1960s. King led the 1955–56 bus boycott in Montgomery, Alabama, helped bring together the Southern Christian Leadership Conference in 1957, and played a major role in the 1963 March on Washington, in which he gave his famous "I Have a Dream" speech. Can you name any other leaders who might be considered transformational? What leadership characteristics did they exhibit?

During the second phase, those who are still acceptable to the group may vie for leadership. Sometimes one contender will become an informal leader because the group faces a crisis that this member recognizes and is better able to help the group remedy than others are. At other times, a contender may become an informal leader because one or more members of the group have come to trust this person and openly support that person as a leader.

In some groups, most members will eventually recognize one or more informal leaders. For example, one leader might be particularly attuned to group relationships and may help to keep conflict at healthy levels. The other leader may be skilled at keeping the group on track and moving through the agenda during meetings. Students are often interested in how they can show leadership in a group. Because leadership is demonstrated through communication behaviors, following these recommendations can help you emerge as a leader.

needed for task accomplishment and be sure to perform many of those functions.

Transformational Leadership

This approach emphasizes being a visionary, helping the group to set goals and motivating, if not inspiring, the group to achieve its goals (Wilson, 2005). Transformational leaders are creative, charismatic, and inspire others (Barge, 1994). Famous leaders such as Gandhi or Martin Luther King would be considered transformational leaders. To engage in this leadership approach, you will want to focus on the big picture, help the group to see things in a novel way, and energetically promote the group's goals.

Types of Leaders

A group will often have more than one leader. Many groups have a designated formal leader, an assigned, appointed, or elected leader who is given legitimate power to influence others. During its work life, a group may have only one formal leader, but several people may play leadership roles. Informal leaders are members of the group whose authority to influence stems from the power they gain through their interactions in the group. Informal leaders do not have legitimate power; rather, their influence comes from their expertise or the extent that other group members like and respect them.

1. **Actively participate in discussions.** When members do not participate, others may view them as disinterested or uninformed. Indicate your interest and commitment to the group by participating in the group's discussions.

formal leader
an assigned, appointed, or elected leader who is given legitimate power to influence others

informal leaders
members of the group whose authority to influence stems from the power they gain through their interactions in the group

2. **Come to group meetings prepared.** Uninformed members rarely achieve leadership, whereas those who demonstrate expertise often emerge as leaders.

3. **Actively listen to the ideas and opinions of others.** Because leadership requires analyzing what a group needs, the leader must understand the ideas and needs of members. When you actively listen, you also demonstrate your willingness to consider a point of view different from your own.

4. **Avoid stating overly strong opinions.** When other members of the group perceive that someone is strongly opinionated or inflexible, they are less likely to accept that person as a leader.

5. **Stimulate creative and critical thinking.** When members bring original ideas and insights to a group or when they help the group to examine reasoning and evidence before making decisions, they increase their likelihood of emerging as leaders.

6. **Actively manage meaning.** People who offer vision or a perspective on the task at hand will often emerge as a leader. If you have a mental map or framework that can move the group to see things a certain way, offer it.

Gender and Leadership

In her book on communication, gender, and culture, Julia Wood (2007) explains that leadership, especially in workplaces, is often linked with stereotypically masculine styles of communicating, including independence, competitiveness, assertiveness, and confidence rather than stereotypically feminine styles of communication such as cooperation, collaboration, attentiveness, supportiveness, inclusion, and deference. If masculine behaviors are equated with leadership, then women who communicate in more feminine ways may not be recognized as leaders. Yet, research does not support the position that only masculine styles of communicating contribute to effective leadership. Effective leadership depends on both the task-oriented behaviors associated with masculinity and the maintenance or people-related behaviors associated with femininity. Some situations call for a directive, take-charge style of leadership, while other situations call for cooperative leadership, which motivates and empowers others. A good leader should be able to demonstrate a full range of behaviors (Claes, 2002).

Another complicating factor of gendered leadership is the persistent research finding that leadership behaviors are evaluated differently based on the sex of the person using the behavior (Valian, 1998; Rhode, 2003). The same behavior may be perceived differently, depending on whether it is performed by a woman or a man. For example, a group member says, "I think we are repeating the same points here. Let's move on to the next agenda item." If the speaker is a woman, the comment may be seen as bossy or dominating. If a man makes the same comment, he may be seen as helpful and skilled in task-oriented roles. Because of gender expectations that women should be friendly, accommodating, and supportive, women who do not behave this way may be perceived negatively. Ironically, though, because assertive, directive, and competitive behaviors are associated with masculinity, sometimes when women use these behaviors, they are judged as behaving in too masculine a fashion. Similarly, if a man reacts emotionally in a leadership role, he may be perceived as weak or lacking credibility rather than being valued for an honest reaction. An emotional reaction from a female leader would likely be regarded as appropriate or typical.

So leaders should be aware that their behaviors will be judged, in part, through a gendered lens. This knowledge may help in understanding why group members sometimes react to leaders in the ways that they do. Some flexibility in communicating in both stereotypically masculine and feminine ways is necessary for all leaders.

> Leadership behaviors are evaluated differently based on the sex of the person using the behavior.

LO⁴ Leading Group Meetings

In addition to performing task and maintenance roles in a decision-making meeting, there are duties to be completed before the meeting begins. By performing these jobs before leading a meeting, you can make sure that meeting time is spent productively and little time is wasted. When running a meeting, you should complete these five tasks.

Leadership Responsibilities Before the Meeting

1. Define and communicate the meeting purpose.
2. List specific outcomes that should be produced from the meeting.
3. Communicate a starting and ending time for the meeting and stick to it.
4. Send out a detailed agenda.
5. Make physical or technology arrangements.

Before the Meeting

1. **Define and communicate the meeting purpose.** It can be frustrating to be expected to attend a meeting for which you do not know the purpose. Participants in a meeting can prepare beforehand if they know the specific purpose of the meeting. They can also bring necessary materials to the meeting. For example, if the upcoming meeting of teachers involves curriculum planning, the purpose should be defined even more clearly. The memo announcing the meeting might say: "We will examine our existing curriculum goals and course topics as they relate to state curriculum requirements in the area of science."

2. **List specific outcomes that should be produced from the meeting.** Even with a clearly stated meeting goal, participants may not know what tasks should be accomplished or what decisions should be made during the meeting. Listing specific outcomes keeps the meeting focused on clear goals and serves to keep the group on track. For example, the meeting leader might specify, "By the end of the meeting we should have a written statement of eleventh- and twelfth-grade science goals that meet state requirements."

3. **Communicate a starting and ending time for the meeting and stick to it.** To use time efficiently and to be fair to those members who arrive on time, meetings should begin promptly. By waiting for latecomers, meeting leaders enable members to be late in the future because they know that the meeting will be delayed until everyone arrives. Likewise, in the workplace, people have very busy schedules and need to know when a meeting will end. The meeting leader should closely monitor time during the meeting to make sure it ends on time.

4. **Send out a detailed agenda.** The agenda should include the date, time, and location of the meeting, and the topics to be discussed, with an approximate amount of time allocated to each agenda item; see Figure 11.1. This schedule of topics and times will allow the discussion to proceed efficiently and will keep the group discussion focused on concrete items. This agenda is useful also for

> > Meetings where the purpose is not well defined can be frustrating. Do you think the people in this picture have a good idea of their meeting's purpose?

Figure 11.1

Agenda for Internet Course Committee

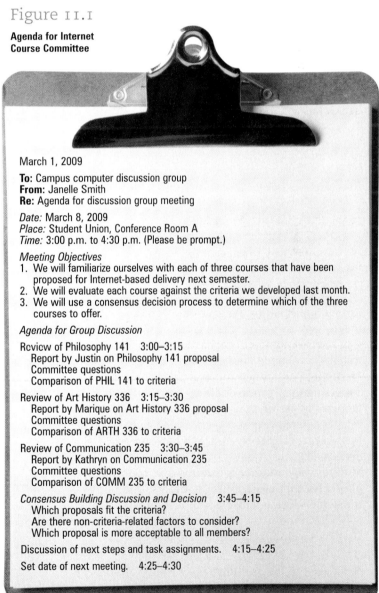

March 1, 2009

To: Campus computer discussion group
From: Janelle Smith
Re: Agenda for discussion group meeting

Date: March 8, 2009
Place: Student Union, Conference Room A
Time: 3:00 p.m. to 4:30 p.m. (Please be prompt.)

Meeting Objectives
1. We will familiarize ourselves with each of three courses that have been proposed for Internet-based delivery next semester.
2. We will evaluate each course against the criteria we developed last month.
3. We will use a consensus decision process to determine which of the three courses to offer.

Agenda for Group Discussion

Review of Philosophy 141   3:00–3:15
 Report by Justin on Philosophy 141 proposal
 Committee questions
 Comparison of PHIL 141 to criteria

Review of Art History 336   3:15–3:30
 Report by Marique on Art History 336 proposal
 Committee questions
 Comparison of ARTH 336 to criteria

Review of Communication 235   3:30–3:45
 Report by Kathryn on Communication 235
 Committee questions
 Comparison of COMM 235 to criteria

Consensus Building Discussion and Decision   3:45–4:15
 Which proposals fit the criteria?
 Are there non-criteria-related factors to consider?
 Which proposal is more acceptable to all members?

Discussion of next steps and task assignments.   4:15–4:25

Set date of next meeting.   4:25–4:30

participants who cannot attend the entire meeting or guests who need not be present for the whole meeting. With prior knowledge of which agenda items will be discussed when, meeting participants can attend at the crucial point in time.

5. **Make physical or technology arrangements.** This may include reserving a meeting room, arranging for a particular seating format, and ordering meeting supplies or food. Or for a virtual meeting, arrangements may include working with technical support to plan for audio- or videoconferencing equipment and informing remote locations of their technical requirements.

Leadership Responsibilities During the Meeting

1. Review and modify the agenda.
2. Monitor roles members assume and consciously play roles that are unfilled by others.
3. Monitor the agenda and time so that the group stays on schedule.
4. Monitor conflicts and intervene as needed.
5. Periodically check to see if the group is ready to make a decision.
6. Implement the group's decision rules.
7. Before ending the meeting, summarize decisions and assignments.
8. Ask the group to decide if and when another meeting is needed.

During the Meeting

1. **Review and modify the agenda.** Begin the meeting by reviewing the agenda and modifying it based on members' suggestions. Because things can change between when an agenda is distributed and when the meeting is held, reviewing the agenda ensures that the group is working on items that are still important and relevant. Reviewing the agenda also gives members a chance to control what is to be discussed.

2. **Monitor roles members assume and consciously play roles that are unfilled by others.** The role of the leader during a discussion is to provide the task or maintenance roles that the group lacks. Leaders need to maintain awareness of what specific roles are needed by the group at a specific time. For example, if the leader notices that some people are talking more than their fair share and that no one else is trying to draw out quieter members, the leader should assume the gatekeeper role and ask reluctant members to comment on the discussion.

3. **Monitor the agenda and time so that the group stays on schedule.** It is easy for a group to get bogged down in a discussion or to go off on tangents. Although another group member may serve as the orienter, it is the leader's responsibility to make sure that the group stays on track with the agenda.

4. **Monitor conflicts and intervene as needed.** A healthy level of conflict should be encouraged in the group so that issues are fully examined. But if the conflict level becomes dysfunctional, the leader may need to perform a harmonizing role so that relationships are not unduly strained.

5. **Periodically check to see if the group is ready to make a decision.** The leader of the group should listen for agreement and move the group into its formal decision process when the leader senses that discussion is no longer adding insight.

6. **Implement the group's decision rules.** The leader is responsible for overseeing that the decision-making rule the group has agreed to is used. If the group is deciding by consensus, the leader must make sure that all members feel that the chosen alternative is one that they can support. If the group is deciding by majority rule, the leader calls for the vote and tallies the results.

7. **Before ending the meeting, summarize decisions and assignments.** To bring closure to the meeting and to make sure that each member is clear about what has been accomplished, the leader should summarize what has happened in the meeting. The leader also should reiterate task assignments made during the meeting and review what is left to accomplish or decide.

8. **Ask the group to decide if and when another meeting is needed.** Ongoing groups should be careful not to meet just for the sake of meeting. Leaders should clarify with members when, and if, future meetings are necessary. The overall purposes of future meetings will dictate the agenda that will need to be prepared.

Meeting Follow-Up

1. **Review the meeting outcomes and process.** A good leader learns how to be more effective by reflecting on and analyzing how well the previous meeting went. Leaders need to think about whether the meeting accomplished its goals and whether group cohesion was improved or damaged in the process.

2. **Prepare and distribute a summary of meeting outcomes.** Although some groups have a member who serves as the note taker and who distributes minutes, many groups rely on their leaders to do this. A written record of what was agreed to, what was accomplished, and next steps serve to remind group members of the work they have to do. If the group has a recorder, the leader should check to make sure that minutes are distributed in a timely manner.

3. **Repair damaged relationships through informal conversations.** If the debate during the meeting

>> Effective leaders hold informal conversations after the meeting to repair damaged relationships. Is this easy for you to do?

©IMAGE STATE/JUPITER IMAGES

has been heated, it is likely that some people have damaged their relationships with others or left the meeting angry or hurt. Leaders can help repair relationships by seeking out these participants and talking with them. Through empathetic listening, leaders can soothe hurt feelings and spark a recommitment to the group.

4. **Follow up with members to see how they are progressing on items assigned to them.** When participants have been assigned specific task responsibilities, the leader should check with them to see if they have encountered any problems in completing those tasks.

LO^5 Evaluating Group Effectiveness

There is an old saying that goes, "A camel is a horse built by a committee." Although this saying is humorous, for some groups it is also true. If we are to avoid ending up with camels when we want horses, we need to understand how to assess a group's effectiveness and how to improve group processes based on those evaluations. Groups can be evaluated on the quality of the decision, the quality of role taking, and the quality of leadership.

The Decision

That a group meets to discuss an issue does not necessarily mean that it will arrive at a decision. As foolish as it may seem, some groups thrash away for hours, only to adjourn without having reached a conclusion. Of course, some groups discuss such serious problems that a decision cannot be made without several meetings. In such cases, it is important that the group adjourn with a clear understanding of what the next step will be. When a group "finishes" its work without arriving at some decision, however, the result is likely to be frustration and disillusionment. The Group Effectiveness Rating Sheet in Figure 11.2 provides one method for evaluating the quality of a group's decision based on three major aspects of groups: group characteristics, member relationships, and problem-solving ability.

Individual Participation and Role Behavior

Although a group will struggle without leadership, it may not be able to function at all without members who are willing and able to meet the task and maintenance functions for the group. The Participation and Role Behavior Rating Sheet in

Figure 11.3 provides one method for evaluating the behavior and role taking of each participant.

Leadership

Some group discussions are leaderless, although no discussion should be without leadership. If there is an appointed leader—and most groups have one—evaluation can focus on that individual. If the group is truly leaderless, the evaluation should consider attempts at leadership by various members or focus on the apparent leader who emerges from the group. The Leader Behavior Rating Sheet in Figure 11.4 provides one method for evaluating the behavior and role taking of the meeting leader.

Summary

When individuals interact in groups, they assume roles. A role is a specific pattern of behavior that a member of the group performs based on the expectations of other members.

There are three types of roles: task-oriented roles, maintenance roles, and self-centered roles. Members select the roles they will play based on how roles fit with their personality, what is required of them by virtue of a position they hold, and what roles the group needs to have assumed that are not being played by other members. One role that is of particular importance to effective group functioning is the leadership role.

Leadership is the process of influencing members to accomplish goals. Leadership is viewed through various perspectives including traits, situations, functions, and transformations. Groups may have a single leader, but more commonly leadership is shared among group members. Groups may have both formal and informal leaders. Formal leaders have formal authority given to them either by some entity outside of the group or by the group members themselves. Informal leaders emerge during a two-stage process. Individuals who want to become recognized as informal leaders in a group should come to group meetings prepared, actively participate in discussions, actively listen to others, avoid appearing bossy or stating overly strong opinions, and manage the meaning for other participants by framing.

Using the forms provided, you can evaluate groups on the quality of the decision, the quality of note taking, and the quality of leadership.

©INDEX STOCK IMAGERY/JUPITER IMAGES

>> **Highly effective groups can keep from building camels when they really need horses.**

Figure 11.2

Group Effectiveness Rating Sheet

Rate the group as a whole on each of the following questions using this scale:
1 = always, 2 = often, 3 = sometimes, 4 = rarely, 5 = never.

Group Characteristics

_____ 1. Did the group have a clearly defined goal to which most members were committed?

_____ 2. Did the group's size fit the tasks required to meet its goals?

_____ 3. Was group member diversity sufficient to ensure that important viewpoints were expressed?

_____ 4. Did group cohesiveness aid in task accomplishment?

_____ 5. Did group norms help accomplish goals and maintain relationships?

_____ 6. Was the physical setting conducive to accomplishing the work?

Member Relationships

_____ 1. Did members feel valued and respected by others?

_____ 2. Were members comfortable interacting with others?

_____ 3. Did members balance speaking time so that all members participated?

_____ 4. Were conflicts seen as positive experiences?

_____ 5. Did members like and enjoy each other?

Group Problem Solving

_____ 1. Did the group take time to define its problem?

_____ 2. Was high-quality information presented to help the group understand the problem?

_____ 3. Did the group develop criteria before suggesting solutions?

_____ 4. Were the criteria discussed sufficiently and based on all of the information available?

_____ 5. Did the group use effective brainstorming techniques to develop a comprehensive list of creative solution alternatives?

_____ 6. Did the group fairly and thoroughly compare each alternative to all solution criteria?

_____ 7. Did the group follow its decision rules in choosing among alternatives that met the criteria?

_____ 8. Did the group arrive at a decision that members agreed to support?

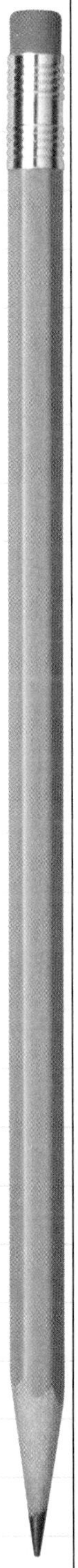

Figure 11.3

Participation and Role Behavior Rating Sheet

Name of Participant:

For each characteristic listed below, rate the participant on a scale of 1 to 5:

1 = excellent, 2 = good, 3 = average, 4 = fair, 5 = poor.

Meeting Behavior

_____ 1. Prepared and knowledgeable

_____ 2. Contributed ideas and opinions

_____ 3. Actively listened to the ideas of others

_____ 4. Politely voiced disagreement

_____ 5. Completed between-meeting assigned tasks

Performance of Task-Oriented Roles

_____ 1. Acted as initiator

_____ 2. Acted as information or opinion giver

_____ 3. Acted as information or opinion seeker

_____ 4. Acted as analyzer

_____ 5. Acted as orienter

Performance of Maintenance Roles

_____ 1. Acted as gatekeeper

_____ 2. Acted as encourager

_____ 3. Acted as harmonizer

Avoidance of Self-Centered Roles

_____ 1. Avoided acting as aggressor

_____ 2. Avoided acting as joker

_____ 3. Avoided acting as withdrawer

_____ 4. Avoided acting as blocker

Qualitative Analysis

Based on the quantitative analysis above, write a two- to five-paragraph analysis of the person's participation. Be sure to give specific examples of the person's behavior to back up your conclusions.

Figure 11.4

Leader Behavior Rating Sheet

Was there a formal group leader? Yes _____ No _____

If yes, name this person: _____

Who were the informal leaders of the group?

a. _____

b. _____

c. _____

Which of these leaders was most influential in helping the group meet its goals?

_____

Rate this leader on each of the following questions using a scale of 1 to 5: 1 = always, 2 = often, 3 = sometimes, 4 = rarely, 5 = never.

_____ 1. Demonstrated commitment to the group and its goals.

_____ 2. Actively listened to ideas and opinions of others.

_____ 3. Adapted his or her behavior to the immediate needs of the group.

_____ 4. Avoided stating overly strong opinions.

_____ 5. Managed meaning for the group by framing issues and ideas.

_____ 6. Was prepared for all meetings.

_____ 7. Kept the group on task and on schedule.

_____ 8. Made sure that conflicts were handled effectively.

_____ 9. Implemented the group's decision rules effectively.

_____ 10. Worked to repair damaged relationships.

_____ 11. Followed up after meetings to see how members were progressing on assignments.

Developing Your Topic and Doing Your Research

Learning Outcomes

LO^1 Discuss how to identify topics for your speech

LO^2 Understand how to analyze the audience

LO^3 Understand how to analyze the setting

LO^4 Discuss topic selection

LO^5 Identify and write out the specific goals of your speech

LO^6 Develop strategies for locating and evaluating information sources and primary research

LO^7 Identify and select relevant information

LO^8 Explain how to record information

> **"**When you are able to express your ideas to an audience, you are empowered.**"**

How do you feel about the prospect of speaking in front of a crowd? You may be taking this course as part of a graduation requirement and the thought of giving a speech can be overwhelming. On the other hand, you may feel very confident about it. In either case, developing public speaking skills is important. Why? Because when you are able to express your ideas to an audience, you are empowered. In a public forum, an effective speaker can stimulate and influence the thinking of others in ways that can improve their lives and the lives of those around them. In the workplace, effective public speaking skills are essential to advancement. From presenting oral reports and proposals, to responding to questions or training other workers, management-level and professional employees spend much of their work lives in activities that include or draw on public speaking skills.

Luckily, public speaking skills are not inborn; they are learned. So in the chapters that follow, we will be explaining how you can improve your public speaking through careful preparation. In chapters 12 through 15, you will learn a simple five-step process that will enable you to quickly and successfully prepare for the speeches you give. These steps are: (1) determine a specific speech goal that is adapted to the audience and occasion; (2) gather and evaluate material for use in the speech; (3) organize and develop the material in a way that is best suited to the audience and speech goal; (4) adapt the material to the needs of the specific audience; and (5) practice presenting the speech. In the final two chapters we go beyond this basic process and explain how to develop and organize informative and persuasive speeches.

In real-life settings, people are invited to speak because they have expertise in a particular subject or have some relationship to the audience. Nevertheless, expert speakers will still use the five action steps as they prepare their speeches.

In this chapter, we explain how to complete the first and second action steps: (1) identifying a specific speech goal that meets the needs of the audience and occasion, and (2) gathering and evaluating material for use in the speech.

What do you think?

Speaking in front of a crowd makes me nervous.

Strongly Disagree						Strongly Agree
1	2	3	4	5	6	7

©PHOTOS.COM/JUPITER IMAGES

©IMAGE 100/JUPITER IMAGES

Action Step 1: Determine a Specific Speech Goal That Is Adapted to the Audience and Occasion

To prepare an appropriate specific goal for your speech, you must first identify topics you'd be interested in speaking about, analyze your audience and setting, and then select your topic.

LO¹ Identify Topics

What do you know? What has interested you enough so that you have gained some expertise? Our speech topics should come from subject areas in which we already have some knowledge and interest. What is the difference between subject and topic? A **subject** is a broad area of expertise, such as movies, cognitive psychology, computer technology, or the Middle East. A **topic** is a specific aspect of a subject. It is narrow and focused, allowing a speaker to state a main idea and thoroughly explain, support, or defend it in the space of a speech. So, if your broad area of expertise is movies, you might feel qualified to speak on a variety of topics such as how the

subject
a broad area of knowledge

topic
some specific aspect of a subject

Academy Awards nomination process works; the relationships between movie producers, directors, and distributors; and how technology is changing movie production.

List Subjects

You can identify potential subjects for your speeches by simply listing those areas that (1) are important to you and (2) you know something about. These areas will probably include your vocation or area of formal study (major, prospective profession, or current job), your hobbies or leisure activities, and special interests (social, economic, educational, or political concerns). So, if retailing is your actual or prospective career, skateboarding is your favorite activity, and problems of illiteracy, substance abuse, and immigration are your special concerns, then these are subject areas from which you can identify topics for your speeches.

At this point, it is tempting to think, "Why not just talk on a subject that I know an audience wants to hear?" But in reality, all subject areas can interest an audience when speakers use their expertise or insight to enlighten the audience on a particular subject.

Figure 12.1 contains examples of subjects that students in two classes at the University of Cincinnati listed under (1) major or vocational interest, (2) hobby or activity, and (3) issue or concern.

Figure 12.1

why ppl should/shouldn't get married.

Student Subject Lists

Major or Vocational Interest	Hobby or Activity	Issue or Concern
communication	soccer	crime
disc jockey	weight lifting	governmental ethics
marketing	music	environment
public relations	travel	media impact on society
elementary school teaching	photography	censorship
sales	mountain biking	same-sex marriage
reporting	hiking	taxes
hotel management	volleyball	presidential politics
physics	tennis	cloning
fashion design	tracing your family tree	global warming
law	backpacking	child abuse
human resources	horseback riding	road rage
computer programming	sailing	illiteracy
nurse	swimming	effects of smoking
doctor	magic	women's rights
politics	gambling	abortion

Action Step 1a: Brainstorm for Topics

1. Divide a sheet of paper into three columns. Label column 1 with your major or vocation, such as "Art History," label column 2 with a hobby or an activity, such as "Chess," and label column 3 with a concern or an issue, such as "Water Pollution."
2. Working on one subject column at a time, quickly brainstorm a list of at least 15 related topics for each column.
3. Place a check mark next to the three topics in each list that you would most enjoy speaking about.
4. Keep these lists for future use in choosing a topic for an assigned speech.

Brainstorm for Topic Ideas

Because a topic is a specific aspect of a subject, from one subject you can identify many topics. A quick way to identify numerous topics is through brainstorming—an uncritical, nonevaluative process of generating associated ideas. Concerning the subject of tennis, for example, a person who plays tennis may brainstorm a list that includes the types of serves, net play, the types of courts, player rating systems, and equipment improvements. Once you have lists of topic ideas, you will be able to develop speeches you might give on that subject for this course and other occasions.

LO² Analyze the Audience

Because speeches are given for a particular audience, before you can finally decide on a topic you need to identify your prospective audience. An audience analysis is a study of the intended audience for your speech. This information will help you select one topic from your list that is appropriate for most audience members. You will also use your audience analysis in audience adaptation, the process of tailoring your information to the specific speech audience.

Identify Audience Analysis Information Needs

Audience analysis begins by gathering information that will allow you to know how audience members

Table 12.1

Demographic Audience Analysis Questions

Age:	Average age and age range?
Educational level:	Percentage with high school, college, or postgraduate education?
Gender:	Percentages of men and women?
Occupation:	Single (or dominant) occupation or industry or diverse occupations and industries?
Socioeconomic background:	Percentage lower, medium, upper income?
Ethnicity:	Dominant culture of group, if any? Other co-cultures represented?
Religion:	Religions represented? Is one preponderant?
Community:	Single neighborhood, city, state, country? Or mixed?
Language:	Common spoken language? Other first languages shared by a significant minority?

are alike and different from you and from each other. You will want to gather data that help you understand basic audience characteristics or demographics. Table 12.1 presents a list of questions you can use to obtain necessary demographic information.

You will also want to collect subject-related audience data, including: how knowledgeable audience members are in your subject area, their initial level of interest in the subject, their attitude toward the subject, and their attitude toward you as a speaker. Once you determine what your audience already knows about your subject, you can eliminate familiar topics that might bore them and choose a topic that will present them with new information and new insights. When you understand the initial level of interest that audience members have regarding your subject, you can choose a topic that builds on that interest, or you will need to adapt your material so that it captures their interest. Understanding your audience's attitude toward your subject is especially important when you want to influence their beliefs or move them to action. Because there is a limit to how persuasive any one speech can be, knowing your audience members' attitudes toward your subject will enable you to choose a topic that affects your audience's position without alienating them.

brainstorming
an uncritical, nonevaluative process of generating associated ideas

audience analysis
the study of the intended audience for your speech

audience adaptation
the active process of developing a strategy for tailoring your information to the specific speech audience

Gather Audience Data

There are four main methods you can use to gather the information you need for an audience analysis:

1. **Conduct a Survey.** Although it is not always feasible, the most direct and most accurate way to collect audience data is to survey the audience. A **survey** is a questionnaire designed to gather information from people. Some surveys are done as interviews; others are written forms that are completed by audience members. Survey questions or items can be: two-sided items (respondents choose between two answers), multiple response items (respondents choose between several items), scaled items (respondents choose between levels of intensity in a response), or open-ended items (respondents reply in any way they see fit). Figure 12.2 gives examples of each type of question.

2. **Informally Observe.** If the members of the audience are people whom we know, such as classmates or coworkers, we can learn a lot about them by just watching. For instance, after a couple of classes, we can determine the approximate average age of the class members, the ratio of men to women, and the general cultural makeup. As we listen to classmates talk, we learn about their knowledge of, and interest in, certain issues.

3. **Question a Representative.** When we are invited to make a speech, we can ask the contact person for audience information.

> **survey**
> a questionnaire designed to gather information from people

Methods for Gathering Audience Data

1. Conduct a survey.
2. Informally observe.
3. Question a representative.
4. Make educated guesses.

You should specifically ask for data that are somewhat important for you as you choose a topic or work to adapt your material. For example, if your subject is ethanol, you would want to know if the audience members have a basic understanding of chemistry.

4. **Make Educated Guesses.** If you can't get information in any other way, you can make informed guesses based on indirect data such as the general profile of people in a certain community or the kinds of people likely to attend the event or occasion.

Action Step 1b: Analyze Your Audience

1. Decide on the audience characteristics (demographics and subject-specific information that you need in order to choose a topic and adapt to your audience).
2. Choose a method for gathering audience information.
3. Collect the data.

Figure 12.2

Sample Survey Questions

Two-sided question
Are you
_____ a man?
_____ a woman?

Question with multiple responses
Which is the highest educational level you have completed?
_____ less than high school
_____ high school
_____ attended college
_____ associate's degree
_____ bachelor's degree
_____ master's degree
_____ doctorate degree
_____ postdoctorate

Scaled items
How much do you know about Islam?

not much   a little   some   quite a lot   detailed
                                                    knowledge

Open-ended item
What do you think about labor unions?

LO³ Analyze the Setting

The location and occasion make up the speech setting. Answers to several questions about the setting should also guide your topic selection and other parts of your speech planning.

1. **What are the special expectations for the speech?** Every speaking occasion is surrounded by expectations. At an Episcopalian Sunday service, for example, the congregation expects the minister's sermon to have a religious theme. Likewise, at a national sales meeting, the field representatives expect to hear about new products. For your classroom speeches, a major expectation is that your speech will meet the assignment.

2. **What is the appropriate length for the speech?** The time limit for classroom speeches is usually quite short, so you will want to choose a topic that is narrow enough to be accomplished in the brief time allowed. For example, "Two Major Causes of Environmental Degradation" could be presented as a 10-minute speech, but "A History of Human Impact on the Environment" could not. Speakers who speak for more or less time than they have been scheduled can seriously interfere with the program of an event and lose the respect of both their hosts and their audience.

3. **How large will the audience be?** Although audience size may not directly affect the topic you select, it will affect how you adapt your material and how you present the speech. For example, if the audience is small (up to about 50), you can talk without a microphone and move about if you choose to do so. For larger audiences, you will have a microphone that may limit your range of movement.

4. **Where will the speech be given?** Rooms vary in size, shape, lighting, and seating arrangements. Some are a single level, some have stages or platforms, and some have tiered seating. The space affects the speech. For example, in a long narrow room, you may have to speak loudly to be heard in the back row. The brightness of the room and the availability of shades may affect what kinds of visual aids you can use. So you will want to know and consider the layout of the room as you plan your speech. At times, you might request that the room be changed or rearranged so that the space is better suited to your needs.

5. **What equipment is necessary to give the speech?** Would you like to use a microphone, podium, flip chart, overhead or slide projector and screen, or a hookup for your laptop computer during your speech? If so, you need to check with your host to make sure that the equipment can be made available to you. In some cases, the unavailability of equipment may limit your topic choice. Regardless of what arrangements have been made, however, experienced speakers expect that something may go wrong and are always prepared with alternative plans. For example, although

setting
the occasion and location for your speech

> >How do the setting and the occasion dictate what a speaker will talk about at a graduation ceremony?

©BOB DAEMMRICH/PHOTOEDIT

Analyzing the Setting

1. What are the special expectations for the speech?
2. What is the appropriate length for the speech?
3. How large will the audience be?
4. Where will the speech be given?
5. What equipment is necessary to give the speech?

computer-mediated visual aids can be very effective, there are often technological glitches that interfere with their use, so many speakers prepare overheads of key presentation slides and bring them along as backup.

LO⁴ Select a Topic

Armed with your topic lists and the information you have collected on your audience and setting, you are ready to select an appropriate topic. Are there some topics on your list that are too simple or too difficult for this audience? Eliminate them. Are some topics likely to bore the audience and you can't think of any way to pique their interest. Eliminate them. How does the audience's demographic profile mesh with each topic? Are some ill suited to this demographic profile? Eliminate them. At the end of this process you should have several topics that would be appropriate for your audience.

Now consider the setting. Are some of the remaining topics inappropriate for the expectations of the audience or too broad for the time allocated, or do they require equipment that is unavailable to you in this setting? If so, eliminate them.

From the topics that still remain after considering the audience and the setting, you should choose the one that you would find most enjoyable to share with the audience as your speech topic.

general speech goal
the intent of your
speech

LO⁵ Write a Speech Goal

With a speech topic established, you are now ready to identify the general goal of your speech and to write a goal statement that specifies what you hope your audience will gain as a result of listening to you.

Identify Your General Goal

The **general goal** of a speech indicates the type of audience response that is expected if the speech is successful. Speeches intend to entertain, inform, or persuade. If they are effective, then audience members are amused, enlightened, or convinced. Although any speech may have elements of each type of goal, overall, only one of these is the primary aim of the speaker. For example, the general goal of Conan O'Brien's opening monologue is to entertain, even though it may include controversial topical material presented in a way that is clearly supportive of one side. Likewise, a politician's stock stump campaign speech has the general goal of persuading the audience to vote for the candidate, even though it contains material that informs the audience about the issues and may use humor to belittle the platform of the rival.

In this book, we focus on speeches that have goals to inform and to persuade; these are the kinds of speeches that you are most likely to be asked to present in academic, professional, and community settings.

Phrase a Specific Goal Statement

The specific goal, or specific purpose of your speech, is a single statement that identifies the exact response you want from the audience as a result of listening to this speech. A specific goal statement for an informative speech usually specifies whether you want the audience to learn about, understand, or appreciate the topic. "I would like the audience to understand the four major criteria used for evaluating a diamond" is a goal statement for an informative speech. A specific goal statement for a persuasive speech specifies whether you want the audience to accept the belief that you are presenting: "I want my audience to believe that the militarization of space is wrong," or to act a certain way: "I want my audience to donate money to the United Way." Figure 12.3 gives further examples of informative and persuasive speech goals.

To create a well-worded specific goal statement, we should follow these guidelines:

1. **Write a first draft of your speech goal, using a complete sentence that specifies the type of response you want from the audience.** Julia, who has been concerned with and is knowledgeable about the subject of illiteracy, drafts the following statement of her general speech goal: "I want my audience to be informed about the effects of illiteracy." Julia's draft is a complete sentence, and it specifies the response she wants from the audience: to understand the effects of illiteracy. Her phrasing tells us that she is planning to give an informative speech.

2. **Revise the draft statement until it focuses on the particular audience reaction that is desired.** The draft, "I want my audience to understand illiteracy," was a good start, but it is an extremely broad statement. Just what is it about illiteracy that Julia wants the audience to understand? She narrows the statement to read, "I want my audience to understand three effects of illiteracy." This version is more specific than her first draft, but it still does not clearly capture her intention, so she revises it further to read, "I would like the audience to understand three effects of illiteracy in the workplace." Now the goal is limited not only by Julia's focus on the specific number of effects, but also by her focus on a specific situation. If Julia wanted to persuade her audience, her specific goal might be worded: "I want my audience to believe that illiteracy is a major problem."

3. **Make sure that the goal statement contains only one central idea.** Suppose Julia had written the following specific goal statement: "I want the audience to understand the nature of illiteracy and innumeracy." This would need to be revised because it includes two distinct ideas: understanding the nature of illiteracy and understanding the nature of innumeracy. Although these problems may be related, because both make it difficult for people to function in society, the root causes of illiteracy and innumeracy are different. As a result, it would be difficult for a speaker to adequately address both within one speech. So Julia needs to realize that this statement really includes two topic ideas and she needs to choose between them. If your goal statement includes the word "and," you may have more than one idea and will need to narrow your focus.

specific speech goal
a single statement of the exact response the speaker wants from the audience

Figure 12.3

Informative and Persuasive Speech Goals

Informative Goals	
Increase understanding:	I want my audience to understand the three basic forms of a mystery story.
Increase knowledge:	I want my audience to learn how to light a fire without a match.
Increase appreciation:	I want my audience to appreciate the intricacies of spider-web designs.
Persuasive Goals	
Reinforce belief:	I want my audience to maintain its belief in drug-free sports.
Change belief:	I want my audience to believe that SUVs are environmentally destructive.
Motivate to act:	I want my audience to join Amnesty International.

Action Step 2: Gather and Evaluate Material to Use in the Speech

To select and then use the most effective information to support your speech, you must be able to locate and evaluate appropriate sources of information, identify and select the information most relevant to your speech, draw information from multiple cultural perspectives, and then record the information in a way that will help you prepare for and present your speech.

LO⁶ Locate and Evaluate Information Sources

How can you quickly find the best information related to your specific speech goal? It depends. Speakers usually start by assessing their own knowledge, experience, and personal observations. Then they move on to secondary resources (many of which are available at the library) and electronically search for relevant books, articles, general references, and websites. Occasionally, when other resources do not have the information needed, speakers may have to conduct their own studies by surveying people, reading original documents, interviewing experts, or experimenting.

Personal Knowledge, Experience, and Observation

secondary research
the process of locating information about your topic that has been discovered by other people

If you have chosen to speak on a topic you know something about, you are likely

> **When other resources do not have the information needed, speakers may have to conduct their own studies by surveying people, reading original documents, interviewing experts, or experimenting.**

to have material that you can use as examples and personal experiences in your speech. For instance, musicians have special knowledge about music and instruments, entrepreneurs know about starting up their own businesses, and marine biologists have knowledge about marine reserves. So Erin, a skilled rock climber, can draw material from her own knowledge and experience for her speech on "Rappelling Down a Mountain."

For many topics, the knowledge you've gained from experience can be supplemented with careful observation. If, for instance, you are planning to talk about how a small claims court works or how churches help the homeless find shelter and job training, you can learn more about each of these by attending small claims sessions or visiting a church's outreach center. By focusing attention on specific behaviors and taking notes of your observations, you will have a record of specifics that you can use in your speech.

Secondary Research

Secondary research is the process of locating information about your topic that has been discovered by other people. Libraries house various sources of secondary research. Most libraries store information about their holdings in electronic databases. Users retrieve the information at computer terminals in the library or over the Internet. If you don't know how to access your school's library resources online, you can call the help desk at your library. If you have difficulty using library search tools, you can probably take a short seminar offered at your library or you can ask a research librarian for help. Secondary resources include the following types of materials.

Books

If your topic has been around for at least six months, there are likely to be books written about it. To find them, you can do a key word search of the online library book catalog.

Articles

Articles, which may contain more current or highly specialized information on your topic than a book would, are published in **periodicals**—magazines and journals that appear at fixed periods. Today, most libraries subscribe to electronic databases that index periodical articles. Check with your librarian to learn what electronic indexes your college or university subscribes to.

Newspapers

Newspaper articles are excellent sources of facts about and interpretations of both contemporary and historical issues. Three electronic newspaper indexes that are most useful if they are available to you are (1) *National Newspaper Index,* which indexes five major newspapers: the *New York Times,* the *Wall Street Journal,* the *Christian Science Monitor,* the *Washington Post,* and the *Los Angeles Times;* (2) *Newsbank,* which provides not only the indexes but also the text of articles from more than 450 U.S. and Canadian newspapers; and (3) InfoTrac College Edition's *National Newspaper Index.*

Statistical Sources

Statistical sources present numerical information on a wide variety of subjects. When you need facts about demography, continents, heads of state, weather, or similar subjects, access one of the many single-volume sources that report such data. Two of the most popular sources in this category are *The Statistical Abstract of the United States* (now available online), which provides reference material for numerical information and various aspects of American life, and *The World Almanac and Book of Facts.*

Biographical References

When you need accounts of a person's life, from thumbnail sketches to reasonably complete essays, you can turn to one of the many biographical references that are available. In addition to full-length books and encyclopedia entries, consult such books as *Who's Who in America* and *International Who's*

Who. Your library may also carry *Contemporary Black Biography, Dictionary of Hispanic Biography, Native American Women, Who's Who of American Women, Who's Who Among Asian Americans,* and many more.

Books of Quotations

A good quotation can be especially provocative as well as informative, and there are times when you want to use a quotation from a respected person.

Government Documents

If your topic is related to public policy, government documents may provide you with useful information.

Internet-Based Resources

In addition to printed resources (which may be accessed online) there are electronic journals (not available in print), hosted websites, newsgroups (bulletin boards), personal web pages,

periodicals
magazines and journals that appear at fixed intervals

and blogs that exist in cyberspace and may have information you can use in your speech.

Primary Research

Primary research is the process of conducting your own study to acquire information for your speech. It should be the option of last resort in satisfying your information needs because it is much more labor intensive and time consuming than secondary research, and in the professional world, it is much more costly. If, after making an exhaustive search of secondary sources, you cannot locate the information you need, you might consider getting it through one of the following primary research methods.

Surveying

You can gather information directly from a group of people through the use of a questionnaire.

Interviewing

You can locate someone who is an acknowledged expert on your topic and ask for their opinions on your topic.

Examining Artifacts or Original Documents

Although the information you need may not have been published, it may exist in an original unpublished source (anything from ancient manuscripts to company files) or there may be an object that you can view to get the information you need.

Experimenting

You can design a study to test a hypothesis that you have. Then, based on your analysis, you can report the results in your speech.

Evaluate Sources

Information sources vary in the accuracy, reliability, and validity of the information they present. So before you use the information from a source in your speech, you will want to evaluate it. Three criteria you can use are authority, objectivity, and currency.

Authority

The first test of a resource is the expertise of its author and/or the reputation of the publishing or sponsoring organization. When an author is listed, you can check the author's credentials through biographical references or by seeing if the author has a home page listing professional qualifications. Use the electronic periodical indexes or check the Library of Congress to see what else the author has published in the field (see *Using Cyber Resources*, 2000).

On the Internet, you will find information that is anonymous or credited to someone whose background is not clear. In these cases, your ability to trust the information depends on evaluating the qualifications of the sponsoring organization. On the Internet, URLs ending in ".gov" (governmental), ".edu" (educational), and ".org" are noncommercial sites with institutional publishers. The URL ".com" indicates that the sponsor is a for-profit organization. If you do not know whether you can trust the sources, then do not use the information.

Objectivity

Although all authors have a viewpoint, you will want to be wary of information that is overly slanted. Documents that have been created under the sponsorship of some business, government, or public interest groups should be carefully scrutinized for obvious biases or good "public relations" fronts. To evaluate the potential biases in articles and books, read the preface or identify the thesis statement. These often reveal the author's point of view. When evaluating a website with which you are unfamiliar, look for the purpose of the website. Most home pages contain a purpose or mission statement that can help you understand why the site was created. Armed with this information, you are in a better position to recognize the biases that may be contained in the information. Remember, at some level all Web pages can be seen as "infomercials," so always be concerned with who created this information and why (Kapoun, 2000).

Currency

In general, newer information is more accurate than older. So when evaluating your sources, be sure to consult the latest information you can find. One of the reasons for using web-based sources is that they can provide more up-to-date information than printed sources (Munger et al., 2000). But just because a source is found online does not mean that the information is timely. To determine how current the information is, you will need to find out when the book was published, the article was written, the study was conducted, or the article was placed on the web or revised. Web page dates are usually listed at the end of the article. If there are no dates listed, you have no way of judging how current the information is.

primary research
the process of conducting your own study to acquire information for your speech

LO⁷ Identify and Select Relevant Information

The information that you find in your sources may include factual statements, expert opinions, and elaborations.

Factual Statements

Factual statements are those that can be verified. "A recent study confirmed that preschoolers watch an average of 28 hours of television a week," and "Johannes Gutenberg invented printing from movable type in the 1400s" are both statements of fact that can be verified. One way to verify whether the information is factual is to check it against material from other sources on the same subject. Never use any information that is not carefully documented unless you have corroborating sources. Factual statements may be statistics or examples.

1. **Statistics.** Statistics are numerical facts. "Only five out of every ten local citizens voted in the last election" or "The cost of living rose 0.6 percent in January of 2006," can provide impressive support for a point, but when they are poorly used in the speech, they may be

boring and, in some instances, downright deceiving. So you should:

- Use only statistics that you can verify to be reliable. Taking statistics from only the most reliable sources and double-checking any startling statistics with another source will guard against the use of faulty statistics.

- Use only recent statistics so your audience will not be misled.

- Use statistics comparatively. One number does not reveal much, but when compared with another number, it can show growth, decline, gain, loss, and so on.

- Use statistics sparingly. A few pertinent numbers are far more effective than a battery of statistics.

2. **Examples.** Specific instances that illustrate or explain a general factual statement are examples. Examples are useful because they provide concrete detail that makes a general statement more meaningful to the audience. One or two short examples like the following are often enough to help make a generalization meaningful: "One way a company increases its power is to buy out another company. Recently, K-Mart bought out Sears and thereby became a much larger company with many more products and outlets." "Professional billiard players practice many long hours every day. Jennifer Lee practices as many as 10 hours a day when she is not in a tournament."

Expert Opinions

Expert opinions are interpretations and judgments made by an authority in a particular subject area. At times, they augment facts

factual statements
statements that can be verified

statistics
numerical facts

examples
specific instances that illustrate or explain a general factual statement

expert opinions
interpretations and judgments made by authorities in a particular subject area

by helping to interpret what they mean or put them in proper perspective. "Watching 28 hours of television a week is far too much for young children, but may be OK for adults," and "The invention of printing from movable type was for all intents and purposes the start of mass communication" are opinions. Whether they are expert opinions depends on who made the statements. An **expert** is a person who has mastered a specific subject, usually through long-term study, and who is recognized by other people in the field as being a knowledgeable and trustworthy authority.

Elaborations

Both factual information and expert opinions can be elaborated upon through anecdotes and narratives, comparisons and contrasts, or quotable explanations and opinions.

Anecdotes and Narratives

Anecdotes are brief, often amusing stories; **narratives** are accounts, personal experiences, tales, or lengthier stories. Because holding audience interest is important in a speech and because audience attention is likely to be captured by a story, anecdotes and narratives are worth looking for, creating, and using. The key to using stories is to make sure that the point of the story directly states or reinforces the point you make in your speech. Good stories and narratives may be humorous, sentimental, suspenseful, or dramatic.

Comparisons and Contrasts

One of the best ways to give meaning to new ideas or facts is through comparison and contrast. **Comparisons** illuminate a point by showing similarities, whereas **contrasts** highlight differences. Although comparisons and contrasts may be literal, like comparing and contrasting the murder rates in different countries or during different eras, they may also be figurative such as:

- In short, living without health insurance is as much of a risk as having uncontrolled diabetes or driving without a safety belt (Nelson, 2006, p. 24). *(comparison)*

- If this morning you had bacon and eggs for breakfast, I think it illustrates the difference. The eggs represented "participation" on the part of the chicken. The bacon represented "total commitment" on the part of the pig! (Durst, 1989, p. 325). *(contrast)*

©FOODPIX/JUPITER IMAGES

Quotations

At times, the information you find will be so well stated that you might want to directly quote it in your speech. Because the audience is interested in listening to your ideas and arguments, you should avoid using too lengthy or too many quotations. But when you find that an author or expert has worded an idea especially well, you may want to directly quote it and then verbally acknowledge the person who said or wrote it. Using quotations or close paraphrases without acknowledging the source is **plagiarism**, the unethical act of representing another person's work as your own.

Draw Information from Multiple Cultural Perspectives

How facts are perceived and what opinions are held often are influenced by a person's cultural background. Therefore, it is important to draw your information from culturally diverse perspectives by seeking sources that have differing cultural orientations and by interviewing experts with diverse cultural backgrounds. For example, when Carrie was preparing for her speech on proficiency testing in grade schools, she purposefully searched for articles written by noted Hispanic, Asian, African American, and European American authors. In addition, she interviewed two local school superintendents—one from an urban district and one from a suburban dis-

expert
a person who has mastered a specific subject, usually through long-term study

anecdotes
brief, often amusing stories

narratives
accounts, personal experiences, tales, or lengthier stories

comparisons
illuminate a point by showing similarities

contrasts
highlight differences

plagiarism
the unethical act of representing another author's work as your own

trict. Because she consciously worked to develop diverse sources of information, Carrie felt more confident that her speech would more accurately reflect all sides of the debate on proficiency testing.

LO⁸ Record Information

As you find facts, opinions, and elaborations that you want to use in your speech, you need to record information accurately and keep a careful account of your sources so they can be cited appropriately.

Prepare Note Cards

How should you keep track of the information you plan to use? Although it may seem easier to record all material from one source on a single sheet of paper (or to photocopy source material), sorting and arranging material is much easier when each item is recorded separately. So it is wise to record information on note cards, which allow you to easily find, arrange, and rearrange each item of information as you prepare your speech.

A note card should be prepared for each factual statement, expert opinion, or elaboration that you find. To prepare a note card, begin by identifying a key word or category heading that captures the main idea of this piece of information and identifies the subcategory to which the information belongs. Next, record the specific fact, opinion, or elaboration statement. Any part of the information item that is quoted directly from the source should be enclosed

with quotation marks. Finally, record the information you will need to complete the bibliographic citation for your source list.

The exact bibliographic citation you will record depends on the type of source the information came from and the style sheet (MLA, APA, etc.) you are using. Generally for a book, you will record the names of authors, title of the book, the place of publication and the publisher, the date of publication, and the page or pages from which the information is taken. For a periodical or newspaper, you will record the name of the author (if given), the title of the article, the name of the publication, volume and issue number, the date, and the page number from which the information is taken. For online sources, include the URL for the website, the heading under which you found the information, and the time and date that you accessed the site. Be sure to record enough source information so that you can relocate the material if you need to. Figure 12.4 provides a sample note card.

The number of sources and note cards that you will need depends, in part, on the type of speech you

Figure 12.4

A Sample Note Card

Topic:
Bird Flu
Heading: Mortality Rate
From 2003 until August 14, 2006 there have been 139 laboratory confirmed deaths worldwide from avian flu.

Google: Bird Flu.
"Cumulative Number of Confirmed Human Cases of Avian Influenza A/(H5N1) Reported to WHO, August 14, 2006." World Health Organization.
http://www.who.int/csr/disease/avian_influenza/country/cases_table_2006_08_14/en/index.html
Accessed 7:21 p.m. EDT August 14, 2006.

are giving and your own expertise. For a narrative/personal experience, you obviously will be the main, if not the only, source. For informative reports and persuasive speeches, however, speakers ordinarily draw from multiple sources. For a five-minute speech on bird flu in which you plan to talk about causes, symptoms, and means of transmission, you might have two or more note cards under each heading. Moreover, the note cards should come from a number of different sources. Selecting and using information from several sources allows you

to develop an original approach to your topic, insures a broader research base, makes it more likely that you will uncover the various opinions related to your topic, and reduces the likelihood that you will plagiarize the ideas of another.

Cite Sources in Speeches

In your speeches, as in any communication in which you use ideas that are not your own, you need to acknowledge the sources of your ideas and statements. Specifically mentioning your sources helps the audience evaluate the content and also adds to your credibility. In addition, citing sources will give concrete evidence of the depth of your research. Failure to cite sources, especially when you are presenting information that is meant to substantiate a controversial point, is unethical.

In a written report, ideas taken from other sources are credited in footnotes; in a speech, these notations must be included in your verbal statement of the material. Although you do not want to clutter your speech with long bibliographical citations, be sure to mention the sources of your most important information. Figure 12.5 gives several examples of appropriate source citations.

Figure 12.5

Appropriate Speech Source Citations

"Thomas Friedman, noted international editor for the *New York Times*, stated in his book *The Lexis and the Olive Tree* . . ."
"In an interview with *New Republic* magazine, Governor Arnold Schwarzenegger stated . . ."
"According to an article about the 9/11 Commission Report in last week's *Newsweek* magazine . . ."
"In the latest Gallup poll cited in the February 10 issue of *Newsweek* . . ."
"But to get a complete picture we have to look at the statistics. According to the 2006 *Statistical Abstract*, the level of production for the European Economic Community rose from . . ."
"In a speech on business ethics delivered to the Public Relations society of America last November, Preston Townly, CEO of the Conference Board, said . . ."

Test coming up? Now what?

With COMM you have a multitude of study aids at your fingertips. After reading the chapters, check out these ideas for further help.

Chapter in Review Cards include all learning outcomes, definitions, and visual summaries for each chapter.

Printable Flash Cards give you three additional ways to check your comprehension of key communication concepts.

Other great ways to help you study include **Speech Builder Express 3.0™**, **Interactive Quizzing, Downloads, Games and Simulations,** and **Interactive Video Activities**.

You can find it all at **4ltrpress.cengage.com/comm**

Organizing *Your* Speech

Learning Outcomes

LO **1**   Describe methods for developing the body of your speech

LO **2**   Explain how to create an introduction

LO **3**   Explain how to prepare a conclusion

LO **4**   Examine guidelines for listing sources

LO **5**   Develop a method for reviewing the outline

> **❝** *Although every speech should have an introduction, a body, and a conclusion, not all speeches that have these components are well organized.* **❞**

How often have you heard a speech that was packed with interesting information and delivered in a way that held your attention, but when you reflected on what was said, you found it difficult to state what the speaker's main ideas were, or even what the overall goal of the speech was? Although every speech should have an introduction, a body, and a conclusion, not all speeches that have these components are well organized. So, we listen to a speech and find that even though we have been entertained for the moment, the speaker's words have no lasting impact on us. Well-constructed speeches have impact. When we have finished listening to a speech, we must remember not only the opening joke, or a random story, but we must also remember to think about the main ideas that the speaker presented. In this chapter, we describe the third of the five action steps: Organize and develop speech material to meet the needs of your particular audience. As you follow these steps, you will find that you are able to prepare a speech that will not only maintain your audience's interest, but will help your audience understand and remember what you have said.

Introduction

1st Main Point

2nd Main Point

3rd Main Point

Conclusion

Action Step 3: Organize and Develop Speech Material to Meet the Needs of Your Particular Audience

Organizing, the process of selecting and structuring ideas you will present in your speech, is guided by your audience analysis. During organizing you (1) develop a thesis statement for the speech tailored to the information needs or persuasive disposition of your audience; (2) select and tailor the speech's main ideas and supporting materials so they

organizing
the process of selecting and arranging the main ideas and supporting material to be presented in the speech in a manner that makes it easy for the audience to understand

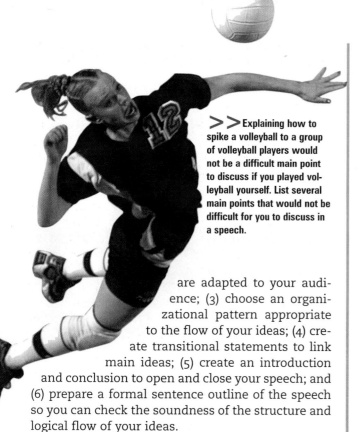

>> Explaining how to spike a volleyball to a group of volleyball players would not be a difficult main point to discuss if you played volleyball yourself. List several main points that would not be difficult for you to discuss in a speech.

are adapted to your audience; (3) choose an organizational pattern appropriate to the flow of your ideas; (4) create transitional statements to link main ideas; (5) create an introduction and conclusion to open and close your speech; and (6) prepare a formal sentence outline of the speech so you can check the soundness of the structure and logical flow of your ideas.

LO¹ Developing the Body of the Speech

Once you have analyzed the audience, developed a speech goal, and assembled a body of information on your topic, you are ready to craft the body of your speech by (a) determining the main points; (b) writing a thesis statement; (c) outlining the body of the speech; (d) selecting and ordering supporting material (examples, statistics, illustrations, quotations, and so on) that elaborates on or supports each of your main points; and (e) preparing sectional transitions.

Determining Main Points

The main points of a speech are complete sentence statements of the two to five central ideas that you want to present in your speech. You will want to limit the number of main points in your speech so your audience members can keep track of your ideas and so you can develop each idea with an appropriate amount of supporting material. Usually, the difference between a 5-minute speech and a 25-minute speech with

main points
complete sentence representations of the main ideas used in your thesis statement

the same speech goal will not be the number of main ideas that are presented, but rather, the extent to which each main point is developed.

With some topics and goals, determining the main points is easy. Erin, who plays Division I volleyball for her college, doesn't need to do much research for her speech on how to spike a volleyball. And because she will be speaking to a group of volleyball players, it was easy for her to group the actions into three steps: the proper approach, a powerful swing, and effective follow-through.

But for other topics and goals, determining main points is more difficult. For example Emming wants to speak on choosing a credit card. His specific goal statement is: "I want the audience to understand the criteria for choosing a credit card." As he did his research, he uncovered numerous interesting facts related to the topic, but he has had trouble figuring out how to group these ideas. When you find yourself in Emming's shoes, you will need to do further work to determine the main ideas you want to present.

How can you proceed? First, begin by listing the ideas that you have found that relate to your specific goal. Like Emming, you may be able to list as many as nine or more. Second, eliminate ideas that your audience analysis suggests that this audience already understands. Third, check to see if some of the ideas can be grouped together under a broader concept. Fourth, eliminate ideas for which you do not have strong support in the sources you consulted. Fifth, eliminate any ideas that might be too complicated for this audience to comprehend in the time you have to explain them. Finally, from the ideas that remain, choose three to five that are the most important for your audience to understand if you are to accomplish your specific speech goal.

Let's look at how Emming used these steps to identify the main points for his speech on criteria for choosing a credit card. To begin with, Emming had some thoughts about possible main ideas for the speech, but it wasn't until he completed most of his research, sorted through what he had collected, and thought about it that he was able to choose his main points. First, he listed ideas (in this case nine) that were discussed in the research materials he had found about choosing a credit card:

what is a credit card

interest rates

credit ratings

convenience

discounts

annual fee

institutional reputation

©AP PHOTO/RODNEY WHITE

©RICHARD LEWISOHN/IMAGE SOURCE

Action Step 3a: Determining Main Points

To determine three to five main ideas or main points that you will present in your speech:

1. List all of the ideas you have found that relate to the specific goal of your speech.
2. If there are more than five:
   a. Draw a line through each of the ideas that you believe the audience already understands, or that you have no supporting information for, or that just seem too complicated for the time allowed.
   b. Look for and combine ideas that can be grouped together under a larger heading.
3. From those ideas that remain, choose the two to five that you think will make the best main points for your audience.

frequent flyer points

rebates

Second, Emming eliminated the idea "what is a credit card" because he knew that his audience already understood this. This left him with eight ideas—far too many for his first speech. Third, Emming noticed that several of the ideas seemed to be related. "Discounts," "frequent flyer points," and "rebates" are all types of incentives that card companies offer to entice people to choose their card. So Emming grouped these three ideas together under the single heading of "incentives." Fourth, Emming noticed that he had uncovered considerable information on interest rates, credit ratings, discounts, annual fees, rebates, and frequent flyer points, but had very little information on convenience or institutional reputation, so he crossed out these ideas.

Finally, Emming considered each of the six remaining ideas in light of the five-minute time requirement he faced. He decided to cross out "credit ratings" because, although people's credit ratings influence the types of cards and interest rates for which they might qualify, Emming believed that he could not adequately explain this idea in the short time available. In fact, he believed that explaining how a credit rating was made to this audience might take longer than five minutes and wasn't really as basic as some of the other ideas he had listed.

This process left Emming with three broad-based points that he could develop in his speech: interest rates, annual fee, and incentives. So, if you find that you want to talk about a topic that includes numerous forms, types, categories, and so on, follow

Writing a Thesis Statement

A **thesis statement** is a sentence that states the specific goal and the main points of the speech. Thus, your thesis statement provides a blueprint from which you will organize the body of your speech.

Now let's consider how you arrive at this thesis statement. Recall that Emming determined three main ideas that he wanted to talk about in his speech on choosing a credit card: interest rates, annual fee, and incentives. Based on his specific goal and the main points he had determined, Emming was able to write the thesis statement: "Three criteria you should use to find the most suitable credit card are level of real interest rate, annual fee, and advertised incentives."

Outlining the Body of the Speech

Once you have a thesis statement, you can begin to outline your speech. A **speech outline** is a sentence representation of the hierarchical and sequential relationships between the ideas presented in the speech. Your outline may have three hierarchical levels of information: main points (noted by the use of Roman numerals), subpoints that support a main point (noted by the use of capital letters), and sometimes sub-subpoints to support subpoints (noted by Arabic numbers). Figure 13.1 on the following page provides the general form of how the speech outline system looks.

You will want to write your main points and subpoints in complete sentences, to clarify the relationships between main points and subpoints. Once you have worded each main point and determined its relevant subpoints, you will choose a pattern of organization that fits your thesis. The sequential order in which you will present your main points will depend on the pattern of organization that you choose.

Wording Main Points

Recall that Emming determined that interest rates, annual fee, and advertised inducements are the three major criteria for finding a suitable credit card and his thesis statement was: Three criteria you should

thesis statement
a sentence that identifies the topic of your speech and the main ideas you will present

speech outline
a sentence representation of the hierarchical and sequential relationships between the ideas presented in a speech

use to find the most suitable credit card are level of real interest rate, annual fee, and advertised incentives. So Emming might write a first draft of the main points of his speech like this:

I. Examining the interest rate is one criterion that you can use to find a credit card that is suitable for where you are in life.
II. Another criterion that you can use to make sure you find a credit card that is suitable for where you are in life is to examine the annual fee.
III. Finding a credit card can also depend on weighing the advertised incentives, which is the third criterion that you will want to use to be sure that it is suitable for where you are in life.

Study these statements. Do they seem a bit vague? Sometimes, the first draft of a main point is well expressed and doesn't need additional work. More often, however, we find that our first attempt doesn't quite capture what we want to say. So we need to rework the statements to make them clearer. Testing our main points with two questions can help us as we revise.

1. *Does the main point statement specify how it is related to the goal?* Based on this question, Emming revised his main points like this:

I. **A low interest rate is one criterion that you can use to select a credit card that is suitable for where you are in life.**
II. **Another criterion that you can use to make sure you find a credit card that is suitable for where you are in life is to look for a card with no annual fee or a very low one.**

parallel
wording in more than one sentence that follows the same structural pattern, often using the same introductory words

III. Finding a credit card can also depend on weighing the value of the advertised incentives against the increased annual cost or interest rate, which is the third criterion that you will want to use to be sure that it is suitable for where you are in life.

2. *Are the main points parallel in structure?* Main points are **parallel** to each other when their wording follows the same structural pattern, often using the same introductory words. Parallel structure helps the audience recognize main points by recalling a pattern in the wording. Based on this, Emming revised his main points to make them parallel:

I. **The first criterion for choosing a credit card is to select a card with a relatively low interest rate.**
II. **A second criterion for choosing a credit card is to select a card with no annual fee or a low annual fee.**
III. **A third criterion for choosing a credit card is to weigh the value of the advertised incentives against the increased annual cost or interest rate.**

Figure 13.1

General Form for a Speech Outline

©COMSTOCK IMAGES/JUPITER IMAGES

```
I. Main point one
   A. Subpoint A for main point one
      1. Sub-subpoint one for subpoint A of main point one
      2. Sub-subpoint two for subpoint A of main point one
   B. Subpoint B of main point one
      1. Sub-subpoint one for subpoint B of main point one
      2. Sub-subpoint two for subpoint B of main point one
II. Main point two
   A. Subpoint A for main point two
      1. Sub-subpoint one for subpoint A of main point two
      2. Sub-subpoint two for subpoint A of main point two
   B. Subpoint B of main point two
      1. Sub-subpoint one for subpoint B of main point two
      2. Sub-subpoint two for subpoint B of main point two
      3. Sub-subpoint three for subpoint B of main point two
   C. Subpoint C of main point two
      1. Sub-subpoint one for subpoint C of main point two
      2. Sub-subpoint two for subpoint C of main point two
      3. Sub-subpoint three for subpoint C of main point two
III. Main point three
   A. Subpoint A for main point three
      1. Sub-subpoint one for subpoint A of main point three
      2. Sub-subpoint two for subpoint A of main point three
   B. Subpoint B of main point three
      . . . and so on.
```

Selecting an Organizational Pattern for Main Points

A speech can be organized in many different ways. Your objective is to find or create the structure that will help the audience make the most sense of the material. The speech pattern you select will guide the order in which you present your main points. Although speeches may follow many types of organization, there are three fundamental patterns for beginning speakers to learn: time, or sequential, order; topic order; and logical reasons order.

1. *Time, or sequential, order.* **Time**, or **sequential, order** arranges main points by a chronological sequence or by steps in a process. Thus, when you are explaining how to do something, how to make something, how something works, or how something happened, you will want to use time order. Erin's speech on how to spike a volleyball is an example of time order (good approach, powerful swing, good follow-through). As the following example illustrates, the sequence of main points is as important for audiences to remember as the ideas of the main points.

   Thesis Statement: The four steps involved in developing a personal network are to analyze your current networking potential, to position yourself in places for opportunity, to advertise yourself, and to follow up on contacts.

   I. First, analyze your current networking potential.
   II. Second, position yourself in places for opportunity.
   III. Third, advertise yourself.
   IV. Fourth, follow up on contacts.

   Although the use of "first," "second," and so on, is not a requirement when using a time order, their inclusion serves as markers that help audience members understand the importance of sequence.

2. *Topic order.* **Topic order** arranges the main points of the speech by categories or divisions of a subject. This is a common way of ordering main points because nearly any subject may be subdivided or categorized in many different ways. The order of the topics may go from general to specific, least important to most important, or some other logical sequence.

   In the example below, the topics are presented in the order that the speaker believes is most suitable for the audience and speech goal, with the most important point presented last and the second most important point presented first.

   Thesis Statement: Three proven methods for ridding our bodies of harmful toxins are reducing animal foods, hydrating, and eating natural whole foods.

   I.   One proven method for ridding our bodies of harmful toxins is reducing our intake of animal products.
   II. A second proven method for ridding our bodies of harmful toxins is eating more natural whole foods.
   III. A third proven method for ridding our bodies of harmful toxins is keeping well hydrated.

3. *Logical reasons order.* **Logical reasons order** is used when the main points are the rationale or proof that support the thesis. For example:

   Thesis Statement: Donating to the United Way is appropriate because your one donation covers many charities, you can stipulate which specific charities you wish to support, and a high percentage of your donation goes to charities.

   I. When you donate to the United Way, your one donation covers many charities.

time order (sequential order) organizing the main points by a chronological sequence, or by steps in a process

topic order organizing the main points of the speech by categories or divisions of a subject

logical reasons order used when the main points provide proof supporting the thesis statement

>>If you were giving a speech on the phenomenon of soldiers creating blogs about their combat experiences, what organizational pattern do you think would best suit your speech?

©AP/JULIE JACOBSON

II. **When you donate to the United Way, you can stipulate which charities you wish to support.**

III. **When you donate to the United Way, you know that a high percentage of your donation will go directly to the charities you've selected.**

Although these three organizational patterns are the most basic ones, in Chapters 16 and 17 you will be introduced to several other patterns that are appropriate for informative and persuasive speaking.

Selecting and Outlining Supporting Material

Although the main points provide the basic structure or skeleton of your speech, whether your audience understands, believes, or appreciates what you have to say usually depends on supporting material—information used to develop main points. You can identify supporting material by sorting the note cards you have prepared during your research into piles that correspond to each of your main points. The goal is to see what information you have that can help you develop each point. When Emming did this, he discovered that for his first point on choosing a credit card with a low interest rate, he had the following support:

- Most "Zero Percent" cards carry an average of 8 percent after a specified period.

- Some cards carry as much as 21 percent after the first year.

- Some cards offer a "grace period" before interest charges kick in.

- Department store interest rates are often higher than bank rates.

- Variable rate means that the interest rate can change from month to month.

- Fixed rate means the interest rate will stay the same.

- Many companies offer "Zero Percent" for up to 12 months.

- Some companies offer "Zero Percent" for a few months.

Once you have listed each of the supporting items, look for relationships between them that will allow you to group ideas under a broader heading and eliminate ideas that don't really belong. Then select the ideas that best support the main idea and develop them into complete sentences. When Emming did this, he came up with two statements that grouped the information he had found in support of his first main point. These two became his subpoints. He also had material that supported each subpoint. So he expanded his outline to include this material.

Here is Emming's outline:

I. The first criterion for choosing a credit card is to select a card with a lower interest rate.
   A. Interest rates are the percentages that a company charges you to carry a balance on your card past the due date.
      1. Most credit cards carry an average of 8 percent.

2. Some cards carry as much as 21 percent.
3. Many companies quote low rates (0%–3%) for a specific period.
   B. Interest rates can be variable or fixed.
   1. A variable rate means that the percent charged can vary from month to month.
   2. A fixed rate means that the rate will stay the same.

The outline includes supporting points of a speech, but it does not include all the development. For instance, Emming might use personal experiences, examples, illustrations, anecdotes, statistics, and quotations to elaborate on a main point or subpoint. But these are not detailed on the outline. Emming will choose these developmental materials later as he considers how to verbally and visually adapt to his audience. We will consider this in the next chapter.

Preparing Section Transitions

Once you have outlined your main points, subpoints, and potential supporting material, you will want to consider how you will move smoothly from one main point to another. Transitions are words, phrases, or sentences that show the relationship between or bridge two ideas. Transitions act like tour guides leading the audience from point to point through the speech. Section transitions are complete sentences that show the relationship between or bridge major parts of the speech. They may summarize what has just been said or preview the next main idea. For example, suppose Kenneth has just finished the introduction of his speech on antiquing tables and is now ready to launch into his main points. Before stating his first main point he might say, "Antiquing a table is a process that has four steps. Now let's consider the first one." When his listeners hear this transition, they are signaled to mentally prepare to listen to and remember the first main point. When he finishes his first main point, he will use another section transition to signal that he is finished speaking about step one and is moving on to discuss step two: "Now that we see what is involved in cleaning the table, we can move on to the second step."

You might be thinking that this sounds repetitive or patronizing, but section transitions are important for two reasons. First, they help the audience follow the organization of ideas in the speech. If every member of the audience were able to pay complete attention to every word, then perhaps section transitions would not be needed. But as people's attention rises and falls during a speech, they often find themselves wondering where they are. Section transitions give us a mental jolt and say, "Pay attention."

Second, section transitions are important in helping us retain information. We may well remember something that was said once in a speech, but our retention is likely to increase markedly if we hear something more than once. Good transitions are important in writing, but they are even more important in speaking. If listeners get lost or think they have missed something, they cannot check back as they can with writing.

In a speech, if we forecast main points, then state each main point, and use transitions between each point, audiences are more likely to follow and remember the organization.

On your speech outline, section transitions are written in parentheses and at the junctures of the speech.

transitions
words, phrases, or sentences that show the relationship between or bridge ideas

Action Step 3e: Preparing Section Transitions

Prepare section transitions to appear as parenthetical statements before or after each main point. Using complete sentences:

1. Write a transition from your first main point to your second.
2. Write a transition from each of your remaining main points to the one after it.
3. Add these transitional statements to your outline.

TRANSITIONS MOVE YOUR AUDIENCE ALONG WITH YOU.

©STOCK IMAGE/JUPITER IMAGES

Fast Facts— Useful Landmarks

During the 1800s, American pioneers travelling to the Pacific Northwest along the Oregon Trail used landmarks such as Chimney Rock, in what is now the western part of Nebraska, to make sure they were on the right path. In the same way, section transitions in a speech can help keep the audience on track and reel them back in if they get lost.

LO² Creating the Introduction

Now that the body of the speech has been developed, you can decide how to begin your speech. Because the introduction establishes your relationship with your audience, you will want to develop two or three different introductions and then select the one that seems best for this particular audience. Although your introduction may be very short, it should gain audience attention and motivate audience members to listen to all that you have to say. An introduction is generally about 10 percent of the length of the entire speech, so for a five-minute speech (approximately 750 words), an introduction of 60 to 85 words is appropriate. A common problem for beginning speakers is to plan an introduction that is too time consuming, which causes them to deliver a speech that is too long.

Goals of the Introduction

An introduction should get audience's attention and introduce the thesis. In addition, effective introductions also begin to establish speaker credibility, set the tone for the speech, and create a bond of goodwill between the speaker and the audience.

Getting Attention

An audience's physical presence does not guarantee that audience members will actually listen to your speech. Your first goal, then, is to create an opening that will win your listeners' attention by arousing their curiosity and motivating them to continue listening. In the next section of this chapter, we discuss six types of attention-getting devices you can use to get the audience's attention and also to stimulate their interest in what you have to say.

Stating the Thesis

Because audiences want to know what the speech is going to be about, it's important to state your thesis, which will introduce them to the main points of your speech. For his speech about romantic love, after Miguel gained the audience's attention, he introduced his thesis, "In the next five minutes, I'd like to explain to you that romantic love consists of three elements: passion, intimacy, and commitment." Stating main points in the introduction is necessary unless you have some special reason for not revealing the details of the thesis. For instance, after getting the attention of his audience Miguel might say, "In the next five minutes, I'd like to explain the three aspects of romantic love," a statement that specifies the number of main points, but leaves stating specifics for transition statements immediately preceding main points. Now let's consider three other goals you might have for your introduction.

Establishing Your Credibility

If someone hasn't formally introduced you before you speak, the audience members are going to wonder who you are and why they should pay attention to what you have to say. So another goal of the introduction may be to begin to build your credibility. For instance, it would be natural for an audience to question Miguel's qualifications for speaking on the topic of romantic love. So after his attention-getting statement he might say, "I became interested in this topic last semester, when I took an interdisciplinary seminar on romantic love, and I am now doing an independent research project on commitment in relationships."

Setting a Tone

The introductory remarks may also reflect the emotional tone that is appropriate for the topic. A humorous opening will signal a lighthearted tone; a serious opening signals a more thoughtful or somber tone. For instance, a speaker who starts with a rib-tickling, ribald story is putting the audience in a lighthearted, devil-may-care mood. If that speaker then says, "Now let's turn to the subject of abortion (or nuclear war, or ethnic genocide)," the audience will be confused by the preliminary introduction that signaled a far different type of subject.

Creating a Bond of Goodwill

In your first few words, you may also establish how an audience will feel about you as a person. If you're enthusiastic, warm, and friendly and give a sense that what you're going to talk about is in the audience's best interest, it will make them feel more comfortable about spending time listening to you.

For longer speeches, you will have more time to accomplish all five goals in the introduction. But for shorter speeches, like those that you are likely to be giving in class, you will first focus on getting attention and stating the thesis; then you will use very brief comments to try to build your credibility, establish an appropriate tone, and develop goodwill.

Methods of Attention Gaining

The ways to gain your audience's attention as you begin a speech are limited only by your imagination. In this section, we describe six common methods you can use to get and excite your audience's interest in your topic: startling statements, rhetorical questions, personal references, quotations, stories, and suspense.

Startling Statement

A startling statement grabs your listeners' attention by shocking them in some way. Because of the shock of what has been said, audience members stop what they were doing or thinking about and focus on the speaker. The following example illustrates the attention-getting effect of a startling statement:

> By 2030—less than [25] years from now—the world's energy needs will be almost 50 percent greater than they were last year. That is a startling statistic, especially when you consider that 80 percent of that growth will come from one subset—developing countries.

> Developing countries in Asia alone will see energy demand increase by over 150 percent in the period from 2000 to 2030. This growing demand for energy reflects a growing demand worldwide [because] of a higher standard of living. Meeting [the demand] will require massive investment, access to resources, and a continued focus on technology (Tillerson, 2006, p. 441).

In less than a minute, this 99-word introduction grabs attention and leads into the speech.

Rhetorical Question

Asking a rhetorical question—a question seeking a mental rather than a vocal response—is another appropriate opening for a short speech. Notice how a student began her speech on counterfeiting with these three short, rhetorical questions:

> What would you do with this 20-dollar bill if I gave it to you? Take your friend to a movie? Treat yourself to a pizza and drinks? Well, if you did either of these things, you could get in big trouble—this bill is counterfeit!

> Today I want to explain the extent of counterfeiting in America and what our government is doing to curb it.

This short opening that can be stated in less than 30 seconds gets attention and leads into the speech.

Personal Reference

A statement that can personalize the topic for audience members will quickly establish how the topic is in the individual's self-interest. In addition to getting attention, a personal reference can be especially effective at engaging listeners as active participants in a speech. A personal reference opening, like this one on exercise, may be suitable for a speech of any length:

> Say, were you panting when you got to the top of those four flights of stairs this morning? I'll bet there were a few of you who vowed you're never going to take a class on the top floor of this building again. But did you ever stop to think that maybe the problem isn't that this class is on the top floor? It just might be that you are not getting enough exercise.

> Today I want to talk with you about how you can build an exercise program that will get you and keep you in shape, yet will only cost you three hours a week, and not one red cent!

This 112-word opening, which can be presented in less than a minute, not only gets attention, but also personalizes the topic in a way that helps motivate listeners to pay attention.

rhetorical question
a question seeking a mental rather than a vocal response

>>A good quotation—or a good story—helps grab your reader's attention.

©AP/THE TRUTH, JENNIFER SHEPHARD

he made it safely across, and everybody cheered. "Who believes I can ride a bicycle across?" and they all said "Don't do it, you'll fall!" But he got on his bicycle and made it safely across. "Who believes I can push a full wheelbarrow across?" Well, by this time the crowd had seen enough to make real believers of them, and they all shouted, "We do! We do!" At that he said, "Okay . . . Who wants to be the first to get in?"

Well, that's how many investors feel about companies who have adopted the philosophy that balancing the interests of all stakeholders is the true route to maximum value. They go from skeptics to believers—but are very reluctant to get in that wheelbarrow.

What I would like to do this afternoon is share with you Eastman's philosophy [about that] practice, and then I'll give you some results (Deavenport, 1995, p. 49).

Quotation

A particularly vivid or thought-provoking quotation makes an excellent introduction to a speech of any length, especially if you can use your imagination to relate the quotation to your topic. For instance, in his introduction, notice how Thomas "Byron" Thames, M.D., Member, Board of Directors, AARP, uses a quotation to get the attention of his audience:

W. C. Fields was fond of saying, "There comes a time in a man's life when he must take the bull by the horns and face the situation." Well, ladies and gentlemen, the time has come for those of us with a stake in our nation's health care system to "take the bull by the horns and face the situation" regarding today's out-of-control health care costs (Thames, 2006, p. 315).

A good quotation not only gets attention; it also motivates the audience to listen carefully to what the speaker is going to talk about.

Stories

A story is an account of something that has happened. Most people enjoy a well-told story. So, if you have uncovered an interesting story in your research that is related to the goal of the speech, consider using it for your introduction.

Unfortunately, many stories are lengthy and can take more time to tell than is appropriate for the length of your speech, so only use a story if you can abbreviate it to fit your speech length. Notice how the following story captures attention and leads into the topic of the speech, balancing stakeholder interests.

A tightrope walker announced that he was going to walk across Niagara Falls. To everyone's amazement,

Suspense

An introduction that is worded so that what is described remains uncertain or mysterious will excite the audience. When you begin your speech in a way that gets the audience to thinking, "What is she leading up to?" you have created suspense. The suspenseful opening is especially valuable when the topic is one that an audience does not already have an interest in hearing. Consider the attention-getting value of this introduction:

It costs the United States more than $116 billion per year. It has cost the loss of more jobs than a recession. It accounts for nearly 100,000 deaths a year. I'm not talking about cocaine abuse—the problem is alcoholism. Today I want to show you how we can avoid this inhumane killer by abstaining from it.

Notice that by putting the problem "alcoholism" at the end, the speaker encourages the audience to try to anticipate the answer. And because the audience may well be thinking "narcotics," the revelation that the answer is alcoholism is likely to be much more effective.

LO^3 Preparing the Conclusion

Shakespeare said, "All's well that ends well." A strong conclusion will summarize the main ideas and will leave the audience with a vivid impression of what they have learned. Even though the conclusion will be a relatively short part of the speech—seldom more than 5 percent (35 to 40 words for a five-minute speech)—it is important that your conclusion be carefully planned.

Just as with your speech introduction, you should prepare two or three conclusions and then choose the one you believe will be the most effective with your audience.

Summary of Main Points

Any effective speech conclusion is likely to include a summary of the main points. In very short speeches, a summary may be the only conclusion that is necessary. Thus, a short, appropriate ending for an informative speech on how to improve your grades might be: "So I hope you now understand that three techniques in helping you improve your grades are to attend classes regularly, to develop a positive attitude toward the course, and to study systematically." Likewise, a short ending for a persuasive speech on why you should lift weights might be: "So, remember that three major reasons why you should consider lifting weights are to improve your appearance, to improve your health, and to accomplish both with a minimum of effort."

Leaving Vivid Impressions

Although summaries achieve the first goal of an effective conclusion, a speaker may need to develop additional material designed to achieve the second goal: leaving the audience with a vivid impression. Vivid impressions can be created in variety of ways. Their purpose is to give the audience one memorable image that serves as an emotional summary of the speech. The following represent two ways to create vivid impressions.

Story

For longer informative or persuasive speeches, speakers may also look for stories or other types of material that can further reinforce the message of the speech. Here we will give you one example of such a story. In his speech on corporate responsibility in the Hispanic business community, Solomon D. Trujillo (2002, p. 406) ends with a story that dramatizes the importance of acting now:

> In closing, there's an old tale called "The Four Elements" from the Hispanic Southwest by my friend Rudolfo Anaya that captures my message.
>
> In the beginning, there were four elements on this earth, as well as in man. These basic elements in man and earth were Water, Fire, Wind and Honor. When the work of the creation was completed, the elements decided to separate, with each one seeking its own way. Water spoke first and said: "If you should ever need me, look for me under the earth and in the oceans." Fire then said: "If you should

need me you will find me in steel and in the power of the sun." Wind whispered: "If you should need me, I will be in the heavens among the clouds." Honor, the bond of life, said: "If you lose me, don't look for me again—you will not find me."

So it is for corporate responsibility. Once lost, honor cannot be replaced. It is the right thing to do . . . it is right for business . . . it is inseparable in our interdependent world. Let's act now to bring Hispanic issues to the forefront of America's agenda.

Appeal to Action

The appeal to action is a common way to end a persuasive speech. The appeal describes the behavior that you want your listeners to follow after they have heard your arguments. Notice how Llewellyn H. Rockwell, Jr. concludes his speech on Iraq and the Democratic Empire (2006, p. 302) with a strong appeal to action:

> In the first, by the Left and the Democrats, we are asked to think of the state as an expansive Good Samaritan who clothes, feeds, and heals people at home and abroad, but fail to notice that this Samaritan ends up not helping people but enslaving its clients. In the second, as offered by the Right and the Republicans, we are asked to think of the state as an expansive Solomon with all power to right a wrong and bring justice and faith to all peoples at home and abroad. They completely fail to notice that Solomon ends up behaving more like Caesar Augustus and his successors. Are you independent minded? Reject these two false alternatives. Do you love freedom? Embrace peace. Do you love peace? Embrace private property. Do you love and defend civilization? Defend and protect us against all uses of Power, the evil against which we must proceed ever more boldly.

By their nature, appeals are most relevant for persuasive speeches, especially when the goal is to motivate an audience to act.

appeal describes the behavior you want your listeners to follow after they have heard your arguments

LO⁴ Listing Sources

Regardless of the type or length of speech, you'll want to prepare a list of the sources you are going to use in the speech. Although you may be required to prepare this list for the speeches you give in this course and other courses you take, in real settings, this list will enable you to direct audience members to the specific source of the information you have used, and will allow you to quickly find the information at a later date. The two standard methods of organizing source lists are (1) alphabetically by author's last name or (2) by content category, with items listed alphabetically by author within each category. For speeches with a short list, the first method is efficient. But for long speeches with a lengthy source list, it is helpful to group sources by content categories.

There are many formal bibliographic style formats you can use in citing sources (for example, MLA, APA, Chicago, CBE). And the "correct" form differs by professional or academic discipline. Check to see if your instructor has a preference about which style you use in class.

Regardless of the particular style, however, the specific information you need to record differs depending on whether the source is a book, a periodical, a newspaper, or an Internet source or website. The elements that are essential to all are author, title of article, title of publication, date of publication, and page numbers. Figure 13.2 gives examples of Modern Language Association (MLA) citations for the most commonly used sources.

Action Step 3h helps you compile a list of sources used in your speech. Figure 13.3 gives an example of this activity completed by a student in this course.

Action Step 3h: Compiling a List of Sources

Record the list of sources you used in the speech.

1. Review your note cards, separating those with information you have used in your speech from those you have not.
2. List the sources of information used in the speech by copying the bibliographic information recorded on the note card.
3. For short lists, organize your list alphabetically by the last name of the first author. Be sure to follow the form shown in Figure 13.3. If you did not record some of the bibliographic information on your note card, you will need to revisit the library, database, and so on, to find it.

Figure 13.2

Examples of the MLA Citation Form for Speech Sources

Book
Shell, G. Richard. *Bargaining for Advantage: Negotiation Strategies for Reasonable People*. New York: Penguin Books, 2006.

Edited Book
Jens Lautrup Norguard. "Intercultural Alternatives: Critical Perspectives on Intercultural Encounters in Theory and Practice." *Intercultural Ethics*. Eds. Maribel Blaseo and Jan Gustafsson. New York: Mc-Graw Hill, 2004. 193–214.

Magazine
Poniewozik, James. "How to Create a Heavenly Host." *Time* 21 June 2006: 63.

Academic Journal
Barge, J. Kevin. "Reflexibility and Managerial Practice." *Communication Monographs* 71:1 (Mar. 2004): 70–96.

Newspaper
Bergin, Kathy. "A New Orleans Revival Plan." *The Chicago Tribune* 31 May 2006: A3.

Electronic Article
Friedman, Thomas L. "Connect the Dots." *New York Times* 25 Sept. 2003. http://www.nytimes.com/2003/09/25/opinion/25FRIED.html.

Electronic Site
Osterweil, Neil and Michael Smith. "Does Stress Cause Breast Cancer?" *WEB M.D.Health* 24 Sept. 2003. http://my.webmd.com/contents/article/74/89170.htm?z=3734_00000_1000_ts_01.

Observation
Schoenling Brewery. Spent an hour on the floor observing the use of various machines in the total process and employees' responsibilities at each stage. 22 April 2006.

Interviews
Mueller, Bruno. Personal interview with diamond cutter at Fegel's Jewelry. 19 March 2006.

LO⁵ Reviewing the Outline

Now that you have created all of the parts of the outline, it is time to put them together in complete outline form and edit them to make sure the outline is well organized and well worded. Use this checklist to complete the final review of the outline before you move into adaptation and rehearsal.

☑ *Have I used a standard set of symbols to indicate structure?* Main points are indicated by Roman numerals, major subdivisions by capital letters, minor subheadings by Arabic numerals, and further subdivisions by lowercase letters.

☑ *Have I written main points and major subdivisions as complete sentences?* Complete sentences help you to see (1) whether each main point actually develops your speech

Figure 13.3

Student Response to Action Step 3h

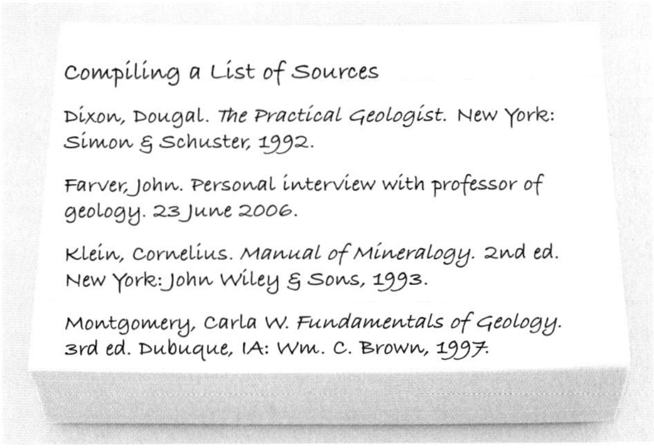

> Compiling a List of Sources
>
> Dixon, Dougal. *The Practical Geologist.* New York: Simon & Schuster, 1992.
>
> Farver, John. Personal interview with professor of geology. 23 June 2006.
>
> Klein, Cornelius. *Manual of Mineralogy.* 2nd ed. New York: John Wiley & Sons, 1993.
>
> Montgomery, Carla W. *Fundamentals of Geology.* 3rd ed. Dubuque, IA: Wm. C. Brown, 1997.

©GREG WHITE/IMAGE SOURCE

goal and (2) whether the wording makes your intended point. Unless the key ideas are written out in full, it will be difficult to follow the next guidelines.

✔ *Do main points and major subdivisions each contain a single idea?* This guideline ensures that the development of each part of the speech will be relevant to the point. Thus, rather than

I. **The park is beautiful and easy to get to.**

divide the sentence so that both parts are separate:

I. **The park is beautiful.**
II. **The park is easy to get to.**

The two-point example sorts out distinct ideas so that the speaker can line up supporting material with confidence that the audience will see and understand its relationship to the main points.

✔ *Does each major subdivision relate to or support its major point?* This principle, called subordination, insures that you don't wander off point and confuse your audience. For example:

©MIAMI HERALD/MCT/LANDOV

I. **Proper equipment is necessary for successful play.**
   A. **Good gym shoes are needed for maneuverability.**
   B. **Padded gloves will help protect your hands.**
   C. **A lively ball provides sufficient bounce.**
   D. **And a good attitude doesn't hurt.**

Notice that the main point deals with equipment. A, B, and C (shoes, gloves, and ball) all relate to the main point. But D, attitude, is not

equipment and should appear somewhere else, if at all.

✔ *Are potential subdivision elaborations indicated?* Recall that it is the subdivision elaborations that help to build the speech. Because you don't know how long it might take you to discuss these elaborations, it is a good idea to include more than you are likely to use. During rehearsals, you may discuss each a different way.

✔ *Does the outline include no more than one-third the total number of words anticipated in the speech?* An outline is only a skeleton of the speech—not a complete manuscript with letters and numbers attached. The outline should be short enough to allow you to experiment with different methods of development during practice periods and to adapt to audience reaction during the speech itself. An easy way to judge whether your outline is about the right length is to estimate the number of words that you are likely to be able to speak during the actual speech and compare this to the number of words in the outline (counting only the words in the outline minus speech goal, thesis statement, headings, and list of sources). Because approximate figures are all you need, to compute the approximate maximum words for your outline, start by assuming a speaking rate of 160 words per minute. (Last term, the speaking rate for the majority of speakers in my class was 140 to 180 words per minute.) Thus, using the average of 160 words per minute, a three- to five-minute speech would contain roughly 480 to 800 words, and the outline should be 160 to 300 words. An 8- to 10-minute speech, roughly 1,280 to 1,600 words, should have an outline of approximately 426 to 533 words.

FINAL LOOK

Now that we have considered the various parts of an outline, let us put them together for a final look. The outline in Figure 13.4 illustrates the principles in practice. The commentary to the right of the outline relates each part of the outline to the guidelines we have discussed.

Figure 13.4

Sample Complete Outline

OUTLINE	ANALYSIS

OUTLINE

Specific Goal: I would like the audience to understand the major criteria for finding a suitable credit card.

Introduction

I. How many of you have been hounded by credit card vendors outside the Student Union?
II. Today I want to share with you three criteria you need to consider carefully before you decide on a particular credit card.

Thesis Statement: Three criteria that will enable audience members to find the credit card that is most suitable for them are level of real interest rate, annual fee, and advertised incentives.

Body

I. The first criterion for choosing a credit card is to select a card with a lower interest rate.
   A. Interest rates are the percentages that a company charges you to carry a balance on your card past the due date.
      1. Most credit cards carry an average of 8%.
      2. Some cards carry an average of as much as 21%.
      3. Many companies offer 0% interest rates for up to 12 months.
      4. Other companies offer 0% interest rates for a few months.
   B. Interest rates can be variable or fixed.
      1. Variable rates mean that the rate will change from month to month.
      2. Fixed rates mean that the rate will stay the same.
(Now that we have considered interest rates, let's look at the next criterion.)

II. A second criterion for choosing a suitable credit card is to select a card with no or a low annual fee.
   A. The annual fee is the cost the company charges you for extending you credit.
   B. The charges vary widely.
      1. Some cards advertise no annual fee.
      2. Most companies charge fees that average around 25 dollars.
(After you have considered interest and fees, you can weigh the benefits that the company promises you.)

III. A third criterion for choosing a credit card is to weigh the incentives.
   A. Incentives are extras that you get for using a particular card.
      1. Some companies promise rebates.
      2. Some companies promise frequent flyer miles.
      3. Some companies promise discounts on "a wide variety of items."
   B. Incentives don't outweigh other criteria.

Conclusion

I. So, getting the credit card that's right for you may be the answer to your dreams.
II. But only if you exercise care in examining interest rates, annual fee, and perks.

Sources

Bankrate Monitor. 25 Sept. 2007. http://www.Bankrate.com.

Haddad, Charles. "Congratulations, Grads—You're Bankrupt: Marketing Blitz Buries Kids in Plastic Debt." *BusinessWeek* 21 May 2001: 48.

Hennefriend, Bill. "Credit Card Blues." *Office Pro* Oct. 2004: 17–20.

McGuire, William. "Protect Your Credit Card." *Kiplinger's* Dec. 2004: 88.

Rose, Sarah. "Prepping for College Credit," *Money* Sept. 1998: 156–7.

ANALYSIS

Write your specific goal at the top of the page. Refer to the goal to test whether everything in the outline is relevant.

The heading *Introduction* sets the section apart as a separate unit. The introduction attempts to (1) get attention and (2) lead into the body of the speech as well as establish credibility, set a tone, and gain goodwill.

The thesis statement states the elements that are suggested in the specific goal. In the speech, the thesis serves as a forecast of the main points.

The heading *Body* sets this section apart as a separate unit. In this example, main point I begins a topical pattern of main points. It is stated as a complete sentence.

The two main subdivisions designated by A and B indicate the equal weight of these points. The second-level subdivisions—designated by 1, 2, and 3 for the major subpoint A, and 1 and 2 for the major subpoint B—give the necessary information for understanding the subpoints.

The number of major and second-level subpoints is at the discretion of the speaker. After the first two levels of subordination, words and phrases may be used in place of complete sentences for elaboration.

This transition reminds listeners of the first main point and forecasts the second.

Main point II, continuing the topical pattern, is a complete meaningful statement paralleling the wording of main point I. Furthermore, notice that each main point considers only one major idea.

This transition summarizes the first two criteria and forecasts the third.

Main point III, continuing the topical pattern, is a complete meaningful statement paralleling the wording of main points I and II.

Throughout the outline, notice that main points and subpoints are factual statements. The speaker adds examples, experiences, and other developmental material during practice sessions.

The heading *Conclusion* sets this section apart as a separate unit. The content of the conclusion is intended to summarize the main ideas and leave the speech on a high note.

A list of sources should always be a part of the speech outline. The sources should show where the factual material of the speech came from. The list of sources is not a total of all sources available—only those that were used, directly or indirectly. Each of the sources is shown in proper form.

Speak Up!

Adapting
Verbally and Visually

Learning Outcomes

LO¹ Discuss the adaptation of your speech information to your audience

LO² Discuss the adaptation of your visual material to your audience

> **“***The skill of adapting involves both verbally adapting and visually adapting by preparing visual aids that facilitate audience understanding.***”**

An effective speech is one that is adapted to the specific audience. You will recall that in Chapter 12, we defined **audience adaptation** as the process of customizing your speech to your specific audience. We explained that audience adaptation depends on audience analysis, and so Action Step 1b asked you to prepare an audience analysis. You used the results of your audience analysis for identifying your topic, deciding on a specific purpose, and selecting main points. Now you are going to learn how to use your audience analysis as you develop that speech. In this chapter, we will look at the fourth Action Step: Adapt the verbal and visual material to the needs of your specific audience. You will use your knowledge of your audience as you consider what specific verbal material you will present and how you will represent that material visually.

What do you think?

There's no way to make a speech more engaging for the audience: either they're interested or they aren't.

Strongly Disagree						Strongly Agree
1	2	3	4	5	6	7

Action Step 4: Adapt the Verbal and Visual Material to the Needs of Your Specific Audience

The skill of adapting involves both verbally adapting and visually adapting by preparing visual aids that facilitate audience understanding.

LO¹ Adapting to Your Audience Verbally

As you are choosing the supporting material for your speech, you will want to select material that demonstrates how this speech (1) is relevant to the audience, (2) helps the audience to comprehend the information, (3) establishes common ground between you and the audience, (4) enhances your credibility and the credibility of the material you are presenting, (5) is appropriate for the audience's initial attitudes, and (6) is culturally sensitive to the diversity in the audience.

Relevance

As you work to adapt your speech to your audience, your first challenge will be to demonstrate **relevance** in the speech so that audience members view the speech goal as important to them. Listeners pay attention to and are interested in ideas when they have a personal impact (speak to the question, "What does this have to do with me?") and are bored when they don't see how

audience adaptation
the process of customizing your speech material to your specific audience

relevance
adapting the information in the speech so that audience members view it as important to them

financial investment that a diamond represents. Well, today I'm going to help you out by explaining criteria for evaluating the quality of diamonds.

Establish Proximity

Your listeners are more likely to be interested in information that has proximity, a relationship to their personal "space." Psychologically, we pay more attention to information that affects our "territory" than to information that we perceive as remote. So your audience is likely to be more attentive to information when it is related to them, their families, their neighborhoods, and/or their city, state, or country. You have probably heard speakers say something like this: "Let me bring this closer to home by showing you . . ." and then make their point by using a local example. As you review the supporting material you have collected during your research, you will want to look for statistics and examples that have proximity for your audience. For example, if you give a speech on the difficulties the EPA is having cleaning up Super Fund sites, you will want to find and use statistics and other material showing what is being done at Super Fund sites in your area.

Demonstrate Personal Impact

When you present information on a topic that can have a serious physical, economic, or psychological impact on audience members, they will be interested in what you have to say. For example, notice how your classmates' attention picks up when your instructor says that what is said next "will definitely be on the test." Your instructor understands that this economic impact (not paying attention can "cost") is enough to refocus most students' attention on what is being said.

As you prepare your speech, you will want to incorporate ideas that create personal impact for your audience. In a speech about toxic waste, you might show a serious physical impact by providing statistics on the effects of toxic waste on the health of people in your state. You may be able to demonstrate serious economic impact by citing the cost to the taxpayers of a recent toxic waste cleanup in your city. Or you might be able to illustrate a serious psychological impact by finding and recounting the stresses faced by one family (that is demographically similar to the audience) with a long-term toxic waste problem in their neighborhood.

Information Comprehension

Although your audience analysis helped you select a topic that was appropriate for your audience's current knowledge level, you will still need to adapt the information you present so that audience members

what is being said relates to them. You can help the audience perceive your speech as relevant by including supporting material that is timely, proximate, and has a personal impact.

Establish Timeliness

Listeners are more likely to be interested in information they perceive as timely—they want to know how they can use the information *now*. In a speech on "The criteria for evaluating the quality of diamonds," presented to a college-aged audience, the introduction below ties the topic to an issue that is timely for most members and therefore piques their interest.

> Most of us have dreamed about shopping for that special diamond that will seal our relationship to our beloved for all time. Well, the day when that becomes a reality is closer each day and I wonder if you're really ready to make such a big decision. No, I'm not talking about the emotional commitment. I'm talking about making the

timely
showing how information is useful now or in the near future

proximity
a relationship to personal space

can easily follow what you are saying and remember it when you are through. Six techniques that can aid you are (1) orienting or refamiliarizing the audience with basic information, (2) defining key terms, (3) creating vivid examples to illustrate new concepts, (4) personalizing information, (5) comparing unfamiliar ideas with those the audience recognizes, and (6) using multiple methods of development.

Orient the Audience

When listeners become confused or have forgotten basic information, they lose interest or do not understand what is being said. So you will want to quickly review the basic ideas that are critical to understanding the speech. For example, if your speech concerns U.S. military involvement in Iraq, you can be reasonably sure that everyone in your audience is aware that the United States and Great Britain were participants in the coalition, but many may not remember the other countries that participated. So before launching into the roles of various countries, remind your listeners by listing the nations that have provided troops, and where they have been stationed.

There may be, however, some audience members who do not need the reminder, so to avoid offending them by appearing to talk down at them and to save face for those who need the reminder, you should acknowledge that they probably already remember the information. Phrases such as: "As you will remember . . . ," "As we all probably learned in high school . . . ," and "As we have come to find out . . ." are ways of prefacing reviews so that they are not offensive.

Define Key Terms

Words have many meanings, so you ensure audience members' comprehension of ideas by defining the key terms that may be unfamiliar to them or are critical to understanding your speech. This becomes especially important when you are using familiar words whose commonly accepted meanings have been altered. For instance, in a speech on the four major problems faced by functionally illiterate people in the workplace, it will be important to your audience to understand what you mean by "functionally illiterate." So early in the speech, you can offer your definition. "By 'functionally illiterate,' I mean people who have trouble accomplishing simple reading and writing tasks."

Illustrate New Concepts with Vivid Examples

Vivid examples help audience members understand and remember abstract, complex, and novel material. From one vivid example, we are better able to understand a more complicated concept. So as you prepare your speech, you will want to adapt by choosing real or hypothetical examples and illustrations to help your audience understand the new information you present. For example, in the definition we used above, the description "having trouble accomplishing simple reading and writing tasks" can be made more vivid when accompanied by the following example: "For instance, a functionally illiterate person could not read and understand the directions on a prescription label that states: 'Take three times a day with a glass of water. Do not take on an empty stomach.'"

Personalize Information

We **personalize** information by presenting it in a frame of reference that is familiar to the audience. Devon, a student at the University of California, is preparing to give a speech on how the Japanese economy affects U.S. markets at the student chapter of the American Marketing Association. He wants to help his audience understand geographic data about Japan. He could just quote the following statistics from the 2001 World Almanac:

> Japan is small and densely populated. The nation's 126 million people live in a land area of 146,000 square miles, giving them a population density of 867 persons per square mile.

Although this would provide the necessary information, it is not adapted to an audience consisting of college students in California, a large state in the United States. Devon can easily adapt the information to the audience by putting it in terms that are familiar to this student audience.

> Japan is a small, densely populated nation. Its population of 126 million is less than half that of the *United States*. Yet the Japanese are crowded into a land area of only 146,000 square miles— roughly the same size as *California*. In fact, Japan

personalize presenting information in a frame of reference that is familiar to the audience

>> What points would you make in a speech on local, state, and federal elections to make the topic relevant for your classmates?

packs 867 persons into every square mile of land, whereas in the *United States* we average about 74 persons per square mile. Overall, then, Japan is about 12 times as crowded as the USA.

In order for Devon to personalize the information above, he had to find the statistics on the U.S. and California. If Devon were speaking to an audience from another state of the country, he could adapt to them by substituting information from that state.

Compare Unknown Ideas with Familiar Ones

An easy way to adapt your material to your audience is to compare your new ideas with ones the audience already understands. For example, if I want an audience of Generation Xers to feel the excitement that was generated when telegrams were first introduced, I might compare it to the change that was experienced when e-mail became widely available. In the speech on functional illiteracy, if you want the audience of literates to sense what functionally illiterate people experience, you might compare it to the experience of surviving in a country where one is not fluent in the language.

Use Multiple Methods for Developing Criteria

People vary in how they learn, so you will want to develop your ideas in different ways. Some people learn best with detailed explanations, some need precise definitions or vivid examples, others learn through statistics, and still others will benefit from a well-designed visual aid.

Let's look at how you might use multiple methods to develop an idea. Suppose the point you are trying to make is: "For the large numbers of Americans who are functionally illiterate, understanding simple directions can be a problem." Here's an example that develops this idea:

For instance, a person who is func-

tionally illiterate might not be able to read or understand a label that states: "Take three times a day after eating."

Now look at how much richer the meaning becomes when we build the statement by adding statistics and additional examples:

A significant number of Americans are functionally illiterate. That is, about 35 million people or about 20 percent of the adult population have serious difficulties with common reading tasks. They cannot read well enough to understand how to prepare a dish from a recipe, how to assemble a simple toy from the printed instructions, or which bus to catch to go across town from the signs at the bus stop. Many functionally illiterate people don't read well enough to follow the directions on a prescription that reads: "Take three times a day after eating."

Common Ground

Each person in the audience is unique, with differing knowledge, attitudes, philosophies, experiences, and ways of perceiving the world. They may or may not know others in the audience. So it is easy for them to assume that they have nothing in common with you or with other audience members. Yet when you speak, you will be giving one message to that diverse group. **Common ground** is the background, knowledge, attitudes, experiences, and philosophies that are shared by audience members and the speaker. Effective speakers use the audience analysis to identify areas of similarity; then they use the adaptation techniques of using personal pronouns, asking rhetorical questions, and drawing on common experiences to create common ground.

Use Personal Pronouns

The simplest way of establishing common ground is to use **personal pronouns**: "we," "us," and "our," so speakers can acknowledge commonalities between themselves and members of the audience. For example, in a speech given to an audience whose members are known to be sympathetic to legislation limiting violence in children's programming on TV, notice the effect of using a personal pronoun:

I know that most *people* are worried about the effects that violence on TV is having on young children.

I know that most of *us* worry about the effects that violence on TV is having on young children.

common ground
the background, knowledge, attitudes, experiences, and philosophies that are shared by audience members and the speaker

personal pronouns
"we," "us," and "our" pronouns that refer directly to members of the audience

>> In what ways do you think the speaker in this situation could create common ground with the audience?

©ERNST WRBA/ALAMY

By using "us" instead of "most people," the speaker includes the audience members and this gives them a "stake" in listening to what is to follow.

Ask Rhetorical Questions

A **rhetorical question** is one whose answers are obvious to audience members and to which they are not really expected to reply. Rhetorical questions create common ground by alluding to information that is shared by audience members and the speaker. They are often used in the introduction to a speech, but can also be effective as transitions and in other parts of the speech. For instance, notice how this transition, phrased as a rhetorical question, creates common ground:

> When you have watched a particularly violent TV program, have you ever asked yourself, "Did they really need to be this graphic to make the point"?

Rhetorical questions are meant to have only one answer that highlights similarities between audience members and leads them to be more interested in the content that follows.

Draw from Common Experiences

You can develop common ground by selecting and presenting personal experiences, examples, and illustrations that embody what you and the audience have in common. For instance, in a speech about the effects of television violence, you might allude to a common viewing experience:

> Remember how sometimes at a key moment when you're watching a really frightening scene in a movie, you may quickly shut your eyes? I remember doing that over and over again. I vividly remember slamming my eyes shut during the snake scenes in *Indiana Jones*.

To be able to create material that draws on common experiences, you must study the audience analysis to understand how you and audience members are similar in the exposure you have had to the topic or in other areas that you can then compare to your topic.

Adapting your information so that it speaks directly to your specific audience, creating common ground, takes time and thought. But well-adapted speeches never leave an audience wondering, "What does this have to do with me?" Research has shown a significant effect of adaptation, or "immediacy," on building attention and ensuring audience retention of information.

Speaker Credibility

Credibility is the confidence that an audience places in the truthfulness of what a speaker says. Some famous people are widely known as experts in a particular area and have proven to be trustworthy and likeable. When these people give a speech, they don't have to adapt their remarks to establish their credibility. However, for most of us, even though we may be given a formal introduction that attempts to acquaint the audience with our credentials and character prior to our speech, we will still need to adapt our remarks in the speech so that we can build audience confidence in the truthfulness of what we are saying. Three adaptation techniques that can affect how credible we are perceived are demonstrating knowledge and expertise, establishing trustworthiness, and displaying personableness.

Demonstrate Knowledge and Expertise

When the audience perceives you to be a knowledgeable expert, it will perceive you as credible. Their assessment of your **knowledge and expertise** depends on how well you convince them that you are qualified to speak on this topic. You can demonstrate your knowledge and expertise through direct and indirect means.

You directly establish expertise when you disclose your experiences with your topic, including formal education, special study, demonstrated skill, and your "track record." Audience members will also assess your expertise through indirect means such as how prepared you seem and how much you demonstrate your firsthand involvement by using personal examples and illustrations. Audiences have an almost instinctive sense of when a speaker is "winging

rhetorical questions
questions phrased to stimulate a mental response rather than an actual spoken response on the part of the audience

credibility
the level of trust that an audience has or will have in the speaker

knowledge and expertise
how well you convince your audience that you are qualified to speak on

CHAPTER 14 Adapting Verbally and Visually **183**

it," and most audiences distrust a speaker who does not appear to have command of the material. Speakers who are overly dependent on their notes or who "hem and haw," fumbling to find ways to express their ideas, undermine the confidence of the audience. When your ideas are easy to follow and are clearly expressed, audience members perceive you to be more credible.

Similarly, when the audience hears a speech in which the ideas are developed through specific statistics, high-quality examples, illustrations, and the personal experiences of the speaker, they are likely to view the speaker as credible. Recall how impressed you are with instructors who always seem to have two or three perfect examples and illustrations and who are able to recall statistics without looking at their notes. Compare this to your experiences with instructors who seem tied to the textbook and don't appear to know much about the subject beyond their prepared lecture. In which instance do you perceive the instructor to be more knowledgeable?

Therefore, as you prepare, you will want to adapt want you say so that you directly and indirectly demonstrate your expertise and knowledge.

Establish Trustworthiness

Your **trustworthiness** is the extent to which the audience can believe that what you say is accurate, true, and in their best interests. The more your audience sees you as trustworthy, the more credible you will be. People assess others' trustworthiness by judging their character and their motives. So you can establish yourself as trustworthy by following ethical standards and by honestly explaining what is motivating you to speak.

As you plan your speech, you need to consider how to demonstrate your character: that you are honest, industrious, dependable, and a morally strong person. For example, when you credit the source of

trustworthiness
both character and apparent motives for speaking

personableness
the extent to which you project an agreeable or pleasing personality

your information as you speak, you confirm that the information is true—that you are not making it up—and you signal your honesty by not taking credit for someone else's ideas. Similarly, if you present the arguments evenly on both sides of an issue, instead of just the side you favor, audience members will see you as fair-minded.

How trustworthy you seem to be will also depend on how the audience views your motives. If people believe that what you are saying is self-serving rather than in their interest, they will be suspicious and view you as less trustworthy. Early in your speech, then, it is important to show how audience members will benefit from what you are saying. For example, in his speech on toxic waste, Brandon might describe how one community's ignorance of the dangers of toxic waste disposal allowed a toxic waste dump to be located in their community, with subsequent serious health issues. He can then share his motive by saying something like: "My hope is that this speech will give you the information you need to thoughtfully participate in decisions like these that may face your community."

By adapting your material so that it highlights your strong character and pure motives, you can establish your trustworthiness.

Display Personableness

We have more confidence in people that we like. **Personableness** is the extent to which you project an agreeable or pleasing personality. The more your listeners like you, the more likely they are to believe what you tell them. We quickly decide how much we like a new person based on our first impressions of them. As a speaker who is trying to build credibility with an audience, you should look for ways to adapt your personal style to one that will help the audience like you and perceive you as credible.

Besides dressing in a way that is appropriate for the audience and occasion, you can increase the chance that the audience will like you by smiling at individual audience members before beginning your remarks and by looking at individuals as you speak, acknowledging them with a quick nod. You can also demonstrate personableness by using humor, especially self-deprecating remarks.

>> **Many people considered the late Pope, John Paul II, trustworthy. Why do you think that is?**

Initial Audience Attitudes

Initial audience attitudes are predispositions for or against a topic, usually expressed as an opinion. Meeting initial audience attitudes means framing a speech in a way that takes into account how much the audience knows and their attitude toward the topic. As part of your audience analysis, you identified the initial attitude that you expected most of your audience members to have toward your topic. During your speech preparation, you will be challenged to adapt the material you plan to present so that it takes this attitude into account.

Although adapting to listeners' attitudes is obviously important for persuasive speeches, it is also important for informative speeches. For example, although a speech on refinishing wood furniture is meant to be informative, you may face an audience whose initial attitude is that refinishing furniture is difficult and complicated, or you may face an audience of young homeowners who are addicted to HGTV and who are really looking forward to your talk. Although the process you describe in both instances would be the same, how you approached explaining the steps in furniture refinishing would need to take the audience's initial disposition into account. Suppose you know that you have an audience of young, new-home owners and have found out through a simple show of hand that most of them enjoy watching HGTV. Then you will want to play upon their interest as you speak, or refer to some of the most popular shows on HGTV. If, however, you have an audience that initially views refinishing furniture as complicated and boring, then you will need to adjust what you say to develop their interest and convince them that the process is simpler than they initially thought. In Chapter 17, "Persuasive Speaking," we will examine strategies for dealing with listeners' attitudes in depth.

Language and Cultural Differences

Western Europeans' speaking traditions inform the approach to public speaking we discuss in this book. However, public speaking is a social and cultural act so, as you would expect, public speaking practices and their perceived effectiveness vary. As they prepare and present speeches, speakers from various cultures and subcultures draw on the traditions of their speech communities. Speakers who address audiences comprised of people from ethnic and language groups different from their own face two additional challenges of adaptation: being understood when speaking in a second language and having

> Public speaking is a social and cultural act, so public speaking practices and their perceived effectiveness vary. As they prepare and present speeches, speakers from various cultures and subcultures draw on the traditions of their speech communities.

limited common experiences on which to establish common ground.

Overcome Linguistic Problems

When the first language spoken by the audience is different from that of the speaker, who is trying to speak their language, audience members often cannot understand what the speaker is saying due to mispronunciations, accents, vocabulary mistakes, and idiomatic speech meaning. Fear of making these mistakes can make second-language speakers self-conscious. But most audience members are more tolerant of mistakes made by second-language speakers than they are of those made by native speakers. Likewise, most audience members will work hard to understand a second-language speaker.

Nevertheless, when you are speaking in a second language, you have the additional responsibility to make your speech as understandable as possible. You can help your audience by speaking more slowly and articulating as clearly as you can. By slowing your speaking rate, you give yourself additional time to pronounce seemingly awkward sounds and choose words whose meanings you know. You also give your audience members additional time to "adjust their ear" so that they can more easily process what you are saying.

One of the best ways to improve when you are giving a speech in a second language is to practice the speech in front of friends and associates who are native speakers. These "trial audience members" should be instructed to take note of words and phrases that are mispronounced or misused. Then they can work with you to correct the pronunciation or to choose other words that better express your idea. Also, keep in mind that the more you practice speaking the language, the more comfortable you will

initial audience attitudes
predispositions for or against a topic, usually expressed as an opinion

Action Step 4a: Adapting to Your Audience Verbally

The goal of this activity is to help you plan how you will verbally adapt your material to the specific audience.

Write your thesis statement.

Review the audience analysis that you completed in Action Steps 1b and 1c. As you review the speech outline that you completed in Action Steps 3a–3h, plan the supporting material you will use to verbally adapt to your audience by answering the following questions:

1. How can I adapt this material so that it is relevant to this audience by showing that it is timely, proximate, and has a personal impact on them?
2. How can I make this material easier for the audience to comprehend by orienting them, defining key terms, using vivid examples, personalizing the information, comparing unknowns with what is known, and using diverse methods of development?
3. How can I establish common ground by using personal pronouns, asking rhetorical questions, and drawing from common experiences?
4. How can I establish my credibility by demonstrating my knowledge and expertise, my trustworthiness, and my personableness?
5. How can I adapt to the language and cultural differences that exist between me and the audience?

become with the language and with your ability to relate to the audience members.

Choose Culturally Sensitive Material

Although overcoming linguistic problems can seem daunting, those whose cultural background differs significantly from that of their audience members also face the challenge of having few common experiences from which to draw. Much of our success in adapting to the audience hinges on establishing common ground and drawing on common experiences. But when we are speaking to audiences who are vastly different from us, we must learn as much as we can about the culture of our audience so that we can develop the material in a way that is meaningful to them. This may mean conducting additional library research to find statistics, examples, and so on that are meaningful to the audience. Or it may require us to elaborate on ideas that would be self-explanatory in our own culture. For example, suppose that Maria, a Mexican American exchange student, was giving a personal narrative speech on the quinceañera party she had when she turned 15 for her speech class at Yeshiva University in Israel. Because

visual aid
a form of speech development that allows the audience to see as well as to hear information

students in Israel have no experience with the Mexican coming-of-age tradition of quinceañera parties, they would have trouble understanding the significance of this event unless Maria was able to use her knowledge of the Bar Mitzvah and Bat Mitzvah coming-of-age ritual celebrations in Jewish culture and relate it to those.

LO² Adapting to Audiences Visually

As you adapt your speech to the specific needs of your audience, consider what visual material will help audience members understand and remember the material you present.

A **visual aid** is a form of speech development that allows the audience to see as well as hear information. You'll want to consider using visual aids; they enable you to adapt to an audience's level of knowledge because they can clarify and dramatize your verbal message. Visual aids also help audiences retain the information over long periods because people will be able to remember more when they use both their eyes and their ears rather than their ears alone.

Types of Visual Aids

Before you can choose visual aids to use for a specific speech, you need to recognize the various types of visual aids from which you can choose. Visual aids range from those that are simple to use and readily available from an existing source, to those that require practice to use effectively and must be custom produced for your specific speech. In this section, we describe the types of visual aids that you can consider using as you prepare your speech.

>> **How is this person using visual aids in his presentation, and how do you think they help him communicate his point to the audience?**

Objects

An **object** is a three-dimensional representation of an idea you are communicating. Objects make good visual aids (1) if they are large enough to be seen by all audience members, and (2) when they are small enough to carry to the site of the speech. A volleyball or a braided rug are objects that would be appropriate in size for most classroom-sized audiences. A cell phone might be OK if the goal was simply to show a phone, but might be too small if the speaker wanted to demonstrate how to key in certain specialized functions.

On occasion, you can be an effective visual aid object. For instance, through descriptive gestures, you can show the height of a tennis net; through your posture and movement, you can show the motions involved in the butterfly swimming stroke; and through your attire, you can illustrate the native dress of a different country.

Models

When an object is too large to bring to the speech site or too small to be seen (like the cell phone), a three-dimensional model is appropriate. In a speech on the physics of bridge construction, a scale model of a suspension bridge would be an effective visual aid. Likewise, in a speech on genetic engineering, a model of the DNA double helix might help the audience understand what happens during these microscopic procedures.

Still Photographs

If an exact reproduction of material is needed, enlarged still photographs are excellent visual aids. In a speech on "smart weapons," enlarged before-and-after photos of target sites would be effective in helping the audience understand the pinpoint accuracy of these weapons.

Slides

Like photographs, slides allow you to present an exact visual image to the audience. The advantage of slides over photographs is that the size of the image can be manipulated on-site so that they are easy for all audience members to see. In addition, if more than one image is to be shown, slides eliminate the awkwardness associated with manually changing photographs. The remote-control device allows you to smoothly move from one image to the next and to talk about each image as long as you would like. One drawback to using slides, however, is that in most cases the room must be darkened for the slides to be viewed. In this situation, it is easy for the slides to become the focal point for the audience. Many novice speakers are tempted to look and talk to the slides rather than to the audience. Moreover, to use slides, you must bring a projector to class with you.

Film and Video Clips

You can use short clips from films and videos to demonstrate processes or to expose audiences to important people. But because effective clips generally run one to three minutes, for most classroom speeches they are ineffective and inappropriate because they dominate the speech and the speaker. In longer speeches when clips are used, speakers must ensure that the equipment needed is available and operative. This means performing a dry run on-site with the equipment prior to beginning the speech.

Simple Drawings

Simple drawings are easy to prepare. If you can use a compass, a straightedge, and a measure, you can draw well enough for the purposes of most speeches. For instance, if you are making the point that water-skiers must hold their arms straight, with the back straight and knees bent slightly, a stick figure (see Figure 14.1) will illustrate the point. Stick figures may not be as aesthetically pleasing as professional drawings or photographs, but to demonstrate a certain concept they can be quite effective. In fact, elaborate, detailed drawings may not be worth the time and effort and actual photographs may be so detailed that they obscure the point you wish to make.

Once a drawing is prepared, it can be scanned and used as part of a PowerPoint presentation, or as an overhead, or the drawing can be used freestanding if it is enlarged and prepared

object
a three-dimensional representation of an idea you are communicating

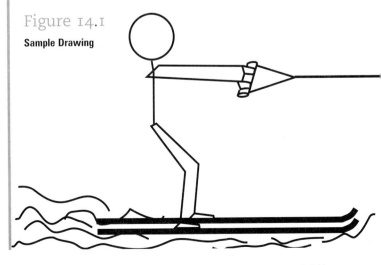

Figure 14.1

Sample Drawing

Figure 14.2

Sample Map

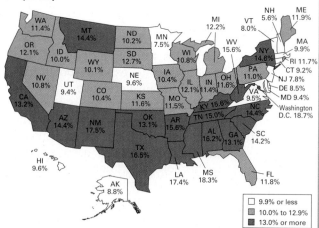

Source: Poverty in the United States: 2005, U.S. Census Bureau, September 2006, Table 19, http://www.census.gov/hhes/www/ poverty/histpov/hstpov19.html. Rates are averaged for 2003, 2004, and 2005 to provide more reliable figures.

on poster board or foamcore. Obviously, you will want to prepare drawings that are easily seen by all audience members. Drawings should be prepared on poster board or foamcore so that they remain rigid and are easy to display.

Maps

Like drawings, maps are relatively easy to prepare. Simple maps allow you to orient audiences to landmarks (mountains, rivers, and lakes), states, cities, land routes, weather systems, and so on. Commercial maps are available, but simple maps are relatively easy to prepare and can be customized so that audience members are not confused by visual information that is irrelevant to your purposes. Like drawings, maps can be used as part of PowerPoint presentations, as overheads, or as freestanding items. Figure 14.2 is a good example of a map that focuses on weather systems.

Figure 14.3

Sample Word Chart

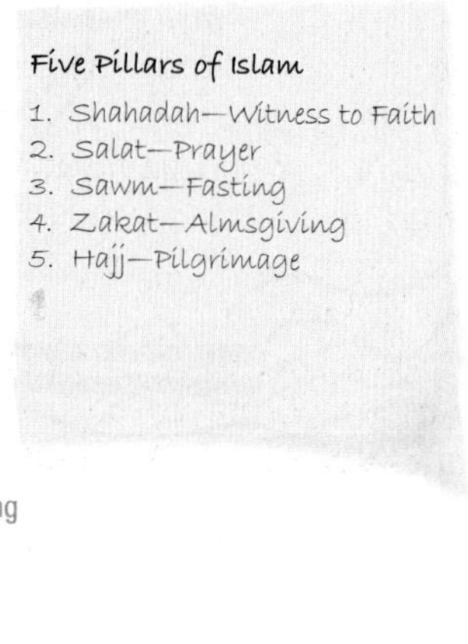

Five Pillars of Islam

1. Shahadah—Witness to Faith
2. Salat—Prayer
3. Sawm—Fasting
4. Zakat—Almsgiving
5. Hajj—Pilgrimage

Charts

A **chart** is a graphic representation that distills a lot of information and presents it to an audience in an easily interpreted visual format. Word charts and flow charts are the most common.

A **word chart** is used to preview, review, or highlight important ideas covered in a speech. In a speech on Islam, a speaker might make a word chart that lists the five pillars of Islam, as shown in Figure 14.3. An outline of speech main points can become a word chart.

A **flow chart** uses symbols and connecting lines to diagram the progressions through a complicated process. Organizational charts are a common type of flow chart that shows the flow of authority and chain of command in an organization. The chart in Figure 14.4 illustrates the organization of a student union board.

In a PowerPoint presentation, you can design the chart so that each part is displayed as you talk about it. If overheads are used, multiple transparencies can be "stacked" so that each transparency adds information that appears on the screen. You can also create the same effect by using a large newsprint pad with a series of charts in which additional information is added on succeeding pages. Then mount the pad on an easel and, as you are talking, flip the pages to reveal more information as you discuss it.

Graphs

A **graph** is a diagram that presents numerical information. Bar graphs, line graphs, and pie graphs are the most common forms of graphs.

A **bar graph** is a chart that presents information using a series of vertical or horizontal bars. It can show relationships between two or more variables at the same time or at various times on one or more dimensions. For instance, in a speech on fluctuations of economy, the bar graph in Figure 14.5 shows the increases for clothing exports from China from 1998 to 2006.

Figure 14.4

Sample Organizational Chart

charts
graphic representations that present information in easily interpreted formats

word charts
used to preview, review, or highlight important ideas covered in a speech

flow charts
use symbols and connecting lines to diagram the progressions through a complicated process

graph
a diagram that compares information

bar graphs
charts that present information using a series of vertical or horizontal bars

Figure 14.5

Sample Bar Graph

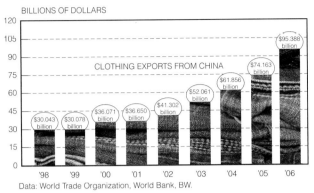

Data: World Trade Organization, World Bank, BW.

Sources: http://www.wto.org/english/res_e/statis_e/its2001_e/chp_4_e.pdf
http://www.wto.org/english/res_e/statis_e/its2004_e/its04_bysector_e.pdf
http://www.wto.org/english/res_e/statis_e/its2007_e/its07_merch_trade_product_e.pdf

A **line graph** is a chart that represents the changes in one or more variables over time through use of a line or series of lines. In a speech on the population of the United States, for example, the line graph in Figure 14.6 helps by showing the population increase, in millions, from 1810 to 2000.

A **pie graph** is a chart that shows the relationships among parts of a single unit. In a speech on comparative family net worth, a pie graph such as the one in Figure 14.7 on the next page could be used to show the percentage of U.S. households that have achieved various levels of net worth.

Most spreadsheet computer programs allow you to prepare colorful graphs easily and to compare the data arrayed as a bar, line, or pie graph. This allows you to choose which display you think will be most effective for your presentation. If you prepare your graphs on the computer, you will be able to insert

Figure 14.6

Sample Line Graph

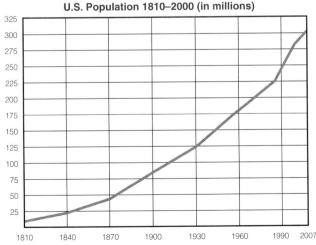

Source: factfinder.census.gov

them into a PowerPoint slide or print them onto an overhead transparency.

When choosing or preparing graphs, make sure that labels are large enough to be read easily by audience members

Methods for Displaying Visual Aids

Once you have decided on the specific visual aids for your speech, you will need to choose the method you will use to display them. There are trade-offs to be considered when choosing a method. Methods for displaying visual aids vary in the type of preparation they require, the amount of specialized training needed to use them effectively, and the professionalism they convey. Some methods, such as writing on a chalkboard, require little advanced preparation. Other methods, such as computer-generated presentation aids, can require extensive preparation. Similarly, it's easy to use an object or a flip chart, but you will need training to properly set up and run a slide or PowerPoint presentation. Finally, the quality of your visual presentation will affect your perceived credibility. A well-run, computer-generated presentation is impressive, but technical difficulties can make you look ill prepared. Hand-prepared charts and graphs that are hastily or sloppily developed mark you as an amateur, whereas professional-looking visual aids enhance your credibility. Speakers can choose from the following methods.

Computer-Mediated Presentations

Today, in many educational and professional settings, audiences expect speakers to use computer-mediated visual aids. PowerPoint, Adobe Persuasion, and Lotus Freelance are popular presentation software. Using these programs, you can create your visual aids on your computer, download them to a disk or CD-ROM, and then use them on a computer/projector or monitor system at your speech site. Additionally, through the Internet you can find, download, and store your own library of images. Presentation software typically allows you to insert an image from your library into your presentation. Using a computer scanner, you can also digitize a photograph from a book or magazine and transfer it to your computer library.

The visuals you create can be displayed directly onto a screen or TV monitor

line graphs
charts that indicate changes in one or more variables over time

pie graphs
charts that help audiences visualize the relationships among parts of a single unit

Figure 14.7

Sample Pie Graph

U.S. Annual Income Distribution by Household (2006)

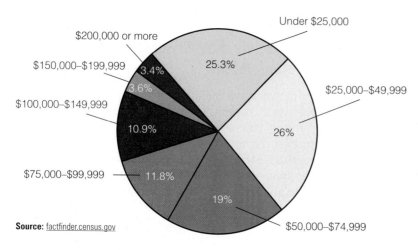

- $200,000 or more — 3.4%
- $150,000–$199,999 — 3.6%
- $100,000–$149,999 — 10.9%
- $75,000–$99,999 — 11.8%
- Under $25,000 — 25.3%
- $25,000–$49,999 — 26%
- $50,000–$74,999 — 19%

Source: factfinder.census.gov

as a computer "slide show," and they also can be used to create slides, overhead transparencies, or handouts. Visual aids developed with presentation software give a very polished look to your speech and allow you to develop complex multimedia presentations.

Today, most colleges and universities offer classes in developing and using presentation software and have dedicated classrooms or portable roll-around carts that house the equipment needed to present computer-mediated visuals.

Preparing visual aids with presentation software is time consuming. Smoothly presenting a computerized visual presentation takes practice. But if you start simply, over time you will become more adept at creating professional-quality visuals. Well-developed and well-presented computer-mediated visual aids greatly enhance audience perceptions of speaker credibility. *Caution:* computer-mediated presentations can be addicting. Many novices overuse them, so instead of having visual aids (visuals that "aid"

the speaker's ideas), the visuals become the show and the speaker is relegated to the role of projectionist (Ayres, 1991, pp. 73–79).

Overhead Transparencies

An easy way to display drawings, charts, and graphs is to transfer them to an acetate film and project them onto a screen via an overhead projector. With a master copy of the visual, you can make an overhead transparency using a copy machine, thermograph, color lift, or if the master is a computer document, with a computer printer. Transparencies are easy and inexpensive to make, and the overhead needed to project them is easy to operate and likely to be available at most speech sites. Overheads work well in nearly any setting, and unlike other types of projections, they don't require dimming the lights in the room. Moreover, overheads can be useful for demonstrating a process because it is possible to write, trace, or draw on the transparency while you are talking. The size at which an overhead is projected can also be adjusted to the size of the room so that all audience members can see the image.

Flip Charts

A **flip chart**, a large pad of paper mounted on an easel, can be an effective method for presenting visual aids. Flip charts (and easels) are available in many sizes. For a presentation to four or five people, a small tabletop version works well; for a larger audience, a larger sized pad (30" × 40") is needed.

Flip charts are prepared before the speech; you use colorful markers to record the information. At times, a speaker may record some of the information before the speech begins and then add information while speaking.

When preparing flip charts, leave several pages between each visual on the pad. If you discover a mistake or decide to revise, you can tear out that sheet without disturbing the order of other visuals you may have prepared. After you have the visuals, tear out all but one sheet between each chart. This blank sheet

flip chart
a large pad of paper mounted on an easel; it can be an effective method for presenting visual aids

serves as both a transition page and a cover sheet. Because you want your audience to focus on your words and not on visual material that is no longer being discussed, you can flip to the empty page while you are talking about material not covered by charts. Also, the empty page between charts ensures that heavy lines or colors from the next chart will not show through.

For flip charts to be effective, information that is handwritten or drawn must be neat and appropriately sized. Flip chart visuals that are not neatly done detract from speaker credibility. Flip charts can comfortably be used with smaller audiences (less than 100 people), but are not appropriate for larger settings. It is especially important when creating flip charts to make sure that the information is written large enough to be comfortably seen by all audience members.

Poster Boards

The easiest method for displaying simple drawings, charts, maps, and graphs is by preparing them on stiff cardboard or foamcore. Then the visual can be placed on an easel or in a chalk tray when it is referred to during the speech. Like flip charts, poster boards must be neat and appropriately sized. They are also limited in their use to smaller audiences.

Chalkboards and Smart Boards

Because the chalkboard is a staple in every college classroom, many novice (and ill-prepared) speakers rely on this method for displaying their visual aids. The smart board serves the same purpose as a chalkboard but can display an image of a computer's desktop via projector, which can be drawn on and manipulated either from the computer or from the board itself.

Unfortunately, the chalkboard is easy to misuse and to overuse. Moreover, chalkboards are not suitable for depicting complex material. So writing on a chalkboard is appropriate to use for very short items of information that can be written in a few seconds. Nevertheless, being able to use a chalkboard effectively should be a part of any speaker's repertoire.

Chalkboards should be written on prior to speaking or during a break in speaking. Otherwise, the visual is likely to either be illegible or partly obscured by your body as you write. Or you may end up talking to the board instead of to the audience. If you need to draw or write on the board while you are talking, you should practice doing it. If you are right-handed, stand to the right of what you are drawing. Try to face at least part of the audience while you work. Although it may seem awkward at first, your effort will allow you to maintain contact with your audience and will allow the audience to see what you are doing while you are doing it.

"Chalk talks" are easiest to prepare, but they are the most likely to result in damage to speaker credibility. It is the rare individual who can develop well-crafted visual aids on a chalkboard. More often, chalkboard visuals signal a lack of preparation.

Handouts

At times, it may be useful for each member of the audience to have a personal copy of the visual aid. In these situations, you can prepare handouts: material printed or drawn on sheets of paper. On the plus side, you can prepare handouts quickly, and all the people in the audience can have their own professional-quality material to refer to and take with them from the speech. On the minus side is the distraction of distributing handouts and the potential for losing audience members' attention when you want them to be looking at you. Before you decide to use handouts, carefully consider why a handout is superior to other methods. If you decide on handouts, you may want to distribute them at the end of the speech.

Criteria for Choosing Visual Aids

Now that you understand the various types of visual aids and the methods you can use to display them, you have to decide what content needs to be depicted and the best way to do this. In this section, we focus on some of the key questions you need to answer to help you make visual aid choices.

1. **What are the most important ideas the audience needs to understand and remember?** These ideas are ones you may want to enhance with visual aids. Visual aids are likely to be remembered. So, you will want to make sure

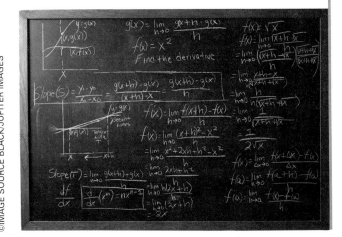

that what you present visually is what you want your audience to remember.

2. **Are there ideas that are complex or difficult to explain verbally but would be easy for members to understand visually?** The old saying that one picture is worth a thousand words is true. At times, we can help our audience by providing a visual explanation. Demonstrating the correct way to hold a golf club is much easier and clearer than simply describing the positioning of each hand and finger.

3. **How many visual aids are appropriate?** Unless you are doing a slide show in which the total focus of the speech is on visual images, the number of visual aids you use should be limited. For the most part, you want the focus of the audience to be on you, the speaker. You want to use visual aids when their use will hold attention, exemplify an idea, or help the audience remember. For each of these goals, the more visual aids used, the less value they will contribute. For a five-minute speech, using three visual aids at crucial times will get attention, exemplify, and stimulate recall far better than using six or eight.

   There is another reason for keeping the visual aids to a small number. A couple of well-crafted visual aids could maximize the power of your statements, whereas several poorly executed or poorly used visual aids could actually detract from the power of your words.

4. **How large is the audience?** The kinds of visual aids that will work for a small group of 20 or less differ from the kinds that will work for an audience of 100 or more. For an audience of 20 or less, as in most of your classroom speeches, you can show relatively small objects and use relatively small models and everyone will be able to see. For larger audiences, you'll want projections that can be seen from 100 or 200 feet away with ease.

5. **Is necessary equipment readily available?** At times, you may be speaking in an environment that is not equipped for certain visual displays. At many colleges and universities, most rooms are equipped with only a chalkboard, an overhead projector, and electrical outlets. If you want to use other equipment, you will have to bring it yourself or reserve it through the appropriate university media office. Be prepared! When you have scheduled equipment from an outside source, you need to prepare yourself for the possibility that the equipment may not arrive on time or may not work the way you thought it did. Call ahead, get to your speaking

>> **Make sure you take into account your audience size when choosing your equipment.**

©AP PHOTO/REX ARBOGAST

location early, and have an alternative visual aid to use, just in case.

6. **Is the time involved in making or getting the visual aid and/or equipment cost effective?** Visual aids are supplements. Their goal is to accent what you are doing verbally. If you believe that a particular visual aid will help you better achieve your goal, then the time spent is well worth it.

You'll notice that most of the visual aids we've discussed can be obtained or prepared relatively easily. But because some procedures are more complicated, we might find ourselves getting lost in making some of them. Visual aids definitely make a speech more interesting and engaging. However, I've found that the best advice is to keep it simple.

Use the following guidelines when choosing visual aids:

- Take a few minutes to consider your visual aid strategy. Where would some kind of visual aid make the most sense? What kind of visual aid is most appropriate?

- Adapt your visuals to your situation, speech topic, and audience needs.

- Choose visuals with which you are both comfortable and competent.

- Check out the audiovisual resources of the speaking site before you start preparing your visual aids.

- Be discriminating in the number of visual aids you use and the key points that they support.

Principles for Designing Effective Visual Aids

However simple you may think your visual aids will be, you still have to carefully design them. The visual aids that you are most likely to design for a classroom presentation are charts, graphs, diagrams, and drawings written on poster board or flip charts or projected on screens using overheads or slides. In this section, we will suggest eight principles for designing effective visual aids. Then, we'll look at several examples that illustrate these principles.

Use a Print or Type Size That Can Be Seen Easily by Your Entire Audience

If you're designing a hand-drawn poster board, check your lettering for size by moving as far away from the visual aid you've created as the farthest person in your audience will be sitting. If you can read the lettering and see the details from that distance, then both are large enough; if not, draw another sample and check it for size.

When you project a typeface from an overhead onto a screen, the lettering on the screen will be much larger than the lettering on the transparency itself. So, what's a good rule of thumb for overhead lettering? Try 36-point type for major headings, 24-point for subheadings, and 18-point for text. Figure 14.8 on the next page shows how these sizes look on paper. The 36-point type will project to about two to three inches on the screen; 24-point will project to about one to two inches; 18-point will project to about one inch. Most presentational software will prompt you if you have chosen a font size that is too small.

Use a Typeface That Is Easy to Read and Pleasing to the Eye

Modern software packages, such as Microsoft Word, come with a variety of typefaces (fonts). Yet only a few of them will work well in projections. In general, avoid fonts that have heavy serifs or curlicues. Figure 14.8 also shows a sample of four standard typefaces in regular and boldface 18-point size. Most other typefaces are designed for special situations.

Which of these typefaces seem easiest to read and most pleasing to your eye? Perhaps you'll decide that you'd like to use one typeface for the heading and another for the text. In general, you will not want to use more than two typefaces—headings in one, text in another. You want the typefaces to call attention to the material, not to themselves.

Use Upper- and Lowercase Type

The combination of upper- and lowercase is easier to read. Some people think that printing in all capital letters creates emphasis. Although that may be true in some instances, ideas printed in all capital letters are more difficult to read—even when the ideas are written in short phrases (see Figure 14.8).

Limit the Lines of Type to Six or Less

You don't want the audience to spend a long time reading your visual aid—you want them listening to you. Limit the total number of lines to six or fewer and write points as phrases rather than as complete sentences. The visual aid is a reinforcement and summary of what you say, not the exact words you say. You don't want the audience to have to spend more than six or eight seconds "getting" your visual aid.

Include Only Items of Information That You Will Emphasize in Your Speech

We often get ideas for visual aids from other sources, and the tendency is to include all the material that was original. But for speech purposes, keep the aid as simple as possible. Include only the key information and eliminate anything that distracts or takes emphasis away from the point you want to make.

Because the tendency to clutter is likely to present a special problem on graphs, let's consider two graphs that show college enrollment by age of students (Figure 14.9 on page 195), based on figures reported in *The Chronicle of Higher Education*. The graph on the left shows all 11 age categories mentioned; the graph on the right simplifies this information by combining age ranges with small percentages. The graph on the right is not only easier to read, but it also emphasizes the highest percentage classifications.

Make Sure Information Is Laid Out in a Way That Is Aesthetically Pleasing

Layout involves leaving white space around the whole message, indenting subordinate ideas, and using different type sizes as well as different treatments, such as bolding and underlining.

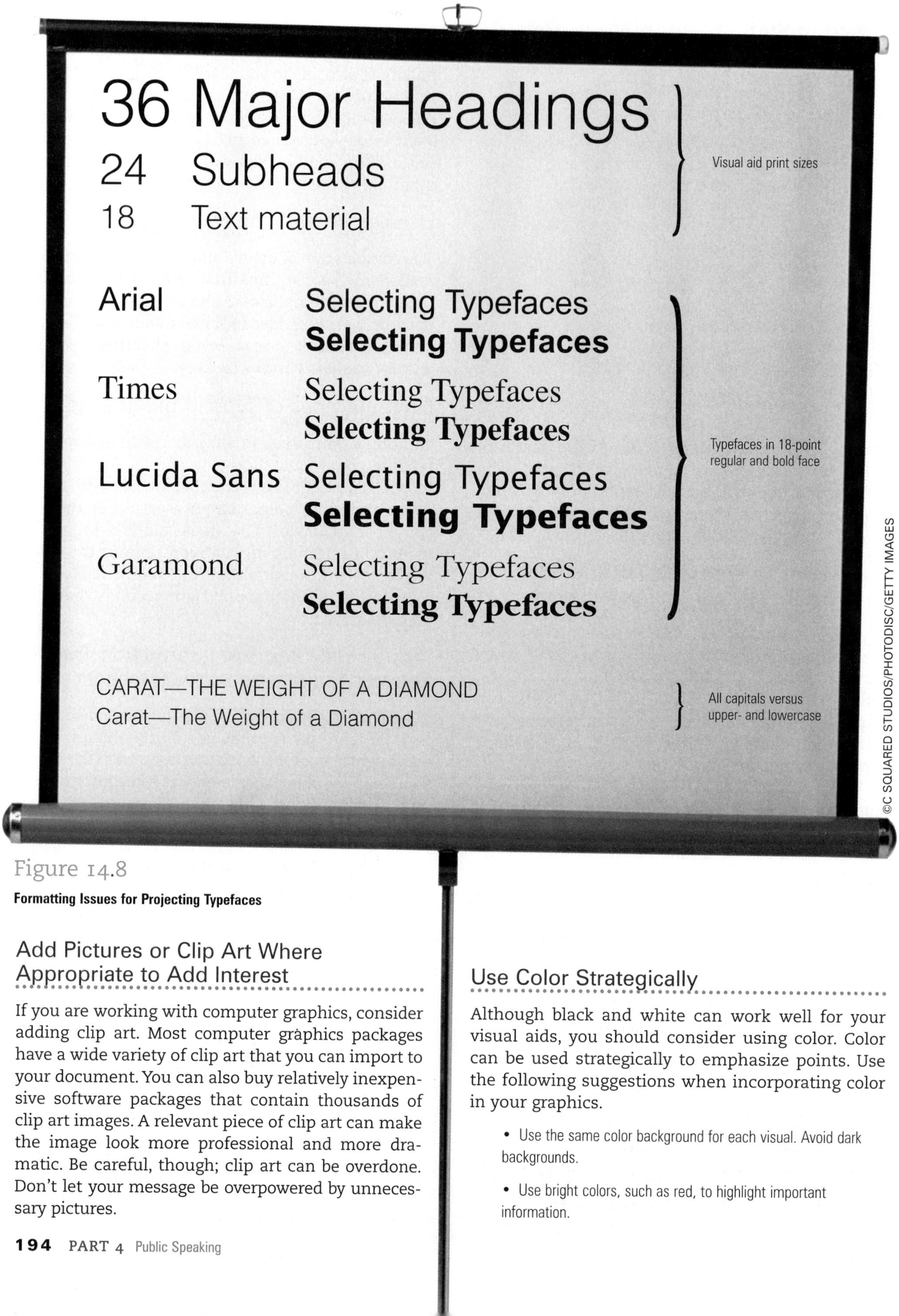

Figure 14.8

Formatting Issues for Projecting Typefaces

Add Pictures or Clip Art Where Appropriate to Add Interest

If you are working with computer graphics, consider adding clip art. Most computer graphics packages have a wide variety of clip art that you can import to your document. You can also buy relatively inexpensive software packages that contain thousands of clip art images. A relevant piece of clip art can make the image look more professional and more dramatic. Be careful, though; clip art can be overdone. Don't let your message be overpowered by unnecessary pictures.

Use Color Strategically

Although black and white can work well for your visual aids, you should consider using color. Color can be used strategically to emphasize points. Use the following suggestions when incorporating color in your graphics.

- Use the same color background for each visual. Avoid dark backgrounds.

- Use bright colors, such as red, to highlight important information.

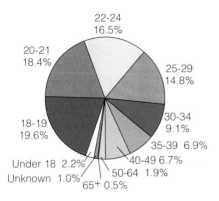

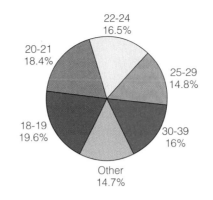

Figure 14.9

Comparative Graphs: College Enrollments by Age of Students

- Use black or deep blue for lettering, especially on flip charts.

- When using yellow or orange for lettering, outline the letters with a darker color because unless outlined, they can't be seen well from distance.

- Use no more than four colors; two or three are even better.

- When you want to get into more complex color usage, use a color wheel to select harmonizing colors.

- Don't crowd. Let the background color separate lettering and clip art.

- Always make a quick template before you prepare your visual aids. Pretend you are your audience. Sit as far away as they will be sitting, and evaluate the colors you have chosen for their readability and appeal.

Let's see if we can put all of these principles to work. Figure 14.10 contains a lot of important information that the speaker has presented, but notice how unpleasant this is to the eye. As you can see, this visual aid ignores all principles. However, with some thoughtful simplification, this speaker could produce the visual aid shown in Figure 14.11, which sharpens the focus by emphasizing the key words (reduce, reuse, recycle), highlighting the major details, and adding clip art for a professional touch.

Now that you have created a plan for using visual aids in your speech and understand the principles for creating high-quality visual aids, you are in a position to visually adapt your speech to your particular audience. In the next chapter, we describe a process for practicing your speech. You will want to have your visual aids ready to use during your practice sessions.

Figure 14.10

A Cluttered and Cumbersome Visual Aid

> ### I WANT YOU TO REMEMBER THE THREE R'S OF RECYCLING
>
> **Reduce the amount of waste people produce like overpacking or using material that won't recycle.**
>
> **Reuse by relying on cloth towels rather than paper towels, earthenware dishes rather than paper or plastic plates, and glass bottles rather than aluminum cans.**
>
> **Recycle by collecting recyclable products, sorting them appropriately, and getting them to the appropriate recycling agency.**

Figure 14.11

A Simple but Effective Visual Aid

CHAPTER 15

Learning Outcomes

LO¹ Discuss public speaking apprehension

LO² Identify the physical elements that affect the delivery of your speech

LO³ Describe characteristics of a conversational presentation style

LO⁴ Identify different types of speech delivery

LO⁵ Discuss methods of rehearsing for your speech

LO⁶ Determine criteria for evaluating speeches

Overcoming
Speech Apprehension
by Practicing Delivery

> **"** *The difference between a good speech and a great speech is often how well it is delivered.* **"**

The difference between a good speech and a great speech is often how well it is delivered. Although delivery can't compensate for a poorly researched, poorly organized, or poorly developed speech, it can take a well-researched, well-organized, and well-developed speech and make it a powerful vehicle for accomplishing your speech goal. Although some people seem to be naturally fluent and comfortable speaking to a group, most of us are a bit frightened about the prospect and not really comfortable with our abilities to effectively present our ideas.

What do you think?

The more I practice a speech, the more comfortable I feel.

Strongly Disagree   Strongly Agree
1   2   3   4   5   6   7

Action Step 5: Practice Your Speech Wording and Delivery

In this chapter, we're going to explain the fifth action step: Practice your speech. We begin by discussing stage fright or public speaking apprehension, which most of us face. Then we will explain the physical elements of effective delivery and the characteristics that are the hallmark of a conversational delivery style. Next, we describe three modes of speech delivery that someone might use to deliver a speech. Then we introduce you to a speech practice process designed to make your rehearsal sessions productive. Finally we explain criteria you can use to evaluate your speeches and others you might hear and, as an example, we apply the criteria to a sample student speech.

LO¹ Public Speaking Apprehension

People probably have feared speaking in public since they first began doing it. So if you're a bit unnerved, you are in good company. And those of us who teach others to speak have been concerned with helping students like you overcome their fears almost as long. Public speaking apprehension, a type of communication anxiety (or nervousness), is the level of fear you experience when anticipating or actually speaking to an audience.

public speaking apprehension
a type of communication anxiety (or nervousness); the level of fear you experience when anticipating or actually speaking to an audience

©ALAN OLIVER/ALAMY

Almost all of us have some level of public speaking apprehension, but about 15 percent of the U.S. population experiences high levels of apprehension (Richmond & McCroskey, 1995, p. 98). Today, we benefit from the results of a significant amount of research that has studied public speaking apprehension and methods for helping us overcome it.

Symptoms and Causes

The signs of pubic speaking apprehension vary from individual to individual, and symptoms range from mild to debilitating. Symptoms include physical, emotional, and cognitive reactions. Physical signs may be stomach upset (or butterflies), flushed skin, sweating, shaking, light-headedness, rapid or heavy heartbeats, and verbal disfluencies including stuttering and vocalized pauses ("like," "you know," "ah," "um," and so on). Emotional symptoms include feeling anxious, worried, or upset. Symptoms can also include specific negative cognitions or thought patterns. For example, a highly apprehensive person might dwell on thoughts such as "I'm going to make a fool of myself," or "I just know that I'll blow it."

The level of public speaking apprehension we feel varies over the course of speaking. In an article written some years ago, researchers identified three phases of reaction that speakers proceed through: anticipation reaction, confrontation reaction, and adaptation reaction (Behnke & Carlile, 1971, p. 66). **Anticipation reaction** is the level of anxiety you experience prior to giving the speech, including the ner-

anticipation reaction
the level of anxiety you experience prior to giving the speech, including the nervousness you feel while preparing and waiting to speak

confrontation reaction
the surge in your anxiety level that you feel as you begin your speech

adaptation reaction
the gradual decline of your anxiety level that begins about one minute into the presentation and results in your anxiety level declining to its pre-speaking level in about five minutes

vousness you feel while preparing and waiting to speak. Your **confrontation reaction** is the surge in your anxiety level that you feel as you begin your speech. This level begins to fall about a minute or so into your speech and will level off at your pre-speaking level about five minutes into your presentation. Your **adaptation reaction** is the gradual decline of your anxiety level that begins about one minute into the presentation and results in your anxiety level declining to its pre-speaking level in about five minutes.

The causes of public speaking apprehension are still being studied, but several sources have been suggested, including the idea that speaking apprehension may be inborn. Two other explanations for apprehension are negative reinforcement and underdeveloped skills.

Negative reinforcement concerns how others have responded to your public speaking endeavors in the past. If you experienced negative reactions, you will probably be more apprehensive about speaking in public than if you had been praised for your efforts (Motley, 1997, p. 2). But these feelings do not have to handicap future performances.

Underdeveloped skills (or "skill deficit" theory) was the earliest explanation for apprehension and continues to receive the attention of researchers. It suggests that many of us become apprehensive because we don't understand or perform the basic tasks associated with effective speech making. Luckily, in the past several chapters you have studied the Action Step process, which is designed to give you the skills you need to be successful.

Although knowing the skills of speech making is critical for reducing your apprehension, there are additional ways to manage and reduce your apprehension.

Managing Your Apprehension

Many of us believe that we would be better off if we could be totally free from nervousness and apprehension. But based on years of study, Prof. Gerald Phillips has concluded that nervousness is not necessarily negative. He noted that "learning proceeds best when the organism is in a state of tension" (1977, p. 37). In fact, it helps to be a little nervous to do your best: If

Managing Your Apprehension

1. Recognize that despite your apprehension, you can make it through your speech.
2. Realize that listeners may not perceive that you are anxious or nervous.
3. Understand that with careful preparation and rehearsal, apprehension will decrease.

you are lackadaisical about giving a speech, you probably will not do a good job (Motley, 1997, p. 27).

Research also has confirmed that although most students in speaking courses experience apprehension, nearly all learn to cope with the nervousness (Phillips, 1977, p. 37). So how does this apply to you?

1. **Recognize that despite your apprehension, you can make it through your speech.** Very few people are so afflicted by public speaking apprehension that they are unable to function. You may not enjoy the "flutters" you experience, but you can still deliver an effective speech. In the years we've been teaching, we've only had two students who were so frightened that they were unable to give the speech. We have seen speakers forget some of what they planned to say, and some have strayed from their planned speech, but they all finished speaking. Moreover, we have had students who reported being scared stiff who actually gave excellent speeches.

2. **Realize that listeners may not perceive that you are anxious or nervous.** Some people increase their apprehension because they mistakenly think the audience will detect their fear. But the fact is that audience members are seldom aware of how nervous a person is. For instance, a classic study found that even speech instructors greatly underrate the amount of stage fright they believe a person has (Clevenger, 1959, p. 136).

3. **Understand that with careful preparation and rehearsal, apprehension will decrease.** If you follow the Speech Plan Action Steps that you have learned in this text, you will find yourself paying less attention to your apprehension as you become engrossed in the challenges of communicating with your particular audience. Moreover, by practicing for a speech, you'll reduce the anxiety you can expect to have if you are "winging it." A study by Kathleen Ellis reinforces previous research findings that students who believe they are competent speakers experience less public speaking apprehension than those who do not (Ellis, 1995, p. 73).

Techniques for Reducing Apprehension

Because there are multiple causes for our public speaking apprehension, there are multiple methods that can help us reduce our overall speech anxiety and also several specific techniques we can employ during a speech that are designed to control our nervousness in the moment.

Techniques for Reducing Apprehension

1. Visualization
2. Systematic desensitization
3. Public speaking skills training

1. **Visualization** is a method that reduces apprehension by helping you develop a mental picture of yourself giving a masterful speech. Joe Ayres and Theodore S. Hopf, two scholars who have conducted extensive research on visualization, have found that if people can visualize themselves going through an entire speech-preparation and speech-making process, they will have a much better chance of succeeding when they are speaking (1990, p. 77).

Visualization has been used extensively with athletes to improve sports performances. In a study of players trying to improve their foul-shooting percentages, players were divided into three groups. One group never practiced, another group practiced, and a third group visualized practicing. As we would expect, those who practiced improved far more than those who didn't. What seems amazing is that those who only visualized practicing improved almost as much as those who practiced (Scott 1997, p. 99). Imagine what happens when you visualize and also practice!

By visualizing the process of speech making, people seem to lower their general apprehension and they also report fewer negative

visualization
a method that reduces apprehension by helping you develop a mental picture of yourself giving a masterful speech

> >**What things do you think this athlete does to mentally prepare herself for her competition? Do you think these methods could be effective in preparing to give a speech?**

3. **Public speaking skills training** is the systematic teaching of the skills associated with the processes involved in preparing and delivering an effective public speech, with the intention of improving speaking competence and thereby reducing public speaking apprehension.

Skills training is based on the assumption that some of our anxiety about speaking in public is due to our realization that we do not know how to be successful—that we lack the knowledge and behaviors to be effective. Therefore, if we learn the processes and behaviors associated with effective speech making, then we will be less anxious (Kelly, Phillips, & Keaen, 1995, pp. 11–13). Public speaking skills include those associated with the processes of goal analysis, audience and situation analysis, organization, delivery, and self-evaluation (ibid).

All three of the methods for reducing public speaking apprehension have been successful at helping people reduce their anxiety. Researchers are just beginning to conduct studies to identify which techniques are most appropriate for a particular person. A study conducted by Karen Kangas Dwyer suggests that the most effective program for combating apprehension is one that uses a variety of techniques, but individualizes these so that the techniques are used in an order that corresponds to the order in which the individual experiences apprehension (Dwyer, 2000). So, for example, when facing a speaking situation, if your immediate reaction is to think worrisome thoughts ("I don't know what I'm suppose to do," or "I'm going to make a fool out of myself"), which then lead you to feel nervous, you would be best served by first undergoing skills techniques. Another person who immediately feels the physical sensations (like nausea, rapid heartbeat, and so on) before thinking about the event would benefit from first learning systematic desensitization techniques; working with visualization or receiving skills training could follow. So to reduce your public speaking apprehension, you may need to use all three techniques, but use them in an order that matches the order in which you experience apprehension.

LO² Elements of Delivery

The physical elements that affect the delivery of your speech are your voice, articulation, and bodily action.

Voice

Your voice is the vehicle that communicates the words of your speech to the audience. How you sound to your audience emphasizes, supplements, and, at

thoughts when they actually speak (Ayres, Hopf, and Ayres, 1994, p. 256). So, you will want to use visualization activities as part of your speech preparation.

2. **Systematic desensitization** is a method that reduces apprehension by gradually having you visualize increasingly more frightening events. The process involves consciously tensing and then relaxing muscle groups, to learn how to recognize the difference between the two states. Then, while in a relaxed state, you imagine yourself in successively more stressful situations—for example, researching a speech topic in the library, practicing the speech out loud to a roommate, and finally, giving a speech. The ultimate goal of systematic desensitization is to have us transfer the calm feelings we attain while visualizing to the actual speaking event. Calmness on command—and it works.

systematic desensitization
a method that reduces apprehension by gradually having you visualize increasingly more frightening events

public speaking skills training
the systematic teaching of the skills associated with the processes involved in preparing and delivering an effective public speech, with the intention of improving speaking competence and thereby reducing public speaking apprehension

times, even contradicts the meaning of the words you speak. As a result, the sound of your voice affects how successful you are in getting your ideas across. To use your voice well, it helps to understand how it works. The four major characteristics of voice are pitch, volume, rate, and quality. You can control these characteristics to create vocal variety and emphasis that will help communicate your meaning effectively.

Pitch refers to scaled highness or lowness of the sound a voice makes. Your voice is produced in the larynx by the vibration of your vocal folds. To feel this vibration, put your hand on your throat at the top of the Adam's apple and say "ah." Now, just as the pitch of a guitar string is changed by making it tighter or looser, so the pitch of your voice is changed by tightening and loosening the vocal folds. Natural pitch varies from person to person, but adult men generally have voices pitched lower than children and adult women. On average, people have a comfortable pitch range of more than an octave, which is eight full notes of a musical scale.

Most of us speak at a pitch range that is appropriate for us. Some people however, have pitch difficulties—that is, they have become accustomed to talking in tones that are either above or below their natural pitch. If you suspect that you have developed pitch difficulty, your instructor can refer you to a speech therapist who can help you readjust to your normal pitch. For most of us, when we speak, the question is not whether we have a satisfactory pitch range, but whether we are using our pitch range to help us communicate our thoughts.

Volume is the degree of loudness of the tone you make as you normally exhale, your diaphragm relaxes, and air is expelled through the trachea. When you speak, you can increase the force of the expelled air on the vibrating vocal folds by contracting your abdominal muscles. This greater force

behind the air you expel increases the volume of your tone.

To feel how these muscles work, place your hands on your sides with your fingers extended over the stomach. Say "ah" in a normal voice. Now say "ah" as loudly as you can. If you are making proper use of your muscles, you should feel an increase in stomach contractions as you increase volume. If you feel little or no stomach muscle contraction, you are probably trying to gain volume from the wrong source. This can result in tiredness, harshness, and lack of sufficient volume to be heard in a large room.

Regardless of your size, you can speak louder. If you are normally soft-spoken, you may have trouble talking loudly enough to be heard by an audience, so you will need to increase pressure from your abdominal area while you are talking.

Rate is the speed at which you talk. In normal conversations, most people speak between 130 and 180 words per minute, but the rate that is best in a speech is determined by whether listeners can understand what you are saying. Usually, even a very fast rate of talking is acceptable if the ideas are not new and complex and when words are well articulated, with sufficient vocal variety and emphasis.

If you are told you speak too rapidly or too slowly, you may need to change your speaking rate. To do this, start by computing your speaking rate when reading written passages. First, read aloud for exactly three minutes. When you have finished, count the number of words you have read and divide by three to compute the number of words you read per minute. If you perceive that your reading rate significantly varied from the 130- to 180-word-per-minute range, then reread the same passage for another three-minute period, consciously decreasing or increasing the number of words you read. Again, count the words and divide by three.

At first, it may be difficult to change speed significantly, but with practice, you will see that you can read much more quickly or much more slowly when you want to. You may find that a different rate, whether faster or slower, will sound strange to you. To show improvement in your normal speaking, you have to learn to adjust your ear to a more appropriate rate of speed. If you practice daily, within a few weeks you should be able to accustom your ear to changes so that you can vary your rate with the type of material you read. As you gain confidence in your ability to alter your rate, you can practice

pitch
the scaled highness or lowness of the sound a voice makes

volume
the degree of loudness of the tone you make as you normally exhale, your diaphragm relaxes, and air is expelled through the trachea

rate
the speed at which you talk

with portions of speeches. You will talk more quickly when material is easy or when you are trying to create a mood of excitement; you will talk more slowly when the material is difficult or when you are trying to create a somber mood.

Quality is the tone, timbre, or sound of your voice. The best vocal quality is a clear and pleasant tone. Difficulties with quality include nasality ("talking through your nose" on vowel sounds), breathiness (too much escaping air during phonation), harshness (too much tension in the throat and chest), and hoarseness (a raspy sound). If you think your voice has one of these undesirable qualities, ask your instructor. If your instructor believes you need help, ask for a referral to a speech therapist, whose extensive knowledge of vocal anatomy and physiology can pinpoint your problem and help you correct it. (Many colleges have speech therapists on staff to work with students.)

Articulation

Articulation is using the tongue, palate, teeth, jaw movement, and lips to shape vocalized sounds that combine to produce a word. Articulation should not be confused with **pronunciation**—the form and accent of various syllables of a word. In the word "statistics," for instance, articulation refers to the shaping of the ten sounds (s-t-a-t-i-s-t-i-k-s); pronunciation refers to the grouping and accenting of the sounds (sta-tis'-tiks).

Many speakers suffer from minor articulation problems such as adding a sound where none appears (athalete for athlete), leaving out a sound where one occurs (libary for library), transposing sounds (revalent for relevant), and distorting sounds (truf for truth). Although some people have consistent articulation problems that require speech therapy (such as substituting *th* for *s* consistently in speech), most of us are guilty of habitual carelessness that is easily corrected.

Two of the most troublesome articulation problems for public speakers are slurring sounds (running sounds and words together) and leaving off word endings. Most spoken English contains some slurring of sounds. For instance, most English speakers are likely to say "tha-table," instead of "that table," because it is simply too difficult to make two *t*

sounds in a row. But some people slur sounds and drop word endings to excess, making it difficult for listeners to understand. "Who ya gonna see?" for "Who are you going to see?" illustrates both of these errors.

If you have a mild case of "sluritis" caused by not taking time to form sounds clearly, you can make considerable improvement in articulation by taking 10 to 15 minutes three days a week to read passages aloud, and trying to overaccentuate each sound. Some teachers advocate "chewing" your words—that is, making sure that lips, jaw, and tongue move carefully for each sound you make. As with most other problems of delivery, to improve, speakers must work conscientiously for days, weeks, or months, depending on the severity of the problem. Constant mispronunciation can give the impression that a speaker is unintelligent, so it is important to learn to articulate clearly.

A major concern of speakers from different cultures and different parts of the country is their **accent**—the articulation, inflection, tone, and speech habits typical of the natives of a country, a region, or even a state or city. Everyone speaks with some kind of an accent, because "accent" means any tone or inflection that differs from the way others speak. Natives of a particular city or region in the U.S. will speak with inflections and tones that they believe are "normal" for North American speech, for instance, people from the Northeast who drop the *r* sound (saying ca for car) or people from the South who "drawl." But when they visit a different city or region, they will be accused of

©DESIGN PICS INC./ALAMY

Do you "chew" your words?

quality
the tone, timbre, or sound of your voice

articulation
using the tongue, palate, teeth, jaw movement, and lips to shape vocalized sounds that combine to produce a word

pronunciation
the form and accent of various syllables of a word

accent
the articulation, inflection, tone, and speech habits typical of the natives of a country, a region, or even a state or city

having an "accent," because the people living in the city or region they visit hear inflections and tones that they perceive as *different* from their own speech.

When should people work to lessen or eliminate an accent? Only when the accent is so "heavy" or different from audience members that they have difficulty in communicating effectively, or if they expect to go into teaching, broadcasting, or other professions where an accent may have an adverse effect on their performance.

Bodily Action

When you deliver a speech, your meaning also depends on how your nonverbal bodily actions supplement the message of your voice. The nonverbal characteristics that affect your delivery are your facial expressions, gestures, movement, poise, and posture.

Facial Expressions

Your facial expressions, eye movement, and mouth movement convey your personableness. Audiences expect your expressions to vary and to be appropriate to what you are saying. Speakers who do not vary their facial expressions during their speech, but who wear deadpan expressions, perpetual grins, or scowls will be perceived by their audience as boring, insincere, or stern. Audiences respond positively to natural facial expressions that reflect what you are saying and how you feel about it.

Gestures

Your gestures are the movements of your hands, arms, and fingers that describe and emphasize what you are saying. Some of us gesture a lot in our casual conversations, while others do not. If gesturing does not come easily to you, don't force yourself to gesture in a speech. Some people who normally use gestures find that, when giving a speech, they aren't able to gesture because they have clasped their hands behind their backs, put their hands in their pockets, or gripped the speaker's stand, and are unable to gracefully pry them free to gesture. As a result, they weirdly wiggle their elbows or appear stiff. To avoid this problem, when you speak, leave your hands free so that they can be available to gesture as you normally do.

Movement

Movement refers to motion of the entire body. Some speakers stand perfectly still throughout an entire

> As a general rule, anything that calls attention to itself is negative, and anything that helps reinforce an important idea is positive.

speech. Others are constantly on the move. In general, it is probably best to remain in one place unless you have some reason for moving. A little movement, however, adds action to a speech, so it may help hold attention. Ideally, movement should help to focus on a transition, emphasize an idea, or call attention to a particular aspect of a speech. Avoid such unmotivated movement as bobbing, weaving, shifting from foot to foot, or pacing from one side of the room to the other. At the beginning of your speech, stand up straight on both feet. If you find yourself in some peculiar posture during the course of the speech, return to the upright position, with your weight equally distributed on both feet.

Posture

Your posture refers to the position or bearing of the body. In speeches, an upright stance and squared shoulders communicate a sense of poise to an audience. Speakers who slouch may give an unfavorable impression of themselves, including the impression of limited self-confidence and an uncaring attitude. As you practice, be aware of your posture and adjust it so that you remain upright, with your weight equally distributed on both feet.

Poise

Poise refers to assurance of manner. A poised speaker is able to avoid mannerisms that distract the audience, such as taking off or putting on glasses, jiggling pocket change, smacking the tongue, licking the lips, or scratching the nose, hand, or arm. As a general rule, anything that calls attention to itself is negative, and anything that helps reinforce an important idea is positive. Likewise, a poised speaker is able to control behaviors that accompany speech nervousness. Later in the chapter, we present several techniques you can use to reduce your nervousness.

Although all of these vocal characteristics and bodily actions may be difficult for speakers with

facial expression
eye and mouth movement

gestures
movements of your hands, arms, and fingers that describe and emphasize what you are saying

movement
motion of the entire body

posture
the position or bearing of the body

poise
assurance of manner

specific handicaps to achieve, all speakers need to practice so that they are as effective at using their voice and body to create a conversational quality to their speaking as they can be.

LO³ Conversational Style

As you practice and deliver your speech, you will want to use your voice, articulation, and bodily action so that your presentation seems natural. A **conversational style** is an informal style of presenting a speech so that your audience feels you are talking with them, not at them. Five hallmarks of a conversational style are enthusiasm, vocal expressiveness, spontaneity, fluency, and eye contact.

Enthusiasm

Enthusiasm is excitement or passion about your speech. If sounding enthusiastic does not come naturally to you, it will help if you have a topic that really excites you. Even normally enthusiastic people can have trouble sounding enthusiastic when they choose an uninspiring topic. Then, focus on how your listeners will benefit from what you have to say. If you are convinced that you have something worthwhile to communicate, you are likely to feel and show more enthusiasm.

To validate the importance of enthusiasm, think of how your attitude toward a class differs depending on whether the professor's presentation says: "I'm really excited to be talking with you about geology (history, English lit)" or "I'd rather be anywhere than talking to you about this subject." A speaker who looks and sounds enthusiastic will be listened to, and that speaker's ideas will be remembered.

Vocal Expressiveness

Vocal expressiveness refers to the contrasts in pitch, volume, rate, and quality that affect the meaning an audience gets from the sentences you speak. Read the following sentence:

"We need to prosecute abusers."

What did the writer intend the focus of that sentence to be? Without hearing it spoken, it is difficult to say. Why? Because it is the vocal expressiveness that helps us understand meanings. Read the sentence aloud four times. Each time, **emphasize** (give a different shade of expressiveness to) a different word, and listen to how it changes the meaning. The first time, emphasize *We*; the second time, emphasize *need*; and so forth. Notice how each time you emphasize a different word, you subtly change the meaning of the sentence. The first time, the emphasis is on who should act. The second time, it is on the urgency and nonvoluntary nature of what is to be done. The third time, the emphasis is on what is to be done, and the final time the emphasis is on who needs to be acted upon. So, if you want to make sure that the audience understands your message, your voice must be expressive enough to delineate shades of meaning.

A total lack of vocal expressiveness produces a **monotone**—a voice in which the pitch, volume, and rate remain constant, with no word, idea, or sentence differing significantly from any other. Although few of us speak in a true monotone, many of us severely limit ourselves when we speak in public and use only two or three pitch levels and relatively unchanging volume and rates. An actual or near monotone makes it difficult for an audience to maintain attention and can diminish the chances that your audience will understand what you are saying. So as you rehearse, you will want to work at developing vocal variety in what you are saying.

Spontaneity

Spontaneity is a naturalness that does not seem rehearsed or memorized. A spontaneous speech delivery is fresh; it sounds as if the speaker is really thinking about both the ideas and the audience as he or she speaks. In contrast, labored speech sounds like a rote recitation and decreases the audience's attention to both speaker and speech.

Audiences often perceive a lack of spontaneity when speakers have memorized their speeches, because people who try to memorize often have to struggle so hard to remember the words that their delivery tends to become laborious. Although talented actors can make lines that they have spoken literally hundreds of times sound spontaneous and vocally expressive, most novice public speakers cannot.

How can you make your outlined and practiced speech still sound spontaneous? Learn the *ideas* of

conversational style
an informal style of presenting a speech so that your audience feels you are talking with them, not at them

enthusiasm
excitement or passion about your speech

vocal expressiveness
the contrasts in pitch, volume, rate, and quality that affect the meaning an audience gets from the sentences you speak

emphasis
giving different shades of expressiveness to words

monotone
a voice in which the pitch, volume, and rate remain constant, with no word, idea, or sentence differing significantly from any other

spontaneity
a naturalness that does not seem rehearsed or memorized

>> Making eye contact with your audience helps ward off boredom.

the speech instead of trying to memorize its words—you will maintain your spontaneity. Suppose someone asks you about the route you take on your drive to work. Because you are familiar with the route, you can present it spontaneously. You have never written out the route, nor have you memorized it—you simply know it. You develop spontaneity in public speaking by getting to know the ideas in your speech as well as you know the route you take to work. Study your outline and absorb the material you are going to present, and then enjoy talking with the audience about it.

Fluency

Effective delivery is also **fluent**—speech that flows easily, without hesitations and vocal interferences. Although most of us are occasionally guilty of using some vocal interferences such as *er, uh, well, OK, you know,* and *like.* These interferences become a problem when they are perceived by others as excessive and when they begin to call attention to themselves, thereby preventing listeners from concentrating on meaning.

Eye Contact

Eye contact is looking directly at the people to whom we are speaking. In speech making, it involves looking at people in all parts of an audience throughout

a speech. As long as you are looking at someone (those in front of you, in the left rear of the room, in the right center of the room, and so on) and not at your notes or the ceiling, floor, or window, everyone in the audience will perceive you as having good eye contact with them.

Maintaining eye contact is important for several reasons.

1. **Maintaining eye contact helps audiences concentrate on the speech.** If speakers do not look at us while they talk, we are unlikely to maintain eye contact with them. This break in mutual eye contact often decreases concentration on the speaker's message.
2. **Maintaining eye contact increases the audience's confidence in you, the speaker.** Just as you are likely to be skeptical of people who do not look you in the eye as they converse, so too audiences will be skeptical of speakers who do not look at them. Eye contact is perceived as a sign of sincerity. Speakers who fail to maintain eye contact with audiences are perceived almost always as ill at ease and often as insincere or dishonest (Burgoon et al., 1986).
3. **Maintaining eye contact helps you gain insight into the audience's reaction to the speech.** Because communication is two-way, your audience is speaking to you at the same time you are speaking to it. In conversation, the audience's response is likely to be both verbal and nonverbal; in public speaking, the audience's response is more likely to be shown by nonverbal cues alone. Audiences that pay attention are likely to look at you with varying amounts of intensity. Listeners who are bored yawn, look out the window, slouch in their chairs, and may even sleep. If audience members are confused, they will look puzzled; if they agree with what you say or understand it, they will nod their

fluency
speech that flows easily, without hesitations and vocal interferences

eye contact
looking directly at the people to whom we are speaking

Why Is Maintaining Eye Contact Important?

1. Maintaining eye contact helps audiences concentrate on the speech.
2. Maintaining eye contact increases the audience's confidence in you, the speaker.
3. Maintaining eye contact helps you gain insight into the audience's reaction to the speech.

heads. By monitoring your audience's behavior, you can adjust by becoming more animated, offering additional examples, or moving more quickly through a point. If you are well prepared, you will be better equipped to make the adjustments and adapt to the needs of your audience.

One way of ensuring eye contact during your speech is to gaze at various groups of people in all parts of the audience throughout the speech. To establish effective eye contact, mentally divide your audience into small groups scattered around the room. Then, at random, talk for four to six seconds with each group. Eventually, you will find yourself going in a random pattern in which you look at all groups over a period of a few minutes. Using such a pattern helps you avoid spending a disproportionate amount of your time talking with those in front of you or in the center of the room.

LO⁴ Types of Delivery

Speeches vary in the amount of content preparation and the amount of practice that you do ahead of time. Each of these factors influences how a speech can be delivered. The three most common types of delivery are impromptu, scripted, and extemporaneous.

Impromptu Speeches

At times, you may be called on to speak "on the spot," with no notice or time to prepare. At a business meeting or in a class, you may be called upon to share what you know about a topic of interest. An **impromptu speech** is one that is delivered with only seconds or minutes of advance notice for preparation and is usually presented without referring to notes of any kind. You may have already been called on in this class to give an impromptu speech, so you know the pressure that comes with this type of speaking.

You can improve your impromptu performances by practicing mock impromptu speeches. For example, if you are taking a class in which the professor calls on students at random to answer questions, you can prepare by anticipating the questions

>> The amount of content preparation and necessary practice time influence the type of speech delivery that you should use.

©SUSAN VAN ETTEN

that might be asked on the readings for the day and practice giving your answers. Over time, you will become more adept at organizing your answers and thinking on your feet.

Scripted Speeches

At the other extreme, there are situations in which you might carefully prepare a complete written manuscript of each word you will speak in your presentation. Then you will either memorize the text or read the text to the audience from a printed document or teleprompter. A **scripted speech** is one that is prepared by creating a complete written manuscript and delivered by rote memory or reading a written copy.

Obviously, effective scripted speeches take a great deal of time to prepare because both an outline and a word-for-word transcript must be prepared and perhaps memorized. When scripted speeches are memorized, you face the increased anxiety caused by fear of forgetting your lines. When you read a scripted speech, you must become adept at looking at the script with your peripheral vision so that you don't appear to be reading and can maintain eye contact with your audience.

impromptu speeches
speeches that are delivered with only seconds or minutes of advance notice for preparation and usually presented without referring to notes of any kind

scripted speeches
speeches that are prepared by creating a complete written manuscript and delivered by rote memory or by reading a written copy

Because of the time and skill required to effectively prepare and deliver a scripted speech, scripted speeches are usually reserved for important occasions that have grave consequences. Political speeches, keynote addresses at conventions, commencement addresses, and CEO remarks at annual stockholder meetings are examples of occasions when a scripted speech might be worth the effort.

Extemporaneous Speeches

Most speeches, whether at work, in the community, or in class, are delivered extemporaneously. An **extemporaneous speech** is researched and planned ahead of time, but the exact wording is not scripted and will vary from presentation to presentation. When speaking extemporaneously, you may refer to simple notes you have prepared to remind you of the ideas you want to present and the order in which you want to present them.

Extemporaneous speeches are the easiest to give effectively. Unlike impromptu speeches, when speaking extemporaneously, you are able to prepare your thoughts ahead of time, have notes to prompt you, and practice what you might actually say. Yet, unlike scripted speeches, extemporaneous speeches do not require as lengthy a preparation process to be effective. In the next section of this chapter, we describe how to rehearse successfully for an extemporaneous speech.

LO⁵ Rehearsal

Rehearsing is practicing the presentation of your speech aloud. In this section, we describe how to schedule your preparation and practice, prepare and use notes, and handle your visual aids, and we provide guidelines for effective rehearsal.

Scheduling and Conducting Rehearsal Sessions

Inexperienced speakers often believe they are ready to present the speech once they have finished their outline. But a speech that is not practiced is likely to be far less effective than it would have been had you given yourself sufficient practice time. In general, if you are not an experienced speaker, try to complete the outline at least two days before the speech is to be presented so that you have sufficient practice time to revise, evaluate, and mull over all aspects of the speech. Figure 15.1 provides a useful timetable for preparing a classroom speech.

Is it really necessary to practice a speech out loud? A study by Menzel and Carrell (1994) supports this notion and concludes that "The significance of rehearsing out loud probably reflects the

extemporaneous speeches speeches that are researched and planned ahead of time, although the exact wording is not scripted and will vary from presentation to presentation

rehearsing practicing the presentation of your speech aloud

JUNE

Figure 15.1

Timetable for Preparing a Speech

SUNDAY	MONDAY	TUESDAY	WEDNESDAY	THURSDAY	FRIDAY	SATURDAY
1	2	3	4 Select Topic; Begin Research (7 Days Before)	5 Continue Research (6 Days Before)	6 Outline Body of Speech (5 Days Before)	7 Work on Introduction and Conclusion (4 Days Before)
8 Finish Outline; Find Additional Material if Needed; Have all Visual Aids Completed (3 Days Before)	9 First Rehearsal Session (2 Days Before)	10 Second Rehearsal Session (1 Day Before)	11 Give Speech (Due Date)	12	13	14

fact that verbalization clarifies thought. As a result, oral rehearsal helps lead to success in the actual delivery of a speech" (p. 23).

Preparing Speaking Notes

Prior to your first rehearsal session, prepare a draft of your speech notes. **Speech notes** are a word or phrase outline of your speech, including hard-to-remember information such as quotations and statistics designed to help trigger memory. The best notes contain the fewest words possible written in lettering large enough to be seen instantly at a distance.

To develop your notes, begin by reducing your speech outline to an abbreviated outline of key phrases and words. Then, if you have details in the speech for which you must have a perfectly accurate representation—such as a specific example, a quotation, or a set of statistics—add these in the appropriate spot. Finally, indicate exactly where you plan to show visual aids.

Making speaking notes not only provides you with prompts when you are speaking, but also helps you cement the flow of the speech's ideas in your mind.

For a three- to five-minute speech, you will need only one or two 3 × 5 note cards to record your speaking notes. In longer speeches, you might need one card for the introduction, one for each main point, and one for the conclusion. If your speech contains a particularly important and long quotation or a complicated set of statistics, you can record this information in detail on separate cards. Figure 15.2 shows how Emming could represent his complete outline (shown on page 176 of Chapter 13) on two 3 × 5 note cards.

During practice sessions, use the notes as you would in the speech. If you will use a podium, set the notes on the speaker's stand or, alternatively, hold them in one hand and refer to them only when needed. How important is it to construct good note cards? Speakers often find that the act of making a note card is so effective in helping cement ideas in the mind that during practice, or later during the speech itself, they do not need to use the notes at all.

Using Visual Aids during the Speech

Many speakers think that once they have prepared good visual aids, they will have no trouble using them in the speech. However, many speeches with good visual aids have become a shambles because

speech notes
word or phrased outlines of your speech

Figure 15.2

Sample Note Cards

Note Card 1
Intro
How many hounded by vendors?
Three criteria: 1 IR, 2 Fee, 3 Inducements

Body
1st C: Examine interest rates
IRs are % that a company chooses to carry balance
✓ Average of 8%
✓ As much as 21%
✓ Start as low as 0 to 8%—but contain restrictions
IRs variable or fixed
✓ Variance—change month to month
✓ Fixed—stay same
(Considered IRs: look at next criterion)

Note Card 2
2d C: Examine the annual fee—charges vary
✓ Some no annual fee
✓ Most companies average around $25
(After considered interest and fees, weigh benefits)
3d C: Weigh inducements
✓ Rebates
✓ Freq flier miles
✓ Discounts
Inducements not outweigh other factors
Conclusion
So 3 criteria: IRs, annual fees, inducements

the aids were not well handled. You can avoid problems by following these guidelines:

1. **Carefully plan when to use visual aids.** Indicate on your outline (and mark on your speaking notes) exactly when you will display each visual aid and when you will remove it. Practice introducing visual aids, handling them until you can use them comfortably and smoothly.
2. **Consider audience needs carefully.** As you practice, consider eliminating any visual aid that does not contribute substantially and directly to the audience's attention to, understanding of, or retention of the key ideas in the speech.
3. **Show a visual aid only when talking about it.** Because visual aids will draw audience attention, practice displaying them only when

Guidelines for Using Visual Aids

1. Carefully plan when to use visual aids.
2. Consider audience needs carefully.
3. Show a visual aid only when talking about it.
4. Describe specific aspects of the visual aid while showing it.
5. Display visual aids so that everyone in the audience can see them.
6. Talk to your audience, not to the visual aid.
7. Carefully consider the disadvantages of passing objects through the audience.

you are talking about them, and then remove visual aids from sight when they are no longer the focus of attention.

A single visual aid may contain several bits of information. To keep audience attention where you want it, you can prepare the visual aid so that you only expose the portion of the visual aid that you are currently discussing.

4. **Describe specific aspects of the visual aid while showing it.** Practice helping your audience to understand the visual aid by verbally telling your audience what to look for, describing various parts, and interpreting figures, symbols, and percentages.

5. **Display visual aids so that everyone in the audience can see them.** It's frustrating not to be able to see a visual aid. So, if you hold the visual aid, practice positioning it away from your body and pointing it toward all parts of the audience. If you place your visual aid on a chalkboard or easel or mount it in some way, practice standing to one side and pointing with the arm nearest the visual aid. If it is necessary to roll or fold the visual aid, bring some transparent tape to mount it to the chalkboard or wall so that it does not unroll or wrinkle. If you are projecting your visual aid, try to practice in the space where you will give your speech so you will know how to position the equipment so that the image is the appropriate size and in focus. If you cannot practice ahead of the date, be sure to arrive early enough on the day of the presentation to practice quickly with the equipment you will use.

6. **Talk to your audience, not to the visual aid.** Although you will want to acknowledge the visual aid by looking at it occasionally, it is important to keep your eye contact focused on your audience. When speakers become too engrossed in their visual aids, looking at the aid instead of at the audience, audience members can become bored. So as you practice, resist the urge to stare at your visual aid.

7. **Carefully consider the disadvantages of passing objects through the audience.** People look at, read, handle, and think about whatever they hold in their hands. While they are so occupied, they are not likely to be listening to you. So if you have a powerful and essential visual aid that must be passed, consider what you will do to maintain audience focus on what you are saying.

Practicing the Speech

Just as with any other activity, effective speech making requires practice, and the more you practice, the better your speech will be. During practice sessions,

>> What are the risks of using living things as visual aids?

©SUSAN VAN ETTEN

you have three major goals. First, you will practice wording your ideas so they are vivid and emphatic. Second, you will practice your speech by working with your voice and body so that your ideas are delivered with enthusiasm, appropriate emphasis, and spontaneity. Third, you will practice using visual aids. As part of each practice you will want to analyze how well it went and set goals for the next practice session. Let's look at how you can proceed through several practice rounds.

First Practice

Your initial rehearsal should include the following steps:

1. Audiotape your practice session. If you do not own a recorder, try to borrow one. You may also want to have a friend sit in on your practice.

2. Read through your complete sentence outline once or twice to refresh memory. Then put the outline out of sight and practice the speech using only the note cards you have prepared.

3. Make the practice as similar to the speech situation as possible, including using the visual aids you've prepared. Stand up and face your imaginary audience. Pretend that the chairs, lamps, books, and other objects in your practice room are people.

4. Write down the time that you begin.

5. Begin speaking. Regardless of what happens, keep going until you have presented your entire

speech. If you goof, make a repair as you would have to do if you were actually delivering the speech to an audience.

6. Write down the time you finish. Compute the length of the speech for this first rehearsal.

Analysis

Listen to the tape and look at your complete outline. How did it go? Did you leave out any key ideas? Did you talk too long on any one point and not long enough on another? Did you clarify each of your points? Did you adapt to your anticipated audience? (If you had a friend or relative listen to your prac-

---

Action Step 5a: Rehearsing Your Speech

The goal of this activity is to rehearse your speech, analyze it, and rehearse it again. One complete rehearsal includes a practice, an analysis, and a second practice.

1. Find a place where you can be alone to practice your speech. Follow the six points of the first practice as listed above.
2. Listen to the tape. Review your outline as you listen and then answer the following questions.

    Are you satisfied with how well:
    The introduction got attention and led into the speech? _____
    Main points were clearly stated? _____ And well developed? _____
    Material adapted to the audience? _____
    Section transitions were used? _____
    The conclusion summarized the main points? _____ Left the speech on a high note? _____
    Visual aids were used? _____
    Ideas were expressed vividly? _____ And emphatically? _____
    You maintained a conversational tone throughout? _____

    Sounded enthusiastic? _____ Sounded spontaneous? _____ Spoke fluently? _____

    List the three most important changes you will make in your next practice session:
    One: _____
    Two: _____
    Three: _____
3. Go through the six steps outlined for the first practice again. Then assess: Did you achieve the goals you set for the second practice? _____
    Reevaluate the speech using the checklist and continue to practice until you are satisfied with all parts of your presentation.

---

tices, have him or her help with your analysis.) Were your note cards effective? How well did you do with your visual aids? Make any necessary changes before your second rehearsal.

Second Practice

Repeat the six steps outlined for the first rehearsal. By practicing a second time right after your analysis, you are more likely to make the kind of adjustments that begin to improve the speech.

Additional Practices

After you have completed one full rehearsal session, consisting of two practices and analysis, put the speech away until that night or the next day. Although you should rehearse the speech at least one more time, you will not benefit if you cram all the practices into one long rehearsal time. You may find that a final practice right before you go to bed will be very helpful; while you are sleeping, your subconscious will continue to work on the speech. As a result, you are likely to find significant improvement in your mastery of the speech when you practice again the next day.

How many times you practice depends on many variables, including your experience, your familiarity with the subject, and the length of your speech.

LO^6 Criteria for Evaluating Speeches

In addition to learning to prepare and present speeches, you are learning to evaluate (critically analyze) the speeches you hear. From an educational standpoint, critical analysis of speeches provides the speaker with both an analysis of where the speech went right and where it went wrong, and it also gives you, the critic, insight into the methods that you want to incorporate or, perhaps, avoid in presenting your own speeches.

Although speech criticism is context specific (analyzing the effectiveness of an informative demonstration speech differs from analyzing the effectiveness of a persuasive action speech), in this section we look at criteria for evaluating public speaking in general. Classroom speeches are usually evaluated on the basis of how well the speaker has met specific criteria of effective speaking.

In Chapters 12 through 15, as you have been learning the Action Steps, you have also been learning the criteria by which speeches are measured. The critical assumption is that if a speech has good content that is well organized and adapted to the audience, and if it is delivered well, it is likely to achieve its goal. Thus, you can evaluate any speech by answering questions that relate to the basics of content, organization, and presentation. Figure 15.3 is a diagnostic speech checklist. You can use this checklist to analyze your first speech during your rehearsal period and to critique sample student speeches at the end of this chapter.

Sample Speech: Chinese Fortune Telling

Adapted from a Speech by Chung-Yan Man, Collin County Community College*

1. Review the outline and adaptation plan developed by Chung-Yan Man in preparing his speech on Chinese fortune telling.
2. Then read the transcript of Chung-Yan's speech.
3. Use the Speech Critique Checklist from Figure 15.3 to help you evaluate this speech.
4. Write a paragraph of feedback to Chung-Yan describing the strengths of his presentation and what he might do next time to be more effective.

You can complete this activity with the Speech Critique Checklist in Figure 15.3, which you can download online.

Adaptation Plan

1. **Key aspects of audience.** The majority of listeners are not familiar with Chinese culture and have had little exposure to Chinese mysticism.
2. **Establishing and maintaining common ground.** My main way of establishing common ground will be by using personal pronouns.
3. **Building and maintaining interest.** Because interest is not automatic, I will provide a variety of examples to pique audience interest.
4. **Audience knowledge and sophistication.** Because most of the class is not familiar with Chinese fortune telling, I will introduce them to the three most common forms of fortune telling. I believe that by repeating key points and by using a variety of examples, the audience will be more likely to retain the information.

*Used with permission of Chung-Yan Man

Figure 15.3

Speech Critique Checklist

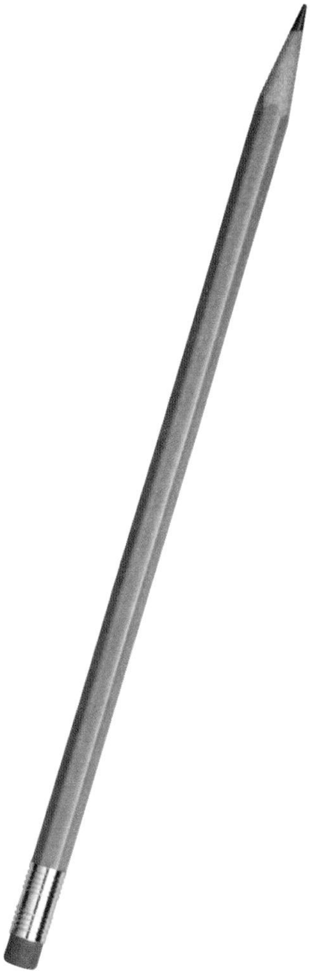

Thinking Critically about Speeches
Check all items that were accomplished effectively.

Content
- [ ] 1. Was the goal of the speech clear?
- [ ] 2. Did the speaker have high-quality information?
- [ ] 3. Did the speaker use a variety of kinds of developmental material?
- [ ] 4. Were visual aids appropriate and well used?
- [ ] 5. Did the speaker establish common ground and adapt the content to the audience's interests, knowledge, and attitudes?

Organization
- [ ] 6. Did the introduction gain attention and goodwill for the speaker, and did it lead into the speech?
- [ ] 7. Were the main points clear, parallel, and in meaningful complete sentences?
- [ ] 8. Did transitions lead smoothly from one point to another?
- [ ] 9. Did the conclusion tie the speech together?

Presentation
- [ ] 10. Was the language clear?
- [ ] 11. Was the language vivid?
- [ ] 12. Was the language emphatic?
- [ ] 13. Did the speaker sound enthusiastic?
- [ ] 14. Did the speaker show sufficient vocal expressiveness?
- [ ] 15. Was the presentation spontaneous?
- [ ] 16. Was the presentation fluent?
- [ ] 17. Did the speaker look at the audience?
- [ ] 18. Were the pronunciation and articulation acceptable?
- [ ] 19. Did the speaker have good posture?
- [ ] 20. Was speaker movement appropriate?
- [ ] 21. Did the speaker have sufficient poise?

Based on these criteria, evaluate the speech as (check one):
- [ ] excellent, [ ] good, [ ] satisfactory, [ ] fair, [ ] poor.

5. **Building credibility.** Because I am Chinese, the audience will assume that I am familiar with the culture, and I will reinforce this as I speak.
6. **Audience attitudes.** The audience is likely to be curious but skeptical.
7. **Adapting to audiences from different cultures and language communities.** Because most audience members come from a different culture and language community than I do and are unfamiliar with these practices, I will be careful to describe these techniques in everyday language.
8. **Using visual aids to enhance audience understanding and memory.** I will show an overhead transparency of the palm of a hand, a transparency of a face, and samples of the sticks used in joss stick fortune telling.

Speech Outline: Chinese Fortune Telling

General purpose: To inform.

Speech goal: I want my audience to appreciate three different kinds of Chinese fortune telling.

Introduction
I. Do you want to know what your future will be?
II. In general, people want to know the future, because knowledge of the future means control of the future.
III. As you know, I am from Hong Kong and I have experienced the mysterious and unique practice of fortune telling in the traditional Chinese culture.
IV. So, today I am going to going to talk about three different forms of Chinese fortune telling.

Body
I. One kind of Chinese fortune telling you may have heard of is palm reading.
  A. Palm reading, also termed palmistry, is the process of foretelling one's future by the imprints and marks on the palm.
    1. Palmistry is based upon the interpretation of the general characteristics of one's hands.
    2. Palmistry focuses on the study of lines, their patterns, and other formations and marks that appear on the palms and fingers. (*Overhead 1: Picture of palm with heart, head, and life lines labeled.*)
  B. Palmistry is divided into two subfields: the palm itself and the fingers.
    1. The three principle lines on your palm are heart, head, and life lines: if lines are deep, clear, and have no interruptions, it is a sign of a smooth and successful life.
    2. Fingers are also important in palm reading: length of the index and ring figure each indicates different beliefs.

Transition: So now that you have understood the basic ideas of palm reading, let us go on to a second kind of Chinese fortune telling, face reading.

II. The Chinese believe that the face can also be used to predict the future and fortune of an individual.
  A. Face reading is the Chinese art of predicting a person's future and fortunes by analyzing the different elements of his or her face. (*Overhead 2: Simple line drawing of a Chinese face.*)
    1. The major facial features that are used in developing the fortune are the nose, mouth, forehead, eyebrows, and eyes.
    2. The face shapes show basic constitution and attributes.
  B. Balance and proportion are important in face reading, as in paintings.

Transition: The final type of Chinese fortune telling uses joss sticks—you may be least familiar with this practice.

III. The oldest known method of fortune telling in the world is the use of fortune-telling sticks.
  A. It is to give an indication of the possibilities of the future instead of exactly what will happen.
  B. This method, which is part of religious practice, takes place in a temple.
    1. A believer selects numbered sticks from a bamboo case containing 78 sticks.
    2. Prayers burn joss sticks, then kneel before the main altar.

Conclusion
I. In conclusion, when people know more about Chinese fortune telling, they begin to understand that these methods are quite scientific and, to a certain extent, accurate.
II. So, I hope what you have learned today about palmistry, face reading, and joss sticks will give you an appreciation for Chinese culture and fortune-telling practices.

Works Cited
Bright, Maura. "Chinese Face Reading for Health Diagnosis and Self Knowledge." 2001. The Wholistic Research Company. 18 Oct. 2005. http://www.wholisticresearch.com/info/artshow.php3?artid=96.

Chan, King-Man Stephen. *Fortune Telling.* May. 2005. Chinese University of Hong Kong. 15 Oct. 2005. http://www.se.cuhk.edu.hk/~palm/chinese/fortune/.

"Fortune Telling." *Chinese Customs.* 2003. British Born Chinese. 17 Oct. 2005. http://www.britishbornchinese.org.uk/pages/culture/customs/fortunetelling.html.

"Most Popular." *Wong Tai Sin Temple.* 18 Oct. 2005. Hong Kong Tourism Board. 18 Oct. 2005. http://www.discoverhongkong.com/eng/touring/popular/ta_popu_wong.jhtml.

"What Is Palmistry?" 2004. *Palmistry.* 16 Oct. 2005. http://www.findyourfate.com/palmistry/palmistry.htm.

Speech and Analysis

Speech

Let me ask you a question: Do you want to know what your future will be? Don't all of us want to know? A lot of people want to know what the future will bring, because knowing it means that you can control the future. I am from Hong Kong, and in China we can tell the future. Well, actually, we can experience the mysterious and unique practice of fortune telling that is part of traditional Chinese culture. Today I am going to talk about three different kinds of Chinese fortune telling: the palm reading, the face reading, and the fortune-telling sticks.

One kind of Chinese fortune telling is palm reading. According to Stephen Chan in his web article "Fortune Telling," palm reading is the process of foretelling one's future by examining and interpreting the imprints, marks, and other general characteristics of one's hands. Palm reading, which is also known as palmistry, is divided into two subfields: the palm itself and each of the fingers. Take a look at your palm for a minute. The "What Is Palmistry?" page on FindYourFate.com tells us that the three principle lines on your palm are your heart, head, and life lines—the heart line is the long line up at the top of your palm; the head line is the line just below it that also runs across your palm; and the life line is the line running from the bottom of your palm and kind of arcing toward your thumb. If these lines are deep, clear, and have no breaks or interruptions, it is a sign of a smooth and successful life. The length, shape, and spacing of the fingers are also important aspects of a palm reading. For example the lengths of the index and ring fingers indicate different aspects of your personality, such as whether or not you are a leader, artistic, or reckless in nature.

So now that you understand the basic ideas of palm reading, let's move on to a second kind of Chinese fortune telling, face reading. The Chinese believe that the face also can be used to predict the future and fortune of a person. In face reading, the fortune teller analyzes the different elements of a person's face. According to Maura Bright's web page, the major facial features used to determine a person's fortune are the nose, mouth, forehead, eyebrows, and eyes. The shape and condition of the face indicate a person's basic constitution, personality, and attributes. For example, a long, narrow face indicates that you are a leader and an organizer, whereas a short and square face means that you are practical and reliable. The balance and proportion of all your features are also important in face reading, just as they are in paintings.

Last but not least, the Chinese also use fortune-telling joss sticks. This is the oldest known method of

Analysis

These opening rhetorical questions are designed to make the audience curious about the topic.

In this sentence, Chung-Yan establishes his credibility.

His thesis statement previews his three main points: the three types of Chinese fortune telling he will discuss.

His first main point focuses on the first type of fortune telling: palm reading.
Notice how he documents the definition.

He has two subpoints, which he quickly previews before explaining each.
Here he attempts to get the audience involved in identifying the nature of their own palm lines: the heart line, the head line, and the life line.

He encourages the audience to see whether these lines are deep, clear, and without breaks or interruptions. But he doesn't really develop what "interruptions" might mean. The audience is left to guess.

He goes on to note the importance of the length, shape, and spacing of the fingers in palm reading. But again, he doesn't really develop the point.

Chung-Yan's transition signals that he will begin discussing a new type of fortune telling.

Again, he acknowledges the source of his information.

Chung-Yan gives a good example of how face shape is used to predict personal characteristics, but he doesn't explain how individual features or balance and proportion affect one's fortune.

Although better than no transition, this transition is trite and neither summarizes nor previews the main points.

fortune telling in the world. Joss sticks are a type of incense, and they are used to indicate the *possibilities* of the future, instead of *exactly* what will happen. This method of fortune telling, which is part of Chinese folk religious practice, takes place in a temple. As described on the "Most Popular" page of the Hong Kong Tourist Board's website, a believer seeking his or her fortune lights a joss stick, kneels before a main altar and makes a wish, then selects a fortune stick from a bamboo case containing 78 numbered sticks. The fortune seeker exchanges the stick for a piece of paper with the same number on it, and his or her fortune is written on the paper.

In conclusion, when people know more about Chinese fortune telling, they begin to understand that these methods are actually based in scientific fact and, to a certain extent, are accurate. I hope what you have learned today about palmistry, face reading, and joss sticks will give you an appreciation for Chinese culture and traditional fortune-telling practices.

Chung-Yan needed to clarify the difference between a "possibility" and an "exact future." An example would have helped.

Although he explains the process, this point would be made more meaningful with more detail. For example, what type of temple? Is the believer seeking an answer to a particular question, or is this a general fortune?

In this conclusion, Chung-Yan claims that these practices are based on "scientific facts" and are "accurate." Yet nothing in the body of the speech supports this conclusion.

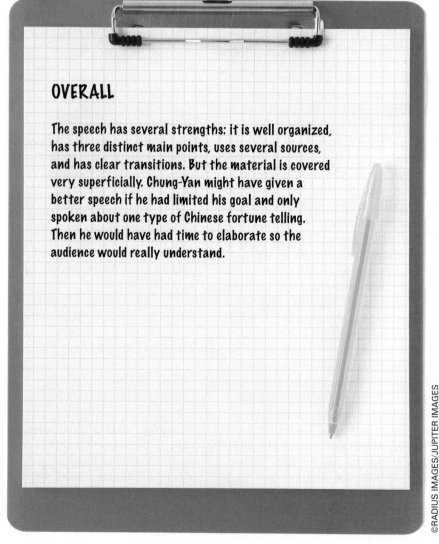

OVERALL

The speech has several strengths: it is well organized, has three distinct main points, uses several sources, and has clear transitions. But the material is covered very superficially. Chung-Yan might have given a better speech if he had limited his goal and only spoken about one type of Chinese fortune telling. Then he would have had time to elaborate so the audience would really understand.

©RADIUS IMAGES/JUPITER IMAGES

Listen Up!

COMM *was designed for students just like you—* busy people who want choices, flexibility, and multiple learning options.

COMM delivers concise, focused information in a fresh and contemporary format. And ... COMM gives you a variety of online learning materials designed with you in mind.

At **4ltrpress.cengage.com/comm**, you'll find electronic resources such as **Printable Flash Cards, Speech Builder Express 3.0™, Interactive Quizzing, Downloads, Games and Simulations,** and **Interactive Video Activities** for each chapter. These resources will help supplement your understanding of core communication concepts in a format that fits your busy lifestyle.

Visit **4ltrpress.cengage.com/comm** to learn more about the multiple COMM resources available to help you succeed!

CHAPTER 16

Learning Outcomes

LO **1** Identify characteristics of effective informative speaking

LO **2** Describe methods for conveying information

LO **3** Discuss common types of informative speeches

Informative Speaking

> **"** *Effective informative speeches are intellectually stimulating, creative, and use emphasis to aid memory.* **"**

In the last four chapters, we described the basic action steps that you will use to prepare any kind of speech. Now in this chapter, we go beyond the basics and focus on the characteristics of good informative speaking and the methods that you can use to develop an effective informative speech.

What do you think?

It's easier for me to remember a joke than facts from the newspaper.

Strongly Disagree					Strongly Agree	
1	2	3	4	5	6	7

An **informative speech** is one that has a goal to explain or describe facts, truths, and principles in a way that stimulates interest, facilitates understanding, and increases likelihood that audiences will remember. In short, informative speeches are designed to educate an audience. Thus, most lectures that your instructors present in class are classified as informative speeches (although, as you are aware, they may range from excellent to poor in quality).

In the first section of this chapter, we focus on three distinguishing characteristic of informing. In the second section, we discuss five methods of informing. And in the final section, we discuss two common types of informative speeches and provide examples of each.

LO¹ Characteristics of Effective Informative Speaking

Effective informative speeches are intellectually stimulating, creative, and use emphasis to aid memory.

Intellectually Stimulating

Information will be perceived by your audience to be **intellectually stimulating** when it is new to them and when it is explained in a way that piques audience curiosity and excites their interest. When we say new information, we mean either that most of your audience is unfamiliar with what you present, or that the way you present the information provides your audience with new insights into a topic with which they are already familiar.

If your audience is unfamiliar with your topic, you should consider how you might tap the audience's natural curiosity. Imagine that you are an anthropology major who is interested in early human forms, not an interest that is widely shared by

informative speech
a speech that has a goal to explain or describe facts, truths, and principles in a way that increases understanding

intellectually stimulating
information that is new to audience members

>>Docents, guides, and interpreters at zoos, museums, and parks work to become experts so they can tailor their presentations to the needs of specific audiences. If you were listening to this docent, what would you want to know?

most members of your audience. You know that in 1991, a 5,300-year-old man, Ötzi, as he has become known, was found perfectly preserved in an ice field in the mountains between Austria and Italy. Even though it was big news at the time, it is unlikely that most of your audience knows much about this. You can draw on their natural curiosity, however, as you present "Unraveling the Mystery of the Iceman," in which you describe scientists' efforts to understand who Ötzi was and what happened to him (Ice Man, http://www.idgonsite.com/drdig/mummy/22.html).

If your audience is familiar with your topic, you will need to identify information that is new to them. Suppose you are a car buff and want to give a speech on SUVs. Because most of your audience is familiar with these cars and their drawbacks, what can you talk about that is likely to be intellectually stimulating to them? You and your audience are aware that SUVs are gas hogs, so you might find out the challenges that manufacturers face when they try to make them more fuel-efficient. As you can see, when your topic is one that the audience is familiar with, your challenge will be to find a new angle that will be intellectually stimulating to them. To do this, choose a goal and develop your speech to present information that challenges most members of your audience to think about what you are saying.

Creative

creative
using information in a way that yields different or original ideas and insights

divergent thinking
thinking that occurs when we contemplate something from a variety of different perspectives

Information will be perceived by your audience to be **creative** when you use information in a way that yields different or original ideas and insights. You may never have considered yourself to be creative, but that may be because you have never worked to develop innovative ideas. Contrary to what you may think, creativity is not a gift that some have and some don't; rather, it is the result of hard work. Creativity comes from good research, time, and divergent thinking.

Creative informative speeches begin with good research. The more you learn about the topic, the more you will have to think about and creatively develop. If all you know about your topic is enough information to fill the time you are allotted, you will be hard pressed to come up with novel ways to approach the information. Speakers who creatively present information do so because they have given themselves lots of material to work with.

For the creative process to work, you also have to give yourself time. So if you want to creatively present the material, you need to decide on your main points and major subpoints at least a couple of days before you speak. This will give you the time to create examples and illustrations, to develop ways of adapting your statistics to the audience, and so on. Rarely do creative ideas come when we are in a time crunch. Instead, they are likely to come when we least expect it, when we're driving our car, preparing for bed, or daydreaming. So the creative process depends on having time to mull over ideas.

For the creative process to work, you have to think divergently. **Divergent thinking** occurs when we contemplate something from a variety of different perspectives. Each perspective may give us at least one new insight that can yield numerous ideas from which we can choose as we work to make our speech creative. Then, with numerous ideas to choose from, we can select the ones that are best suited to our particular audience. Let's look at how divergent thinking can help to identify different approaches to a topic. Suppose you want to give a speech on climatic variation in the United States, and in your research, you ran across the data shown in Figure 16.1.

By looking at the data from different perspectives, you can identify several possible lines of development for your speech. For instance, you might notice that the yearly high temperatures vary less than the yearly low temperatures. Most people wouldn't understand why this is so and would be curious about this. Looking at the data from another perspective, you might spot that it hardly ever rains on the west coast in the summer. In fact, Seattle, a city that most of us consider to be rainy, is shown as receiving less than an inch of rain in July, which is three inches less than any eastern city and five inches less than Miami. Again, an explanation of this anomaly would interest most audience members. Looking at these data yet another way reveals that although most of us might think of July as a month

Figure 16.1

Temperature and Precipitation Highs and Lows in Selected U.S. Cities

City	Yearly Temperature (in degrees Fahrenheit) High	Low	Precipitation (in inches) July	Annual
Chicago	95	−21	3.7	35
Cincinnati	98	−7	3.3	39
Denver	104	−3	1.9	15
Los Angeles	104	40	trace	15
Miami	96	50	5.7	56
Minneapolis	95	−27	3.5	28
New Orleans	95	26	6.1	62
New York	98	−2	4.4	42
Phoenix	117	35	0.8	7
Portland, ME	94	−18	3.1	44
St. Louis	97	−9	3.9	37
San Francisco	94	35	trace	19
Seattle	94	23	0.9	38

that is relatively dry, cities in the Midwest and on the east coast get more than the average rainfall we would expect in July. Again, some audience members might find an explanation of this interesting.

Divergent thought can also help us to create alternative ways to make the same point. Again, using the information in Figure 16.1, we can quickly create two ways to support the point: "Yearly high temperatures in U.S. cities vary far less than yearly low temperatures."

> *Alternative A:* "Of the 13 cities in this table, 10 or 77 percent of them had yearly highs between 90 and 100 degrees. Four or 30 percent had yearly lows above freezing; two or 15 percent had yearly lows between zero and 32 degrees; and seven or 54 percent had low temperatures below zero."

> *Alternative B:* "Cincinnati, Miami, Minneapolis, New York, and St. Louis, cities at different latitudes, all had yearly high temperatures of 95 to 98 degrees. In contrast, the lowest temperature for Miami was 50 degrees, while the lowest temperatures for

Cincinnati, Minneapolis, New York, and St. Louis were -7, -27, -2, -9 degrees, respectively.

Use Emphasis to Aid Memory

If your speech is really informative, your audience will hear a lot of new information but will need your help in remembering the most important. In addition to emphasizing the specific goal and making sure your main points are stated in parallel language, you can use visual aids, repetition, transitions, humor, and memory aids to further highlight important information that you want your audience to remember.

Visual Aids

When we can visualize what we are learning, we remember more than when we only hear. When listening to an informative speech, audiences are more likely to remember information that is presented with visual aids. So your visual aids should be used to emphasize what you want your audience to remember. When choosing your visual aids, be careful not to confuse your audience by presenting exciting visualizations of minor points or details that your audience needn't remember.

Repetition

We remember information that is repeated. Think about it. In class, when you are taking notes, aren't you more likely to write down something that your instructor repeats? So, another easy way to help the audience remember something important is to repeat it. You can repeat the idea word-for-word ("The first dimension of romantic love is passion—that's passion.") or you can paraphrase the idea ("The first dimension of romantic love is passion. That is, it can't really be romantic love if there is no sexual attraction."). Be careful not to overdo repetition, because it can become boring and counterproductive if used as the sole way of reinforcing important information.

Transitions

Effective transitions can help your audience members identify your organization pattern and differentiate between main ideas and subpoints. In your introduction, you can preview the structure so that audience members will know what to listen for. For example, toward the end of the introduction to a speech on romantic love, the speaker might preview what will be discussed:

> Today, I'm going to explain the three characteristics of romantic love and five ways you can keep romantic love alive.

©AP PHOTO/CRAIG LENIHAN

Then, as the speaker moves from describing the characteristics to discussing the how-to's, the speaker might use a transition to summarize and orient the audience:

So, there are three characteristics of romantic love: passion, intimacy, and commitment. Now let's see how people keep love alive.

Again, as the speaker moves into the conclusion, a good transition will remind the audience of the main ideas and signal that the speech is coming to a close:

Today, I've told you that romantic love is comprised of passion, intimacy, and commitment. You've also learned how engaging in small talk, being supportive, and openly sharing ideas and feelings, in addition to self-development and relationship rituals, can keep the romantic flame burning . . .

Effective transitions emphasize your main ideas and help the audience to remember them.

Humor

We remember things that are funny. So, effective speakers use humor to emphasize important ideas. For example, in a speech on reducing stress, one of the speaker's main points was "Keep things in perspective." To emphasize the point, he told the following story:

A problem that seems enormous at the moment can be perceived as less stressful when put in perspective. For instance, there was a man who went to the racetrack and in the first race bet two dollars on a horse that had the same name as the elementary school he had attended. The horse won and the man won 10 dollars. In each of the next several races, he continued with his "system"—betting on "Apple Pie," his favorite dessert, and "Kathie's Prize," his wife's name. And he kept on winning, each time betting all that he had made on the subsequent race. By the end of the sixth race, he had won 700 dollars. He was about to leave when he noticed that in the seventh race, "Seventh Veil" was scheduled to race from the number seven position, and was currently going off at odds of seven to one. Well, he couldn't resist. So he took the entire 700 dollars and bet it on the horse . . . who sure enough, came in seventh. When he got home his wife asked, "How did you do at the track today?" to which he calmly replied, "Not too bad; I lost two dollars." Now that's perspective!

Verbal Memory Aids

You can emphasize ideas and help your audience remember them by using such verbal memory aids as mnemonics and acronyms.

Mnemonics is a system of improving memory by using formulas. For example, if you can word your main points so that a key word in each point starts with the same letter, then you can point out this mnemonic to your audience. For example, in an informative speech on diamonds, the four criteria for evaluating a diamond—weight, clarity, tint, and shape—might be recast into "the four C's" of carat, clarity, color, and cut.

Similarly you might develop an **acronym**, a word formed from the first letter of a series of words to emphasize the ideas. In a speech on effective goal setting, a speaker might say that "useful goals are **SMART**—**S**pecific, **M**easurable, **A**ction-Oriented, **R**easonable, and **T**ime Bound." Now that you understand the characteristics of effective informative speeches, let's look at the different methods you can use to inform your audience about your topic.

LO² Methods of Informing

We can inform through description, definition, comparison and contrast, narration, and demonstration. Let's look more closely at each of these patterns.

Description

Description is the informative method used to create an accurate, vivid, verbal picture of an object, geographic feature, setting, or image. If the thing that is to be described is simple and familiar (like a light bulb or a river), the description may not need to be detailed. But if the thing to be described is complex and unfamiliar (like a sextant or holograph), the description will need to be more exhaustive. Descriptions are, of course, easier if you have a visual aid, but verbal descriptions that are clear and vivid can create mental pictures that are equally informative. To describe something effectively, you can explain its size, shape, weight, color, composition, age, condition, and spatial organization. Although your description may focus on only a few

{ **Fast Facts—A Description of the Sistine Chapel** }

The Sistine Chapel is 134 feet long and 44 feet wide with a 68 foot vaulted ceiling. The interior of the chapel holds a 6:2:3 ratio of length:width:height, a classical ratio that was commonly a feature in Renaissance architecture. The middle tier of the side walls is decorated by two parallel series of frescoes depicting the life of Moses and the life of Christ. Above them, along the upper tier of the windows, is the *Gallery of Popes*. On the wall above the alter is painted Michelangelo's *The Last Judgment*. The ceiling, also by Michelangelo, features *The Ancestors of Christ,* a series of alternating male and female prophets, and at the top of the vault, nine scenes from Genesis, including *The Creation of Adam*.

of these features, each is helpful to consider as you create your description.

You can describe size subjectively as large or small and objectively by noting the specific numerical measures. For example, you can describe a book subjectively as large, or point out that it is 9 by 6 inches with 369 pages.

You can describe shape by reference to common geometric forms like round, triangular, oblong, spherical, conical, cylindrical, rectangular, and so on, or by reference to the shapes of well-known objects such as by saying, "the lower peninsula of Michigan can be described as a left-handed mitten." Shape is made more vivid by using adjectives, such as smooth, jagged, and so on.

You can describe weight subjectively as heavy or light and objectively by pounds and ounces or grams, kilograms, milligrams, or karats, and so on.

You can describe color by coupling a basic color with a common familiar object. For instance, instead of describing something as puce or ocher, you might do better by describing the object as "eggplant purple" or "clay pot orange."

You can describe the composition of something by indicating what it is actually made of, such as by saying the building was made of brick, concrete, wood, or siding. Or, an object may described as what it appears to be, such as by saying it looks "metallic," even if it is made of plastic rather than metal.

You can describe something by its age and by its condition. For example,

mnemonics
a system of improving memory by using formulas

acronyms
words formed from the first letter of a series of words

description
the informative method used to create an accurate, vivid, verbal picture of an object, geographic feature, setting, or image

describing a city as ancient and well kept gives rise to different mental pictures than does describing a city as old and war torn.

Finally, when you describe, you need to follow one spatial organization pattern going from top to bottom, left to right, outer to inner, and so on. A description of the Sistine Chapel might go from the floor to the ceiling, for example.

Definition

Definition is a method of informing that explains something by identifying its meaning. There are four ways that you can use to explain what something means.

First, you can define a word or idea by classifying it and differentiating it from similar ideas. For example, in a speech on vegetarianism, you might use information from the Vegan Society's website (http://www.vegansociety.com) to develop the following explanation of a "vegan." "A vegan is a vegetarian who is seeking a lifestyle free from animal products for the benefit of people, animals, and the environment. Vegans eat a plant-based diet free from all animal products including milk, eggs, and honey. Vegans also don't wear leather, wool, or silk and avoid other animal-based products."

Second, you can define a word by explaining its derivation or history. For instance, the word *vegan* is made up from the beginning and end of the word VEGetariAN and was coined in the U.K. in 1944 when the Vegan Society was founded. Offering this etymology will help your audience to remember the meaning of vegan.

Third, you can define a word by explaining its use or function. When you say, "A plane is a hand-powered tool that is used to smooth the edges of wooden board," you are defining this tool by indicating its use.

The fourth, and perhaps the quickest way you can define something, is by using a familiar synonym or antonym. A **synonym** is a word that has the same or similar meaning; an **antonym** is a word that is a direct opposition. So if you wanted to give a quick definition of a "vegan," you could use the word "vegetarian," a synonym.

definition
a method of informing that explains something by identifying its meaning

synonym
a word that has the same or similar meaning

antonym
a word that is a direct opposition

comparison and contrast
a method of informing that explains something by focusing on how it is similar and different from other things

narration
a method of informing that explains something by recounting events

Comparison and Contrast

Comparison and contrast is a method of informing that explains something by focusing on how it is similar and different from other things. For example, in a speech on vegans, you might want to tell your audience how vegans are similar and different from other types of vegetarians. You can point out that like all vegetarians, vegans don't eat meat, but that unlike semi-vegetarians, they also do not eat fish or poultry. Like lacto-vegetarians, vegans don't eat eggs, but unlike this group and the lacto-ovo vegetarians, vegans also don't use dairy products. So of all vegetarians, vegans have the most restrictive diets.

As you will remember, comparisons and contrasts can be figurative or literal. So you can use metaphors and analogies in explaining your ideas as well as making actual comparisons.

Narration

Narration is a method of informing that explains something by recounting events. Narration of autobiographical or biographical events as well as myths, stories, and other accounts can be effective ways to explain an idea. Narrations usually have four parts. First, the narration orients the listener to the event to be recounted by describing when and where the event took place and by introducing the important people or characters. Second, once listeners are oriented, the narration explains the sequence of events that led to a complication or problem, including details that enhance the development. Third, the narration discusses how the complication or problem affected the key people in the narrative. Finally, the narration recounts how the complication or problem was solved. The characteristics of a good narration include a strong "story line; use of descriptive language and detail that enhance the plot, people, setting, and events; effective use of dialogue; pacing that builds suspense; and a strong voice (Baerwald, http://ccweb.norshore.wednet.edu/writingcorner/narrative.html). The effectiveness of the narration will depend on how much your audience can identify with the key people in the story.

Narrations can be presented in a first-, second-, or third-person voice. When you use first person, you report what you have personally experienced or observed. "Let me tell you about the first time I tried to become a vegetarian . . ." might be the opening for a narrative story told in first person. When you use second person, you place your audience "at the scene" and use the pronouns "you" and "your." "Imagine that you have just gotten off the plane in Pakistan. You look at the signs, but can't read a thing.

Which way is the terminal? . . ." When you use third person, you describe to your audience what has happened, is happening, or will happen to other people. "When the immigrants arrived at Ellis Island, the first thing they saw was . . ."

Demonstration

Demonstration is a method of informing that explains something by showing how something is done, by displaying the stages of a process, or by depicting how something works. Demonstrations range from very simple with a few easy-to-follow steps (like how to make an international phone call), to very complex (such as explaining how to make ethanol). Regardless of whether the topic is simple or complex, effective demonstrations require expertise, developing a hierarchy of steps, and using visual language and aids.

In a demonstration, your experience with what you are demonstrating is critical. Expertise gives you the necessary background to supplement bare-bones instructions with personal, lived experience. Why are TV cooking shows so popular? Because the chef doesn't just read the recipe and do what it says. Rather, while performing each step, the chef shares tips about what to do that won't be mentioned in any cookbook. It is the chef's experience that allows the chef to say that one egg will work as well as two, or that you can't substitute margarine for butter.

In a demonstration, you organize the steps into a time-ordered hierarchy so that your audience will be able to remember the sequence of actions accurately. Suppose that you want to demonstrate the steps in using a touch screen voting machine. If, rather than presenting 14 separate points, you group them under the four headings of I. Get ready to vote, II. Vote, III. Review your choices, and IV. Cast your ballot, chances are much higher that the audience will be able to remember most if not all the items in each of the four groups.

Although you could explain a process with only words, most demonstrations actually show the audience the process or parts of the process. If what you

are explaining is relatively simple, you can demonstrate the entire process from start to finish. However if the process is lengthy or complex, you may choose to pre-prepare material so that although all stages in the process are shown, not every single step is completed as the audience watches.

Effective demonstrations require practice. Remember that under the pressure of speaking to an audience, even the simplest task can become difficult (did you ever try to thread a needle with 25 people watching you?). As you practice, you will want to consider the size of your audience and the configuration of the room. Be sure that all of the audience can actually see what you are doing. You may find that your demonstration takes longer than the time limit you have been given. In these cases, you might want to pre-prepare a step or two.

LO³ Common Types of Informative Speeches

Although you can give a speech that uses any of the methods of informing as the primary framework for organizing an informative speech, two of the most common informative speech types are process speeches and expository speeches.

Process Speeches

The goal of a process speech is to demonstrate how something is done or made, or how it works. Effective process speeches require you to carefully delineate the steps in the process and the order in which they occur. Then steps are grouped and concrete explanations for each step and substep are developed. Because it is based on demonstration, a process speech will likely use visual aids and/or full or modified demonstrations.

For example, Allie is a floral designer and has been asked by her former art teacher to speak on the basics of floral arrangement to a high school art class. The teacher has given her five minutes for her presentation. In preparing for the speech, Allie recognized that in five minutes she could not complete arranging one floral display of any size, let alone help students understand how to create various effects. So she opted to physically demonstrate only parts of the process and bring as additional visual aids, arrangements in various stages of completion. For

> Why are TV cooking shows so popular? Because the chef doesn't just read the recipe and do what it says. While performing each step, the chef shares tips about what to do that won't be mentioned in any cookbook.

demonstration
a method of informing that explains something by showing how something is done, by displaying the stages of a process, or by depicting how something works

>> Effective process speeches require you to carefully delineate the steps in the process and the order in which they occur.

example, the first step in floral arranging is to choose the right vase and frog. So she brought in vases and frogs of various sizes and shapes to display as she explained how to choose a vase and frog based on the types of flowers to be used and the visual effect that is desired. The second step is to prepare the basic triangle of blooms, so she began to demonstrate how to place the flowers she had brought to form one triangle. Rather than hurrying and trying to get everything perfect in the few seconds she had, however, she also brought out several other partially finished arrangements that were behind a draped table. These showed other carefully completed triangles that used other types of flowers. The third step was adding additional flowers and greenery to complete an arrangement and bring about various artistic effects. Again, Allie actually demonstrated how to place several blooms, and then, as she described them, she brought out several com-

expository speech
an informative presentation that provides carefully researched, in-depth knowledge about a complex topic

pleted arrangements that illustrated various artistic effects. Even though Allie did not physically perform all of each step, her visual presentation was an excellent demonstration of floral arranging.

Although some process speeches require you to demonstrate, others are not suited to demonstrations, but use visual aids to help the audience "see" the steps in the process. In a speech on making iron, it wouldn't be practical to demonstrate the process; however, a speaker would be able to greatly enhance the verbal description by showing pictures or drawings of each stage.

In process speeches, the steps are the main points and the speech is organized in time order, so that earlier steps are discussed before later ones.

Expository Speeches

An **expository speech** is an informative presentation that provides carefully researched, in-depth knowledge about a complex topic. For example, "understanding the health care debate," "the origins and classification of nursery rhymes," "the sociobiological theory of child abuse," and "viewing gangsta rap as poetry" are all topics on which you could give an interesting expository speech. Lengthy expository speeches are known as lectures.

All expository speeches require that the speaker use an extensive research base for preparing the presentation, choose an organizational pattern that helps the audience understand the material that is discussed, and use a variety of the informative methods we just discussed to sustain the audience's attention and comprehension of the material presented.

Even college professors who are experts in their fields draw from a variety of source material when they prepare their lectures. You will want to acquire your information from reputable sources. Then as you are speaking, you will want to cite the sources for the information you present. In this way, you can establish the trustworthiness of the information you present and also strengthen your own credibility.

Expository speakers also must choose an organizational pattern that is best suited to the material they will present. Different types of expository speeches are suited to different organizational patterns, so it is up to the speaker to arrange the main points of the speech thoughtfully so they flow in a manner that aids audience understanding and memory.

Finally, a hallmark of effective expository speaking is that it uses various methods of informing for developing material. Within one speech, you may hear the speaker use descriptions, definitions, comparisons and contrasts, narration, and short demonstrations to develop the main points.

Expository speeches include those that explain a political, economic, social, religious, or ethical issue; those that explain events or forces of history; those that explain a theory, principle, or law; and those that explain a creative work.

Exposition of Political, Economic, Social, or Religious Issues

One type of expository speech you might give would help the audience understand the background or context of a political, economic, social, or religious issue. In such a speech, you would explain the forces that gave rise to the issue and are continuing to affect it. You may also present the various positions that are held about the issue and the reasoning behind these positions. Finally, you may discuss various ways that have been presented for the issue to be resolved.

The general goal of your speech is to inform, not to persuade. So you will want to evenly present all sides of controversial issues, without advocating which side is better. You will also want to make sure that the sources you are drawing from are respected and objective in what they report. Finally, you will want to present complex issues in a straightforward manner that helps your audience understand, while not oversimplifying knotty issues.

For example, while researching a speech on drilling for oil and natural gas in Arctic National Wildlife Refuge (ANWR), you need to be careful to consult articles and experts on all sides of this controversial issue and fairly represent and incorporate their views in your outline. Because this is a very complex issue, you will want to discuss all impor- tant aspects of the controversy, including the ecolog- ical, economic, political (national, state, and local), and technological aspects. If time is limited, you may limit the discussion to just one or two of these aspects, but you should at least inform the audience of the other considerations that affect the issue.

Exposition of Historical Events and Forces

A second important type of expository speech is one that explains historical events or forces. History can be fascinating for its own sake, but when history is explained, we can see its relevance for what is hap- pening today. As an expository speaker, you have a special obligation during your research to seek out stories and narratives that can enliven your speech. And you will want to consult sources that analyze the events you will describe so that you are able to describe the impact they had at the time they occurred and the meaning they have today. Although many of us know the historical fact that the United States developed the atomic bomb during World War II, an expository speech on the "Manhattan Project" (as it was known) that drama- tizes the race to produce the bomb and also tells the stories of the main players, would add to our under- standing of the inner workings of "secret," govern- ment-funded research projects and might also place modern arms races and the fear of nuclear prolifer- ation in their proper historical context.

Exposition of a Theory, Principle, or Law

The way we live is affected by natural and man- made laws and principles, and is explained by vari- ous theories. Yet there are many theories, principles, and laws that we do not completely understand or do not understand how they affect us. So an exposi- tory speech can inform us by explaining these important phenomena. As an expository speaker, you will be challenged to find material that explains the theory, law, or principle in language that is understandable to the audience. You will want to search for or create examples and illustrations that demystify esoteric or complicated terminology. Effective examples and comparing unfamiliar ideas with those that the audience already knows can help you explain the law. In a speech on the psychologi- cal principles of operant conditioning, a speaker could help the audience understand the difference between continuous reinforcement and intermittent reinforcement with the following explanation:

> When a behavior is reinforced continuously, each time the person performs the behavior they get the reward, but when the behavior is reinforced inter- mittently, the reward is not always given when the behavior is displayed. Behavior that is learned by

>> This picture from the spring of 2008 is of anti-government protests in Lhasa, Tibet. If you were giving an expository speech about this situation, you might want to identify what these people were protesting about, when and how the conflict originated, and what views have been taken by key figures in the situation, such as the Chinese government and the Dalai Lama. What other factors or consid- erations would you want to take note of?

© AP PHOTO/BINOD JOSHI

continuous reinforcement disappears quickly when the reward no longer is provided, but behavior that is learned by intermittent reinforcement continues for long periods of time, even when not reinforced. Every day you can see the effects of how a behavior was conditioned. For example, take the behavior of putting a coin in the slot of a machine. If the machine was a vending machine, you expect to be rewarded every time you "play." And if the machine doesn't eject the item, you might wonder if the machine is out of order and "play" just one more coin or you might bang on the machine. In any case, you are unlikely to put in more than one more coin. But suppose the machine is a slot machine, or a machine that dispenses instant winner lottery tickets. Now how many coins will you "play" before you stop and conclude that the machine is "out of order"? Why the difference? Because you were conditioned to a vending machine on a continuous schedule, but a slot machine or automatic lottery ticket dispenser "teaches" you on an intermittent schedule.

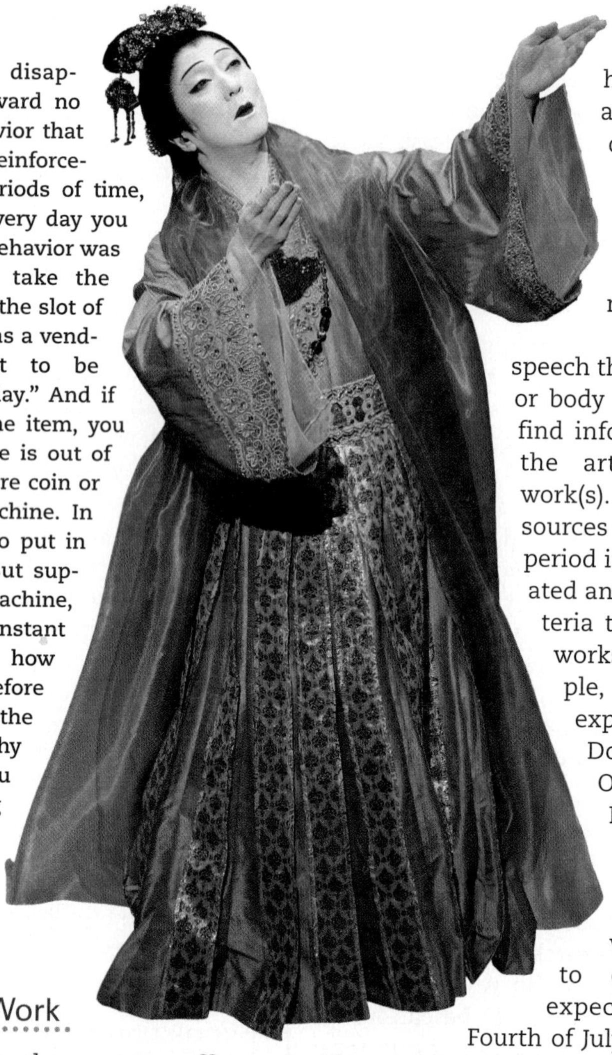

Exposition of Creative Work

Probably every university in the country offers courses in art, theatre, music, literature, and film appreciation. The purpose of these courses is to explain the nature of the creative work and to give the student tools by which to recognize the style, historical period, and quality of a particular piece or group of pieces. Yet most of us know very little about how to understand a creative work, so presentations designed to explain creative works like poems, novels, songs, or even famous speeches can be very instructive for audience members.

When developing a speech that explains a creative work or body of work, you will want to find information on the work and the artist(s) who created the work(s). You will also want to find sources that educate you about the period in which this work was created and inform you about the criteria that critics use to evaluate works of this type. So, for example, if you wanted to give an expository speech on Fredrick Douglas's Fourth of July Oration given in Rochester, New York in 1852, you might need to orient your audience by first reminding them of who Douglas was. Then you would want to explain the traditional expectation that was set for Fourth of July speakers at this point in history. After this, you might want to summarize the speech and perhaps share a few memorable quotes. Finally, you would want to discuss how speech critics view the speech and why the speech is considered to be "great."

Figure 16.2 presents examples of topics for each of the four types of expository speeches.

Figure 16.2

Examples of Expository Speech Topics

Topic Ideas for Political, Economic, Social, or Religious Issues	Topic Ideas for Historical Events, Forces, and People	Topic Ideas for Exposition of Theory, Principle, or Law	Topic Ideas for Expositions of Creative Work
The Bush doctrine of preemption	W. E. B. DuBois	Monetary theory	Jazz
Stem cell research	Gandhi's leadership	Boyle's law	The films of Alfred Hitchcock
Gay marriage	The papacy	Number theory	Impressionist painting
School vouchers	The colonization of Africa	Psychoanalytic theory	The love sonnets of Shakespeare
Mandatory sentencing	Conquering Mt. Everest	Global warming	Salsa dancing
School uniforms	The Vietnam War	Intelligent design	Kabuki theater
Home schooling	The Balfour Declaration	The normal distribution	Inaugural addresses
Immigration	The Republic of Texas	Color theory	Iconography

Sample Expository Speech: The Three C's of Down Syndrome

Adapted from a Speech by Elizabeth Lopez, Collin County Community College*

This section presents a sample expository speech adaptation plan, outline, and transcript given by a student in an introductory speaking course.

1. Review the outline and adaptation plan developed by Elizabeth Lopez in preparing her speech on Down syndrome.
2. Then read the transcript of Elizabeth Lopez's speech.
3. Use the Expository Speech Evaluation Checklist from Figure 16.3 to help you evaluate this speech.
4. Write a paragraph of feedback to Elizabeth Lopez, describing the strengths of her presentation and what you think she might do next time to be more effective.

You can complete this activity with the Expository Speech Evaluation Checklist in Figure 16.3, which you can download online.

Adaptation Plan

1. **Key aspects of audience.** Because audience members have probably seen someone with Down syndrome but don't really know much about it, I will need to provide basic information.
2. **Establishing and maintaining common ground.** My main way of establishing common ground will be by using inclusive personal pronouns (we, us, our).
3. **Building and maintaining interest.** I will build interest by pointing out my personal relationship and interest in Down syndrome and through the use of examples.
4. **Audience knowledge and sophistication.** Because most of the class is not familiar with Down syndrome, I will provide as much explanatory information as I can.
5. **Building credibility.** Early in the speech, I will demonstrate credibility by mentioning my volunteer experience, educational background, and most importantly, my daughter, who has Down syndrome.
6. **Audience attitudes.** I expect my audience to be curious about Down syndrome, but probably uncomfortable with the idea of interacting with people who have the syndrome. So, I will give them information to help them become more knowledgeable and, I hope, less fearful.

*Used with permission of Elizabeth Lopez

Figure 16.3

Expository Speech Evaluation Checklist

You can use this form to critique an expository speech that you hear in class. As you listen, outline the speech and identify which type of expository speech the speaker is giving. Then answer the questions that follow.

Type of Expository Speech (Check One)
- ☐ a political, economic, social, or religious issue
- ☐ historical events or forces
- ☐ a theory, principle, or law
- ☐ a creative work

Primary Criteria
- ☐ 1. Did the speech provide well-researched information on a complex topic?
- ☐ 2. Did the speaker effectively use a variety of methods to convey the information?
- ☐ 3. Did the speaker emphasize the main ideas and important supporting material?
- ☐ 4. Did the speaker use high-quality sources for the information presented?
- ☐ 5. Was the speech well organized, with clearly identifiable main points?
- ☐ 6. Did the speaker present in-depth, high-quality information?

General Criteria
- ☐ 1. Was the specific goal clear?
- ☐ 2. Was the introduction effective in creating interest and introducing the process to be explained?
- ☐ 3. Was the speech organized using time order?
- ☐ 4. Was the language clear, vivid, emphatic, and appropriate?
- ☐ 5. Was the conclusion effective in summarizing the steps?
- ☐ 6. Was the speech delivered enthusiastically, with vocal expressiveness, fluency, spontaneity, and directness?

7. **Adapt to audiences from different cultures and language communities.** Although the audience is diverse and because Down syndrome occurs in all ethnic groups and in both sexes, I won't do anything specific to adapt.
8. **Use visual aids to enhance audience understanding and memory.** I will use several PowerPoint slides to highlight Down syndrome characteristics.

Speech Outline: The Three C's of Down Syndrome

General purpose: To inform

Speech goal: In this speech, I am going to familiarize the audience with the three C's of Down syndrome: its causes, its characteristics, and the contributions people with Down syndrome make.

Introduction

I. In our lifetime, we will encounter many people who, for a variety of reasons, are "different."

II. Today I want to speak to you about one of those differences—Down syndrome.

III. Why do I want to talk about this topic? Because I have a daughter who has Down syndrome.

IV. In this speech, I will discuss with you the three C's of Down syndrome. *(Slide 1: Causes, Characteristics, and Contributions)*

Body

I. To begin, let it be understood what causes Down syndrome.

A. Although Down syndrome is a genetic condition, it is not hereditary.

1. People with Down syndrome have 47 chromosomes instead of the normal 46 (http://www.nads.org).

2. This extra chromosome is caused by a random error in cell division within chromosome 21 prior to conception. *(Slide 2: Chromosome 21)*

3. Although individuals do not inherit the mutant chromosome 21, so neither parent is to blame, once a couple has a child with Down syndrome, the likelihood of reoccurrence with the same two parents is increased. *(Slide 3: Genetic but Not Inherited)*

B. There are approximately 350,000 people living in the U.S. with Down syndrome.

1. Down syndrome occurs in one of every 800 live births, and an unknown number of fetuses with Down syndrome are aborted each year.

2. Women over the age of 35 are most likely to produce chromosome 21–altered eggs, but most children with Down syndrome are born to younger mothers because younger women have a greater percentage of babies.

Transition: Now that you know what causes Down syndrome, I want to describe the key physical and mental differences that people with this syndrome have.

II. People with Down syndrome differ from others both physically and mentally.

A. People with Down syndrome look different, and this syndrome also can create a number of physical health problems. *(Slide 4: Characteristics: Physical and Health Differences)*

1. The major physical differences are facial, such as a flat face, slanted eyes, and a large tongue in conjunction with a small mouth, but people with Down syndrome also experience low muscle tone.

2. The major health concerns include heart defects, hearing loss, vision loss, and a weaker immune system.

B. Second, people with Down syndrome are also mentally different, experiencing developmental delays, cognitive impairments, and emotional precociousness. *(Slide 5: Characteristics)*

1. The delayed developmental characteristics of Down syndrome are speech, cognitive, and motor skills.

2. The cognitive developmental characteristics of children with Down syndrome are varied among children with Down syndrome.

3. People with Down syndrome are emotionally precocious.

Transition: Now that you understand what Down syndrome is and how people with the syndrome differ from others, I would like to explain the special and unique ways that people with Down syndrome contribute to others.

III. People with Down syndrome positively affect their families and communities. *(Slide 6: Contributions)*

A. What are the positive contributions people with Down syndrome make in families?

1. Families with a child who has Down syndrome often include a tighter marriage and more compassionate siblings.

2. Families with a child who has Down syndrome also tend to experience a higher degree of acceptance in their communities.

B. People with Down syndrome contribute to their communities.

1. Children with Down syndrome who are mainstreamed in classrooms teach their peers to value differences.

2. Many adults with Down syndrome in the workplace are role models of dedication and perseverance.

Conclusion

I. To review, now you know that Down syndrome is caused by a preconception change in chromosome 21 that causes people with Down syndrome to be physically and mentally different, and you also know that many people with Down syndrome make positive contributions to society.

II. So, the next time you encounter someone with Down syndrome, I hope you'll remember what you have learned so you can enjoy getting to know this person rather than being afraid.

Works Cited

Faragher, R. Down syndrome: it's a matter of quality of life. *Journal of Intellectual Disability Research*, October 2005, 49:761–765. *Academic Search Premier.* EBSCOE Host Research Databases. Collin County Community College District. Accessed October 7, 2005 at www.web27.epnet.com.

Helders, Paul. Children with Down syndrome. 2005: 141. *Academic Search Premier.* EBSCOE Host Research Databases. Collin County Community College District. Accessed October 7, 2005 at www.web27.epnet.com.

"Information and Resources," National Down Syndrome Society. Accessed October 7, 2005 at www.ndss.org.

National Association for Down syndrome. Accessed October 7, 2005 at www.nads.org.

Rietveld, Christine. Classroom learning experiences by new children with Down syndrome. *Journal of Intellectual and Developmental Disability*, September 2005, 30:127–138. *Academic Search Premier.* EBSCOE Host Research Databases. Collin County Community College District. Accessed October 7, 2005 at www.web27.epnet.com.

Speech and Analysis

Speech

In our lifetimes, we will encounter many people who, for a variety of reasons, are considered "different" by those who consider themselves "normal." Today I want to speak to you about one of those things that makes people seem different: Down syndrome. Why do I want to talk about this topic? In part, because I have volunteered with mentally disabled children for many years, I am pursuing a professional career in special education, and I'd like to share with you what I've been learning. But, more importantly, I have a toddler daughter who has Down syndrome, and I've found from personal experience that when people know more about what makes my daughter different, they're more accepting of her and of people who are different in other ways.

In this speech, I'd like to share with you some basic information about this syndrome—I call them the three C's. First, I will discuss what causes Down syndrome. Then I will explain the typical characteristics that differentiate people with Down syndrome from others. Finally, I will describe the positive contributions that people with Down syndrome make in their families and communities.

To begin, let me explain what causes Down syndrome. Contrary to what some people believe, Down syndrome is not hereditary—it is a genetic condition. According to the website for the National Association for Down Syndrome, people with Down syndrome have 47 chromosomes instead of the normal 46. This extra chromosome is produced by a random error in cell division within chromosome 21 prior to conception. Because you don't inherit the mutant chromosome 21, neither parent is to "blame," so to speak, for producing a child with Down syndrome. However, once a couple has a child with Down syndrome, the likelihood that the same two parents could have another child with the same syndrome increases.

Analysis

Elizabeth opens with a statement about normal and different, then quickly introduces her topic.

She immediately establishes her credibility by showing that she has worked with children with Down syndrome, and she also has a daughter who has the syndrome.

She concludes her introduction by using a mnemonic device, the three C's, to preview her main points.

Here, Elizabeth clearly explains that although Down syndrome is a genetic condition, it is not an inherited one. Her PowerPoint slide is simple and visually reinforces her point.

According to the National Down Syndrome Society website, there are approximately 350,000 people with Down syndrome in the United States. Down syndrome occurs in one of about every 800 live births, and an unknown number of fetuses with Down syndrome are aborted each year. Many of us have heard that older women are more likely to have babies with Down syndrome. It's true that women over the age of 35 are most likely to produce chromosome 21–altered eggs, but, really, most Down syndrome children are born to younger mothers because younger women have a greater percentage of babies.

Having established its genetic cause, Elizabeth elaborates and explains more about the prevalence of Down syndrome and which parents are likely to have children with Down syndrome.

Now that I've talked about what causes Down syndrome, let me describe the main physical and mental characteristics that differentiate people with Down syndrome from others. Of course, one of the first things people notice about people with Down syndrome is that they look different, but Down syndrome can also create a number of health problems. The major physical differences we notice first are facial characteristics, like a flat face, slanted eyes, and a large tongue in a small mouth, although not all people with the syndrome have all of these facial features. But people with Down syndrome also often experience low muscle tone and more problematic health concerns like heart defects, hearing loss, vision loss, and a weak immune system.

Here Elizabeth uses a good transition in which she reinforces two of her C's: causes and characteristics.

People with Down syndrome are also mentally different from the rest of us. According to R. Faragher in his article on Down syndrome in the *Journal of Intellectual Disability Research*, they experience developmental delays, mostly affecting their speech, cognitive, and motor skills. The degree of delays in cognitive development varies quite a bit among children with Down syndrome. As Christine Rietveld explains in her article on Down syndrome in the *Journal of Intellectual and Developmental Disability*, some children with Down syndrome are able to be mainstreamed and attend public school with other children, some need to attend special education classes in mainstream schools, and others need more specialized programs outside of regular schools.

Here Elizabeth cites one of the sources of her information.

People with Down syndrome are also emotionally precocious, which means that they often seem emotionally mature for their age and have few inhibitions about expressing their emotions. If you have spent time with a child who has Down syndrome, you know what it means to be loved unconditionally.

Elizabeth could have developed this characteristic a bit more, perhaps by giving an example.

Now that you know a little more about what characterizes people with Down syndrome, I'd like to explain the special and unique ways that these people contribute to others. As many of us who live with people with Down syndrome know, there's no doubt that they have a positive effect on their families and

Again, Elizabeth uses a transition that reinforces two of the C's that define her main points: characteristics and contributions.

Although Elizabeth begins by telling the audience that she has a child with Down syndrome, she misses the opportunity to personalize this point. She might have further

communities. As R. Faragher explains, parents of a child with Down syndrome often have a very close, tightly knit marriage—they learn to come together in support of their child who has the syndrome and of their children who don't have Down syndrome, and they learn to rely on each other more to raise a child with special needs. In addition, the siblings of children with Down syndrome are often more compassionate because they understand what it's like to be viewed as "different." Families with a child who has Down syndrome also often experience a higher degree of acceptance in their communities. It's easy for people to become fond of a child with Down syndrome because they tend to be happy, loving kids who express affection easily. And when people feel fond of a child with Down syndrome, they also feel protective and accepting of the child's family.

developed it by giving personal examples of how her daughter has contributed to her family.

In turn, people with Down syndrome often make important contributions to their communities, just as many of us do. For example, such children who are mainstreamed in classrooms teach their peers to value differences and to develop compassion and empathy for people who are not necessarily like everyone else. As adults, many people with Down syndrome are role models of dedication and perseverance in the workplace—I'll bet at least a few of you have encountered a cheerful and professional person with Down syndrome who has helped you in a store or who works with you in an office setting.

Again, specific examples would have aided the development of her point.

In review, now you know that Down syndrome is caused by a change in chromosome 21 before conception, and that this results in people with Down syndrome having several different physical and mental characteristics. But you also know that people with the syndrome often make positive contributions to their families and communities. So, the next time you encounter someone with Down syndrome, I hope you'll remember what you have learned and that you enjoy getting to know this person as a unique and interesting individual.

In this conclusion, she reviews the three C's of causes, characteristics, and contributions, helping us remember what her speech was about.

Overall

All in all, this is a well-presented, informative speech with sufficient documentation.

Learning Outcomes

LO¹ Examine the Elaboration Likelihood Model

LO² Consider writing persuasive speech goals as propositions

LO³ Discuss the effects of emotional appeals on audience involvement

LO⁴ Discuss organizational patterns for persuasive speeches

Persuasive
Speaking

> ## "What determines how well we listen to and how carefully we evaluate the hundreds of persuasive messages we hear each day?"

Although it is easy to get excited about a powerful speech, real-life attempts to persuade others require the speaker to be knowledgeable about forming arguments and adapting them well to the needs of the audience. A **persuasive speech** is one that has a goal to influence the beliefs and/or behavior of audience members. It is, perhaps, the most demanding speech challenge. You will need to use all of the skills you have studied and developed so far. You will also need to build arguments that are convincing to your audience, use emotion to increase your audience's involvement with your topic, develop your credibility by demonstrating goodwill, use incentives to motivate your audience when you want them to take action, and choose an effective organizational strategy. In this chapter, you will learn how to prepare an effective persuasive speech. We begin by presenting a widely accepted theoretical model that explains how people process persuasive messages. Then, based on this model, we describe how you can meet the challenge of developing an effective persuasive speech.

LO¹ How People Process Persuasive Messages: The Elaboration Likelihood Model (ELM)

Do you remember times when you listened carefully and thoughtfully to an idea someone was trying to convince you about? Do you remember consciously thinking over what had been said and making a deliberate decision? Do you remember other times when you only half-listened and made up your mind quickly based on your "gut" feeling about the truthfulness of what had been said? What determines how well we listen to and how carefully we evaluate the hundreds of persuasive messages we hear each day? Richard Petty and John Cacioppo developed a now widely accepted model that explains how likely people are to spend time evaluating information (such as the arguments they hear in a speech) in an *elaborate* way, using their critical thinking skills, rather than processing information in a simpler, less critical manner. Called the Elaboration Likelihood Model (ELM), this theory can be used by speakers to develop persuasive speeches that will be influential with audience members, regardless of how they process information.

The model suggests that people process information in one of two ways. One way is intense and more time consuming. People using this "central route" listen carefully, think about what is

persuasive speech
a speech that has a goal to influence the beliefs or behavior of audience members

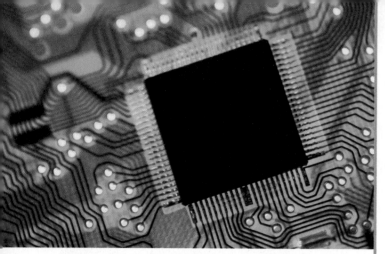

>> Sometimes we process information through the central route, and sometimes through the peripheral route. What factors do you think might influence whether you ought to use one over the other?

said, and may even mentally elaborate on the message. The second way, called the "peripheral route," is a shortcut that relies on simple cues such as a quick evaluation of the speaker's credibility, or a gut check on what the listener feels about the message.

According to the ELM model, the importance we attribute to an issue determines whether we use the central route or the peripheral route. When we feel involved in an issue, we are willing to expend the energy necessary for processing on the central route. When the issue is less important to us, we take the peripheral route. So, how closely your audience members will follow your arguments depends on how involved they feel with your topic. For example, if you have a serious chronic illness that is expensive to treat, you are more likely to pay attention to and evaluate for yourself any proposals to change your health care benefits. If you are healthy, you will probably quickly agree with suggestions from someone you perceive to be credible, or go along with a proposal that seems compassionate.

proposition
a declarative sentence that clearly indicates the speaker's position on the topic

The ELM model also suggests that when we form attitudes as a result of central processing (critical thinking), we are less likely to change our minds than when our attitudes have been formed based on peripheral cues. You can probably remember times when you were swayed at the moment by a powerful speaker, but later upon reflection, regretted your action and changed your mind. Likewise, based on information you have heard and spent time thinking about, you probably have some strongly held beliefs that are not easily changed.

When you prepare a persuasive speech, you will draw on the ELM model theory by developing your topic so that you increase the likelihood of your audience members feeling personally involved with the topic. You will want to develop sound reasons so that audience members who use the central, critical thinking approach to your speech will find your arguments convincing. For members who are less involved, you will want to appeal to their emotions and include information that enables them to see you as credible. In the rest of this chapter, we describe how you can adapt the speech plan Action Step process to help you accomplish the model's objectives.

LO² Writing Persuasive Speech Goals as Propositions

A persuasive speech's specific goal is stated as a proposition. A proposition is a declarative sentence that clearly indicates the speaker's position on the topic. For example, "I want to convince my audience that smoking causes cancer." The goal of persuasive speech to get the audience to agree with what the speaker is advocating. The goal may focus on what the audience's attitude or belief should be or how the audience should act. Figure 17.1 provides examples of propositions aimed at changing an attitude or belief and propositions aimed at audience action.

Figure 17.1

Examples of Propositions of Attitude/Belief and Action

Propositions of Attitude/Belief	Propositions of Action
I want my audience to believe that the city should build a downtown entertainment center.	I want my audience to vote for the tax levy to build a downtown entertainment center.
I want my audience to believe that more funding is needed for cancer research.	I want my audience to donate money to the American Cancer Society.
I want my audience to believe that recycling is necessary to reduce waste.	I want my audience to order and use the recycling bins available to them in their neighborhoods.

Tailoring Your Proposition to Your Audience

As you consider your topic and the proposition you will argue, you'll want to understand the opinions your audience members currently have about your topic.

Audience member opinions about your speech topic can range from highly favorable to highly opposed and can be visualized as lying on a continuum like the one pictured in Figure 17.2. Even though an audience will include individuals whose opinions fall nearly every point along the distribution, generally audience members' opinions tend to cluster in one area of the continuum. For instance, the opinions of the audience represented in Figure 17.2 cluster around "mildly opposed," even though a few people were more hostile and a few others had favorable opinions.

You will use the cluster point to classify your audience's initial attitude toward your topic as "opposed" (opposed to a particular belief or action or holding an opposite point of view), "no opinion" (uninformed, neutral, or apathetic), or "in favor" (already supportive of a particular belief or action) and you will consider this initial opinion as you develop your proposition and speech.

>> Is it more challenging to try to change the attitude of a hostile audience, or to persuade people who are neutral to give money to a cause?

©TIM BOYLE/GETTY IMAGES

Opposed

If your audience is very much opposed to your goal, it is unrealistic to believe that you will be able to change its attitude from "opposed" to "in favor" in only one short speech. So, you should consider a proposition that moves your audience in the direction that you would like, but does not expect it to make a complete change. For example, when you determine that your audience is likely to be totally opposed to the proposition: "I want to convince my audience that gay marriage should be legalized," you may rephrase your goal to: "I want to convince my audience to believe that committed gay couples should be able to have the same legal protection that is afforded to committed heterosexual couples through state-recognized marriage."

When you believe your listeners are only mildly opposed to your topic, you will need to understand their resistance and present arguments to overcome it. Your goal should be to provide them with strong reasons that support your position, including evidence that would counter other attitudes. Your proposition might be phrased: "I want to convince my audience that gay marriage will benefit society."

Neutral

When you perceive that your audience is neutral, you need to consider whether it is uninformed, impartial, or apathetic about your topic. When it is **uninformed**, that is, they do not know enough about a topic to have formed an opinion, you will need to provide the basic arguments and information that they need to become informed. Make sure that each of your reasons is really well supported with good information. When your audience is **impartial**, that is, the audience knows the basics about your topic but still has no opinion, you will want to provide more elaborate or secondary arguments and more robust evidence. When audience members have no opinion because they are apathetic, you will need to find ways to personalize the topic for them so that they see how it relates to them or their needs.

uninformed
not knowing enough about a topic to have formed an opinion

impartial
knowing the basics about a topic but still having no opinion about it

apathetic
having no opinion because one is uninterested, unconcerned, or indifferent to a topic

NO

Highly opposed	Opposed	Mildly opposed	Neither in favor nor opposed	Mildly in favor	In favor	Highly in favor
2	2	11	1	2	2	0

YES

Figure 17.2

Sample Opinion Continuum

In Favor

When your audience is only mildly in favor of your proposal, your task is to reinforce and strengthen its beliefs. An audience whose beliefs favor your topic will still benefit from an elaboration of the reasons for holding these beliefs. The audience may also become further committed to the belief by hearing additional or new reasons and more recent evidence that supports it.

When your audience strongly agrees with your position, then you can consider a proposition that builds on that belief and moves the audience to act on it. So, for example if the topic is gay marriage, and your audience poll shows that most audience members strongly favor the idea, then your goal may be: "I want my audience members to walk in Saturday's march in support of gay marriage."

Developing Arguments That Support Your Proposition

Persuasive speeches are composed of reasons and evidence that are used to make arguments in support of the proposition. Once you have identified a proposition tailored to your audience, you will use the research you have acquired to help you choose the main points of the speech. In a persuasive speech, the main points are reasons that support the proposition; the supporting materials presented are evidence that buttress the reasons.

Finding Reasons to Use as Main Points

Reasons are main point statements that summarize several related pieces of evidence and show *why* you should believe or do something. For example, suppose your speech proposition is: "I want the audience to believe home ownership is good for a society." Based on your research, you develop six potential reasons:

> **reasons**
> main point statements that summarize several related pieces of evidence and show why you should believe or do something

   I. Home ownership builds strong communities.

   II. Home ownership reduces crime.

   III. Home ownership increases individual wealth.

   IV. Home ownership increases individual self-esteem.

   V. Home ownership improves the value of a neighborhood.

   VI. Home ownership is growing in the suburbs.

Once you have a list of reasons, you can weigh and evaluate each and choose the three or four that have the highest quality. You can judge the quality of each reason by asking the following questions:

1. **Is the reason directly related to proving the proposition?** Sometimes, we find information that can be summarized into a reason, but that reason doesn't directly argue the proposition. For instance, you may have uncovered a lot of research that supports the notion that "Home ownership is growing in the suburbs." Unfortunately, it isn't clear how the growth of home ownership in the suburbs benefits society as a whole. So when choosing a reason, eliminate those that are only tangentially related to your proposition.

2. **Do I have strong evidence to support a reason?** A reason may sound impressive, but in your research you may not have been able to find solid evidence that supports it. Because the audience will assess whether they accept your reason based on the evidence you present, eliminate reasons for which you do not have strong support. For example, the second reason, "Home ownership reduces crime," sounds like a good one; but if the only proof you have is an opinion that is expressed by one person whose expertise is questionable, or if, in your research, you discover that although crime is lower in areas with high home ownership, there is little evidence to suggest a cause-and-effect relationship, you should eliminate this reason from consideration.

3. **Will this reason be persuasive for this audience?** Suppose that you have a lot of factual evidence to support the reason, "Home ownership encourages self-esteem." This reason might be very persuasive to an audience of social workers, psychologists, and teachers, but less important to an audience of financial planners, bankers, and economists. So once you are convinced that your reasons are related to the proposition and have strong evidence to support them, choose to use

as main points of your speech the three or four that you believe will be most persuasive for your particular audience.

Selecting Evidence to Support Reasons

Although a reason may seem self-explanatory, most audience members will not believe it unless they hear information that backs it up. As you researched, you may have discovered more evidence to support a reason than you will be able to use in the time allotted for your speech. So, you will have to select the pieces of evidence you will present. Both facts and opinions can serve as evidence.

Suppose that, in your speech to convince people that Alzheimer's research should be better funded, you want to use the reason "Alzheimer's disease is an increasing health problem in America." The following would be a factual statement that supports the reason: "According to a 2003 article in the *Archives of Neurology*, the number of Americans with Alzheimer's has more than doubled since 1980 and is expected to continue to grow, affecting between 11.3 and 16 million Americans by the year 2050."

Statements from people who are experts on a subject can also be used as evidence to support a reason. For example, the statement "According to the Surgeon General, 'By 2050, Alzheimer's disease may afflict 14 million people a year'" is an expert opinion.

Let's look at an example of how fact and opinion evidence can be used in combination to support a proposition.

> *Proposition:* I want the audience to believe that television violence has a harmful effect on children.

Reason: Television violence desensitizes children to violence.

Support: "In Los Angeles, California, a survey of 50 children between the ages of 5 and 10 who had just watched an episode of *Teenage Mutant Ninja Turtles*, asked the children whether or not violence was acceptable. Thirty-nine of the 50, or about 80 percent of them responded, 'Yes, because it helps you to win fights' (facts). Regardless of the rationale that children express, the fact remains that viewing violence desensitizes children and this can lead to real violence. According to Kirsten Houston, a well-regarded scholar writing in the July 1997 issue of *Journal of Psychology*, "Repeated exposure to media violence is a major factor in the gradual desensitization of individuals to such scenes. This desensitization, in turn, weakens some viewers' psychological restraints on violent behavior" (opinion).

Regardless of whether the evidence is based on opinions or facts, you will want to use the best evidence you have found to support your point. You can use the answers to the following questions to help you select evidence that is likely to persuade your audience:

1. **Does the evidence come from a well-respected source?** This question involves both the people who offered the opinions or compiled the facts and the book, journal, or Internet sources in which they were reported. Just as some people's opinions are more reliable than others, some printed and Internet sources are more reliable than others. Be especially careful of undocumented information. Eliminate evidence that comes from a questionable, unreliable, or biased source.

2. **Is the evidence recent; if not, is it still valid?** Things change, so information that was accurate for a particular time period may or may not be valid today. As you look at your evidence, consider when the evidence was gathered. Something that was true five years ago may not be true today. A trend that was forecast a year ago may have been revised since then. A statistic that was reported last week may be based on data that were collected three years ago. So whether it is a fact or an opinion, you want to choose evidence that is valid today. For example, the evidence "The total cost of caring for individuals with Alzheimer's is at least $100 billion according to the Alzheimer's Association and the National Institute on Aging," was cited in a 2003 NIH publication. But it is based on information from a study

conducted using 1991 data that were updated to 1994 data before being published. As a result, we can expect that today, annual costs would be higher. If you choose to use this evidence, you should disclose the age of the data used in the study and indicate that today, the costs would be higher.

3. **Does the evidence really support the reason?** Just as reasons need to be relevant to the proposition, evidence needs to be relevant to the reason. Some of the evidence you have found may be only indirectly related to the reason and should be eliminated in favor of evidence that provides more central support.

4. **Will this evidence be persuasive for this audience?** Finally, just as when you select your reasons, you will want to choose evidence that your particular audience is likely to find persuasive. So, if you have your choice of two quotations from experts, you will want to use the one from the person your audience is likely to find more credible.

Types and Tests of Arguments

An **argument** is the logical relationship between the proposition and the reasons or between the reasons and the evidence. So far, we have concentrated on choosing propositions, reasons, and supporting evidence, but if your audience is not convinced that your evidence provides a convincing argument for your reason, they will not agree with it. And if your audience doesn't buy the argument form from your reasons, they will not support your proposition.

Several kinds of argument links can be developed, as follows:

argument
the logical relationship between the proposition and the reasons or between the reasons and the evidence

arguing by example
support a claim by providing one or more individual examples

arguing by analogy
support a claim with a single comparable example that is significantly similar to the subject of the claim

1. **Arguing by example.** You are **arguing by example** when the reasons you offer are examples of the proposition or when the evidence you offer provides examples of the reason you state. For example, if you say, "Anyone who studies can get "A's," and offer as evidence: "Tom, Jane, and Josh studied and they all got 'A's," you would be making an argument by example. The general form of an argument by example is that "what is true in some instances/examples is true in all instances." When arguing by example, you can make sure that your argument is valid by answering the following questions: "Were enough instances (examples) cited so that listeners understand that they are not isolated or handpicked examples? Were the instances typical and representative? Are the negative instances really atypical?" If the answer to any of these questions is "No," then consider making your argument in a different way.

2. **Arguing by analogy.** You are arguing by analogy when you support your reason with a single comparable example that is so significantly similar to the subject that it offers strong proof. For example, if you support your proposition that "the Cherry Fork Volunteer Fire Department should hold a raffle to raise money for three portable defibrillator units" by saying, "the Mack Volunteer Fire Department, which is similar to Cherry Fork, held a raffle and raised enough money for four units," you would be arguing by analogy. The general form of an argument by analogy is "What is true or will work in one set of circumstances is true or will work in a comparable set of circumstances." When arguing by analogy, make sure your argument is valid by answering these questions: "Are the subjects really comparable?" "Are the Cherry Fork and Mack Fire

©BRAND X PICTURES/GETTY IMAGES

Departments really similar in all important ways?" If they are not, then your argument is not valid. "Are any of the ways that the subjects are dissimilar important to the conclusion?" If so, the reasoning is not sound.

3. **Arguing from causation.** You are **arguing from causation** when you cite evidence that one or more events always or almost always brings about, leads to, creates, or prevents a predictable event or set of effects. If you support your proposition "The wheat crop will have a lower yield than last year" by saying, "We've had a very dry spring," you would be arguing from causation. Your argument can be boiled down to "The lack of sufficient rain causes a poor crop." The general form of a causal argument can be stated: If A, which is known to bring about B, has happened, then we can expect B to occur. To make sure your causal arguments are sound, you should answer the following questions: "Are the events alone enough to cause the stated effect?" "Do other events accompanying the events cited actually cause the effect?" "Is the relationship between causal events and effect consistent?" If the answer to one of these questions is "No," the reasoning is not sound.

4. **Arguing by sign.** You are **arguing by sign** when you offer as a reason to support your proposition or as evidence to support your reason, that events have occurred that are outward signals of the truth of your proposition or reason. For example, you might support your point that the recession is worsening by noting that the local soup kitchens have experienced an increase in the number of people they are serving. Your argument would be "Longer lines at soup kitchens are a sign of the worsening recession." To test this kind of argument, you should ask, "Does the sign cited always or usually signal the conclusion drawn?" "Are a sufficient number of signs present?" and "Are contradictory signs also in evidence?"

Avoiding Fallacies of Reasoning

As you are developing your reasons and the arguments that you will make, you should check to make sure that your reasoning is appropriate for the particular situation. This will allow you to avoid fallacies or errors in your reasoning. Three common fallacies to avoid include:

1. **Hasty generalization.** A **hasty generalization** is a fallacy that presents a generalization that is either not supported with evidence or is supported with only one weak example. Because

©PETRA WEGNER/ALAMY

the supporting material that is cited should be representative of all the supporting material that could be cited, enough supporting material must be presented to satisfy the audience that the instances are not isolated or handpicked. Because you can find an example or statistic to support almost anything, avoiding hasty generalizations requires you to be confident that the instances you cite as support are typical and representative of your claim. For example, someone who argued, "All Akitas are vicious dogs," whose sole piece of evidence was "My neighbor had an Akita and it bit my best friend's sister," would be guilty of a hasty generalization. It is hasty to generalize about the temperament of a whole breed of dogs based on a single action of one dog.

2. **False cause.** A false cause occurs when the alleged cause fails to be related to, or to produce the effect. Just because two things happened

arguing from causation
support a claim by citing events that have occurred to bring about the claim

arguing by sign
support a claim by citing information that signals the claim

hasty generalization
a fallacy that presents a generalization that is either not supported with evidence or is supported with only one weak example

false cause
a fallacy that occurs when the alleged cause fails to be related to, or to produce, the effect

one after the other, does not mean that the first necessarily caused the second. Just as people who blame monetary setbacks or illness on crossing paths with black cats or broken mirrors, you need to be careful that you don't take coincidental events or signal events and present them as causal.

3. **Ad hominem argument.** An **ad hominem argument** supports a claim by attacking or praising the character of someone or something. Ad hominem literally means "to the man." For example, if Jamal's support for his claim that his audience should buy an Apple computer was that Steve Jobs, the founder and current president of Apple Computer, is a genius, he would be making an ad hominem argument. Jobs's intelligence isn't really a reason to buy a particular brand of computer. Television commercials that feature celebrities using the product are often guilty of ad hominem reasoning.

LO³ Increasing Audience Involvement through Emotional Appeals

As you will recall, the ELM model suggests that people are more likely to listen to and think about information when they are involved in the topic. We are more likely to be involved in a topic when we have an emotional stake in it. As a speaker, if you can give your audience an emotional stake in what you are saying, they are more likely to listen to and think about your arguments. You can increase your audience members' involvement by evoking negative or positive emotions in your speeches (Nabi, 2002, p. 292).

Negative emotions are disquieting, so when people experience them, they look for ways to eliminate the discomfort. During your speech, you can arouse negative feelings in your audience so that they will listen to your proposition, which should provide a way for the audience to alleviate the discomfort. There are numerous negative emotions that you might tap; the five most common are fear, guilt, shame, anger, and sadness. Notice in the following statement how "fear" personalizes the statistics on

heart disease and peaks your interest in listening to what the speaker has to say:

> One out of every three Americans age 18 and older has high blood pressure. It is the primary cause of stroke, heart disease, heart failure, kidney disease, and blindness. It triples a person's chance of developing heart disease, and boosts the chance of stroke seven times and the chance of congestive heart failure six times. Look at the person on your right, look at the person on your left. If they don't get it, chances are, you will. Today, I'd like to convince you that you are at risk of developing high blood pressure.

Positive emotional involvement can also lead audience members to more carefully consider your proposition and arguments. When you evoke positive emotions, audience members will look for ways to sustain or further enhance the feeling. Five of the most common emotions that you can evoke so that audience members listen to and process what you have to say include: happiness/joy, pride, relief, hope, and compassion. For example, notice how the speaker used the emotion of "pride" to peak interest in a speech designed to get the audience to sign up for an alternative spring break experience with Habitat for Humanity:

> Imagine you are an Olympian who has won your event and now stand on the podium with a medal around your neck as they play your national anthem. Imagine opening your mail and finding out that you have gotten into the number-one ranking graduate program in the country. Now imagine that you are standing on the front porch of a brand new home that you have helped to build and are being hugged by the mother of four children who, thanks to your selfless work, will no longer have to share a one bedroom fifth floor walk-up. Imagine the pride? How long has it been since you felt so good? Well folks, that's just what you'll experience and much more when you sign up to work with the Habitat for Humanity House being constructed in your community.

Cueing Your Audience through Credibility: Demonstrating Goodwill

Even when you have tried to involve your audience in your topic, not everyone will choose to listen carefully and evaluate and elaborate on what you have said. Some will still choose to pay minimal attention to your arguments and instead will use simple cues and process your message. The most important cues that people use when they process information

As a speaker, if you can give your audience an emotional stake in what you are saying, they are more likely to listen to and think about your arguments.

ad hominem argument
a fallacy that occurs when one attacks the person making the argument, rather than the argument itself

>> Based on an audience analysis of the people in this photo, what personal issues do you think you might address to build goodwill with them?

along the peripheral route is the credibility of the speaker. In Chapter 14, we discussed three speaker characteristics (expertise, trustworthiness, and personableness) that audience members pay attention to when evaluating credibility. A fourth characteristic, goodwill, is crucial to motivating uninvolved audience members to believe what the speaker is saying. **Goodwill** is the audience perception that the speaker understands, empathizes with, and is responsive to them. In other words, goodwill is the audience members' belief that the speaker's intentions toward them are for their good. Audience members who perceive the speaker as exhibiting goodwill toward them are more willing to believe what the speaker is saying.

You can demonstrate that you understand your audience by personalizing your information. Information you gleaned from your audience analysis can help you with this. For example, Meg, a union rep trying to convince the membership to accept a new contract change to health care benefits, might build goodwill by personalizing one aspect of the proposal:

> I know that about 40 percent of you have little use for eye care, which is part of the new package. But for the 60 percent of you who wear glasses or have dependents who wear glasses, this plan will not only pay for your annual eye exam, but it will also pay 30 percent of the cost of new glasses or 25 percent of the new cost of contact lenses. This will mean about $250 in your pocket each year, and with less overtime predicted for this year, that's a real benefit.

Speakers demonstrate goodwill by showing that they understand their audience and also by empathizing with them. Empathizing requires you to go beyond understanding and to identify emotionally with audience members' views. This doesn't

mean, however, that you accept their views as your own. It does mean that you acknowledge them as valid. Even when your speech is designed to change audience members' views, the sensitivity you show to their feelings will demonstrate goodwill. For example the union rep might demonstrate empathy by saying:

> I can imagine what it will be like for some of you who, under this new plan, will go to the drugstore and find that there is now a high co-pay required for a drug you take that is no longer on the formulary. But I also guarantee that the plan formulary will have drugs that your doctor can prescribe that will be direct substitutes, or you will be able to appeal the co-pay.

Finally, to demonstrate goodwill, you will want to show your responsiveness to the audience. **Being responsive** is showing care about the audience by acknowledging feedback from the audience, especially subtle negative cues. The union rep can demonstrate responsiveness by referencing feedback that the membership had provided earlier:

> Before we started negotiations, we surveyed you asking what changes you wanted to see in the health care program. Seventy-five percent of you said that your number-one concern was keeping the office visit co-pay at $10, and in this contract we were able to do that.

Or, if she notices that some members of the audience are looking disgusted and shaking their heads, she might respond:

> I can see that some of you are disappointed with the increase in premiums. So am I. I wish we could have done better on this issue. But the fact is, health care costs have risen 15 percent nationwide this year, and our usage has exceeded this average.

By establishing goodwill, you enhance your credibility with the audience, which is especially important for those audience members who are not personally involved with your topic.

Motivating Your Audience to Act through Incentives

When your speech proposition is aimed at influencing your audience members' attitudes or beliefs, you will use emotional appeals to encourage the audience to become involved with your topic. But when you want to influence your audience to

goodwill
the audience perception that the speaker understands, empathizes with, and is responsive to them

being responsive
showing care about the audience by acknowledging feedback from the audience, especially subtle negative cues

act on what you have said, you will need to provide motivation by showing how what you are asking them to do will meet their needs. Motivation, "forces acting on or within an organism to initiate and direct behavior" (Petri, 1996, p. 3), is often a result of incentives that meet needs.

An incentive is a reward promised if a particular action is taken or goal is reached (Petri, 1996, p. 3). Incentives can be physical (food, shelter, money, sex), psychological (self-esteem, peace of mind), or social (acceptance, popularity, status) rewards.

Incentives are only valuable to the extent that they can satisfy a need that is felt by the audience and their value must not be outweighed by costs associated with the action.

Using Incentives to Satisfy Unmet Needs

Incentives are more likely to motivate people when they satisfy a strong but unmet need. Various ways for categorizing needs have been developed to help us understand types of needs. One of the most widely recognized is Maslow's hierarchy of needs. Abraham Maslow divided people's needs into five categories, illustrated in Figure 17.3: (1) physiological needs, including food, drink, and life-sustaining temperature; (2) safety and security needs, including long-term survival and stability; (3) belongingness and love needs, including the need to identify with friends, loved ones, and family; (4) esteem needs—ego gratification including the quest for material goods, recognition,

> In theory, a person cannot be motivated to meet an esteem need of gaining recognition until basic physiological, safety, and belongingness and love needs have been met.

motivation
forces acting on or within an organism to initiate and direct behavior

incentive
a reward promised if a particular action is taken or goal is reached

and power or influence; (5) cognitive needs; (6) aesthetic needs; and (7) self-actualization needs, including the need to develop one's self to realize one's full potential and engage in creative acts (Maslow, 1954, 80–92). Maslow believed that these needs were hierarchical; that is, that your "lower order" needs had to be met before you would be motivated by "higher order" needs. In theory, then, a person cannot be motivated to meet an esteem need of gaining recognition until basic physiological, safety, and belongingness and love needs have been met.

The hierarchical nature of needs is still debated because there is evidence that at times, some people will sacrifice lower order needs to satisfy higher order ones. Nevertheless, as a speaker, when you can tie the incentives that accompany your proposal with unmet audience needs, you increase the likelihood that the audience will take the action you are proposing. Let's see how this could work in the volunteering for literacy speech with a college student audience. Suppose that, during the speech, you point out that people who volunteer 30 hours or more a

Figure 17.3

Maslow's Hierarchy of Needs

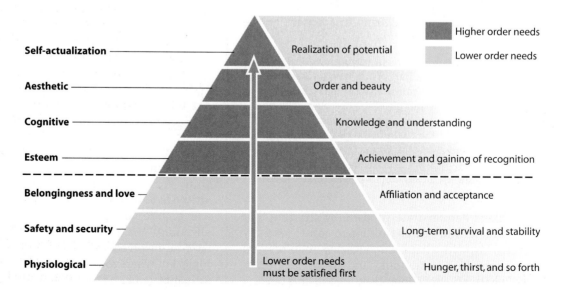

- Self-actualization — Realization of potential
- Aesthetic — Order and beauty
- Cognitive — Knowledge and understanding
- Esteem — Achievement and gaining of recognition
- Belongingness and love — Affiliation and acceptance
- Safety and security — Long-term survival and stability
- Physiological — Hunger, thirst, and so forth

Higher order needs
Lower order needs

Lower order needs must be satisfied first

©TIM GRAHAM/GETTY IMAGES

year receive a recognition certificate and are invited to attend a private dinner with the stars of the hot band that will be headlining the big spring campus concert. After announcing this you add,

> I know that although most of you care about literacy, you're thinking about what else you could do with that hour. But the really cool part of spending your time as a literacy volunteer is that you will feel good about yourself because you have improved someone's life, and you also will be able to list this service and recognition on your résumé. As a bonus, you'll get to brag to your friends about having dinner with several celebrities.

In the first part of this short statement, you have enumerated three incentives that are tied to volunteering: a physical incentive (an award certificate), a psychological incentive of enhanced self-concept (I feel good about myself because I have helped someone else), and a social incentive (having dinner with an elite group and meeting celebrities). In the second part you have also tied each incentive to a need that it can satisfy. With enhanced résumés, people are more likely to get jobs that provide money for food and shelter. If by helping someone else, we feel better about ourselves, then we have met a self-actualization need. And by attending the private dinner, we might satisfy both esteem needs and belongingness needs.

Outweighing Costs

As you prepare your speech, you must be concerned with presenting the incentives that meet the needs of your audience, and you also need to understand the potential costs for audience members who act in line with your proposal. For example, in the literacy speech, one obvious cost is the hour of free time each week that might subtract from time audience members currently spend with their friends or family. This could create a potential deficit in their belongingness

need. To address this concern, you might point out, "Now I know you might be concerned about the time this will take away from your friends or family, but relax. Your friends and family are likely to understand and admire you (esteem need substitute for belongingness). Also, at the Literacy Center, you're going to have time before the tutoring starts to meet other volunteers (belongingness) and they are some really cool people (esteem). I know a couple who just got engaged and they met through their volunteering (big-time belongingness)."

If, through your audience analysis, you discover that you cannot relate your proposition to meeting basic audience needs or if the analysis reveals that the costs associated with your proposition would outweigh the incentives, then you probably need to reconsider what you are asking the audience to do. For example, if you discover that most of your audience members are overcommitted and have little free time to take on volunteer activity, then it is probably unrealistic to think you will be able to convince them to volunteer an hour a week. So, you may need to modify your proposition and persuade them to donate a book or money to buy a book for the literacy library.

Finally, if your incentives are to motivate your audience, the audience must be convinced that there is a high likelihood that if they act as you suggest, they will receive the incentives. It is important, therefore, that you discuss only those incentives that you have strong reason to believe are closely tied to the action you are requesting and are received by almost all people who act in the recommended way. Although there is an annual award given to the literacy volunteer who has donated the most time that year, mentioning this in your speech is unlikely to motivate the audience because only one person receives it, and the cost is very high.

So when you want to move an audience to action, you need to understand their needs and explain the incentives they can receive by taking the action you suggest. You also need to make sure that the incentives you mention fulfill unmet needs in the audience.

LO⁴ Organizational Patterns for Persuasive Speeches

Having developed a proposition, selected evidence to support your reasons, identified ways to increase audience involvement through emotional appeals, determined how you will enhance your credibility by developing goodwill, and identified the incentives you will use to motivate your audience, you are ready to choose a pattern to organize your speech. The most common patterns for organizing persuasive speeches include statement of reasons, problem solution, comparative advantages, criteria satisfaction, and motivated sequence. In this section, we describe and illustrate these persuasive organizational patterns and identify the type of proposition for which they are most commonly used. So that you can contrast the patterns and better understand their use, we will illustrate each pattern by examining the same topic with slightly different propositions that use the same (or similar) reasons.

Statement of Reasons Pattern

The **statement of reasons** is a form of persuasive organization used for proving propositions of fact in which you present your best-supported reasons in a specific order, to increase the likelihood that the audience will accept your argument. For a speech with three reasons or more, place the strongest reason last because this is the reason you believe the audience will find most persuasive. Place the second strongest reason first because you want to start with a significant point. Place the other reasons in between.

Proposition: I want my audience to believe that passing the proposed school tax levy is necessary.

 I. The income will enable the schools to restore vital programs. (second strongest)
 II. The income will enable the schools to give teachers the raises they need to keep up with the cost of living.
 III. The income will allow the community to maintain local control and will save the district from state intervention. (strongest)

Comparative Advantages Pattern

The **comparative advantages pattern** is a form of persuasive organization used for arguing a proposi-

tion of value when the goal is to prove that something has more value than something else. A comparative advantages approach to a school tax proposition would look like this:

Proposition: I want my audience to believe that passing the school tax levy is better than not passing it. (compares the value of change to the status quo)

 I. Income from a tax levy will enable schools to reintroduce important programs that had to be cut. (advantage 1)
 II. Income from a tax levy will enable schools to avoid a tentative strike by teachers who are underpaid. (advantage 2)
 III. Income from a tax levy will enable us to retain local control of our schools, which will be lost to the state if additional local funding is not provided. (advantage 3)

Criteria Satisfaction

The **criteria satisfaction pattern** seeks audience agreement on criteria that should be considered when evaluating a particular idea and then shows how the proposition that the speaker is advocating satisfies the criteria. A criteria satisfaction pattern is especially useful when your audience is opposed to your proposition, because it approaches the proposition indirectly by first focusing on the criteria that the audience may agree with before introducing the specific solution. A criteria satisfaction organization for the school levy would look like this:

Proposition: I want my audience to believe that passing a school levy is a good way to fund our schools.

 I. We can all agree that a good school funding method must meet three criteria:
   A. A good funding method results in the reestablishment of programs that have been dropped due to budget constraints.
   B. A good funding method results in fair pay for teachers.
   C. A good funding method generates enough income to maintain local control, avoiding state intervention.
 II. Passage of a local school tax levy is a good way to fund our schools.
   A. A local levy will allow us to re-fund important programs.
   B. A local levy will allow us to give teachers a raise.
   C. A local levy will generate enough income to maintain local control and avoid state intervention.

statement of reasons pattern a straightforward organization in which you present the best-supported reasons you can find

comparative advantages pattern an organization that allows you to place all the emphasis on the superiority of the proposed course of action

criteria satisfaction pattern an indirect organization that first seeks audience agreement on criteria that should be considered when they evaluate a particular proposition and then shows how the proposition satisfies those criteria

Problem Solution Pattern

The problem solution pattern is an organizational pattern that provides a framework for clarifying the nature of some problem and for illustrating why a given proposal is the best solution. This organization works well when the audience is neutral or only agrees that there is a problem but has no opinion about a particular solution. In a problem solution speech, the claim ("There is a problem that can be solved by X.") is supported by three reasons that take the general form: (1) There is a problem that requires action. (2) Proposal X will solve the problem. (3) Proposal X is the best solution to the problem, because it will lead to positive consequences and minimize or avoid negative ones. A problem solution organization for the school tax proposition might look like this:

Proposition: The current fiscal crisis in the school district can be solved through a local tax levy.

I. The current funding is insufficient and has resulted in program cuts, labor problems resulting from stagnant wages, and a threatened state take-over of local schools. (statement of problem)
II. The proposed local tax levy is large enough to solve these problems. (solution)
III. The proposed local tax levy is the best means of solving the funding crisis.

Motivated Sequence Pattern

The motivated sequence pattern, articulated by Allan Monroe, combines the problem solution pattern with explicit appeals designed to motivate the audience to act. The motivational sequence pattern is a five-point, unified sequence that replaces the normal introduction–body–conclusion model with (1) an attention step, (2) a need step that fully explains the nature of the problem, (3) a satisfaction step that explains how the proposal solves the

>> How would you apply each of the organizational patterns described in this chapter to a speech about rebuilding the wetlands of Louisiana to help reduce the effects of a large hurricane on New Orleans?

©ANDY NELSON/GETTY IMAGES

problem in a satisfactory manner, (4) a visualization step that provides a personal application of the proposal, and (5) an action appeal step that emphasizes the specific direction that listeners' action should take. A motivational pattern for the school tax levy proposition would look like this:

Proposition: I want my audience to vote in favor of the school tax levy on the November ballot.

I. Comparisons of world-wide test scores in math and science have refocused our attention on education. (attention)
II. The shortage of money is resulting in cost-saving measures that compromise our ability to teach basic academic subjects well. (need, statement of problem)
III. The proposed increase is large enough to solve those problems in ways that allow for increased emphasis on academic need areas. (satisfaction, how the proposal solves the problem)
IV. Think of the contribution you will be making to the education of your future children and also to efforts to return our educational system to the world-class level it once held. (visualization of personal application)
V. Here are "Vote Yes" buttons that you can wear to show you are willing to support this much-needed tax levy. (action appeal showing specific direction)

Because motivational patterns are variations of problem solution patterns, the underlying assumption is similar: When the current means are not solving the problem, a new solution that does solve the problem should be adopted.

problem solution pattern
an organization that provides a framework for clarifying the nature of the problem and for illustrating why a given proposal is the best one

motivated sequence pattern
an organization that combines the problem solution pattern with explicit appeals designed to motivate the audience to act

Sample Persuasive Speech: Don't Chat and Drive

Adapted from a Speech by Cedrick McBeth, Collin County Community College*

This section presents a sample persuasive speech adaptation plan, outline, and transcript given by a student in an introductory speaking course.

1. Review the outline and adaptation plan developed by Cedrick McBeth in preparing his speech on cell phones and driving.
2. Then read the transcript of Cedrick McBeth's speech.
3. Use the Persuasive Speech Evaluation Checklist from Figure 17.4 to help you evaluate this speech.
4. Write a paragraph of feedback to Cedrick McBeth describing the strengths of his presentation and what you think he might do next time to be more effective.

You can complete this activity with the Persuasive Speech Evaluation Checklist in Figure 17.4, which you can download online.

Adaptation Plan

1. **Key aspects of audience.** Although the majority of listeners are familiar with the problem of using cell phones while driving, I will present information and arguments to convince them to support legislation banning cell phone use while driving.
2. **Establishing and maintaining common ground.** My main way of establishing common ground will be by using the pronouns "we," "us," and so on.
3. **Building and maintaining interest.** I will use the Manocchio and Peña stories as well as startling statistics to create and maintain attention.
4. **Audience knowledge and sophistication.** Because most of the class is familiar with the general problem of driving while using cell phones, I will present specific statistics that underlie the problem.
5. **Building credibility.** Early in the speech, I will refer to the reading and research I have done on this issue.
6. **Audience attitudes.** Because my classmates are busy commuter students, I believe most own cell phones and use them while driving, so they will be slightly hostile to my proposition.

7. **Adapt to audiences from different cultures and language communities.** Although my audience members are demographically diverse, cell phones are used by most class members and issues are cross-cultural.
8. **Use visual aids to enhance audience understanding and memory.** I will start the speech with a cell phone in hand, as though I were talking and driving.

Speech Outline: Don't Chat and Drive

General purpose: To persuade

Speech goal (proposition): I want to persuade my classmates that cell phones should be prohibited from use while driving an automobile.

Introduction

I. Alexander Manocchio is on trial for vehicular homicide.
II. How many of us in this classroom generally talk on cell phones while driving a car? How many of us take into consideration the dangers of talking on our cell phones while driving a car?
III. What I hope to convince you of today is that using a cell phone while driving an automobile should be prohibited.

Body

I. First, let's see how great a problem cell phone use is while driving.
   A. Overall, cell phone usage has increased tremendously in the last 12 to 14 years.
      1. Statistics show that 168 million people used cell phones as of August 2004.
      2. Compare this figure to the approximately 4.3 million people who used cell phones in 1990.
   B. The jump in cell phone use has been accompanied by the jump in traffic accidents linked to cell phone use.
      1. In 2001, in Texas alone, there were 1,032 accidents with eight fatalities in which cell phone usage was considered a contributing factor.
      2. Regardless of the age or the driving experience of the driver, the risk of collision when using a cell phone is four times higher than when a cell phone is not used by the driver.
   C. Cell phone usage increases the likelihood of fatalities in accidents.
      1. The risk factor for driving while using a cell phone amounts to 6.4 fatalities per million drivers annually.

Figure 17.4

Persuasive Speech Evaluation Checklist

You can use this form to critique a persuasive speech to convince that you hear in class. As you listen to the speaker, outline the speech, paying close attention to the reasoning process the speaker uses. Also note the claims and support used in the arguments and identify the types of appeals being used. Then answer the questions that follow.

Primary Criteria

_____ 1. Was the specific goal phrased as a proposition (were you clear about the position the speaker was taking on the issue)?

_____ 2. Did the proposition appear to be adapted to the initial attitude of most members of the audience?

_____ 3. Were emotional appeals used to involve the audience with the topic?

_____ 4. Were the reasons used in the speech
　　　　　_____ directly related to the proposition?
　　　　　_____ supported by strong evidence?
　　　　　_____ persuasive for the particular audience?

_____ 5. Was the evidence (support) used to back the reasons (claims)
　　　　　_____ from well-respected sources?
　　　　　_____ recent and/or still valid?
　　　　　_____ persuasive for this audience?
　　　　　_____ typical of all evidence that might have been used?
　　　　　_____ sufficient (enough evidence was cited)?

_____ 6. Could you identify the types of arguments that were used?
　　　　　_____ Did the speaker argue by example?　　_____ If so, was it valid?
　　　　　_____ Did the speaker argue by analogy?　　_____ If so, was it valid?
　　　　　_____ Did the speaker argue from causation?　_____ If so, was it valid?
　　　　　_____ Did the speaker argue by sign?　　　_____ If so, was it valid?

_____ 7. Could you identify any fallacies of reasoning in the speech?
　　　　　_____ hasty generalizations
　　　　　_____ arguing from false cause
　　　　　_____ ad hominem attacks

_____ 8. Did the speaker demonstrate goodwill?

_____ 9. If the speech called for the audience to take action,
　　　　　_____ did the speaker describe incentives and relate them to audience needs?
　　　　　_____ did the speaker acknowledge any costs associated with the action?

_____ 10. Did the speaker use an appropriate persuasive organizational pattern?
　　　　　_____ statement of reasons
　　　　　_____ problem solution
　　　　　_____ comparative advantages
　　　　　_____ criteria satisfaction
　　　　　_____ motivated sequence

General Criteria

_____ 11. Was the proposition clear? Could you tell the speaker's position on the issue?

_____ 12. Was the introduction effective in creating interest and involving the audience in the speech?

_____ 13. Was the speech organized using an appropriate persuasive pattern?

_____ 14. Was the language clear, vivid, emphatic, and appropriate?

_____ 15. Was the conclusion effective in summarizing what had been said and mobilizing the audience to act?

_____ 16. Was the speech delivered enthusiastically, with vocal expressiveness, fluency, spontaneity, and directness?

_____ 17. Did the speaker establish credibility?
　　　　　_____ expertise
　　　　　_____ personableness
　　　　　_____ trustworthiness

Overall evaluation of the speech (check one):
_____ excellent _____ good _____ average _____ fair _____ poor

Use the information from this checklist to support your evaluation.

2. The chance that a driver using a cell phone would kill a pedestrian or other motorists is 1.5 per 1 million people.
3. Combining these figures with the 210 million licensed drivers in the U.S. amounts to a risk factor of roughly 1,660 fatalities per year involving cell phone–related accidents.

Transition: Now that we have established that a problem exists, let's look more closely at why cell phone use creates this problem.

II. Using a cell phone while driving is distracting.
   A. First, when accessing or dialing a phone, the driver loses eye contact with the road.
   B. Second, while conversing, mental attention is split between conversation and the ever-changing road conditions.
III. Here are the advantages to prohibiting the use of cell phones while driving.
   A. It would eliminate the sources of mental distraction.
   B. It would eliminate one source of physical distraction.
   C. It would decrease the number of accidents and fatalities.

Conclusion
   I. I've shown you how the increased use of cell phones while driving has led to an increase in accidents and fatalities.
   II. I've explained how cell phones distract drivers.
   III. I've identified a policy that would reduce driver distractions and the accidents they cause.
   IV. A quotation by Patricia Peña shows the effect that one cell phone call can have.

Works Cited
Cellular Telecommunications & Internet Association. November 1997. "An Investigation of the Safety Implications of Wireless Communications in Vehicles."

Dunn, Susan. 2004. "Two Good Reasons Not to Use Your Cell Phone in the Car." *USA Today.* (http://www.americaninsurancedepot.com/protectyourself/cellphones.htm)

Gebler, Dan. 2000. "Cell Phones and Automobiles." *Wireless Newsfactor.* (http://www.uvm.edu/~vlrs/doc/cell_phones.htm)

Greve, Frank. 2000. "Restricting Car Phones is a Difficult Sell in the US." *Philadelphia Inquirer.*

National Conference of State Legislatures. August 1999. "Cell Phones and Driving: 1999 State Legislative Update."

Speech and Analysis

Speech

On June 17, 2006, Alexander Manocchio reached for a ringing cell phone and killed Karyn Cordell and her unborn son. You see, Manocchio was driving a car at the time. Now two people are dead and Alexander's life is in a shambles, all because he answered a phone. Alexander faces two counts of vehicular homicide.

How many of us in this classroom are also guilty of putting lives at risk by talking on cell phones while driving a car? I'll bet almost all of us have done it and many of us do it everyday. But do we ever consider the dangers of talking on our cell phones while driving a car? As I read the statistics and studied this situation, I became convinced that cell phone use while driving has become an unacceptable risk. Today, I hope to convince you that using a cell phone while driving an automobile should be illegal.

Let's begin by establishing that using a cell phone while you're driving has become a serious and growing problem. Overall, cell phone usage has increased tremendously in the last 12 to 14 years. According to the Cellular Telecommunications & Internet Association, as of August 2004, 168 million people used cell phones compared to only 4.3 mil-

Analysis

Cedrick begins with an example that is designed to build our interest in the speech.

He then asks us to consider our behavior.

Here Cedrick begins to establish his credibility.

He then states his goal: to convince you that using a cell phone while driving should be illegal.

Using a problem solution organizational pattern, he begins to establish the problem of using cell phones.

He then goes on to show the dramatic increase in the use of cell phones.

lion in 1990. That's a 390 percent increase. Not surprisingly, according to Vermont Legislative Research Shop, this jump in cell phone use has been accompanied by a jump in traffic accidents linked to cell phone use. According to a 2004 article in *USA Today* by Susan Dunn, in Texas alone during 2001, cell phone usage was considered a contributing factor in 1,032 accidents and resulted in eight fatalities. Regardless of the age or the driving experience of the driver, the risk of being in a collision when using a cell phone is four times higher than when not talking on the phone.

Cell phone usage also increases the likelihood of fatalities. An independent study done in 2002 by the Harvard Center for Risk Analysis found that driving while using a cell phone increases the risk to 6.4 fatalities per million drivers annually. The study also found that the chance that a driver using a cell phone would kill a pedestrian or other motorists was 1.5 per 1 million people. Extrapolating from these figures, with 210 million licensed drivers in the U.S., this amounts to roughly 1,660 fatalities per year stemming from cell phone–related accidents.

So, I'm sure you'll agree that we have a problem. But how does using a cell phone while driving create accidents? Whether we realize it or not, no matter how experienced we are as drivers, we are distracted from paying attention to the road when we use a cell phone while driving. Think about it—when you access your phone or dial a number, you lose eye contact with the road. Even if you use a hands-free phone, your mental attention is split between your conversation and ever-changing road conditions. Being absorbed in a conversation affects your ability to concentrate on driving, which can jeopardize your safety and the safety of pedestrians and people in other cars.

Now let's consider a solution. To eliminate this problem, I recommend that we petition our congressional and state representatives to enact policies that prohibit the use of cell phones while driving a car. Drivers would be required to pull over to a safe place before making a call, and the policy would apply to drivers of all ages. The public would be informed of the policy via mainstream news sources. If this sort of policy were enacted, fewer people would use cell phones while they were driving, they would be less distracted, and the result would be a decrease in the overall number of accidents and fatalities per year.

In conclusion, I've shown you today how the increased use of cell phones over the past several years has led to increased use of cell phones while driving, which in turn has led to an increase in car accidents and fatalities. I've also explained how cell

He then points out that this jump in use has also resulted in a jump in traffic accidents.

He then cites a source to show the results.

With his second point, he shows that the problem is not only the increase in accidents but also the increase in fatalities. Again, he uses statistics to support this claim.

Cedrick's language here is unclear. Although he speaks of "risk," he states raw numbers. Risk is usually stated as a percentage.

At this point, the audience may be losing interest as Cedrick uses one statistic after another, with no references to help ground them.

Notice how here as well as other places in the speech he uses the pronoun we to show that all of us can and may be involved.

Here Cedrick asks the audience members to personalize the process of using cell phones while driving.

Having established the problem, he now offers a solution to eliminate this problem.

His proposal is vague and perhaps a bit overambitious for a speech to a slightly hostile audience.

It might have been better to ask audience members to personally refrain from using cell phones while driving.

In this conclusion he reviews the main points of his speech to reinforce audience memory of what he has said.

phones distract drivers both physically—such as when they look for their phones and dial them—and mentally—such as when their conversation distracts them from their driving. And, finally, I've recommended that we ask the government to enact a policy that would greatly reduce the use of cell phones while driving and thus reduce driver distractions and the accidents they cause.

I began this speech by telling you of Alexander Manocchio, a cell phone user who killed a pregnant woman. I'd like to end by quoting a woman who lost her 2-year-old daughter because a man felt he could safely drive a car while talking on his cell phone:

"My name is Patricia Peña. On November 2, 1999, my 2-year-old daughter Morgan and I were on our way home, when our car was broadsided by another vehicle. Police reports proved that the crash was caused by a driver who was paying more attention to his cell phone than to the road and, as a result, ran a stop sign at 40 miles per hour. Morgan was rushed to the hospital, where she clung to life for the next 16 hours. But she never regained consciousness and was pronounced dead at 4:58 a.m. on November 3rd."

This is just one of many such accidents that have increased with the use of cell phones by drivers. I just pray this never happens to you or someone you love.

Again, notice how his entire speech is given in a way that shows that we are involved, and thus, when we are talking on a cell phone while driving, we need to consider either moving to the side of the road or stating that we should talk later.

He then ends with an emotional appeal, the words of a woman whose daughter died as a result of the driver paying more attention to a cell phone than to the road. Although relevant, the quote does not convey much emotion.

Overall

This is a good persuasive speech of reasons with well-documented use of statistics.

Index

References

Affifi, W. A., & Guerrero, L. K. (2000). Motivations underlying topic avoidance in close relationships. In S. Petronio (Ed.), *Balancing the secrets of private disclosures* (pp. 165-180). Mahwah, NJ: Erlbaum.

Anderson, J. (1988). Communication competency in the small group. In R. Cathcart & L. Samovar (Eds.), *Small group communication: A reader.* Dubuque, IA: Wm. Brown.

Andersen, P. A., Hecht, M. L., Hoobler, G. D., & Smallwood, M. (2003). Nonverbal communication across cultures. In W. B. Gudykunst (Ed.), *Cross-cultural and intercultural communication.* Thousand Oaks, CA: Sage.

Aron, A., Aron, E. N., Tudor, M., & Nelson, G. (2004). Close relationships as including other in the self. In H. T. Reis & C. E. Rusbult (Eds.), *Close relationships* (pp. 365-379). New York: Psychology Press.

Aronson, E. (1999). *The social animal.* New York: Worth.

Axtell, R. E. (1991). *Gestures: The do's and taboos of body language around the world* (rev. ed.). New York: Wiley.

Ayres, J. (1991, June-December). Using visual aids to reduce speech anxiety. *Communication Research Reports,* 73-79.

Ayres, J., & Hopf, T. S. (1990, January). The long-term effect of visualization in the classroom: A brief research report. *Communication Education, 39,* 75-78.

Ayres, J., Hopf, T. S., & Ayres, D. M. (1994, July). An examination of whether imaging ability enhances the effectiveness of an intervention designed to reduce speech anxiety. *Communication Education, 43,* 252-258.

Baerwald, D. Narrative. Northshore School District, http://ccweb.norshore.wednet.edu/writingcorner/narrative.html.

Baker, D. C. (1990). A qualitative and quantitative analysis of verbal style and the elimination of potential leaders in small groups. *Small Group Research, 38,* 13-26.

Bales, R. F. (1971). *Personality and interpersonal behavior.* New York: Holt, Rinehart & Winston.

Balgopal, P. R., Ephross, P. H., & Vassil, T. V. (1986). Self help groups and professional helpers. *Small Group Research, 17,* 123-137.

Barge, J. K. (1994). *Leadership: Communication skills for organizations and groups.* New York: St. Martin's.

Baron, R. A., Bryne, D., & Brascombe, N. R. (2006). *Social psychology* (11th ed.). Boston: Allyn & Bacon.

Bass, B. M. (1981). Traits of leadership: A follow-up to 1970. In R. M. Stogdill (Ed.), *Handbook of Leadership* (pp. 73-96). New York: Free Press.

Baxter, L. (1982). Strategies for ending relationships: Two studies. *Western Journal of Speech Communication, 46,* 223-241.

Beebe, M. B., Anthony, T., Salas, E., & Driskell, J. E. (1994). Group cohesiveness and quality of decision making. *Small Group Research, 25,* 189-204.

Behnke, R. R., & Carlile, L. W. (1971). Heart rate as an index of speech anxiety. *Speech Monographs, 38,* 66.

Berger, C. R., & Brada, J. J. (1982). *Language and social knowledge: Uncertainty in interpersonal relations.* London: Arnold.

Bommelje, R., Houston, J. M., & Smither, R. (2003). Personaltiy characteristics of effective listeners: A five factor perspective. *International Journal of Listening, 17,* 32-46.

Bonito, J. (2000). The effect of contributing substantively on perceptions of participation. *Small Group Research, 31,* 528-553.

Bonvillain, N. (2003). *Language, culture and communication: The meaning of messages.* (4th ed.). Upper Saddle River, NJ: Prentice-Hall.

Boon, S. D. (1994). Dispelling doubt and uncertainty: Trust in romantic relationships. In S. Duck (Ed.), *Dynamics of Relationships* (pp. 86-111). Thousand Oaks, CA: Sage.

Bormann, E. (1990). *Small group communication: Theory and practice.* New York: Harper & Row.

Bostrom, R. (1970). Patterns of communicative interaction in small groups. *Speech Monographs, 37,* 257-263.

Boyd, A. (1999). *How to handle media interviews.* London: Mercury.

Brownell, J. (2002). *Listening: Attitudes, principles, and skills* (2nd ed.). Boston: Allyn & Bacon.

Burgoon, J. K., & Bacue, A. E. (2003). Nonverbal communication skills. In J. O. Greene & B. R. Burleson (Eds.), *Handbook of communication and social interaction skills* (pp. 179-220). Mahwah, NJ: Erlbaum.

Burgoon, J. K., Coker, D. A., & Coker, R. A. (1986). Communicative effects of gaze behavior: A test of two contrasting explanations. *Human Communication Research, 12,* 495-524.

Burgoon, J. K., & Hoobler, G. D. (2002). Nonverbal signals. In M. L. Knapp & J. A. Daly (Eds.), *Handbook of interpersonal communication* (3rd ed., pp. 240-299). Thousand Oaks, CA: Sage.

Burke, K. (1968). *Language as symbolic action.* Berkeley: University of California Press.

Burleson, B. R. (2003). Emotional support skills. In J. O. Green & B. R. Burleson (Eds.), *Handbook of communication and social interaction skills* (pp. 551-594). Mahwah, NJ: Erlbaum.

Burleson, B. R., & Goldsmith, D. J. (1998). How the comforting process works: Alleviating emotional distress through conversationally induced reappraisals. In P. A. Andersen & L. K. Guerrero (Eds.), *Handbook of communication and emotion: Research, theory, applications, and contexts* (pp. 248-280). San Diego, CA: Academic Press.

Carlo-Casellas, I. R. (January 14, 2002). Marketing to US Hispanic Population Requires Analysis of Cultures, p. 9.

Cegala, D. J., & Sillars, A. L. (1989). Further examination of nonverbal manifestations of interaction involvement. *Communication Reports, 2,* 45.

Chen, G. M., & Starosta, W. J. (1998). *Foundations of intercultural communication.* Boston: Allyn & Bacon.

Chuang, R. (2004). An examination of Taoist and Buddhist perspectives on interpersonal conflict, emotions and adversities. In F. E. Jandt (Ed.), *Intercultural communication: A global reader* (pp. 38-50). Thousand Oaks, CA: Sage.

Claes, M. T. (2002). Women, men and management styles. In P. J. Dubeck & D. Dunn (Eds.), *Workplace/women's place: An anthology* (2nd ed., pp. 121-125). Los Angeles: Roxbury.

Clevenger, T., Jr. (1959, April). A synthesis of experimental research in stage fright. *Quarterly Journal of Speech, 45,* 134-145.

Criscito, P. (2000). *Résumés in cyberspace* (2nd ed.). Hauppauge, NY: Barron's Educational Series, Inc.

Cupach, W. R., & Metts, S. (1986). Accounts of relational disclosure: A comparison of marital and non-marital relationships. *Communication Monographs, 53,* 319-321.

Dahl, S. (2004). Intercultural research: The current state of knowledge. Middlesex University Discussion Paper no. 26. Available at SSRN, http://SSRN.com/abstrate=658202.

Darling, A. L., & Dannels, D. P. (2003, January). Practicing engineers talk about the importance of talk: A report on the role of oral communication in the workplace. *Communication Education, 52,* 1-16.

Deavenport, E. W. (1995, July 15). Walking the high wire: Balancing stakeholder interests. *Vital Speeches of the Day,* 595-597.

Demo, D. H. (1987). Family relations and the self-esteem of adolescents and their parents. *Journal of Marriage and the Family, 49,* 705-715.

Dennis, A. R. (1996). Information exchange and use in small group decision making. *Small Group Research, 27,* 532-550.

Derlega, V. J., Metts, S., Petronio, S., & Margulis, S. T. (1993). *Self-disclosure.* Newbury Park, CA: Sage.

Dikel, M. Prepare your resume for e-mailing or posting on the Internet. The Internet-ready resume. Retrieved 9/06/2006 from http://www.rileyguide.com/eresume.html.

Dindia, K., Fitzpatrick, M. A., & Kenny, D. A. (1997). Self-disclosure in spouse and stranger interaction: A social relations analysis. *Human Communication Research, 23,* 388-412.

Dindia, K., & Timmerman, L. (2003). Accomplishing romantic relationships. In J. O. Greene & B. R. Burleson (Eds.), *Handbook of communication and social interaction* (pp. 685-722). Mahwah, NJ: Erlbaum.

Donoghue, P. J., & Seigel, M. E. (2005). *Are you really listening?: Keys to successful communication.* Notre Dame, IN: Sorin Books.

Downey, G., Freitas, A. L., Michaelis, B., & Khouri, H. (2004). The self-fulfilling prophecy in close relationships: Rejection sensitivity and rejection by romantic partners. In H. T. Reis & C. E. Rusbult (Eds.), *Close relationships* (pp. 153-174). New York: Psychology Press.

Duck, S. (1987). How to lose friends without influencing people. In M. E. Roloff & G. R. Miller (Eds.), *Interpersonal processes: New directions in communication research.* Beverly Hills, CA: Sage.

Duck, S. (1999). *Relating to others.* Philadelphia: Open University Press.

Dunkel, P., & Pialorsi, F. (2005). *Advanced listening comprehension: Developing aural and notetaking skills.* Boston: Thomson Heinle.

Durst, G. M. (1989, March 1). The manager as a developer. *Vital Speeches of the Day,* 309-314.

Dwyer, K. K. (2000, January). The multidimensional model: Teaching students to self-manage high communication apprehension by self-selecting treatments. *Communication Education, 49,* 79.

Ekman, P. (1999). Facial expressions. In T. Dalgleish & M. Power (Eds.), *Handbook of cognition and emotions* (pp. 301-320). New York: John Wiley & Sons Ltd.

Ellis, K. (1995, January). Apprehension, self-perceived competency, and teacher immediacy in the laboratory-supported public speaking course: Trends and relationships. *Communication Education, 44,* 64-78.

Encyclopedia.com. (2002). [Online]. Available: www.encyclopedia.com

Estes, W. K. (1989). Learning theory. In A. Lesgold & R. Glaser (Eds.), *Foundations for a psychology of education* (pp. 1-49). Hillsdale, NJ: Erlbaum.

Evans, C., & Dion, K. (1991). Group cohesion and performance: A meta-analysis. *Small Group Research, 22,* 175-186.

Forgas, J. P. (1991). Affect and person perception. In J. P. Forgas (Ed.), *Emotion and social judgments* (pp. 387-406). New York: Pergamon Press.

Forgas, J. P. (2000). Feelings and thinking: Summary and integration. In J. P. Forgas (Ed.), *Feeling and thinking: The role of affect in social cognition* (pp. 387-406). New York: Cambridge University Press.

Gilbert, D., & Kahl, J. A. (1982). *The American class structure: A new synthesis.* Homewood, IL: Dorsey.

Gmelch, S. B. (1998). *Gender on campus: Issues for college women.* New Brunswick, NJ: Rutgers University Press.

Goleman, D. (1998). *Working with emotional intelligence.* New York: Bantam Books.

Gudykunst, W. B., & Kim, Y. Y. (2003). *Communicating with strangers: An approach to intercultural communication* (4th ed.). Boston: Allyn & Bacon.

Hall, B. J. (2002). *Among cultures: The challenge of communication.* Belmont, CA: Wadsworth.

Hall, E. T. (1959). *The silent language.* Greenwich, CT: Fawcett.

Hall, E. T. (1969). *The hidden dimension.* Garden City, NY: Doubleday.

Hattie, J. (1992). *Self-concept.* Hillsdale, NJ: Erlbaum.

Haviland, W. A. (1993). *Cultural anthropology.* Fort Worth, TX: Harcourt, Brace, Jovanovich.

Hayes, J. (2002). *Interpersonal skills at work* (2nd ed.). New York: Routledge.

Henman, L. D. (2003). Groups as systems: A functional perspective. In R. Y. Hirokawa, R. S. Cathcart, L. A. Samovar, & L. D. Henman (Eds.), *Small group communication theory and practice: An anthology* (8th ed., pp. 3-7). Los Angeles: Roxbury.

Hirokawa, R. Y. (1987). Why informed groups make faulty decisions. *Small Group Behavior, 18,* 3-29.

Hirokawa, R. Y. (1988). Group communication and decision-making performance: A continued test of the functional perspective. *Human Communication Research, 14,* 487-515.

Hofstede, G. (1997). *Cultures and organizations: Software of the mind.* New York: McGraw Hill.

Hofstede, G. (1980). *Culture's consequences.* Beverly Hills, CA: Sage.

Hofstede, G. (Ed.) (1998). *Masculinity and femininity: The taboo dimension of national cultures.* Thousand Oaks, CA: Sage.

Hofstede, G. (2000). The cultural relativity of the quality of life concept. In G. R. Weaver (Ed.), *Cultural communication and conflict: Readings in intercultural relations.* Boston: Allyn & Bacon.

Holtgraves, T. (2002). *Language as social action: Social psychology and language use.* Mahwah, NJ: Erlbaum.

Hotz, R. L. (April 15, 1995). Official racial definitions have shifted sharply and often. *Los Angeles Times,* p. A14.

Ice Man, http://www.digonsite.com/drdig/mummy/22.html.

Jackson, R. L. II (Ed.) (2004). *African American communication and identities.* Thousand Oaks, CA: Sage.

Jandt, F. E. (2001). Intercultural communication: An introduction (3rd ed.). Thousand Oaks, CA: Sage.

Janis, I. L. (1982). *Groupthink: Psychological studies of policy decisions and fiascoes.* Boston: Houghton Mifflin.

Johnson, D., & Johnson, F. (2003). *Joining together: Group theory and group skills* (8th ed.). Boston: Allyn & Bacon.

Jones, M. (2002). *Social psychology of prejudice.* Upper Saddle River, NJ: Prentice-Hall.

Jones, R., Oyung, R., & Pace, L. (2005). *Working virtually: Challenges of virtual teams.* Hershey, PA: IRM Press.

Jussim, L. J., McCauley, C. R., & Lee, Y.-T. (1995). Why study stereotype accuracy and inaccuracy? In Y.-T. Lee, L. J. Jussim, & C. R. McCauley (Eds.), *Stereotype accuracy: Toward appreciating group differences* (pp. 3-28). Washington, DC: American Psychological Association.

Kaplan, R. M. (2002). *How to say it in your job search: Choice words, phrases, sentences and paragraphs for résumés, cover letters and interviews.* Patamus, NJ: Prentice-Hall.

Kapoun, J. (2000, January 25). *Teaching undergraduates Web evaluation: A guide for library instruction* [Online]. Available: http://www.ala.org/acrl/undwebev.htm [Accessed October 17, 2001].

Katz, J. E., & Aspden, P. (2004). Social and public policy Internet research: Goals and achievements. www.communitytechnology.org/aspden.

Kelly, L., Phillips, G. M., & Keaen, J. A. (1995). *Teaching people to speak well: Training and remediation of communication reticence.* Cresskill, NJ: Hampton.

Keyton, J. (1993). Group termination: Completing the study of group development. *Small Group Research, 24,* 84-100.

Klyukanov, I. E. (2005). *Principles of intercultural communication.* New York: Pearson.

Knapp, M. L., & Hall, J. A. (2006). *Nonverbal communication in human interaction* (5th ed.). Belmont, CA: Thomson Wadsworth.

Knapp, M. L. & Vangelisti, A. L. (2000). *Interpersonal communication and human relationships* (4th ed.). Boston: Allyn & Bacon.

Koncz, A. (2006). Employers cite communication skills as key, but say many job seekers lack them. *Job Outlook 2006.* Bethlehem, PA: National Association of Colleges and Employers.

Krotz, J. (2006). 6 tips for taking control in media interviews. www.microsoft.com /smallbuiness/resources/management/ leadership_training_6 tips.

Leary, M. R. (2002). When selves collide: The nature of the self and the dynamics of interpersonal relationships. In A. Tesser, D. A. Stapel, & J. V. Wood (Eds.), *Self and motivation: Emerging psychological perspectives* (pp. 119-145). Washington, DC: American Psychological Association.

Listening Factoid. (2003). [Online]. International Listening Association. Available: http://www.listen.org/pages/ factoids.html.

Littlejohn, S. W., & Foss, K. A. (2005). *Theories of human communication.* Belmont, CA: Thomson Wadsworth.

Luckmann, J. (1999). *Transcultural communication in nursing.* New York: Delmar Publishers.

Luft, J. (1970). *Group processes: An introduction to group dynamics.* Palo Alto, CA: Mayfield.

Lulofs, R. S., & Cahn, D. D. (2000). *Conflict: From theory to action* (2nd ed.). Boston: Allyn & Bacon.

Martin, J. N., & Nakayama, T. K. (2000). *Intercultural communication in contexts* (2nd ed.). Mountain View, CA: Mayfield.

Martin, M. M., Anderson, C. M., & Horvath, C. L. (1996). Feelings about verbal aggression: Justifications for sending and hurt from receiving verbally aggressive messages. *Communication Research Reports, 13*(1), 19-26.

Maslow, A. H. (1954). *Motivation and personality.* New York: Harper & Row.

Masters, M. F., & Albright, R. R. (2002). *The complete guide to conflict resolution in the workplace.* New York: Amacom.

Mehrabian, A. (1972). *Nonverbal communication.* Chicago: Aldine.

Menzel, K. E., & Carrell, L. J. (1994). The relationship between preparation and performance in public speaking. *Communication Education, 43,* 17-26.

Michener, H. A., & DeLamater, J. D. (1999). *Social psychology* (4th ed.). Orlando, FL: Harcourt Brace.

Midura, D. W., & Glover, D. R. (2005). *Essentials of teambuilding.* Champaign, IL: Human Kinetics.

Motley, M. (1997). COM Therapy. In J. A. Daly, J. C. McCroskey, J. Ayres, T. Hopf, & D. M. Ayres (Eds.), *Avoiding communication: Shyness, reticence, and communication apprehension* (2nd ed., pp. 379-400). Cresskill, NJ: Hampton Press.

Mruk, C. (1999). *Self-esteem: Research, theory, and practice* (2nd ed.). New York: Springer.

Munger, D., Anderson, D., Benjamin, B., Busiel, C., & Pardes-Holt, B. (2000). *Researching online* (3rd ed.). New York: Longman.

Nabi, Robin L. (2002). Discrete emotions and persuasion. In J. P. Dillard and M. Pfau (Eds.), *The persuasion handbook: Developments in theory and practice* (pp. 291-299). Thousand Oaks, CA: Sage.

Neuleip, J. W. (2006). *Intercultural communication: A contextual approach* (3rd ed.). Thousand Oaks, CA: Sage.

Ogden, C. K., & Richards, I. A. (1923). *The meaning of meaning.* London: Kegan, Paul, Trench, Trubner.

Omdahl, B. L. (1995). *Cognitive appraisal, emotion, and empathy.* Mahwah, NJ: Erlbaum.

Patterson, B. R., Bettini, L., & Nussbaum, J. F. (1993). The meaning of friendship across the life-span: Two studies. *Communication Quarterly, 41,* 145.

Patton, B. R., & Downs, T. M. (2003). *Decision-making group interaction* (4th ed.). Boston: Allyn & Bacon.

Pearson, J. C., West, R. L., & Turner, L. H. (1995). *Gender & communication* (3rd ed.). Dubuque, IA: Brown & Benchmark.

Petri, H. L. (1996). *Motivation: Theory, research, and applications* (4th ed.). Belmont, CA: Wadsworth.

Petronio, S. (2002). *Boundaries of privacy. Dialectics of disclosure.* Albany: State University of New York Press.

Phillips, G. (1977). Rhetoritherapy versus the medical model: Dealing with reticence. *Communication Education, 26,* 34-43.

Rabby, M., & Walther, J. B. (2003). Computer mediated communication effects in relationship formation and maintenance. In D. J. Canary & M. Dainton (Eds.), *Maintaining relationships through communication* (pp. 141-162). Mahwah, NJ: Erlbaum.

Rayner, S. G. (2001). Aspects of the self as learner: Perception, concept, and esteem. In R. J. Riding & S. G. Rayner (Eds.), *Self perception: International perspectives on individual differences,* vol. 2. Westport, CN: Ablex.

Renz, M. A., & Greg, J. B. (2000). *Effective small group communication in theory and practice.* Boston: Allyn & Bacon.

Rhode, D. L. (Ed.) (2003). *The difference "difference" makes: Women and leadership.* Stanford, CA: Stanford Law and Politics.

Richmond, V. P., & McCroskey, J. C. (1995). *Communication: Apprehension, avoidance, and effectiveness* (4th ed.). Scottsdale, AZ: Gorsuch Scarisbrick.

Rockwell, Llewellyn B. (2006, March 1). Iraq and the democratic empire. *Vital Speeches of the Day*, 302.

Rosenfeld, L. B. (2000). Overview of the ways privacy, secrecy, and disclosure are balanced in today's society. In S. Petronio (Ed.), *Balancing the secrets of private disclosures* (pp. 3-18). Mahwah, NJ: Erlbaum.

Rusbult, C. E., Olsen, N., Davis, J. L., & Hannon, P. A. (2004). Commitment and relationship maintenance mechanisms. In H. T. Reis & C. E. Rusbult (Eds.), *Key readings on close relationships* (pp. 287-304). Washington, DC: Taylor & Francis.

Samovar, L. A., & Porter, R. E. (2001). *Communication between cultures* (4th ed.). Belmont, CA: Wadsworth.

Samovar, L. A., Porter, R. E., & McDaniel, E. R. (2007). *Communication between cultures* (6th ed.). Belmont, CA: Thomson Wadsworth.

Samter, W. (2003). Friendship interaction skills across the lifespan. In J. O. Greene & B. R. Burleson (Eds.), *Handbook of communication and social interaction skills* (pp. 637-684). Mahwah, NJ: Erlbaum.

Scott, P. (1997, January-February). Mind of a champion. *Natural Health, 27*, 99.

Shaw, M. E. (1981). *Group dynamics: The psychology of small group behavior* (3rd ed.). New York: McGraw-Hill.

Shimanoff, M. (1992). Group interaction and communication rules. In R. Cathcart & L. Samovar (Eds.), *Small group communication: A reader.* Dubuque, IA: Wm. Brown.

Spitzberg, B. H. (2000). A model of intercultural communication competence. In L. A. Samovar & R. E. Porter (Eds.), *Intercultural communication: A reader* (9th ed., pp. 375-387). Belmont, CA: Wadsworth.

Stewart, C. J., & Cash, W. B. (2000). *Interviewing: Principles and practices* (9th ed.). Dubuque, IA: William C. Brown.

Stewart, L. P., Cooper, P. J., Stewart, A. D., & Friedley, S. A. (1998). *Communication and gender* (3rd ed.). Boston: Allyn & Bacon.

Stiff, J. B., Dillard, J. P., Somera, L., Kim, H., & Sleight, C. (1988). Empathy, communication and prosocial behavior. *Communication Monographs, 55*, 198-213.

Sundstrom, E., DeMeuse, K. P., & Futrell, D. (1990, February). Work teams: Applications and effectiveness. *American Psychologist*, 120-133.

Tannen, D. (1990). *You just don't understand.* New York: HarperCollins.

Taylor, D. A., & Altman, I. (1987). Communication in interpersonal relationships: Social penetration theory. In M. E. Roloff & G. R. Miller (Eds.), *Interpersonal processes: New directions in communication research* (pp. 257-277). Beverly Hills, CA: Sage.

Temple, L. E., & Loewen, K. R. (1993). Perceptions of power: First impressions of a woman wearing a jacket. *Perceptual and Motor Skills, 76*, 345.

Tengler, C. D., & Jablin, F. M. (1983). Effects of question type, orientation, and sequencing in the employment screening interview. *Communication Monographs, 50*, 261.

Terkel, S. N., & Duval, R. S. (Eds.) (1999). *Encyclopedia of ethics.* New York: Facts on File.

Thames, T. B. (2006, March 1). Window of opportunity: The AARP perspective on reforming America's health care system. *Vital Speeches of the Day*, 315.

Thurlow, C., Lengel, L., & Tomic, A. (2004). *Computer mediated communication: Social interaction and the Internet.* Thousand Oaks, CA: Sage.

Tillerson, R. W. (2006, May 6). Economic and environmental solutions in the global energy system. *Vital Speeches of the Day*, 441.

Ting-Toomey, S. (1999). *Communicating across cultures.* New York: Guilford Press.

Ting-Toomey, S., Yee-Jung, K., Shapiro, R., Garcia, W., Wright, T., & Oetzel, J. G. (2000). Cultural/ethnic identity salience and conflict styles. *International Journal of Intercultural Relations, 23*, 47-81.

Trujillo, S. D. (2002, April 15). The Hispanic destiny: Corporate responsibility. *Vital Speeches of the Day*, 406.

Tuckman, B. W. (1965). Developmental sequence in small groups. *Psychological Bulletin, 6393*, 384-399.

Valacich, J. S., George, J. F., Nonamaker, J. F., Jr., & Vogel, D. R. (1994). Idea generation in computer based groups: A new ending to an old story. *Small Group Research, 25*, 83-104.

Valian, V. (1998). *Why so slow? The advancement of women.* Cambridge, MA: MIT Press.

Vegan Society's Web site, http://www.vegansociety.com.

Walther, J. B. (1996). Computer-mediated communication: Impersonal, interpersonal and hyperpersonal interaction. *Western Journal of Communication, 57*, 381-398.

Walther, J. B., & Parks, M. R. (2002). Cues filtered out, cues filtered in: Computer-mediated communication and relationships. In M. C. Knapp & J. A. Daly (Eds.), *Handbook of interpersonal communication* (pp. 529-563). Thousand Oaks, CA: Sage.

Ward, C. C., & Tracy, T. J. G. (2004). Relation of shyness with aspects of online relationship involvement. *Journal of Social and Personal Relationships, 21*, 611-623.

Weaver, J. B. III, & Kirtley, M. B. (1995). Listening styles and empathy. *Southern Communication Journal, 60*, 131-140.

Weiten, W. (1998). *Psychology: Themes and variations* (4th ed.). Pacific Grove, CA: Brooks/Cole.

Wikipedia, http://en.wikipedia.org/wiki/kinesics, 2006.

Wheelen, S. A., & Hochberger, J. M. (1996). Validation studies of the group development questionnaire. *Small Group Research, 27*(1), 143-170.

Widmer, W. N., & Williams, J. M. (1991). Predicting cohesion in a coacting sport. *Small Group Research, 22*, 548-570.

Wilson, G. L. (2005). *Groups in context: Leadership and participation in small groups* (7th ed.). New York: McGraw Hill.

Wolvin, A., & Coakley, C. G. (1996). *Listening* (5th ed.). Dubuque, IA: Brown & Benchmark.

Wood, J. T. (2007). *Gendered lives: Communication, gender, and culture* (7th ed.). Belmont, CA: Wadsworth.

Wood, J. T., & Inman, C. (1993). In a different mode: Recognizing male modes of closeness. *Journal of Applied Communication Research, 21*, 279-295.

Wright, J. W. (2002). *New York Times Almanac.* New York: New York Times.

Young, K. S., Wood, J. T., Phillips, G. M., & Pederson, J. D. (2000). *Group discussion: A practical guide to participation and leadership* (3rd ed.). Prospect Heights, IL: Waveland Press.

Zernpke, R., Raines, C., & Filipczak (2000). *Generations at work.* New York: Amacom.

To help you succeed, we have designed a review card for each chapter.

Chapter in Review

LO¹ communication
the process of creating or sharing meaning in informal conversation, group interaction, or public s...

Here, you'll find the key terms and definitions in the order they appear in the chapter.

participants
individuals who a... and receivers dur...

messages
verbal utterances and nonverbal behaviors to which meaning is attributed during communication

meaning
thoughts in our minds and interpretations of others' messages

symbols
words, sounds, and actions that are generally understood to represent ideas and feelings

encoding
the process of putting our thoughts and feelings into words and nonverbal cues

decoding
the process of interpreting another's message

contexts
the settings in which communication occurs, including what precedes and follows what is said

physical context
its location, the environmental conditions (temperature, lighting, noise level), the dis-

How to Use This Card:

1. Look over the card to preview the new concepts you'll be introduced to in the chapter.

2. Read your chapter to fully understand the material.

3. Go to class (and pay attention).

4. Review the card one more time to make sure you've registered the key concepts. Take the chapter self quiz to test your comprehension.

5. Don't forget, this card is only one of many COMM learning tools available to help you succeed in your communication class.

channel
both the route traveled by the message and the means of transportation

noise
any stimulus that interferes with the process of sharing meaning

physical noise
sights, sounds, and other stimuli in the environment that draw people's attention away from intended meaning

psychological noise
internal distractions based on thoughts, feelings, or emotional reactions to symbols

LO¹ Define the communication process.
We have defined communication as the process of creating or sharing meaning, whether the context is informal conversation, group interaction, or public speaking. The elements of the communication process are participants, messages, context, channels, noise, and feedback.

LO² Discuss communication functions and settings.
Communication plays a role in all aspects of our lives. First, communication serves many important function...ds, to develop and maintain a sense of se... cial obligations, to exchange information, and ...ication occurs in interpersonal, group, publi...ed settings.

In this column, you'll find summary points that give an overview of important concepts.

LO³ Identify communication principles.
Our communication is guided by at least seven principles. First, communication is purposeful. Second, interpersonal communication is continuous. Third, interpersonal communication messages vary in degree of conscious encoding. Messages may be spontaneous, scripted, or constructed. Fourth, interpersonal communication is relational, defining the power and affection between people. Fifth, communication is guided by culture. Sixth, communication has ethical implications. Ethical standards that influence our communication include truthfulness, integrity, fairness, respect, and responsibility. And seventh, interpersonal communication is learned.

LO⁴ Discover how to increase communication competence.
A primary issue in this course is competence—we all strive to become better communicators. Competence is the perception by others that our communication behavior is appropriate as well as effective. It involves a desire to improve our communication, increasing our knowledge of communication, identifying and attaining goals, being able to use various skills, and presenting ourselves as credible and confident communicators. Skills can be learned, developed, and improved, and you can enhance your learning this term by writing goal statements to systematically improve your own skill repertoire.

Chapter 1 Quiz

True/False

Every chapter has a short self-assessment quiz for you to use while reviewing the chapter. You will find the answer key on the back page.

1. Communication can be defi... which meaning is attributed...

2. A primary issue in this course is competence, which is the perception by others that our communication behavior is appropriate as well as effective.

3. Skills are goal-oriented actions or action sequences that we can master and

Prepare for Exams

When it's time to prepare for exams, use the card and the technique to the left to ensure successful study sessions.

...ating without anxiety or

...hers and their ideas, even if you don't agree with them, you are demonstrating the ethical standard of fairness.

internal noise
thoughts and feelings that compete for attention and interfere with the communication process

semantic noise
distractions aroused by certain symbols that take our attention away from the main message

feedback
reactions and responses to messages

LO² interpersonal communication settings
interactions among a small number of people who have relationships with each other

problem-solving group settings
participants come together for the specific purpose of solving a problem or arriving at a decision

public speaking settings
one participant, the speaker, delivers a prepared message to a group or audience who has assembled to hear the speaker

electronically mediated communication settings
involves participants who do not share a physical context but communicate through the use of technology

e-mail
electronic correspondence conducted between two or more users on a network where the communication does not occur in real time

instant messaging (IM)
communication through maintaining a list of people that you can interact with in real time when they are online

text messaging
short, written messages between mobile phones and other handheld electronic devices, exchanged in real time or stored for later retrieval

listservs
electronic mailing lists through the use of e-mail that allow for widespread distribution of information to many Internet users, so online discussions can occur in a delayed time format

chat rooms
interactive message exchange between two or more people where multiple messages are exchanged in real time

weblogs (blogs)
online journals housed on a website

online games
interaction among a group of people in real time to play common board games, games of chance, or fantasy role-playing games

LO³ spontaneous expressions
spoken without much conscious thought

scripted messages
phrasings learned from past encounters that we judge to be appropriate to the present situation

constructed messages
messages put together with careful thought when we recognize that our known scripts are inadequate for the situation

immediacy
the degree of liking or attractiveness in a relationship

Multiple Choice

6. To understand how the process of communication works, we have to describe its essential elements, which are
   a. participants (who), messages (what), context (where), channels (how), presence or absence of noise (distractions), and feedback (reaction).
   b. participants (who), conversation (what), interaction (how), and the interference of white noise (distractions).
   c. public (who), conversation (what), context (where), channels (how), and feedback (distractions).
   d. recipients (who), messages (what), interaction (how), presence or absence of noise (distractions), and feedback (reaction).
   e. partners (who), channels (how), nonverbals (what), and feedback (reaction).

7. Why do we communicate?
   a. To meet our social needs.
   b. To develop and maintain our sense of self.
   c. To develop relationships.
   d. To exchange information and influence others.
   e. All of these answers are correct.

8. In this course you will learn about interpersonal communication settings, which are characterized by
   a. formal interaction among a small number of people.
   b. informal interaction among a small number of people.
   c. participants who come together for the specific purpose of solving a problem or arriving at a decision.
   d. one or more participants who deliver a prepared message to a group or audience.
   e. participants who do not share a physical context but communicate through the use of technology.

9. There are seven principles, or general truths, of communication. Which of the following is not one of them.
   a. Communication has purpose.
   b. Communication is continuous.
   c. Communication messages vary in conscious thought.
   d. Communication messages are always spontaneous expressions.
   e. Communication is relational.

10. Which of the following is not one of the ethical standards that influence our communication and guide behavior:
    a. truthfulness and honesty
    b. integrity
    c. fairness
    d. respect
    e. competence .

Chapter Quiz Answers:
1. E; 2. T; 3. T; 4. F; 5. F; 6. A; 7. E; 8. B; 9. D; 10. E

control
the degree to which one participant is perceived to be more dominant or powerful

culture
systems of knowledge shared by a relatively large group of people

ethics
a set of moral principles that may be held by a society, a group, or an individual

truthfulness and honesty
refraining from lying, cheating, stealing, or deception

moral dilemma
a choice involving an unsatisfactory alternative

integrity
maintaining a consistency of belief and action (keeping promises)

fairness
achieving the right balance of interests without regard to one's own feelings and without showing favor to any side in a conflict

respect
showing regard or consideration for others and their ideas, even if we don't agree with them

responsibility
being accountable for one's actions and what one says

LO⁴ communication competence
the impression that communicative behavior is both appropriate and effective in a given situation

skills
goal-oriented actions or action sequences that we can master and repeat in appropriate situations

credibility
a perception of a speaker's knowledge, trustworthiness, and warmth

social ease
communicating without anxiety or nervousness

Chapter in Review

LO¹ communication
the process of creating or sharing meaning in informal conversation, group interaction, or public speaking

participants
individuals who assume the roles of senders and receivers during an interaction

messages
verbal utterances and nonverbal behaviors to which meaning is attributed during communication

meaning
thoughts in our minds and interpretations of others' messages

symbols
words, sounds, and actions that are generally understood to represent ideas and feelings

encoding
the process of putting our thoughts and feelings into words and nonverbal cues

decoding
the process of interpreting another's message

contexts
the settings in which communication occurs, including what precedes and follows what is said

physical context
its location, the environmental conditions (temperature, lighting, noise level), the distance between communicators, seating arrangements, and time of day

social context
the nature of the relationship that exists between the participants

historical context
the background provided by previous communication episodes between the participants that influence understandings in the current encounter

psychological context
the mood and feelings each person brings to the conversation

cultural context
the values, attitudes, beliefs, orientations, and underlying assumptions prevalent among people in a society

channel
both the route traveled by the message and the means of transportation

noise
any stimulus that interferes with the process of sharing meaning

physical noise
sights, sounds, and other stimuli in the environment that draw people's attention away from intended meaning

psychological noise
internal distractions based on thoughts, feelings, or emotional reactions to symbols

LO¹ Define the communication process.
We have defined communication as the process of creating or sharing meaning, whether the context is informal conversation, group interaction, or public speaking. The elements of the communication process are participants, messages, context, channels, noise, and feedback.

LO² Discuss communication functions and settings.
Communication plays a role in all aspects of our lives. First, communication serves many important functions. People communicate to meet needs, to develop and maintain a sense of self, to develop relationships, to fulfill social obligations, to exchange information, and to influence others. Second, communication occurs in interpersonal, group, public speaking, and electronically mediated settings.

LO³ Identify communication principles.
Our communication is guided by at least seven principles. First, communication is purposeful. Second, interpersonal communication is continuous. Third, interpersonal communication messages vary in degree of conscious encoding. Messages may be spontaneous, scripted, or constructed. Fourth, interpersonal communication is relational, defining the power and affection between people. Fifth, communication is guided by culture. Sixth, communication has ethical implications. Ethical standards that influence our communication include truthfulness, integrity, fairness, respect, and responsibility. And seventh, interpersonal communication is learned.

LO⁴ Discover how to increase communication competence.
A primary issue in this course is competence—we all strive to become better communicators. Competence is the perception by others that our communication behavior is appropriate as well as effective. It involves a desire to improve our communication, increasing our knowledge of communication, identifying and attaining goals, being able to use various skills, and presenting ourselves as credible and confident communicators. Skills can be learned, developed, and improved, and you can enhance your learning this term by writing goal statements to systematically improve your own skill repertoire.

Chapter 1 Quiz

True/False

1. Communication can be defined as verbal utterances and nonverbal behaviors to which meaning is attributed when exchanging messages.

2. A primary issue in this course is competence, which is the perception by others that our communication behavior is appropriate as well as effective.

3. Skills are goal-oriented actions or action sequences that we can master and repeat in appropriate situations.

4. Communication competence means communicating without anxiety or nervousness.

5. When you show regard or consideration for others and their ideas, even if you don't agree with them, you are demonstrating the ethical standard of fairness.

internal noise
thoughts and feelings that compete for attention and interfere with the communication process

semantic noise
distractions aroused by certain symbols that take our attention away from the main message

feedback
reactions and responses to messages

LO² interpersonal communication settings
interactions among a small number of people who have relationships with each other

problem-solving group settings
participants come together for the specific purpose of solving a problem or arriving at a decision

public speaking settings
one participant, the speaker, delivers a prepared message to a group or audience who has assembled to hear the speaker

electronically mediated communication settings
involves participants who do not share a physical context but communicate through the use of technology

e-mail
electronic correspondence conducted between two or more users on a network where the communication does not occur in real time

instant messaging (IM)
communication through maintaining a list of people that you can interact with in real time when they are online

text messaging
short, written messages between mobile phones and other handheld electronic devices, exchanged in real time or stored for later retrieval

listservs
electronic mailing lists through the use of e-mail that allow for widespread distribution of information to many Internet users, so online discussions can occur in a delayed time format

chat rooms
interactive message exchange between two or more people where multiple messages are exchanged in real time

weblogs (blogs)
online journals housed on a website

online games
interaction among a group of people in real time to play common board games, games of chance, or fantasy role-playing games

LO³ spontaneous expressions
spoken without much conscious thought

scripted messages
phrasings learned from past encounters that we judge to be appropriate to the present situation

constructed messages
messages put together with careful thought when we recognize that our known scripts are inadequate for the situation

immediacy
the degree of liking or attractiveness in a relationship

Multiple Choice

6. To understand how the process of communication works, we have to describe its essential elements, which are
   a. participants (who), messages (what), context (where), channels (how), presence or absence of noise (distractions), and feedback (reaction).
   b. participants (who), conversation (what), interaction (how), and the interference of white noise (distractions).
   c. public (who), conversation (what), context (where), channels (how), and feedback (distractions).
   d. recipients (who), messages (what), interaction (how), presence or absence of noise (distractions), and feedback (reaction).
   e. partners (who), channels (how), nonverbals (what), and feedback (reaction).

7. Why do we communicate?
   a. To meet our social needs.
   b. To develop and maintain our sense of self.
   c. To develop relationships.
   d. To exchange information and influence others.
   e. All of these answers are correct.

8. In this course you will learn about interpersonal communication settings, which are characterized by
   a. formal interaction among a small number of people.
   b. informal interaction among a small number of people.
   c. participants who come together for the specific purpose of solving a problem or arriving at a decision.
   d. one or more participants who deliver a prepared message to a group or audience.
   e. participants who do not share a physical context but communicate through the use of technology.

9. There are seven principles, or general truths, of communication. Which of the following is not one of them.
   a. Communication has purpose.
   b. Communication is continuous.
   c. Communication messages vary in conscious thought.
   d. Communication messages are always spontaneous expressions.
   e. Communication is relational.

10. Which of the following is not one of the ethical standards that influence our communication and guide behavior:
    a. truthfulness and honesty
    b. integrity
    c. fairness
    d. respect
    e. competence

Chapter Quiz Answers:

1. F; 2. T; 3. T; 4. F; 5. F; 6. A; 7. E; 8. B; 9. D; 10. E

control
the degree to which one participant is perceived to be more dominant or powerful

culture
systems of knowledge shared by a relatively large group of people

ethics
a set of moral principles that may be held by a society, a group, or an individual

truthfulness and honesty
refraining from lying, cheating, stealing, or deception

moral dilemma
a choice involving an unsatisfactory alternative

integrity
maintaining a consistency of belief and action (keeping promises)

fairness
achieving the right balance of interests without regard to one's own feelings and without showing favor to any side in a conflict

respect
showing regard or consideration for others and their ideas, even if we don't agree with them

responsibility
being accountable for one's actions and what one says

LO⁴ communication competence
the impression that communicative behavior is both appropriate and effective in a given situation

skills
goal-oriented actions or action sequences that we can master and repeat in appropriate situations

credibility
a perception of a speaker's knowledge, trustworthiness, and warmth

social ease
communicating without anxiety or nervousness

LO¹ perception
the process of selectively attending
to information and assigning meaning to it

pattern
a set of characteristics used to differentiate
some things from others

interpret
assigning meaning to information

LO² self-concept
your self-identity

self-esteem
your overall evaluation of your competence
and personal worthiness

role
a pattern of learned behaviors that people use
to meet the perceived demands of a particular
context

self-monitoring
the internal process of observing and regulating your own behavior based on your analysis
of the situation and others' responses to you

incongruence
the gap between our inaccurate self-perceptions and reality

self-fulfilling prophecies
events that happen as the result of being foretold, expected, or talked about

self-talk
the internal conversations we have with
ourselves

LO³ uncertainty reduction
the process of monitoring the social
environment to learn more about self and
others

implicit personality theories
assumptions people have developed about
which physical characteristics and personality
traits or behaviors are associated with another

halo effect
to generalize and perceive that a person has a
whole set of characteristics when you have
actually observed only one characteristic, trait,
or behavior

stereotypes
attributions that cover up individual differences and ascribe certain characteristics to an
entire group of people

prejudice
a rigid attitude that is based on group membership and predisposes an individual to feel,
think, or act in a negative way toward another
person or group

discrimination
a negative action toward a social group or its
members on account of group membership

attributions
reasons we give for others' behavior

LO¹ Discuss the perception process.
Perception is the process of selectively attending to information and
assigning meaning to it. Our perceptions are a result of our selection, organization,
and interpretation of sensory information. Self-concept is our self-identity, the idea or
mental image that we have about our skills, abilities, knowledge, competencies, and
personality. Self-esteem is our overall evaluation of our competence and personal
worthiness. Self-concepts come from interpretations of self based on our own experience and on the reactions and responses of others. The inaccuracy of a distorted
picture of oneself becomes magnified through self-fulfilling prophecies and filtering
messages.

A Sensory Test of Expectation

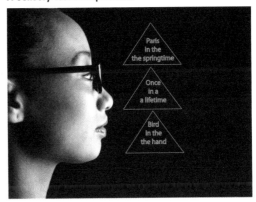

LO² Examine self-perceptions and how they affect communication.
Our self-concept and self-esteem moderate competing internal messages
in our self-talk, influence our perception of others, and influence our personal communication style. Our self-concept is socially constructed by us and by others, and
the different roles we play in various situations create our multiple selves.

LO³ Examine what determines our perception of others.
Perception plays an important role in forming impressions of others. We
form these impressions based on others' physical characteristics and social behaviors, our stereotyping, and our emotional states. Your communication will be most
successful if you do not rely entirely on your own interpretation to determine how
another person feels, what that person is really like, or what you think the person
means by a certain message. You can learn to improve perception if you actively
question the accuracy of your perceptions, seek more information to verify perceptions, talk with the people about whom you are forming perceptions, and realize that
perceptions of people need to change over time.

LO⁴ Describe how we perceive messages.
In addition to perceiving ourself and others, we also use perception to
decode and understand the messages that we receive. As we perceive messages,
the three important factors that affect our perception are the context in which we
receive the message, the language and nonverbal behavior that form the message,
and the skillfulness with which the message was formed.

Perception checking is a communication skill that can help us increase the likelihood that we will share meaning with others. It can help us increase the accuracy of
our self-perceptions, our perceptions of others' behavior, and our perceptions of the
nonverbal parts of the messages that we receive.

LO⁴ perception check
a message that reflects your understanding of the meaning of another person's
nonverbal behavior

Chapter 2 Quiz

True/False

1. The process of selectively attending to information and assigning meaning to it is called perception.

2. Self-concept is your overall evaluation of your competence and personal worthiness.

3. We place a great deal of emphasis on the first experience we have with a particular phenom-enon. For example, if you don't do well in your first attempt at public speaking, your self-per-ception may be that you are not a "natural" at giving speeches.

4. Your communication will be most successful if you rely entirely on your own interpretation, or "gut feeling," to determine what another person is really like or what you think the person means by a certain message.

5. The internal process of observing and regulating your own behavior based on your analysis of the situation and others' responses to you is known as self-monitoring.

Multiple Choice

6. Although we are subject to a constant barrage of sensory stimuli, we focus attention on rel-atively little of it. How we choose depends in part on our needs, interests, and
   a. perceptions.
   b. expectations.
   c. selectivity.
   d. goals.
   e. interpretation.

7. A pattern of learned behaviors that people use to meet the perceived demands of a particu-lar context is called a
   a. role.
   b. self-concept.
   c. personality.
   d. temperament.
   e. persona.

8. Suppose you expect to be rejected when you ask someone out and then behave in ways that lead the person to reject you. This would be an example of
   a. poor self-esteem.
   b. incongruence.
   c. self-fulfilling prophecies.
   d. filtering messages.
   e. perceptions.

9. If you grew up hearing that you were a "slow learner," and then a professor praised you for being a quick study, you may downplay the comment, not really hear it, or discount it entirely. This is an example of
   a. incongruence.
   b. filtering messages.
   c. poor self-perception.
   d. delayed reaction.
   e. self-fulfilling prophecies.

10. Perhaps the most commonly known factor that influences our perception of others is _____, described as "attributions that cover up individual differ-ences and ascribe certain characteristics to an entire group of people."
    a. incongruence
    b. filtering messages
    c. self-fulfilling prophecies
    d. stereotypes
    e. discrimination

Chapter Quiz Answers:

1. T; 2. F; 3. T; 4. F; 5. T; 6. B; 7. A; 8. C; 9. B; 10. D

Chapter in Review

LO¹ language
a body of symbols (most commonly words) and the systems for their use in messages that are common to the people of the same speech community

speech community
a group of people who speak the same language (also called a language community)

words
symbols used by a speech community to represent objects, ideas, and feelings

Sapir–Whorf hypothesis
a theory claiming that language influences perception

denotation
the direct, explicit meaning a speech community formally gives a word

connotation
the feelings or evaluations we associate with a word

syntactic context
the position of a word in a sentence and the other words around it

low-context cultures
cultures in which messages are direct, specific, and detailed

high-context cultures
cultures in which messages are indirect, general, and ambiguous

feminine styles of language
use words of empathy and support, emphasize concrete and personal language, and show politeness and tentativeness in speaking

masculine styles of language
use words of status and problem solving, emphasize abstract and general language, and show assertiveness and control in speaking

LO² specific words
words that clarify meaning by narrowing what is understood from a general category to a particular item or group within that category

concrete words
words that appeal to the senses and help us see, hear, smell, taste, or touch

precise words
words that narrow a larger category

vivid wording
wording that is full of life, vigorous, bright, and intense

simile
a direct comparison of dissimilar things

metaphor
a comparison that establishes a figurative identity between objects being compared

emphasis
the weight or importance given to certain words or ideas

dating information
specifying the time or time period that a fact was true or known to be true

LO¹ Discuss the nature and use of language.
Language is a body of symbols and the systems for their use in messages that are common to the people of the same language community. Language allows us to perceive the world around us. Through language we designate, label, and define; we evaluate, discuss things outside our immediate experience, and talk about language.

The relationship between language and meaning is complex because the meaning of words varies with people, people interpret words differently based on both denotative and connotative meanings, the context in which words are used affects meaning, and word meanings change over time.

Culture and gender influence how words are used and how we interpret others' words. In low-context cultures, messages are direct and language is specific. In high-context cultures, messages are indirect, general, and ambiguous. Societal expectations of masculinity and femininity influence language.

LO² Identify methods for improving language skills.
We can increase language skills by using specific, concrete, and precise language; by developing verbal vividness and emphasis; and by providing details and examples, dating information, and indexing generalizations.

LO³ Understand what is and is not appropriate in speech.
We can speak more appropriately by choosing vocabulary the listener understands, using jargon sparingly, using slang situationally, and demonstrating linguistic sensitivity.

Chapter 3 Quiz

True/False

1. Words are both a body of symbols (called language) and the systems for their use in messages that are common to the people of the same speech community.

2. A speech community is a group of people who speak the same language.

3. Denotation can be defined as the direct, explicit meaning a speech community formally gives a word. Connotation can be defined as the feelings or evaluations we associate with a word.

4. In high-context cultures like the United States and most northern European countries, messages are direct and language is very specific.

5. Masculine styles of language typically use words of status and problem solving, emphasize abstract and general language, and show assertiveness and control in speaking.

Multiple Choice

6. Language affects how people think and what they pay attention to, a concept called
   a. the Littlejohn-Foss hypothesis.
   b. the Sapir-Whorf hypothesis.
   c. perceptual shift.
   d. denotation.
   e. connotation.

indexing generalizations
the mental and verbal practice of acknowledging the presence of individual differences when voicing generalizations

LO³ speaking appropriately
choosing language and symbols that are adapted to the needs, interests, knowledge, and attitudes of the listeners and avoiding language that alienates them

jargon
technical terms understood only by select groups

slang
informal vocabulary used by particular groups in society

generic language
using words that may apply only to one sex, race, or other group as though they represent everyone

nonparallel language
terms are changed because of the sex, race, or other characteristic of the individual

marking
the addition of sex, race, age, or other designations to a description

7. Although language communities vary in the words that they use and in their grammar and syntax systems, all languages serve the same purposes. Which of the following is not one of them?
   a. We use language to designate, label, define, and limit.
   b. We use language to evaluate.
   c. We use language to discuss things outside our immediate experience.
   d. We can use language to talk about language.
   e. All of these are purposes that all languages serve.

8. _____ clarify meaning by narrowing what is understood from a general category to a particular item or group within that category.
   a. General responses
   b. Correct words
   c. Specific words
   d. Descriptive words
   e. Metaphors

9. Which of the following sentences is an example of vivid wording?
   a. Jackson made a great catch.
   b. Emily tried hard to do well in school last year.
   c. Sam fell off his bike and hurt himself.
   d. Casey's bike smashed into the back of the red Mazda, and she went flying into the street, landing face-first on the asphalt.
   e. Haley baked a dessert for her friend's birthday.

10. The weight or importance given to certain words or ideas is
    a. a metaphor.
    b. a simile.
    c. repetition.
    d. emphasis.
    e. communication.

Chapter Quiz Answers:
1. E; 2. T; 3. T; 4. F; 5. T; 6. B; 7. E; 8. C; 9. D; 10. D

LO¹ nonverbal communication behaviors
bodily actions and vocal qualities that typically accompany a verbal message

LO² kinesics
the interpretation of body motions used in communication

gestures
movements of our hands, arms, and fingers that we use to describe or to emphasize

illustrators
gestures that augment a verbal message

emblems
gestures that can substitute for words

adaptors
gestures that respond to a physical need

eye contact (gaze)
how and how much we look at people with whom we are communicating

facial expression
the arrangement of facial muscles to communicate emotional states or reactions to messages

emoticons
typed symbols that convey emotional aspects of an online message

posture
the position and movement of the body

body orientation
posture in relation to another person

haptics
the interpretation of touch

vocalics
the interpretation of a message based on the paralinguistic features

paralanguage
the voiced but not verbal part of a spoken message

pitch
the highness or lowness of vocal tone

volume
the loudness or softness of tone

rate
the speed at which a person speaks

quality
the sound of a person's voice

intonation
the variety, melody, or inflection in one's voice

vocalized pauses
extraneous sounds or words that interrupt fluent speech

proxemics
the interpretation of a person's use of space

LO¹ Identify characteristics of nonverbal communication.
Nonverbal communication refers to the interpretations that are made of bodily actions, vocal qualities, use of space, and self-presentation cues.

LO² Identify channels through which we communicate nonverbally.
Nonverbal communication is continuous, multichanneled, intentional or unintentional, possibly ambiguous, and the primary means by which we convey our emotions. The sources of nonverbal messages include use of body motions (kinesics: gestures, eye contact, facial expression, posture, and touch); use of voice (vocalics: pitch, volume, rate, quality, intonation, and vocalized pauses); and use of space (proxemics: personal space, physical space, and use of artifacts).

Distance Levels of Personal Space in the Dominant U.S. Culture

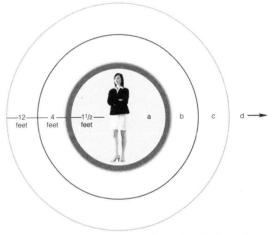

Zone a, **intimate space:** spouses, significant others, family members, and others with whom we have an intimate relationship
Zone b, **personal distance:** friends
Zone c, **social distance:** business associates and acquaintances
Zone d, **public distance:** strangers

LO³ Discuss how our self-presentation affects communication.
People gather information about us based on how they interpret our self-presentation cues. Self-presentation cues include physical appearance (for instance, body shape), clothing and grooming, and use of time (or our temporal orientation).

LO⁴ Examine how nonverbal communication varies based on culture and gender. The nonverbal behaviors that we enact and how we interpret the nonverbal messages of others depends on our culture and gender. Regardless of our cultural background or gender, however, we can become more adept at interpreting others' nonverbal messages we receive by not jumping to conclusions, by considering cultural and gender differences, by paying attention to all aspects of nonverbal communication and their relationship to verbal communication, and by perception checking.

LO⁵ Understand guidelines for improving nonverbal communication.
We can improve our encoding of nonverbal communication by being conscious of the nonverbal behavior we are displaying, by being purposeful or strategic in its use, by making sure that our nonverbal cues do not distract from our message, by making our nonverbal communication match our verbal messages, and by adapting our nonverbal behavior to the situation.

personal space
the distance you try to maintain when you interact with other people

physical space
the physical environment over which you exert control

artifacts
objects and possessions we use to decorate the physical space we control

LO³ **endomorph**
round and heavy body type

mesomorph
muscular and athletic body type

ectomorph
body type that is lean and has little muscle development

chronemics
the interpretation of a person's use of time

monochronic time orientation
a time orientation that emphasizes doing one thing at a time

polychronic time orientation
a time orientation that emphasizes doing multiple things at once

Chapter 4 Quiz

True/False

1. The interpretation of body motions used in communication is called kinesics.

2. Studies show that talkers hold eye contact about 70 percent of the time and listeners only 40 percent of the time.

3. Proxemics is the formal term for the interpretation someone makes of your use of space.

4. Studies show that, regardless of culture or gender, nonverbal communication is always the same.

5. When interpreting nonverbal messages, it's important to automatically know exactly what a particular behavior means so that you'll know how to react appropriately.

Multiple Choice

6. All of the following are characteristics of nonverbal communication *except*
   a. continuous.
   b. multichanneled.
   c. intentional.
   d. unintentional.
   e. unambiguous.

7. Gestures that augment a verbal message are called
   a. emphasizers.
   b. illustrators.
   c. emblems.
   d. kinesics.
   e. adaptors.

8. In Western culture, we shake hands to be sociable and polite, pat a person on the back for encouragement, hug a person to show love, and clasp raised hands to demonstrate solidarity. The interpretation of this kind of touch is called
   a. kinesics.
   b. proxemics.
   c. haptics.
   d. nonverbal communication.
   e. paralanguage.

9. The six vocal characteristics that comprise paralanguage are
   a. pitch, volume, rate, quality, intonation, and vocalized pauses.
   b. vocalics, pitch, volume, haptics, kinesics, and illustrators.
   c. pitch, volume, rate, haptics, intonation, and proxemics.
   d. haptics, expression, vocalics, pitch, quality, and intonation.
   e. expression, quality, vocalics, volume, intonation, and vocalized pauses.

10. There are three general body shapes. The type that is generally muscular and strong, and is believed to be energetic, outgoing, and confident, is called
   a. endomorph.
   b. ectomorph.
   c. mesomorph.
   d. mendomorph.
   e. andromorph.

Chapter Quiz Answers:
1. T; 2. F; 3. T; 4. F; 5. F; 6. E; 7. B; 8. C; 9. A; 10. C

5

Chapter in Review

LO¹ culture shock
the psychological discomfort of adjusting to a new cultural situation

intercultural communication
interaction between people whose cultural assumptions are distinct enough to alter the communication event

dominant culture
the attitudes, values, beliefs, and customs that the majority of people in a society hold in common

co-cultures
groups of people living within a dominant culture but exhibiting communication that is sufficiently different to distinguish them from the dominant culture

ethnicity
a classification of people based on combinations of shared characteristics such as nationality, geographic origin, language, religion, ancestral customs, and tradition

religion
a system of beliefs shared by a group with objects for devotion, rituals for worship, and a code of ethics

social class
an indicator of a person's position in a social hierarchy, as determined by income, education, occupation, and social habits

LO² individualistic culture
emphasizes personal rights and responsibilities, privacy, voicing one's opinion, freedom, innovation, and self-expression

collectivist culture
emphasizes community, collaboration, shared interest, harmony, the public good, and avoiding embarrassment

low uncertainty-avoidance cultures
cultures characterized by greater acceptance of, and less need to control, unpredictable people, relationships, or events

high uncertainty-avoidance cultures
cultures characterized by a low tolerance for, and a high need to control, unpredictable people, relationships, or events

high power distance
the cultural belief that inequalities in power, status, and rank are "natural" and that these differences should be acknowledged and accentuated

low power distance
the cultural belief that inequalities in power, status, and rank should be underplayed and muted

masculine culture
a culture in which people are expected to adhere to traditional sex roles

feminine culture
a culture in which people, regardless of sex, are expected to assume a variety of roles based on the circumstances and their own choices

LO¹ Examine how culture affects communication.
Culture encompasses the values, attitudes, beliefs, orientations, and underlying assumptions prevalent among people in a society. Culture shock refers to the psychological discomfort people have when they attempt to adjust to a new cultural situation. Intercultural communication takes place when people's distinct cultural assumptions alter the communication event. A shared system of meaning exists within the dominant culture, but meanings can vary within co-cultures based on gender, race, ethnicity, sexual orientation, religion, social class, and age.

LO² Discuss how to identify cultural norms and values.
Cultural norms and values vary in systematic ways, and we can understand how similar or different one culture is from others by understanding where the culture is on the dimensions of individualism–collectivism, uncertainty avoidance, power distance, and masculinity–femininity.

Relative Comparison of Dimension Levels Between Ten Countries

Individualsim	High Uncertainty Avoidance	High Power Distance	Masculinity
USA	Japan	Russia	Japan
Netherlands	Russia	China	Germany
France	West Africa	Indonesia	USA
Germany	France	West Africa	Hong Kong
Russia	Germany	France	China
Japan	China	Hong Kong	Indonesia
Hong Kong	Netherlands	Japan	West Africa
China	Indonesia	USA	France
West Africa	USA	Netherlands	Russia
Indonesia	Hong Kong	Germany	Netherlands
Collectivism	**Low Uncertainty Avoidance**	**Low Power Distance**	**Femininity**

Source: G.H. Hofstede, "Cultural Constraints in Management Theories," *Academy of Management Executive* 7, no. 1 (1993): 81–94.

LO³ Explain barriers to effective intercultural communication.
Barriers to intercultural communication include anxiety, assumptions about differences and similarities, ethnocentrism, stereotypes and prejudice, incompatible communication codes, and incompatible norms and values.

LO⁴ Analyze the development of intercultural communication competence.
To develop intercultural communication competence, we need to adopt correct attitudes about intercultural communication. We should learn to tolerate ambiguity, be open-minded, and be altruistic. We can acquire knowledge of other cultures by observing, through formal study, and through cultural immersion. Useful skills for intercultural communication competence are intercultural listening, empathy, and flexibility.

LO³ ethnocentrism
the belief that one's own culture is superior to others

LO⁴ altruism
a display of genuine and unselfish concern for the welfare of others

egocentricity
a selfish interest in one's own needs, to the exclusion of everything else

intercultural empathy
imaginatively placing yourself in the dissimilar other person's cultural world to attempt to experience what he or she is experiencing

flexibility
the ability to adjust your communication to fit the other person and the situation

Chapter 5 Quiz

True/False

1. Intercultural communication can be defined as the psychological discomfort of adjusting to a new cultural situation.

2. The dominant culture of the United States once reflected the values of white, western European, English-speaking, Protestant, heterosexual men, but as we have recognized our diversity, the dominant culture has evolved and incorporated aspects of other cultural groups.

3. People living within a dominant culture but exhibiting communication that is sufficiently different to distinguish them from the dominant culture are called intercultural groups.

4. Individualistic cultures emphasize personal rights and responsibilities, privacy, voicing one's opinion, freedom, innovation, and self-expression. In contract, collectivist cultures place primary value on the interests of the group and group harmony.

5. The United States, Sweden, and Denmark are all examples of low uncertainty-avoidance cultures and are therefore more tolerant of uncertainty in how people behave, in relationships, and in events.

Multiple Choice

6. Which of the following is not one of the major contributors to co-cultures in U.S. society today:
   a. gender
   b. ethnicity
   c. race
   d. political beliefs
   e. sexual orientation

7. Geert Hofstede identified four major dimensions of culture that affect communication. Which of the following is *not* one of them:
   a. individualism–collectivism
   b. religious beliefs
   c. uncertainty avoidance
   d. power distance
   e. masculinity–femininity

8. In cultures characterized by _____, inequalities in power, status, and rank are underplayed and muted.
   a. high power distance
   b. low power distance
   c. masculinity
   d. femininity
   e. individualism

9. Which of the following barriers to effective intercultural communication may occur because a person believes that their own culture is superior to others:
   a. ethnocentrism
   b. assuming similarity or difference
   c. stereotypes and prejudice
   d. incompatible communication codes
   e. incompatible norms and values

10. Competent intercultural communicators overcome cultural barriers by
    a. adopting the correct attitudes toward other cultures.
    b. acquiring accurate information about other cultures' values and practices.
    c. developing specific skills needed to be effective across cultures.
    d. learning to tolerate ambiguity.
    e. All of these answers are correct.

Chapter Quiz Answers:
1. F; 2. T; 3. F; 4. T; 5. T; 6. D; 7. B; 8. B; 9. A; 10. E

Chapter in Review

LO¹ relationships
sets of expectations two people have for their behavior based on the pattern of interaction between them

good relationships
ones in which the interactions are satisfying to and healthy for those involved

acquaintances
people we know by name and talk with when the opportunity arises, but with whom our interactions are largely impersonal

friends
people with whom we have negotiated more personal relationships that are voluntary

close friends (intimates)
people with whom we share a high degree of commitment, trust, interdependence, disclosure, and enjoyment

platonic relationship
an intimate relationship in which the partners are not sexually attracted to each other or do not act on an attraction they feel

romantic relationship
an intimate relationship in which the partners act on their sexual attraction

trust
placing confidence in another in a way that almost always involves some risk

LO² self-disclosure
sharing biographical data, personal ideas, and feelings that are unknown to the other person

feedback
verbal and physical responses to people (and/or their messages) within the relationship

Johari window
a tool for examining the relationship between disclosure and feedback in the relationship

LO³ maintaining a relationship
behaving and communicating in ways that preserve a particular level of closeness or intimacy in a relationship

---

LO¹ Describe the major types of relationships.

Interpersonal communication helps develop and maintain relationships. A good relationship is any mutually satisfying interaction with another person. We have three types of relationships. Acquaintances are people we know by name and talk with, but with whom our interactions are limited in quality and quantity. Friendships are marked by degrees of warmth and affection, trust, self-disclosure, commitment, and expectation that the relationships will endure. Close or intimate friends are those with whom we share a high degree of commitment, trust, interdependence, disclosure, and enjoyment.

LO² Explain how disclosure and feedback affect relationships.

A healthy relationship is marked by a balance of self-disclosure and feedback. The Johari window is a tool for analyzing this balance, categorizing information based on whether it is or is not known by the self and others.

The Johari Window

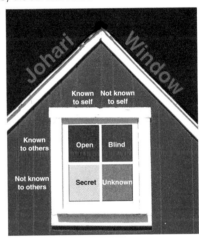

O = Open   S = Secret
B = Blind   U = Unknown

Sample Johrai Windows

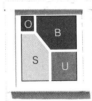

A
low disclosure, low feedback

B
high disclosure, low feedback

C
low disclosure, high feedback

D
high disclosure, high feedback

LO³ Examine levels of communication at various stages in relationships.

Relationships go through a life cycle that includes building and developing, maintaining, and perhaps de-escalating and ending. In the first stage of beginning and developing a relationship, we try to get to know each other to reduce uncertainty, we develop feelings of relaxation and confirmation, and we experience greater levels of disclosure and support. There are various ways to maintain a relationship including spending time together, merging social networks, doing unselfish acts, and exchanging affection, self-disclosure, favors, and support. When relationships start to deteriorate, we tend to recognize feelings of dissatisfaction, notice each other's faults, experience more conflict, discuss only safe topics, and spend less time together. Effective communicators consciously end relationships with direct, open, and honest communication rather than manipulation, withdrawal, or avoidance.

Chapter 6 Quiz

True/False

1. Interpersonal skills help you start, build, and maintain healthy relationships, which are sets of expectations two people have for their behavior based on the pattern of interaction between them.

2. A relationship with someone you know by name and talk with when the opportunity arises, but with whom your interactions are largely impersonal, is considered platonic.

3. Sharing biographical data, personal ideas, and feelings that are unknown to the other person is called feedback.

4. Continuing to spend time with your partner, merging your social networks, and reciprocating unselfish acts are all examples of strategies people use to maintain relationships.

5. Sometimes a relationship may deteriorate simply because the partners are not vigilant in doing those things necessary to maintain the relationship at its current level.

Multiple Choice

6. A relationship with people you share a high degree of commitment, trust, interdependence, and disclosure with, is called
   a. platonic.
   b. intimate.
   c. romantic.
   d. impersonal.
   e. professional.

7. An intimate relationship in which the partners are not sexually attracted to each other or do not act on an attraction they feel is
   a. platonic.
   b. intimate.
   c. romantic.
   d. impersonal.
   e. professional.

8. All of the following are guidelines for meeting other people and developing acquaintance relationships except:
   a. Initiate conversations by introducing yourself.
   b. When you meet someone, refer to the physical context, to your thoughts or feelings, or another person.
   c. Engage in appropriate turn-taking in the conversation.
   d. Be polite.
   e. Be proactive in setting up times to be together.

9. Which of the following is not one of the guidelines for establishing and maintaining trust in an intimate relationship?
   a. Be dependable.
   b. Be responsive to your partner's needs.
   c. Make your comments relevant to what was previously said before you change subjects.
   d. Be an effective partner in conflict by managing it in a collaborative manner.
   e. Be faithful.

10. The Johari window is a tool for examining
    a. the relationship between disclosure and feedback in a relationship.
    b. the level of trust in an intimate relationship.
    c. the gender difference in communication styles.
    d. the strength of a close friendship.
    e. the life cycle of a relationship.

Chapter Quiz Answers:

1. T; 2. F; 3. F; 4. T; 5. T; 6. B; 7. A; 8. E; 9. C; 10. A

Chapter in Review

LO¹ listening
the process of receiving, constructing meaning from, and responding to spoken and/or nonverbal messages

attending
the perceptual process of selecting and focusing on specific stimuli from the countless stimuli reaching the senses

LO² understanding
decoding a message accurately to reflect the meaning intended by the speaker

empathy
intellectually identifying with or vicariously experiencing the feelings or attitudes of another

empathic responsiveness
experiencing an emotional response parallel to, and as a result observing, another person's actual or anticipated display of emotion

perspective taking
imagining yourself in the place of another; the most common form of empathizing

sympathetic responsiveness
feeling concern, compassion, or sorrow for another because of the other's situation or plight

question
a statement designed to get further information or to clarify information already received

paraphrasing
putting into words the ideas or feelings you have perceived from the message

content paraphrase
one that focuses on the denotative meaning of the message

feelings paraphrase
a response that captures the emotions attached to the content of the message

LO³ remembering
being able to retain information and recall it when needed

mnemonic device
any artificial technique used as a memory aid

LO⁴ critical analysis
the process of evaluating what you have heard to determine its truthfulness

factual statements
statements whose accuracy can be verified or proven

inferences
statements made by the speaker that are based on facts or observations

LO¹ List techniques for improving focus in the listening process.
Listening is the complex process that encompasses attending, understanding, remembering, evaluating, and responding with support and comfort.

Attending is the process of selecting and focusing on specific stimuli from the countless ones that we receive. We can be more effective in attending if we (1) get ready both physically and mentally, (2) make the shift from speaker to listener complete (don't rehearse), (3) hear a person out before responding, and (4) observe nonverbal clues.

LO² Examine ways for improving understanding of messages.
Understanding is the process of decoding a message so that the meaning accurately reflects that intended by the speaker. Empathizing, which is identifying with or vicariously experiencing the feelings of another, can increase understanding. We can also increase understanding by asking questions to clarify and get details and by paraphrasing the speaker's content and feelings.

LO³ Discuss how to better retain information.
Remembering is the process of retaining information so it can be recalled when it is needed. By repeating information, using mnemonics, and taking notes, we can increase the likelihood that we will remember what we hear.

LO⁴ Explain how to evaluate and critically analyze the truthfulness of messages.
Critical analysis is the process of evaluating what has been said to determine its truthfulness. Critical analysis is especially important when a speaker is asking you to believe, act on, or support what is being said. One important skill of critical analysis is to separate statements of fact from inferences. Statements of fact should be analyzed to see if they are true. Inferences should be tested to see if they are valid. Three questions can help us to test inferences: (1) What facts support this inference? (2) Is the information really central to the inference? (3) Are there other facts that would contradict the inference?

LO⁵ Identify steps for responding supportively and giving comfort.
Responding with support and comfort helps people feel better about themselves and their behavior. Effective support messages are those that aim to help, accept others, demonstrate concern, show one's willingness to listen and be an ally, acknowledge and validate the speaker's feelings, and encourage elaboration. When we give comfort, we should use messages that clarify our intentions, practice politeness, are other-centered, reframe the situation, and offer advice on issues the speaker cannot seem to resolve.

Giving Comfort

1. Clarifying supportive intentions.
2. Buffering face threats with politeness.
3. Encouraging understanding through other-centered messages.
4. Reframing the situation.
5. Giving advice.

LO⁵ comfort
to help people feel better about themselves and their behavior

supportive messages
comforting statements that have a goal to reassure, bolster, encourage, soothe, console, or cheer up

clarify supportive intentions
openly stating that your goal in the conversation is to help your partner

buffering
cushioning the effect of messages by utilizing both positive and negative politeness skills

positive face needs
the desire to be appreciated and approved, liked, and honored

negative face needs
the desire to be free from imposition or intrusion

other-centered messages
statements that encourage our partners to talk about and elaborate on what happened and how they feel about it

reframing
offering ideas, observations, information, and alternative explanations that might help your partner understand the situation in a different light

giving advice
presenting relevant suggestions and proposals that a person can use to satisfactorily resolve a situation

Chapter 7 Quiz

True/False

1. By using mnemonics and taking notes, we can increase the likelihood that we will understand and make sense of what we have heard.

2. Critical analysis is especially important when a speaker is asking you to believe, act on, or support what is being said.

3. When we give comfort, we should strive to keep our intentions vague and refrain from offering advice on issues the speaker cannot seem to resolve to avoid offending the person.

4. A growing body of research finds that both men and women place a high value on emotional support from their partners in a variety of relationships.

5. Inferences are statements whose accuracy can be verified or proven. For example, the statement "You are reading this sentence," is an inference.

Multiple Choice

6. The process of selecting and focusing on specific stimuli from the countless ones that we receive is called
   a. listening.
   b. attending.
   c. understanding.
   d. remembering.
   e. evaluating.

7. _____ is the process of decoding a message so that the meaning accurately reflects that intended by the speaker.
   a. Listening
   b. Attending
   c. Understanding
   d. Empathizing
   e. Responding

8. Which of the following questions can help us test inference:
   a. What facts support this inference?
   b. Is that information really central to the inference?
   c. Are there other facts that would contradict the inference?
   d. All of these questions help us to test inference.
   e. None of these questions help us to test inference.

9. _____ aim to help, accept others, demonstrate concern, show one's wiliness to listen and be an ally, acknowledge and validate the speaker's feelings, and encourage elaboration.
   a. Empathetic messages
   b. Effective support messages
   c. Intentional messages
   d. Critical analyses
   e. Mnemonics

10. Active listeners are adept at _____, putting into words the ideas or feelings they have perceived from the message.
   a. inference
   b. feedback
   c. paraphrasing
   d. mnemonics
   e. critical analysis

Chapter Quiz Answers:
1. F; 2. T; 3. F; 4. T; 5. F; 6. B; 7. C; 8. D; 9. B; 10. C

Chapter in Review

LO¹ relational dialectics
seemingly opposing forces (open-ness–closedness, autonomy–connection, and novelty–predictability) that occur in all inter-personal relationships

self-disclosure
sharing biographical data, personal experiences, ideas, and feelings

privacy
the right of an individual to keep biographical data, personal ideas, and feelings secret

managing privacy
a conscious decision to avoid disclosure and to withhold information or feelings from a rela-tional partner

report-talk
a way to share information, display knowl-edge, negotiate, and preserve independence

rapport-talk
a way to share experiences and establish bonds with others

LO² describing feelings
the skill of naming the emotions you are feeling without judging them

LO³ describing behavior
accurately recounting the specific behaviors of another without commenting on their appropriateness

praise
describing the specific positive behaviors or accomplishments of another and the effect that behavior has on others

constructive criticism
describing specific behaviors of another that hurt the person or that person's relationships with others

LO⁴ passive behavior
not expressing personal preferences or defending our rights because we fear the cost and are insecure in the relationships, have very low self-esteem, or value the other per-son above ourself

aggressive behavior
belligerently or violently confronting another with your preferences, feelings, needs, or rights with little regard for the situation or for the feelings or rights of others

assertive behavior
expressing your personal preferences and defending your personal rights while respect-ing the preferences and rights of others

LO⁵ interpersonal conflict
when the needs or ideas of one per-son are at odds or in opposition to the needs or ideas of another

LO¹ Discuss the balance between self-disclosure and privacy.
In relationships, seemingly opposing forces of openness–closedness, autonomy–connection, and novelty–predictability naturally occur. Called relational dialectics, these opposites create tension, which must be managed in all interpersonal relationships. Communication through self-disclosure, feedback, assertiveness, and conflict management can assist in managing the dialectical tensions in relationships.

LO² Examine guidelines for disclosing feelings.
Self-disclosure reveals information about ourselves that is unknown to others. Guidelines can help us decide when self-disclosure is appropriate. Sometimes we have legiti-mate reasons for managing our privacy instead of disclosing information. Disclosing feelings can be difficult. We can deal with our feelings by withholding them, displaying them, or skill-fully describing them. Instead of owning our own feelings and ideas, we often avoid disclo-sure by making generalized statements.

LO³ Develop effective ways to give personal feedback.
Personal feedback builds relationships by describing, not evaluating, behavior and its effects. Positive feedback is accomplished through praise. Negative feedback can be delivered effectively through constructive criticism.

LO⁴ Describe assertive behavior.
Assertiveness is the skill of standing up for ourselves in interpersonally effective ways. Passive people are often unhappy as a result of not stating their needs; aggressive people get their ideas and feelings heard but may create other problems through their aggressiveness.

Characteristics of Assertive Behavior

Own your feelings	Assertive individuals acknowledge that the thoughts and feelings expressed are theirs.
Avoid confrontational language	Assertive individuals do not use threats, evalua-tions, or dogmatic language.
Use specific statements directed to the behaviors at hand	Instead of focusing on extraneous issues, assertive individuals use descriptive statements that focus on the issue that is most relevant.
Maintain eye contact and firm body position	Assertive individuals look people in the eye rather than shifting gaze, looking at the floor, swaying back and forth, hunching over, or using other signs that may be perceived as indecisive or lacking conviction.
Maintain a firm but pleasant tone of voice	Assertive individuals speak firmly but at a normal pitch, volume, and rate.
Avoid hemming and hawing	Assertive individuals avoid vocalized pauses and other signs of indecisiveness.

LO⁵ Discuss conflict management styles.
We cope with conflicts in a variety of ways: withdrawing, accommodating, forc-ing, compromising, and collaborating. Although there are positive and negative outcomes of each style, when we are concerned about the long-term relationship and the effectiveness of a solution, collaborating is often most appropriate.

withdrawing

managing conflict by physically or psychologically removing yourself

accommodating

managing conflict by satisfying others' needs
or accepting others' ideas while neglecting
our own

forcing

managing conflict by satisfying your own
needs or advancing your own ideas, with no
concern for the needs or ideas of the other
and no concern for the harm done to the
relationship

compromising

managing conflict by giving up part of what
you want, to provide at least some satisfaction
for both parties

collaborating

managing conflict by fully addressing the
needs and issues of each party and arriving at
a solution that is mutually satisfying

Chapter 8 Quiz

True/False

1. Managing privacy is when you choose to share biographical data, personal experiences, ideas, and feelings with someone else.

2. It is a good idea to continue self-disclosure even when it is not immediately reciprocated because you may be able to draw the other person out and encourage them to trust you more readily.

3. Studies show that people, regardless of culture, gender, or family upbringing, have the same ideas about how much self-disclosure is appropriate.

4. Displaying our feelings can rise to the level of abuse, both verbal and physical. We can use the self-disclosure skill of describing feelings to share them with others in more appropriate ways.

5. Before giving criticism, it's important to ask the person's permission first.

Multiple Choice

6. A conscious decision to withhold information or feelings from a relational partner is called
   a. introversion.
   b. managing privacy.
   c. image management.
   d. self-disclosure.
   e. masking feelings.

7. In *You Just Don't Understand,* Deborah Tannen argues that men are more likely to engage in _____, whereas women engage in _____.
   a. report-talk; rapport-talk
   b. rapport-talk; report-talk
   c. self-disclosure; managing privacy
   d. managing privacy; self-disclosure
   e. negotiation; peacemaking

8. A straight-faced poker player whose expression is impossible to decipher has become a master of
   a. self-disclosure.
   b. rapport-talk.
   c. report-talk.
   d. masking feelings.
   e. managing privacy.

9. Accurately recounting the specific behaviors of another without commenting on their appropriateness is
   a. describing feelings.
   b. disclosing facts.
   c. describing behavior.
   d. report-talk.
   e. constructive criticism.

10. A(n) _____ person has the skill to stand up for him or herself in inter-personally effective ways.
    a. passive
    b. assertive
    c. aggressive
    d. accommodating
    e. collaborating

Chapter Quiz Answers:

1. F; 2. F; 3. F; 4. T; 5. T; 6. B; 7. A; 8. D; 9. C; 10. B

Chapter in Review

LO¹ interview
a planned, structured conversation in which one person asks questions and another person answers them

open questions
broad-based probes that call on the interviewee to provide perspective, ideas, information, feelings, or opinions as he or she answers the question

closed questions
narrowly focused questions that require the respondent to give very brief (one- or two-word) answers

neutral questions
questions that do not direct a person's answer

leading questions
questions that guide respondents toward providing certain types of information and imply that the interviewer prefers one answer over another

primary questions
lead-in questions that introduce one of the major topics of the interview conversation

secondary (follow-up) questions
questions designed to probe the answers given to primary questions

LO² interview protocol
an ordered list of questions that have been selected to meet the specific purpose of the interview

LO⁴ cover letter
a short, well-written letter expressing your interest in a particular job

résumé
a written summary of your skills and accomplishments

electronic cover letters and résumés
these contain the same information as traditional cover letters and résumés but are sent online

LO⁵ talking points
the three or four central ideas you will present as you answer the questions that are asked during a media interview

bridge
a transition you create in a media interview so that you can move from the interviewer's subject to the message you want to communicate

LO¹ Identify different kinds of questions to use in an interview.
Interviewing can be a productive way to obtain information from an expert for a paper, an article, or a speech.

The key skill of interviewing is using questions effectively. Open questions allow for flexible responses; closed questions require very brief answers. Primary questions stimulate response; follow-up questions ask for additional information. Neutral questions allow the respondent free choice; leading questions require the person to answer in a particular way.

LO² Explain how to prepare for and conduct an information interview.
When you are interviewing for information, you will want to define the purpose, select the best person to interview, develop a protocol, and conduct the interview according to the protocol.

LO³ Explain how to conduct a job interview.
Job interviews are a specific type of communication setting, with particular demands for both interviewer and interviewee. When you are interviewing prospective applicants for a job, structure your interview carefully to elicit maximal information about the candidate. Before the interview starts, become familiar with the data contained in the interviewee's application form, résumé, letters of recommendation, and test scores, if available. Be careful how you present yourself, do not waste time, do not ask questions that violate fair employment practice legislation, and give the applicant an opportunity to ask questions. At the end of the interview, explain to the applicant what will happen next in the process.

LO⁴ Explain how to present yourself when being interviewed for a job.
To get an interview, begin by taking the time to learn about the company and prepare an appropriate cover letter and résumé that are designed to motivate an employer to interview you. Electronic letters and résumés have become popular and need special preparation. For the interview itself, you should dress appropriately, be prompt, be alert, look directly at the interviewer, give yourself time to think before answering difficult questions, ask intelligent questions about the company and the job, and show enthusiasm for the position.

Before the Job Interview

1. Do your homework.
2. Based on your research, prepare a list of questions about the organization and the job.
3. Rehearse the interview.
4. Dress appropriately.
5. Plan to arrive on time.
6. Bring supplies.

During the Job Interview

1. Use active listening.
2. Think before answering.
3. Be enthusiastic.
4. Ask questions.
5. Avoid discussing salary and benefits.

After the Job Interview

1. Write a thank-you note.
2. Self-assess your performance.
3. Contact the interviewer for feedback.

LO⁵ Discuss how to participate in a media interview.

To participate in media interviews, prepare by understanding the focus and format of the interview and considering the few main points you want to convey. During the media interview, you should present appropriate nonverbal cues, make clear and concise statements, realize everything you say is on the record, and learn to use bridges as transitions to your message.

Chapter 9 Quiz

True/False

1. Primary questions are the lead-in questions that you use to introduce one of the major topics of the interview conversation.

2. Choosing which people you should interview is not always obvious. You may have to do research to identify them.

3. Interview protocol is how you should act and what you should wear for an interview.

4. It's usually best to ask all of the complex fact questions at the beginning of an interview to get them out of the way and to establish rapport with the other person.

5. It's important to remember to discuss salary and benefits at the beginning of a job interview so you know whether or not to proceed with it.

Multiple Choice

6. "Can you tell me about your job experience?" is an example of a(n)
   a. leading question.
   b. neutral question.
   c. closed question.
   d. unproductive question.
   e. secondary question.

7. "Was your boss as difficult to work with as I've heard he is?" is an example of a(n)
   a. open question.
   b. neutral question.
   c. secondary question.
   d. leading question.
   e. primary question.

8. "Have you taken any courses in marketing?" is an example of a(n)
   a. open question.
   b. closed question.
   c. leading question.
   d. secondary question.
   e. inappropriate question.

9. Getting the interview all begins with
   a. research.
   b. writing a cover letter.
   c. polishing your résumé.
   d. lining up references.
   e. networking.

10. During a media interview, you should
    a. present appropriate nonverbal cues.
    b. make clear and concise statements.
    c. realize everything you say is on the record.
    d. learn to use bridges as transitions to your message.
    e. practice all of these things.

Chapter Quiz Answers:
1. T; 2. T; 3. F; 4. F; 5. F; 6. B; 7. D; 8. B; 9. A; 10. E

LO¹ work group
a collection of three or more people who must interact and influence each other to solve problems and to accomplish a common purpose

group goal
a future state of affairs desired by enough members of the group to motivate the group to work toward its achievement

specific goal
a precisely stated, measurable, and behavioral goal

consistent goals
complementary goals; achieving one goal does not prevent the achievement of another

challenging goals
goals that require hard work and team effort; they motivate group members to do things beyond what they might normally accomplish

acceptable goals
goals to which members feel personally committed

homogeneous group
group in which members have a great deal of similarity

heterogeneous group
group in which various demographics, levels of knowledge, attitudes, and interests are represented

cohesiveness
the degree of attraction members have to each other and to the group's goal

team-building activities
activities designed to help the group work better together

norms
expectations for the way group members will behave while in the group

ground rules
prescribed behaviors designed to help the group meet its goals and conduct its conversations

synergy
a commonality of purpose and a complementariness of each other's efforts that produces a group outcome greater than an individual outcome

face-to-face meeting
a meeting in which all members come together in one physical location to make a decision or solve a problem

virtual meeting
a meeting in which people in various locations use technology to work together on a decision or problem

LO² forming
the initial stage of group development during which people come to feel valued and accepted so that they identify with the group

LO¹ Analyze the characteristics of an effective work group.

Effective work groups meet several criteria: They develop clearly defined goals, have an optimum number of diverse members, work to develop cohesiveness, establish norms, create appropriate environments in face-to-face and virtual meetings, and achieve synergy.

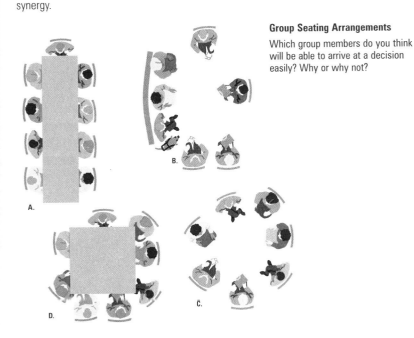

Group Seating Arrangements
Which group members do you think will be able to arrive at a decision easily? Why or why not?

LO² Explain various stages of group development.

Once groups have assembled, they tend to move through five stages of development: forming, getting people to feel valued and accepted so that they identify with the group; storming, clarifying goals while determining the role each member will have in the group power structure; norming, solidifying rules for behavior; performing, overcoming obstacles and meeting goals successfully; and adjourning, assigning meaning to what they have done and determining how to end or maintain interpersonal relations they have developed.

LO³ Explain the steps in group problem solving.

Once the group has reached the performing stage, they begin to move through a series of steps of problem solving, including defining the problem as a question of fact, value, or policy; analyzing the problem; determining solution criteria; identifying possible solutions; evaluating solutions; and deciding.

Methods for Decision Making

1. The expert opinion method
2. The average group opinion method
3. The majority rule method
4. The unanimous decision method
5. The consensus method

storming
the stage of group development during which the group clarifies its goals and determines the roles each member will have in the group power structure

groupthink
a deterioration of mental efficiency, reality testing, and moral judgment that results from in-group pressure

norming
the stage of group development during which the group solidifies its rules for behavior, especially those that relate to how conflict will be managed

performing
the stage of group development when the skills, knowledge, and abilities of all members are combined to overcome obstacles and meet goals successfully

adjourning
the stage of group development in which members assign meaning to what they have done and determine how to end or maintain interpersonal relations they have developed

LO³ **questions of fact**
questions concerned with discovering what is true or to what extent something is true

questions of value
questions that concern subjective judgments of what is right, moral, good, or just

questions of policy
questions that concern what courses of action should be taken or what rules should be adopted to solve a problem

brainstorming
an uncritical, nonevaluative process of generating associated ideas

decision making
the process of choosing among alternatives

Chapter 10 Quiz

True/False

1. "Increase profitability with in-store sales" is an example of a clearly defined goal.

2. In general, as the size of a group grows, so does the complexity it must manage.

3. Synergy is the degree of attraction members have to each other and to the group's goal.

4. Effective groups develop norms that support goal achievement and cohesiveness.

5. Studies show that group meetings should be face-to-face, where all members come together in one physical location to make a decision or solve a problem, in order to be effective.

6. Research shows that all effective work groups follow the same approach to problem solving in which they move linearly through a series of steps to reach consensus.

Multiple Choice

7. All of the following are characteristics of an effective work group *except*
   a. clearly defined goals.
   b. optimum number of diverse members.
   c. a collection of at least two or more people.
   d. cohesiveness.
   e. synergy.

8. A _____ group is one in which various demographics, levels of knowledge, attitudes, and interests are represented.
   a. homogeneous
   b. heterogeneous
   c. cohesive
   d. problem-solving
   e. synergistic

9. All of the following are factors leading to cohesiveness in groups *except*
   a. attractiveness of the group's purpose.
   b. commitment to specific ground rules.
   c. voluntary membership.
   d. feeling free to share opinions.
   e. celebration of accomplishments.

10. The stage of group development during which the group clarifies its goals and determines the roles each member will have in the group power structure is called
    a. forming.
    b. storming.
    c. norming.
    d. performing.
    e. adjourning.

Chapter Quiz Answers:
1. F; 2. T; 3. F; 4. T; 5. F; 6. F; 7. C; 8. B; 9. B; 10. B

LO¹ role
a specific pattern of behavior that one group member performs based on the expectations of other members

task-related roles
specific patterns of behavior that directly help the group accomplish its goals

initiator
a group member who gets the discussion started or moves it in a new direction

information (opinion) giver
a group member who provides content for the discussion

information (opinion) seeker
a group member who probes others for their factual ideas and opinions

analyzer
a group member who probes the content, reasoning, and evidence of members during discussion

orienter
a group member who indicates to the group that it is off track or summarizes points of agreement and disagreement among members

maintenance roles
patterns of behavior that help the group develop and maintain good member relationships, group cohesiveness, and effective levels of conflict

gatekeeper
a group member who ensures that everyone has an opportunity to speak and be heard

encourager
a group member who provides support for the contributions of other team members

harmonizer
a group member who helps the group relieve tension and manage conflict

self-centered roles
patterns of behavior that focus attention on individuals' needs and goals at the expense of the group

aggressor
a group member who seeks to enhance his or her own status by criticizing almost everything or blaming others when things get rough and by deflating the ego or status of others

joker
a group member who attempts to draw attention to himself or herself by clowning, mimicking, or generally making a joke of everything

withdrawer
a group member who meets his or her own goals at the expense of group goals by not participating in the discussion or the work of the group

blocker
a group member who routinely rejects others' views and stubbornly disagrees with emerging group decisions

LO¹ Discuss the roles of members in groups.

When individuals interact in groups, they assume roles. A role is a specific pattern of behavior that a member of the group performs based on the expectations of other members. There are three types of roles: task-oriented roles, maintenance roles, and self-centered roles. Members select the roles they will play based on how roles fit with their personality, what is required of them by virtue of a position they hold, and what roles the group needs to have assumed that are not being played by other members.

Task-Related Roles	Maintenance Roles	Self-Centered Roles
• Initiator	• Gatekeeper	• Aggressors
• Information (opinion) giver	• Encourager	• Jokers
• Information (opinion) seeker	• Harmonizer	• Withdrawers
• Analyzer		• Blockers
• Orienter		

LO² Discuss member responsibilities in group meetings.

Group members need to be prepared for their various responsibilities in group meetings. Group members need to prepare beforehand to participate in meetings, take an active role participating in the meeting, and take necessary steps to follow up after the meeting.

LO³ Examine the importance of leadership in groups.

Leadership is the process of influencing members to accomplish goals. Leadership is viewed through various perspectives including traits, situations, functions, and transformations. Leadership can either be formal or informal. Formal leaders are assigned, appointed, or elected and are given legitimate power to influence others. Informal leaders emerge from the group but are still recognized by the group. Gender plays a role in leadership. Task-oriented behaviors (considered to be more masculine) and maintenance-oriented behaviors (considered to be feminine) are both necessary for effective leadership.

LO⁴ Describe leadership responsibilities in group meetings.

One role that is of particular importance to effective group functioning is the leadership role. Groups may have a single leader, but more commonly leadership is shared among group members. Groups may have both formal and informal leaders. Formal leaders have formal authority given to them either by some entity outside of the group or by the group members themselves. Informal leaders emerge during a two-stage process. Individuals who want to become recognized as informal leaders in a group should come to group meetings prepared, actively participate in discussions, actively listen to others, avoid appearing bossy or stating overly strong opinions, and manage the meaning for other participants by framing.

LO⁵ Examine the process for evaluating group effectiveness.

Using the forms provided in Figures 11.2 through 11.4, you can evaluate groups on the quality of the decision, the quality of note taking, and the quality of leadership. You can also download these forms from www.4ltrpress.cengage.com/comm.

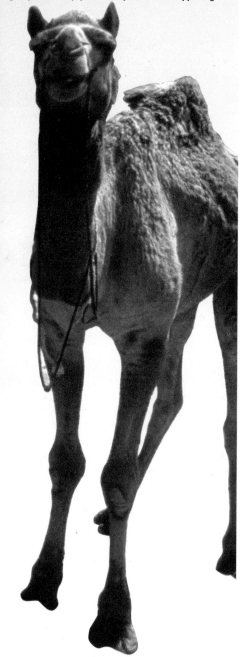

LO³ leadership
a process of influencing members to accomplish group goals

formal leader
an assigned, appointed, or elected leader who is given legitimate power to influence others

informal leaders
members of the group whose authority to influence stems from the power they gain through their interactions in the group

>> **Remember: Ineffective groups build camels when they want to build horses. Understanding the foundations of member roles and leadership in groups will help you to keep that from happening.**

Chapter 11 Quiz

True/False

1. A task-related role is a specific pattern of behavior that one group member performs based on the expectations of other members.

2. Leadership is the process of influencing members to accomplish goals and is viewed through various perspectives including traits, situations, functions, and transformations.

3. Groups always have a single leader.

4. Informal leaders are given authority either by some entity outside of the group or by the group members themselves when the group is initially formed.

5. Repairing damaged relationships through informal conversations may be a necessary step performed during meeting follow-up.

Multiple Choice

6. Which task-related role do you play when you probe the content, reasoning, and evidence of members during the discussion:
   a. initiator
   b. opinion giver
   c. information seeker
   d. analyzer
   e. orienter

7. Which maintenance role do you play when you ensure that everyone has an opportunity to speak and be heard:
   a. gatekeeper
   b. encourager
   c. harmonizer
   d. peacekeeper
   e. initiator

8. Which self-centered role do you play when you routinely reject others' views and stubbornly disagree with emerging group decisions:
   a. aggressor
   b. joker
   c. withdrawer
   d. blocker
   e. bouncer

9. All of the following are ways that people should participate in a group meeting *except*
   a. listen attentively.
   b. stay focused.
   c. play devil's advocate.
   d. dominate the discussion to show your mastery of the material.
   e. ask questions.

10. When running a meeting, be sure to complete each of the following tasks *except*
    a. modify the agenda based on members' suggestions.
    b. monitor roles members assume.
    c. encourage conflict and arguments among group members to elicit everyone's true feelings about the topic at hand, remembering that it's not necessary for the leader to play a harmonizing role.
    d. implement the group's decision rules.
    e. periodically check to see if the group is ready to make a decision.

Chapter Quiz Answers:
1. F; 2. T; 3. F; 4. F; 5. T; 6. D; 7. A; 8. D; 9. D; 10. C

Chapter in Review

LO¹ subject
a broad area of knowledge

topic
some specific aspect of a subject

brainstorming
an uncritical, nonevaluative process of generating associated ideas

LO² audience analysis
the study of the intended audience for your speech

audience adaptation
the active process of developing a strategy for tailoring your information to the specific speech audience

survey
a questionnaire designed to gather information from people

LO³ setting
the occasion and location for your speech

LO⁵ general speech goal
the intent of your speech

specific speech goal
a single statement of the exact response the speaker wants from the audience

LO⁶ secondary research
the process of locating information about your topic that has been discovered by other people

periodicals
magazines and journals that appear at fixed intervals

primary research
the process of conducting your own study to acquire information for your speech

LO⁷ factual statements
statements that can be verified

statistics
numerical facts

examples
specific instances that illustrate or explain a general factual statement

expert opinions
interpretations and judgments made by authorities in a particular subject area

expert
a person who has mastered a specific subject, usually through long-term study

anecdotes
brief, often amusing stories

narratives
accounts, personal experiences, tales, or lengthier stories

LO¹ Discuss how to identify topics for your speech.
Five simple action steps can help you to prepare effective speeches: (1) determine a specific speech goal that is adapted to the audience and occasion; (2) gather and evaluate material to use in the speech; (3) organize and develop the material in a way that is suited to the audience and occasion; (4) adapt the material to fit the needs of the specific audience; and (5) practice presenting the speech.

To accomplish the first action step, determining a specific speech goal, you begin by identifying a topic through listing subjects you are interested in and know something about. Then for each subject, you brainstorm for topic ideas.

LO² Understand how to analyze the audience.
To select an appropriate topic, you need to gather and analyze data about your audience members' information needs. Data should include demographic- and subject-related specifics. You can gather the data by conducting a survey, informally observing, questioning an audience representative, or by making educated guesses.

LO³ Understand how to analyze the setting.
When selecting a topic, you will also want to understand the setting in which you will be speaking and the occasion. You should consider specific expectations of your speech, an appropriate length, the size of the audience, the venue in which you will give the speech, and what equipment you will need in your presentation.

LO⁴ Discuss topic selection.
Based on your audience and setting analyses, you can eliminate topics that would be inappropriate and then select your personal favorite from among the topics that remain.

LO⁵ Identify and write out the specific goals of your speech.
Once you have a topic, you can move on to identify whether your general goal is to entertain, inform, or persuade. Finally, you can develop a specific goal—a single statement that identifies the exact response you want from your audience.

LO⁶ Develop strategies for locating and evaluating information sources and primary research.
The second action step of the speech preparation process is to gather and evaluate material to use in your speech. The three general sources for information include (1) your personal knowledge, experiences, and observations; (2) secondary source research; and (3) primary source research. If you are an expert on your topic, you may already have most of the information you will need to use in your speech. But most of the time you will also need to do secondary research and find resources like books, articles, newspaper accounts, statistics, biographical information, quotations, government documents, and Internet-based information on your topic.

In rare instances, you may need to conduct primary research to get the information you need by surveying, interviewing, examining artifacts or original documents, or conducting experiments. Before you use information that you find, you will want to evaluate it by testing its authority (expertise of the author and reputation of the publication), objectivity, and currency (newness).

LO⁷ Identify and select relevant information.
The information you find will include factual statements (statistics and examples), expert opinions, and elaborations (anecdotes and narratives, comparisons and contrasts, and quotations). As you look at information, you will want to draw from multiple cultural perspectives so that you accurately reflect what is known about your topic.

comparisons
illuminate a point by showing similarities

contrasts
highlight differences

plagiarism
the unethical act of representing another author's work as your own

LO⁸ Explain how to record information.

As you review your sources, you will want to record the information you find on note cards. Each note card should contain only one factual statement, opinion, or elaboration so that you can easily access, sort, and arrange the source material as you prepare the speech. Besides noting the information, you will want to identify it with a key word or category so you can group it with others that are similar. You will also want to note the appropriate bibliographic information so that you can relocate the source if you need to prepare your source list. Finally, on the back of each note card, you should write a short statement citing the source of this fact, opinion, or elaboration that you can use in your speech.

Chapter 12 Quiz

True/False

1. When preparing to give a speech, the first step is to determine a specific speech goal that is adapted to the audience and occasion.

2. Brainstorming is an analytical process of generating ideas and carefully critiquing each one so that you can immediately weed out the ones that aren't practical.

3. The active process of developing a strategy for tailoring your information to the specific speech audience is called audience analysis.

4. The general goal of a speech should always be to inform the audience about your topic.

5. A well-worded specific goal statement should always contain three central ideas.

Multiple Choice

6. A _____ is a broad area of expertise about something such as movies, cognitive psychology, or computer technology.
   a. subject
   b. talking point
   c. topic
   d. main idea
   e. All of these answers are correct.

7. Each of the following questions should be asked about the speech setting to help with speech planning beforehand *except*:
   a. What are the special expectations for the speech?
   b. Will a meal be served before the speech?
   c. What is the appropriate length for the speech?
   d. How large will the audience be?
   e. Where will the speech be given?

8. Books, articles, statistical sources, and biographical references are all examples of
   a. personal knowledge.
   b. experience.
   c. observation tools.
   d. primary research.
   e. secondary research.

9. All of the following are examples of primary research tools *except*
   a. surveys.
   b. interviews.
   c. government documents.
   d. experiments.
   e. examining artifacts or original documents.

10. Before you use information that you find, you will want to evaluate it by testing its authority, objectivity, and
    a. currency.
    b. cultural perspective.
    c. subjectivity.
    d. category.
    e. veracity.

Five Action Steps Toward an Effective Speech Plan

Action Step 1

Determine a Specific Speech Goal That Is Adapted to the Audience and Occasion

(Chapter 12)

Action Step 1

1. Determine a Specific Speech Goal That Is Adapted to the Audience and Occasion

   A: Brainstorm for Topics
   In this activity you will brainstorm topics based on your major or vocation, your hobbies and interests, and issues you are concerned about. Once you've completed your list, you will narrow down the topics you think you would most enjoy speaking about.

   B: Analyze Your Audience
   Identify your audience characteristics, choose a method for gathering audience information, and collect the data.

   C: Understand the Speech Setting
   Talk with the person who arranged your speaking opportunity to gather information about your speech setting.

   D: Select a Topic
   Use the information gathered in Action Steps 1.b and 1.c to narrow down the list you made in 1.a and decide which of the remaining topics you would most enjoy presenting.

   E: Write a Specific Goal
   In this activity, you will draft, revise, and write out your final speech goal.

Action Step 2

Gather and Evaluate Material to Use in the Speech

(Chapter 12)

Action Step 2

2. Gather and Evaluate Material to Use in the Speech

   A: Locate and Evaluate Information Sources
   Use this activity to identify, locate, and evaluate information sources for use in your speech.

   B: Prepare Note Cards: Record Facts, Opinions, and Elaborations
   Using the source material you identified in Action Step 2.a, prepare note cards for each source with specific pieces of information you might wish to use in your speech.

   C: Citing Sources
   Write a brief source citation that you can use in your speech on the back of each note card.

Action Step 3

Organize and Develop Speech Material to Meet the Needs of Your Particular Audience

(Chapter 13)

Action Step 3

3. Organize and Develop Speech Material to Meet the Needs of Your Particular Audience

   A: Determining Main Points
   Use this activity to identify three to five main points that you will present in your speech.

B: Writing a Thesis Statement
Use your goal statement and main points from Action Steps 1.e and 3.a to develop a well-worded thesis statement for your speech.

C: Organizing and Outlining the Main Points of Your Speech
Summarize your main points and choose an organizational pattern to determine the order in which you will present them.

D: Selecting and Outlining Supporting Material
In this exercise you will create a detailed outline for your supporting material.

E: Preparing Section Transitions
Prepare section transitions before or after each main point. Make sure you write them in complete sentences.

F: Writing Speech Introductions
Write three different introductions using the methods for gaining attention discussed in the chapter, then choose one. Include statements addressing the other goals of an effective introduction, and write your introduction in outline form.

G: Creating Speech Conclusions
Write three different conclusions for your speech that summarizes your important points and leaves your audience with a vivid impression or emotional appeal. Choose one of these conclusions, and write it in outline form.

H: Compiling a List of Sources
You will want to create a list of sources based on the note cards from Action Step 2.b that you actually used when you prepared your outline in 3.d. Each item should include all the necessary bibliographic information for each source.

Action Step 4

Adapt the Verbal and the Visual Material to the Needs of Your Specific Audience

(Chapter 14)

Action Step 4

4. Adapt the Verbal and the Visual Material to the Needs of Your Specific Audience

A: Adapting to Your Audience Verbally
Using your audience analysis from Action Steps 1.b and 1.c and the outline from Action Steps 3.a-3.h, create a plan which you will use to verbally adapt your material to your specific audience.

B: Adapting to Your Audience Visually
In this activity you will decide which visual aids you will use in your speech.

Action Step 5

Practice Your Speech Wording and Delivery

(Chapter 15)

Action Step 5

5. Practice Your Speech Wording and Delivery

A: Rehearsing Your Speech
Having finished writing your speech, you will want to rehearse. Follow the rehearsal procedure outlined in Chapter 15, analyze your presentation, and rehearse again. You may continue to rehearse and analyze as many times as you wish until you are satisfied with your presentation.

Chapter in Review

LO¹ organizing

the process of selecting and arranging the main ideas and supporting material to be presented in the speech in a manner that makes it easy for the audience to understand

main points

complete sentence representations of the main ideas used in your thesis statement

thesis statement

a sentence that identifies the topic of your speech and the main ideas you will present

speech outline

a sentence representation of the hierarchical and sequential relationships between the ideas presented in a speech

parallel

wording in more than one sentence that follows the same structural pattern, often using the same introductory words

time order (sequential order)

organizing the main points by a chronological sequence, or by steps in a process

topic order

organizing the main points of the speech by categories or divisions of a subject

logical reasons order

used when the main points provide proof supporting the thesis statement

transitions

words, phrases, or sentences that show the relationship between or bridge ideas

LO² rhetorical question

a question seeking a mental rather than a vocal response

LO³ appeal

describes the behavior you want your listeners to follow after they have heard your arguments

LO¹ Describe methods for developing the body of your speech.

Organizing is the process of selecting and structuring ideas you will present in your speech; it is guided by your audience analysis. Once you have analyzed your audience, created a speech goal, and assembled a body of information on your topic, you are ready to identify the main ideas you wish to present in your speech and to craft them into a well-phrased thesis statement.

Once you have identified a thesis, you will prepare the body of the speech. The body of the speech is hierarchically ordered through the use of main points and subpoints. Once identified, main points and their related subpoints are written in complete sentences, which should be checked to make sure that they are clear, parallel in structure, meaningful, and limited in number to five or less. The sequential relationship between main point ideas and among subpoint ideas depends on the organizational pattern that is chosen. The three most basic organizational patterns are time, topic, and logical reasons order. You will want to choose an organizational pattern that best helps your audience understand and remember your main points. Main point sentences are written in outline form using the organizational pattern selected.

Subpoints support a main point with definitions, examples, statistics, personal experiences, stories, quotations, and so on. These subpoints also appear in the outline below the main point to which they belong. An organizational pattern will also be chosen for each set of subpoints.

Once the outline of the body is complete, transitions between the introduction and the body, between main points within the body, and between the body and the conclusion need to be devised so that the audience can easily follow the speech and identify each main point.

LO² Explain how to create an introduction.

The first step in completing the organization process is creating an introduction. The introduction should get the audience's attention, introduce the thesis, establish credibility, set the tone for the speech, and create goodwill with the audience.

LO³ Explain how to prepare a conclusion.

The second step in completing the organization process is creating a conclusion to summarize the main points of the speech.

LO⁴ Examine guidelines for listing sources.

The third step in the organization process is compiling a list of sources from the bibliographic information you recorded on your research note cards.

LO⁵ Develop a method for reviewing the outline.

The complete draft outline should be reviewed as revised to make sure that you have used a standard set of symbols, used complete sentences for main points and major subdivisions, limited each point to a single idea, related minor points to major points, and made sure the outline length is no more than one-third the number of words of the final speech.

Chapter 13 Quiz

True/False

1. The first step in organizing your speech is to choose an organizational pattern appropriate to the flow of your ideas.

2. The main points of a speech are complete sentence statements of the two to five central ideas that you want to present in your speech.

3. A speech should always be organized according to sequential order.

4. Transitions are the words, phrases, or sentences that show the relationship between or bridge two ideas.

5. An introduction is generally about 10 percent of the length of the entire speech, so for a five-minute speech (approximately 750 words), an introduction of 60 to 85 words is appropriate.

Multiple Choice

6. A sentence that identifies the topic of your speech and the main ideas you will present is called a(n)
   a. thesis statement.
   b. purpose statement.
   c. blueprint.
   d. outline.
   e. guideline.

7. _____ is used in a speech when the main points are the rationale or proof that support the thesis.
   a. A thesis statement
   b. Logical reasons order
   c. Time order
   d. Topic order
   e. Persuasive order

8. Startling statements, rhetorical questions, quotations, and personal references can all be used to
   a. state the thesis.
   b. gain your audience's attention in the introduction.
   c. conclude a speech.
   d. create a bond of goodwill with your audience.
   e. establish your credibility.

9. In the conclusion of a speech, you should
   a. summarize the main points.
   b. read the sources compiled from the bibliographic information recorded on research note cards for the audience.
   c. get the audience's attention.
   d. introduce the thesis.
   e. establish credibility.

10. In the final review of the outline before you move into adaptation and rehearsal, you should ask yourself all of these questions *except:*
    a. Have I used a standard set of symbols to indicate structure?
    b. Have I written main points and major subdivisions as complete sentences?
    c. Do main points and major subdivisions each contain multiple ideas to hold the audience's attention?
    d. Does the outline include no more than one-third the total number of words anticipated in the speech?
    e. Are potential subdivision elaborations indicated?

Chapter Quiz Answers:
1. F; 2. T; 3. F; 4. T; 5. T; 6. A; 7. B; 8. B; 9. A; 10. C

LO¹ **audience adaptation**
the process of customizing your speech material to your specific audience

relevance
adapting the information in the speech so that audience members view it as important to them

timely
showing how information is useful now or in the near future

proximity
a relationship to personal space

personalize
presenting information in a frame of reference that is familiar to the audience

common ground
the background, knowledge, attitudes, experiences, and philosophies that are shared by audience members and the speaker

personal pronouns
"we," "us," and "our" pronouns that refer directly to members of the audience

rhetorical questions
questions phrased to stimulate a mental response rather than an actual spoken response on the part of the audience

credibility
the level of trust that an audience has or will have in the speaker

knowledge and expertise
how well you convince your audience that you are qualified to speak on the topic

trustworthiness
both character and apparent motives for speaking

personableness
the extent to which you project an agreeable or pleasing personality

initial audience attitudes
predispositions for or against a topic, usually expressed as an opinion

LO² **visual aid**
a form of speech development that allows the audience to see as well as to hear information

object
a three-dimensional representation of an idea you are communicating

charts
graphic representations that present information in easily interpreted formats

word charts
used to preview, review, or highlight important ideas covered in a speech

flow charts
use symbols and connecting lines to diagram the progressions through a complicated process

LO¹ Discuss the adaptation of your speech information to your audience.

Audience adaptation is the process of customizing your speech to your specific audience. You need to consider both how to adapt your supporting material as you present it, and you need to consider how to adapt by using visual aids to help the audience understand and remember what you are saying.

First, you adapt to the audience verbally by (1) demonstrating relevance through showing how the information you are presenting is timely, proximate, and has personal impact on the audience; (2) ensuring that your material is easily comprehended by the audience by orienting your audience, defining key terms, illustrating new concepts with vivid examples, personalizing the information to your audience, comparing unknown ideas with those your audience is familiar with, and by using multiple methods for developing your point; (3) establishing common ground by using personal pronouns, asking rhetorical questions, and drawing from common experiences; (4) demonstrating credibility through showing your knowledge and expertise, establishing your trustworthiness, and displaying personableness; and (5) adapting to language and cultural differences through overcoming linguistic problems and choosing culturally sensitive material.

LO² Discuss the adaptation of your visual material to your audience.

Second, you adapt to audiences by developing and using appropriate visual aids. The most common types of visual aids are objects, models, photographs, slides, film and video clips, simple drawings, maps, charts, and graphs. There are various methods speakers can use to display visual aids, including computer-mediated presentation, overhead transparencies, flip charts, poster boards, chalkboards, and handouts. As you plan the visual aids you will use with a speech, consider the time and cost of preparation, the impact on audience understanding and memory, and the effect on speaker credibility.

Criteria for Choosing Visual Aids
1. What are the most important ideas the audience needs to understand and remember?
2. Are there ideas that are complex or difficult to explain verbally but would be easy for members to understand visually?
3. How many visual aids are appropriate?
4. How large is the audience?
5. Is necessary equipment readily available?
6. Is the time involved in making or getting the visual aid and/or equipment cost effective?

Designing Effective Visual Aids
1. Use printing or type size that can be seen easily by your entire audience.
2. Use a typeface that is easy to read and pleasing to the eye.
3. Use upper- and lowercase type.
4. Limit the lines of type to six or less.
5. Include only items of information that you will emphasize in your speech.
6. Make sure information is laid out in a way that is aesthetically pleasing.
7. Add clip art where appropriate.
8. Use color strategically.

Chapter 14 Quiz

True/False

1. In order to be timely, you must adapt the information in the speech so that the audience members view it as important to them.

2. Proximity can be described as the background, knowledge, attitudes, experiences, and philosophies that are shared by audience members and the speaker.

graph
a diagram that compares information

bar graphs
charts that present information using a series of vertical or horizontal bars

line graphs
charts that indicate changes in one or more variables over time

pie graphs
charts that help audiences visualize the relationships among parts of a single unit

flip chart
a large pad of paper mounted on an easel; it can be an effective method for presenting visual aids

3. The simplest way of establishing common ground is to use personal pronouns: "we," "us," and "our," so speakers can acknowledge commonalities between themselves and members of the audience.

4. An example of a rhetorical question could be: "Have you ever worried about the real estate values dropping in your neighborhood because of crime?"

5. Meeting initial audience attitudes means framing a speech in a way that takes into account how much the audience knows and their attitude toward the topic.

Multiple Choice

6. When choosing the supporting material for your speech, it's important to select materials that demonstrate how the speech
   a. is relevant to the audience.
   b. helps the audience comprehend the information.
   c. establishes common ground between you and the audience.
   d. is appropriate for the audience's initial attitudes.
   e. accomplishes all of these things.

7. A speech that includes information about the audience's neighborhood or town is establishing
   a. relevance.
   b. timeliness.
   c. proximity.
   d. personal impact.
   e. credibility.

8. If you are giving a speech about illiteracy and include the sentence, "By 'functionally illiterate,' I mean people who have trouble accomplishing simple reading and writing tasks," you are
   a. defining key terms.
   b. illustrating new concepts with vivid examples.
   c. personalizing information.
   d. talking down to your audience, which may offend them.
   e. comparing unknown ideas with familiar ones.

9. Your _____ is the extent to which the audience can believe that what you say is accurate, true, and in their best interests.
   a. relevance
   b. proximity
   c. expertise
   d. trustworthiness
   e. credibility

10. Which of the following can be used as a visual aid during a speech to indicate changes in one or more variables over time:
    a. bar graph
    b. line graph
    c. pie graph
    d. word chart
    e. flow chart

Chapter Quiz Answers:
1. F; 2. F; 3. T; 4. T; 5. T; 6. E; 7. C; 8. A; 9. D; 10. B

LO¹ public speaking apprehension
a type of communication anxiety (or nervousness); the level of fear you experience when anticipating or actually speaking to an audience

anticipation reaction
the level of anxiety you experience prior to giving the speech, including the nervousness you feel while preparing and waiting to speak

confrontation reaction
the surge in your anxiety level that you feel as you begin your speech

adaptation reaction
the gradual decline of your anxiety level that begins about one minute into the presentation and results in your anxiety level declining to its pre-speaking level in about five minutes

visualization
a method that reduces apprehension by helping you develop a mental picture of yourself giving a masterful speech

systematic desensitization
a method that reduces apprehension by gradually having you visualize increasingly more frightening events

public speaking skills training
the systematic teaching of the skills associated with the processes involved in preparing and delivering an effective public speech, with the intention of improving speaking competence and thereby reducing public speaking apprehension

LO² pitch
the scaled highness or lowness of the sound a voice makes

volume
the degree of loudness of the tone you make as you normally exhale, your diaphragm relaxes, and air is expelled through the trachea

rate
the speed at which you talk

quality
the tone, timbre, or sound of your voice

articulation
using the tongue, palate, teeth, jaw movement, and lips to shape vocalized sounds that combine to produce a word

pronunciation
the form and accent of various syllables of a word

accent
the articulation, inflection, tone, and speech habits typical of the natives of a country, a region, or even a state or city

facial expression
eye and mouth movement

gestures
movements of your hands, arms, and fingers that describe and emphasize what you are saying

LO¹ Discuss public speaking apprehension.
Although speeches may be presented impromptu, by manuscript, or by memory, the material you have been reading is designed to help you present your speeches extemporaneously—that is, carefully prepared and practiced, but with the exact wording determined at the time of utterance.

Even though almost all of us experience public speaking apprehension, only 15 percent or less experience high levels of fear. The signs of speaking apprehension, or stage fright, vary from individual to individual. The causes of apprehension are still being studied—in fact, some speaking apprehension may be inborn. You can learn to manage it by recognizing that despite apprehension, you can make it through your speech by preparing carefully and rehearsing your speech.

Techniques for Reducing Apprehension

1. Visualization
2. Systematic desensitization
3. Public speaking skills training

LO² Identify the physical elements that affect the delivery of your speech.
The major elements of speech delivery are voice (pitch, volume, rate, and quality), articulation (the shaping of sounds to produce words), and bodily action (facial expression, gestures, movement, and posture).

LO³ Describe characteristics of a conversational presentation style.
Effective speakers work to develop a conversational style, the major elements of which are enthusiasm, vocal expressiveness, spontaneity, fluency, and eye contact.

LO⁴ Identify different types of speech delivery.
Three of the most common types of speech delivery are impromptu speaking (talking "on the spot"), scripted speeches (completely written manuscripts), and extemporaneous speaking (speeches that are researched, planned ahead, but not scripted).

LO⁵ Discuss methods of rehearsing for your speech.
Effective delivery also requires rehearsal. Experienced speakers schedule and conduct rehearsal sessions. Once outlines are complete, effective speakers usually rehearse at least twice, often using speech notes on cards that include key phrases and words. In many cases, speakers may use visual aids to help audiences understand and remember the material. To be effective, visual aids need to be carefully planned, shown only when being talked about, and displayed so that all can see. Moreover, effective speakers talk to the audience, not the visual aid.

JUNE

Timetable for Preparing a Speech

SUNDAY	MONDAY	TUESDAY	WEDNESDAY	THURSDAY	FRIDAY	SATURDAY
1	2	3	4 Select Topic; Begin Research (7 Days Before)	5 Continue Research (6 Days Before)	6 Outline Body of Speech (5 Days Before)	7 Work on Introduction and Conclusion (4 Days Before)
8 Finish Outline; find Additional Material if Needed; Have all Visual Aids Completed (3 Days Before)	9 First Rehearsal Session (2 Days Before)	10 Second Rehearsal Session (1 Day Before)	11 Give Speech (Due Date)	12	13	14

movement
motion of the entire body

posture
the position or bearing of the body

poise
assurance of manner

LO³ conversational style
an informal style of presenting a speech so that your audience feels you are talking with them, not at them

enthusiasm
excitement or passion about your speech

vocal expressiveness
the contrasts in pitch, volume, rate, and quality that affect the meaning an audience gets from the sentences you speak

emphasis
giving different shades of expressiveness to words

monotone
a voice in which the pitch, volume, and rate remain constant, with no word, idea, or sentence differing significantly from any other

spontaneity
a naturalness that does not seem rehearsed or memorized

fluency
speech that flows easily, without hesitations and vocal interferences

eye contact
looking directly at the people to whom we are speaking

LO⁴ impromptu speeches
speeches that are delivered with only seconds or minutes of advance notice for preparation and usually presented without referring to notes of any kind

scripted speeches
speeches that are prepared by creating a complete written manuscript and delivered by rote memory or by reading a written copy

extemporaneous speeches
speeches that are researched and planned ahead of time, although the exact wording is not scripted and will vary from presentation to presentation

LO⁵ rehearsing
practicing the presentation of your speech aloud

speech notes
word or phrased outlines of your speech

LO⁶ Determine criteria for evaluating speeches.
In addition to preparing and presenting, you are also learning to evaluate the speeches you hear, focusing on speech content, organization, presentation, and adaptation.

Chapter 15 Quiz

True/False

1. Public speaking apprehension is a rare type of communication anxiety that about 5% of the U.S. population experiences when speaking to an audience.

2. The scaled highness or lowness of the sound a voice makes is its volume.

3. Articulation can be defined as the form and accent of various syllables of a word.

4. Everyone speaks with some kind of an accent, because "accent" means any tone or inflection that differs from the way others speak.

5. You should show a visual aid only when talking about it.

Multiple Choice

6. The surge in your anxiety level that you feel as you begin your speech is
   a. public speaking apprehension.
   b. anticipation reaction.
   c. confrontation reaction.
   d. adaptation reaction.
   e. cognitive reaction.

7. A method that reduces apprehension by gradually having you visualize increasingly more frightening events is called
   a. visualization.
   b. systematic desensitization.
   c. public speaking skills training.
   d. adaptation reaction.
   e. anticipation reaction.

8. The position or bearing of your body while giving a speech is called
   a. articulation.
   b. gestures.
   c. posture.
   d. movement.
   e. poise.

9. All of the following are hallmarks of a conversational style *except*
   a. poise.
   b. vocal expressiveness.
   c. spontaneity.
   d. fluency.
   e. eye contact.

10. Speeches that are researched and planned ahead of time, although the exact wording is not scripted and will vary from presentation to presentation, are called
    a. impromptu.
    b. scripted.
    c. extemporaneous.
    d. practiced.
    e. spontaneous.

Chapter Quiz Answers:
1. F; 2. F; 3. F; 4. T; 5. T; 6. C; 7. B; 8. C; 9. A; 10. C

16

Chapter in Review

LO¹ informative speech
a speech that has a goal to explain or describe facts, truths, and principles in a way that increases understanding

intellectually stimulating
information that is new to audience members

creative
using information in a way that yields different or original ideas and insights

divergent thinking
thinking that occurs when we contemplate something from a variety of different perspectives

mnemonics
a system of improving memory by using formulas

acronyms
words formed from the first letter of a series of words

LO² description
the informative method used to create an accurate, vivid, verbal picture of an object, geographic feature, setting, or image

definition
a method of informing that explains something by identifying its meaning

synonym
a word that has the same or similar meaning

antonym
a word that is a direct opposition

comparison and contrast
a method of informing that explains something by focusing on how it is similar and different from other things

narration
a method of informing that explains something by recounting events

demonstration
a method of informing that explains something by showing how something is done, by displaying the stages of a process, or by depicting how something works

LO³ expository speech
an informative presentation that provides carefully researched, in-depth knowledge about a complex topic

LO¹ Identify characteristics of effective informative speaking.
An informative speech is one that has a goal to explain or describe facts, truths, and principles in a way that stimulates interest, facilitates understanding, and increases likelihood that audiences will remember. In short, informative speeches are designed to educate an audience.

Effective informative speeches are intellectually stimulating, creative, and use emphasis to aid memory. Informative speeches will be perceived as intellectually stimulating when the information is new and when it is explained in a way that excites interest. Informative speeches are creative when they produce new or original ideas or insights. Informative speeches use emphasis to stimulate audience memory.

LO² Describe methods for conveying information.
We can inform by describing something, defining it, comparing and contrasting it with other things, narrating stories about it, or demonstrating it.

Description is used to create verbal pictures of objects, settings, or images discussed in your speech. Definition offers an explanation of something by identifying its meaning through classifying and differentiating it, explaining its derivation, explaining use or function, or by using a synonym. Comparison and contrast demonstrates similarities and differences between your subject and other things. Narration explains something by recounting events. Narration can be presented in a first-, second-, or third-person voice. Demonstration shows how something is done, displays the stages of a process, or depicts how something works.

LO³ Discuss common types of informative speeches.
Two of the most common types of informative speeches are process speeches, which demonstrate how something is done or made, and expository speeches, which provide carefully researched information about a complex topic.

Examples of Expository Speech Topics

Topic Ideas for Political, Economic, Social, or Religious Issues	Topic Ideas for Historical Events, Forces, and People	Topic Ideas for Exposition of Theory, Principle, or Law	Topic Ideas for Expositions of Creative Work
The Bush doctrine of preemption	W. E. B. DuBois	Monetary theory	Jazz
Stem cell research	Gandhi's leadership	Boyle's law	The films of Alfred Hitchcock
Gay marriage	The papacy	Number theory	Impressionist painting
School vouchers	The colonization of Africa	Psychoanalytic theory	The love sonnets of Shakespeare
Mandatory sentencing	Conquering Mt. Everest	Global warming	Salsa dancing
School uniforms	The Vietnam War	Intelligent design	Kabuki theater
Home schooling	The Balfour Declaration	The normal distribution	Inaugural addresses
Immigration	The Republic of Texas	Color theory	Iconography

Chapter 16 Quiz

True/False

1. The goal of an informative speech is to explain or describe facts, truths, and principles in a way that increases understanding.

2. The goal of an expository speech is to demonstrate how something is done or made, or how it works.

3. Effective informative speeches are intellectually stimulating, creative, and use emphasis to aid memory.

4. An acronym is a system of improving memory by using formulas.

5. Information will be perceived by your audience to be intellectually stimulating when it is new to them and when it is explained in a way that piques audience curiosity and excites their interest.

Multiple Choice

6. _____ thinking occurs when we contemplate something from many different perspectives.
   a. Creative
   b. Divergent
   c. Informative
   d. Intellectually stimulating
   e. Outside-the-box

7. You can use visual aids, repetition, transitions, humor, and memory aids to
   a. highlight important information that you want your audience to remember.
   b. encourage divergent thinking.
   c. create an informative speech.
   d. describe the specific goal of the speech.
   e. ensure that your main points are stated in parallel language.

8. A method of informing that explains something by recounting events is called
   a. description.
   b. definition.
   c. comparison and contrast.
   d. narration.
   e. demonstration.

9. All of the following are examples of expository speeches *except*
   a. How to hang crown molding.
   b. The effects of drilling for oil in Arctic National Wildlife Refuge.
   c. The true story behind the "Manhattan Project."
   d. The impact that Martin Luther King, Jr., had on the Civil Rights Movement.
   e. The making of "The Godfather" series.

10. If you give a speech about living a vegan lifestyle and explain the similarities and differences it has with a vegetarian lifestyle, you're using the method of informing known as
    a. description.
    b. definition.
    c. comparison and contrast.
    d. narration.
    e. demonstration.

Chapter Quiz Answers:
1. T; 2. F; 3. T; 4. F; 5. T; 6. B; 7. A; 8. D; 9. A; 10. C